ACCLAIM FOR
RISING TIDE

"[Bryant and Namath's] years together fueled the growing popularity of college football and coincided with the unfolding of the civil rights struggle that emerged as the defining news story of the early 1960s. RISING TIDE weaves the two elements in an informative and entertaining narrative with broad appeal."

—Associated Press

"RISING TIDE reads like an ESPN documentary but packs ten times the information and entertainment value. Its accessible but intelligent prose and deep-probing insights keep interest high throughout its chapters. Football, its impact, events, and mannerisms are flawlessly interwoven with the tumultuous recounts of a politically, socially, and racially evolving South...a fabulous football book."   —*Atlanta Journal-Constitution*

"A lively, highly readable account of two iconic figures...RISING TIDE aspires to be much more than another jock biography. It tells a fascinating story lying at the intersection of football, race, and entertainment...Gridiron fans, particularly those of a certain age, will enjoy this trip down memory lane. So, too, will readers interested in revisiting a nation in transition."

—*Cleveland Plain Dealer*

"[Roberts and Krzemienski] tell a compelling story against a background of racial and political turmoil."

—*Dallas Morning News*

"I didn't think the world needed another Bear Bryant book, but this one digs a little deeper and blitzes me with new info. And to think a Purdue guy wrote it."
　　　　　　　　　　　　　　　　　　　　　　—Dan Jenkins

"The authors do such a colorfully thorough and yet unusually objective job of fly-on-the-wall storytelling about Joe Namath's shenanigans and Bear Bryant's burdens, it's a coin-flip: You might like these characters more than you did before, you might like them less."
　　　　　　　　　　　　　　　　—*Charleston Post and Courier* (SC)

"RISING TIDE is a riveting football story that doubles as first-rate, seminal historical investigation. Building the narrative around Coach Paul 'Bear' Bryant and Joe Namath, the authors interweave early TV and civil rights into the fabric of their story with great grace. An absolutely wonderful read!"
　　　　　　　　　　—Douglas Brinkley, professor of history at
　　　　　　　　　　　　　　Rice University and author of *Cronkite*

"Riveting...exceedingly well-researched and portrayed...Roberts and Krzemienski present a fine profile of Bryant and offer the best treatment of the pre-professional Namath yet printed."
　　　　　　　　　　　　　　　—*Library Journal* (starred review)

"An absolute gem of a book about the twin pillars of white Southern identity: racial segregation and football...RISING TIDE is an expertly written, must-read story of the intersection of athletics and politics."
　　　　　　　　　　—Gerald Early, author of *A Level Playing Field* and
　　　　　　　　　　　　　　winner of the National Book Critics Circle
　　　　　　　　　　　　　　Award for *The Culture of Bruising*

"The authors deliver three-dimensional portraits of both men."
—*Booklist*

"A must-read! RISING TIDE is an electrifying book that hits on all four cylinders: rich Alabama football tradition; North meets South; civil rights movement era; and Coach Bryant's history-making return to his alma mater. The short and long of it: This book is just plain explosive!"
—John Mitchell, Pittsburgh Steelers assistant head coach and defensive line coach

"RISING TIDE will be on the All Time Top Ten List for the Crimson Tide nation, but it is not just another 'fan's book.' Anyone who wants to understand the roots of college football as Big Business will learn from this account of the bond between its two gifted, charismatic, and flawed heroes. As an eyewitness to the Bear-and-Joe-Willie show, I can tell you that Randy Roberts and Ed Krzemienski got it right about how the Tide rolls."
—Howell Raines, author and former executive editor of the *New York Times*

"[This is] a can't-lay-it-down book. In evocative prose, Roberts and Krzemienski recapture the drama, glory, and shame of big-time college sports set in an era of social upheaval. You don't have to be a Crimson Tide fan to enjoy this great read."
—George C. Rable, Charles Summersell Chair in Southern History, University of Alabama

RISING TIDE

TIDE

BEAR BRYANT, JOE NAMATH,
AND DIXIE'S LAST QUARTER

RANDY ROBERTS
AND
ED KRZEMIENSKI

TWELVE

NEW YORK   BOSTON

Twelve
Hachette Book Group
1290 Avenue of the Americas
New York, NY 10104
www.HachetteBookGroup.com

Printed in the United States of America

Originally published in hardcover by Twelve.

First trade edition: August 2014

Twelve is an imprint of Grand Central Publishing.
The Twelve name and logo are trademarks of Hachette Book Group, Inc.

The Hachette Speakers Bureau provides a wide range of authors for speaking events. To find out more, go to www.hachettespeakersbureau.com or call (866) 376-6591.

The publisher is not responsible for websites (or their content) that are not owned by the publisher.

Library of Congress Control Number: 2013939673
ISBN 978-1-4555-2632-1 (pbk.)

For Hoot Owl Hicks (1939–2009) and all of the other passionate fans of the Crimson Tide, the most successful college football team in history

Contents

Like his father (below with daughter Rita), Joe Namath preferred formal attire considered somewhat flashy in the conservative environs of Beaver Falls. (Krzemienski Collection)

Prologue

The Tower

ON A HOT SUMMER DAY IN 1961, Joe Namath arrived at Van De Graaff Field in Tuscaloosa from Beaver Falls clothed in steel-mill chic. He got off the DC-3 wearing a slick, garish one-button large-checked brown suit, tight as a glove and pegged at the shoe line. In his pants pocket was a pocket watch attached by a chain. In the breast pocket was a pack of Kools. Sticking out the corner of his mouth was a toothpick. Faux Ray-Ban shades protected his eyes from the intense Alabama sun. Perched on his head, at what a guy destined to become one of his best friends described as a "perfect fuck-you angle" was a thin-brimmed straw fedora with a pearl stickpin on the side and a lavish white feather protruding from the band. He looked a bit like a pimp or a hustler come to town to set up shop, a tall, round-shouldered, thin-waisted, hugely confident trafficker of something not quite legal.[1]

Carrying the eighteen-year-old's two bags was Howard Schnellenberger, slumped like a derelict who had been sleeping in his clothes and scratching a good four-day growth. "I guess I looked pretty matty," recalled Schnellenberger, a handsome first-year receiver coach who was normally a fastidious dresser. The other members of the Alabama staff who greeted Howard's triumphant return laughed at the scene. "They thought Joe looked like the coach and I looked like the player," Schnellenberger added.[2]

But no matter: Howard Schnellenberger had done his job.

A week earlier, a Maryland assistant coach had called Alabama assistant coach Charlie Bradshaw and told him that the Terrapins' top quarterback recruit had failed to get the 750 score on the Scholastic Aptitude Test (SAT) required for admission to Atlantic Coast Conference schools. The player's name was Joe Namath, and Alabama had a rare opportunity to get him if they moved fast. The truth was that Maryland head coach Tom Nugent wanted to get Joe out of the region altogether. He feared that Namath would land at Notre Dame, Penn State, Miami, Syracuse, Boston College, or some other school that might appear on Maryland's schedule. Nugent knew that Joe was "just too damn good" to have to play against.

Bradshaw, a Kentucky graduate who had recruited the western Pennsylvania region, already knew about Namath. So did Alabama's head coach, Paul "Bear" Bryant, who had stomped over the region plenty, plucking recruits from Pennsylvania steel-mill and coal-mining towns when he had coached at Kentucky in the 1940s and 1950s. George Blanda and Vito "Babe" Parilli, Bear's two great quarterbacks at Kentucky, came from western Pennsylvania. And everyone who followed football knew that Johnny Unitas, the greatest of them all, learned to pass the ball there as well.

During Joe's senior season a couple of Crimson Tide recruiters had paid a visit to his hometown of Beaver Falls. They had listened to stories about the local phenomenon, heard the rumors about his less than wholesome lifestyle, and met the young man himself. Joe was brash and confident, but hardly headed for Sing Sing. But then his high school coach, Larry Bruno, showed the recruiters films of Namath in action. Projected on a bedsheet, the unprofessional, grainy black-and-white flickering images, shot from a high angle, showed a football genius, a boy who had hands almost as big as Sonny Liston's and could throw a football like Whitey Ford threw a baseball. They wanted Namath, but he was not interested in them. Tuscaloosa was simply not on his radar.[3]

Namath chose Maryland instead. But now Maryland had unchosen him, and Alabama had a second chance.

"Go git 'um an' bring 'um hea," Bear told Schnellenberger. Then, digging into a tin of petty cash, Bryant handed him a fistful of traveling money. Schnellenberger was not about to disappoint Coach Bryant. He had played for Bear at Kentucky and knew the coach did not tolerate failure or excuses. Getting the job done was all that mattered. Anything less was unacceptable. "I sure the heck didn't want to go back to Tuscaloosa by myself and have to listen to Coach Bryant talk about it," he recalled.[4]

Schnellenberger flew to Pittsburgh and rented a car. Driving northwest on Ohio River Boulevard, hugging the north side of the river, he meandered through the heartland of industrial America. Every mile he traveled, on both sides of the river, he saw steel mills belching smoke and dumping pollutants into the Coke-bottle green and muddy-gray waters. He passed steel bridge after steel bridge connecting industrial plants to industrial plants, choked with eighteen-wheelers going into and out of the mills. Locals said that that stretch of the river had more bridges than anywhere in the world except Venice—and Venice didn't count, they claimed, because the Venetians called any stick across a puddle a bridge. Schnellenberger saw no stick bridges, nor any romantic covered ones like he would have seen in southeastern Pennsylvania. He saw only the steel veins of industrial America, pulsing with the work of a nation.

Ohio River Boulevard followed the snaking path of the river, past Ambridge with its American Bridge Company; past Aliquippa with its two branches of the Jones & Laughlin Steel Corporation, North Star Transfer Coal Company, and Dravo Corporation; and past Monaca with its Anchor Hocking Glass Corporation. At Rochester the Ohio River intersected with the Beaver River, and Schnellenberger followed Route 18 into New Brighton and over the river into Beaver Falls, where the road became 7th Avenue. Before domestic troubles divided his parents, Joe Namath had lived at the lower end of the street, just a few Hail Mary passes from the river.

The factories along the Ohio and Beaver Rivers did not seem to touch the hills above them, which were as heavily wooded as they must have been when the first English colonists arrived. But the hills and woods were for hunting, not making money. It was the factories that lured Germans, Poles, Italians, Czechs, Hungarians, and other immigrants to the region, and the Catholic churches in Beaver Falls testified to this. Holy Trinity served the Poles, St. Ladislaus the Hungarians, and St. Mary's—the oldest and wealthiest—the Germans.

In the late nineteenth and twentieth centuries the area also became known for the production of football players. Back in the day when Dr. Jock Sutherland contended for national championships at the University of Pittsburgh, it was said that a good recruiter could put together a great team with a bus pass around Allegheny and Beaver Counties. The region turned out players as tough as its steel—while Namath was learning the game, Joe Walton of Beaver Falls and Mike Ditka of Aliquippa were playing for Pitt.

Bear Bryant had chosen Schnellenberger over more experienced recruiters to go to Beaver Falls for a good reason. Joe's older brother Frank had played football at Kentucky in 1955–56,

Schnellenberger's senior year. In scrimmages it had been Frank's unenviable task to block the All-American and All-SECer Schnellenberger. "He just beat the shit out of me," Frank recalled. But the combat had brought the two closer together. Although Frank dropped out of school to take care of a family problem, the two remained friends. Frank, then, was Howard's ace in the hole, the older brotherly voice that could nudge Joe toward Alabama.[5]

Schnellenberger's first problem was just locating the kid. Even with Frank's help, Joe was an elusive character. The recruiter eventually found Namath on the street outside the Blue Room pool hall. "From a visual standpoint Joe didn't look like a typical Alabama player," Schnellenberger said. He looked more like a pool hustler. "He had on a suit that was in vogue at the time—one of those one-button jobs with big wide lapels and a key ring on his pants pocket." His hair was longer, skin darker, and mouth sharper than the boys playing for the Crimson Tide. It was soon clear that although Frank could make introductions, he could not make up Joe's mind. Joe had heard of Bear Bryant, was not sure that he was the right coach for him, and showed not a hint of desperation to jump at an offer. Schnellenberger understood immediately that Joe was no low-hanging fruit ready to be picked. He needed to be convinced, which made Howard nervous. He was sure that at any time recruiters from Notre Dame, Penn State, or some other football school would show up in Beaver Falls.[6]

Schnellenberger had planned poorly and packed worse. He had come to Beaver Falls with too little of Bear's petty cash and none of his own, and only the clothes on his back, anticipating a short trip. He thought he would tell Joe about Alabama and the kid would respond, "Sure, let's go." But it did not work out that way. He stayed almost a week working on the quarterback and his mother—talking to Joe about how pretty the southern belles were in Alabama and to Rose about what good care he would take of "little Joey." It should not have been a hard sell. Alabama was more tangible than Joe's pipe dream of playing big league baseball, and more enticing than a job at the B&W or Moltrup mill. But Rose was wary of the distance, and Joe would not go anywhere without her consent.

It took some time, but finally, maybe just to get rid of him, Rose invited Schnellenberger over for a home-cooked dinner. Chicken and dumplings, her specialty. Joe's favorite. "And they were really good," Schnellenberger attested. The dinner was as good as her blessings. In fact, she went upstairs and packed for her son.[7]

With his recruit in hand, Schnellenberger should have been in tall cotton, and he would have been, except for one thing. He had all but run through Bear's allotment. American Express cards were for fast-lane businessmen and Wall Street types. Football recruiters paid as they went and turned in legitimate receipts when they got home. Bear had given Schnellenberger enough for a few days, not a week. With only change in his pocket he began to write checks from his personal bank account, and assistant coaches' salaries at Alabama ensured that such accounts were not well stocked. Writing a bad check for Namath's plane fare, he began the ordeal of ferrying his prize recruit back to Tuscaloosa.

Everything went fine as far as Atlanta, Schnellenberger said, "but the dag gon connection flight couldn't get out of there because of engine trouble or something." That meant a night at an airport hotel and another bad check. Fortunately, Joe was not a breakfast eater, and Schnellenberger was able to fish ten or fifteen cents out of his pocket to cover a cup of coffee. From Atlanta they flew to Tuscaloosa and the friendly, smiling faces of the other coaches.[8]

It would take days for the checks to arrive at his bank, and as far as he knew there were no warrants for his arrest. Howard

Schnellenberger had accomplished his mission: He had returned to Tuscaloosa with the finest quarterback in Pennsylvania, maybe the entire country. Judging by Joe's behavior, the ease with which he permitted the recruiter to carry his bags and the charm he radiated, he surely must be "the goddamn bell cow" that Bear expected.

Schnellenberger escorted his prize to the practice field. Niceties like late registration and dorm assignments could wait. Joe stood by Schnellenberger watching the Alabama players—and except for a few boys from neighboring southern states, all the players were born and raised in Alabama—tear into each other in the late August heat. The eighteen-year-old wore the expression of a connoisseur who was impressed by few things in life.

High above the practice field, his eyes shielded by an Alabama baseball cap, Bryant watched the activity below. Everything about him accentuated his power. "This must be what God looks like," future Hall of Fame quarterback George Blanda recalled thinking when he first met Bryant at the University of Kentucky. Bart Starr, another future Hall of Famer, had a similar reaction when he heard Bryant speak. "The voice of God," he thought. Bryant fostered this sense of the divine by decreeing that a tower be built for him at the practice field. Alone, every practice, he ascended the tower, watching the action below with a grim coldness, occasionally barking an order, inspecting his minions as they twitched at the sound of his voice as assuredly as if they were puppets attached to strings tied around his fingers. And if something or someone particularly got his gall, he unlatched the chain, came down from the clouds, and intervened directly. "When you heard the chain at the entrance of the tower rattle," assistant coach Dude Hennessey recalled, "you did not want to be in his line of sight."[9]

To the best knowledge of the assistant coaches, no one, not players, coaches, or visiting politicians and dignitaries, had ever been invited up into the tower. On this day, however, something totally unexpected occurred. Bryant took his eyes off the practice field, lifted a bullhorn to his mouth, and summoned Joe up into his sanctuary. It was a command without precedent, a request so shocking that every player and coach on the practice field seemed to be struck dumb. "Je-sus Christ," Schnellenberger thought, "this was why I was sent to Beaver Falls. This guy isn't just another great high school quarterback. He must be in a class by himself."

Watching from below, sweating on the practice field and trying his best to make a good impression, freshman center/linebacker Gaylon McCollough looked toward the tower and wondered who the guy dressed like a mobster with the toothpick in his mouth was. "Who is that character?" he asked one of the graduate assistant coaches. "That's your new quarterback," the assistant replied. McCollough laughed. "Right, he'll last about two days." But there was no denying that Joe was standing where no other player had stood.[10]

In the tower Joe was oblivious to the commotion below. For all he knew, every recruit got summoned to the perch. But out of respect he took off his sunglasses, looked the coach in the eyes, and shook hands. Bryant's eyes sent a shiver through him. They were clear blue and frighteningly intense, with a gaze so steady that a person wanted to look away but feared that it would be a clear signal of weakness. Bear began to talk. With a half smile, mumbling like his mouth was full of marbles, he gesticulated, pointing toward the players below.[11]

Joe was mystified. It was like he was watching a foreign film without subtitles. The only word that seemed like an English cognate was "stud." It was a word that acted as a period to sentences. They talked, but they did not really communicate. Joe struggled to understand what the coach was saying. Not understanding what

Bear was talking about, but relieved that his tone seemed pleasing enough, Joe thought it best just to keep his mouth shut and smile. Eventually, a phrase or two became a trifle clearer: "Ya kin be jes lek themum, just lek themum *studs* rat dun thar." He pointed enthusiastically, repeating, "Jes lek themum **STUDS!**" Joe got the picture. He would be the king stud on a team full of studs.

The meeting that joined the two as allies was also a clash of cultures—North and South, young and old, brash and conservative. Bryant, a man for whom clothes mattered enormously, could not have been unaware that Namath did not look even remotely like the southern boys below him fighting for a place on the team. At a moment when these divisions were beginning to take on colossal meaning, they were fully present, if not perfectly defined, in that tower on that day in Tuscaloosa, Alabama.

When Joe descended from the tower he had only a vague idea about Bear Bryant. Of course, he knew that the successful head coach had a reputation for driving his players hard, and had even heard that as a teenager Bryant had wrestled a traveling carnival bear. But he had no idea what motivated the man. He didn't know that Bryant had grown up in a shack without electricity or running water in Moro Bottom, Arkansas. Bryant had known the hunger pains and humiliation of poverty. He had experienced the muscle-numbing body ache of laboring for hours behind a mule plowing a worked-over field of cotton. He had felt the red-faced shame of attending school in patched clothes and smelling of too much work and too little soap and water. Back then the "city" boys from Fordyce had called him a "hick" and worse, laughing at his high-water pants and clodhopper shoes. And he had never forgotten what the world looked like between the ears of a mule. He had been there, and he was not going back.

Namath had been there too, not behind a mule in Arkansas but in a steel mill, terrified by the clamor and activity, the palpable sense of danger—and even death—lurking everywhere. If Alabama did not work out, he might give professional baseball a try, or even join the military. His brother Sonny and sister Rita had signed up. So had hundreds of other "mill hunkies" from western Pennsylvania. But either way, he was not going back.

Namath's ascension to the top of the tower was a defining moment, electric with importance and meaning. From Joe's first day at the University of Alabama, Bryant had set him apart from the other players. On the practice field Bear had always been above everyone else, physically and metaphorically. He was distant and untouchable, yet all-seeing. Now Joe had climbed the tower to see him and shake his hand and talk with him. Together they had surveyed the field and the team. Or perhaps they had looked into the future.

———

If Bryant seemed to be speaking a foreign language to Namath, Joe quickly realized that Tuscaloosa was a foreign country. He came down the steps of the tower carefully, afraid he might fall in the slick leather-soled dress shoes he was wearing, and crossed the field toward Coach Schnellenberger. Pleased to be back in Tuscaloosa and anticipating a shower and a shave, the recruiter still had to take care of one final detail. Bryant had offered Namath a scholarship, but before Joe could join the team, Schnellenberger had to dot some i's and cross some t's. The National Collegiate Athletic Association (NCAA) required that a prospective player physically leave a college campus if a recruiting trip was to be considered a "visit." Since Joe Namath intended to remain in Tuscaloosa on this, his first trip, it would not count as an official visit if he did not leave the college. If it did not count as an official visit, then the NCAA would view it as an attempt to kidnap a player to prevent him from visiting other schools.[12]

So Schnellenberger took Namath off the campus, giving him his first exposure to Tuscaloosa and the South. They went to the town's Greyhound bus station. At first glance, it appeared to Namath like any other. Its run-down look, uncomfortable wooden benches, and faint smell of urine reminded him of the Beaver Falls station. Schnellenberger said he had to go to the men's room and told Namath to sit on the bench for a minute. Glancing in the direction Schnellenberger was walking, Namath noticed that above the MEN's sign on the bathroom door was another sign that read WHITES. Another door, not far away from the first one, similarly read MEN's, and again above that sign was COLORED. There were similar differentiations for the women's rooms—WHITES and COLORED.

Namath thought briefly of the "colored" people he knew, the ones who were his friends and teammates in Beaver Falls. He knew before coming to Alabama that race relations differed in the South, but he was unprepared for this. The Tuscaloosa bus station gave a face to the South. "Segregated"—that foreign-sounding word that appeared regularly on the evening news and in the daily newspapers in Beaver Falls—became, in an instant, "colored" water, "colored" waiting rooms, and "colored" bathrooms. While he waited for Schnellenberger to return from the room for "white men," he thought, "I am deep into the Deep South."[13]

Even before he was a coach, Bryant showed an appreciation for hats and hard work. Here, Bryant, second from the left, poses with a lawn mower and several of his Alabama teammates in the mid-1930s. In late 1957, he returned to the University of Alabama. (Bryant Museum)

I

"Mama Called"

There's not a spot of ground out there that doesn't have a little of my blood on it.

—Bear Bryant before first spring practice at
Denny Field, 1958

THE NEW COACH had arrived at Friedman Hall early, moving to the front of the deep, narrow room and repeatedly glancing at his watch. He was not about to begin early, and he assuredly would not start a second late. Tardiness for him was the sign of a deep moral failing, an unforgivable character flaw. "It reflected sloppiness and a lack of commitment," Bryant biographer Keith Dunnavant wrote. Finally it was time.[1]

"How many of y'all have girlfriends?"

They were football players, weren't they? Almost all of them had girlfriends, some more than one. Maybe the new coach was just asking a friendly question, a prelude to some clever down-home southern bon mot that would break the ice and get everybody loose and relaxed. Get the new regime off to a good start.

"Well, all y'all who raised your hands might as well pack your bags right now, 'cause you won't have the time to become football players."[2]

No one laughed. Paul "Bear" Bryant's face was only just beginning to develop a crease or two, still decades away from its familiar deeply lined look—almost like a sheet of paper that had been crushed into a tight ball then smoothed into a flat sheet again. In December 1957 Bear was still close to his physical prime. He was forty-four years old, almost six-four, roughly 220 pounds, and ruggedly handsome. Everything about him seemed big and powerful—high forehead, large ears, wide powerful shoulders, thick hamlike hands, sturdy legs. He looked like a coach who could get physical with his biggest players—really get down without pads and go one-on-one with a guard or a tackle and win. He looked it, he could do it, and on occasions when he wanted to make a point, he did it. Even in an expensive tweed suit, a white shirt, and a Countess Mara tie, there was nothing about Coach Bryant that breathed a trace of softness or suggested he couldn't kick the ass of any man within hollering distance.

If there was anyone who doubted that statement, one look into his clear, cold blue eyes would set them straight. He seemed to look at the world with his chin slightly tilted down so that his eyes were skewed up, forcing him to furrow his forehead. It wasn't a calculated expression, but it had a chilling effect. Richmond Flowers Jr., who was recruited by Bryant, recalled that when you talked to Bear you tended to look up at him and he tended to look down at you. Others who knew him agreed: He had a gaze that was difficult to meet, the kind of penetrating intensity that made a man afraid to look into his eyes directly because it might be interpreted as a challenge, and fearful to look away because it might be taken as a lack of resolve.

On the morning of December 9, 1957, every player crammed into a classroom in Friedman Hall, the athletic dorm, was looking at Bryant. They had heard the stories about the coach—the tales about Junction Station in Texas, his take-no-prisoners method of coaching, his record of turning losing programs into winning ones. But they had not seen him in the flesh until that moment. Now, sitting in classroom desk chairs, standing in the aisles and crammed against the walls, some dressed in khakis, penny loafers, argyle socks, and letter jackets, others in slacks, button-down shirts, and V-neck sweaters, they waited for a sign of what was to come.

He talked a little about himself, about why he left Texas A&M, a team that had fallen just a few plays short of winning a national championship, for a team that was setting new records of futility at a proud football school. He had come to Alabama, his alma mater, for one reason, and it wasn't money. No, he said, "I could buy or sell any one of you. I came here to make Alabama a winner again."

And that meant a new philosophy and a fresh start for everybody. He made a guarantee and a promise. "Everything from here on out is going to be first class, which includes living quarters, food, equipment, modes of travel. And my staff and I are going to see that you play first-class football." He said that he was interested in only first-class boys on his team, the kind who regularly wrote letters to their parents, always used "yes, sir" and "no, ma'am," said their prayers at night, and went to church on Sunday. He demanded boys who took pride in how they looked and how they acted, ones who were excited about representing a great school and determined to represent their families and hometowns with real class.

If a boy knew he did not fit Bryant's definition of a first-class player, if he wasn't ready to give maximum effort, Bear had some advice. "If you're not committed to winning ball games, to making your grades, go ahead and get your stuff and move out of the dorm, because it's going to show. Pull out so we can concentrate on the players who want to play."

Beyond that, Bear didn't talk about the x's and o's of football. There would be time for that, and time for them to get to know him and him to get to know them. Right now, he said, "I don't know any of you and I don't want to know anybody.... I'll know who I want to know by the end of spring practice."[3]

———

Bear was in a foul mood, and had been for some time. Coming to Alabama had cost him considerably, and money was the least of it. The chain of events that prompted his move from Texas A&M began far from the football field. In February 1956, after a three-year court battle, Autherine Lucy, a college graduate from Shiloh, Alabama, became the first black student to attend the University of Alabama. Her presence on campus prompted a series of protests, ranging from marches and speeches to violence. Though escorted to classes by university officials, Lucy was pelted with rotten eggs and forced to accept police protection to get off campus. The worst for her came after Alabama upset Vanderbilt in a basketball game. Students departing the game and nonstudents milling around campus formed a mob, chanting, "Hey, Hey, Ho, Ho, Autherine's got to go!" and "Two, four, six, eight, we don't want to integrate!"[4]

The mob blocked traffic and created a public nuisance. Although many of the protesters had no ties to the school, their actions alarmed Alabama's Board of Trustees, who voted first to exclude her from the university and then, after Lucy's lawyers filed a temperate complaint, to permanently expel her from the institution. She had been thrown out of school not for anything she had done but for what she symbolized to others.

Coming in the wake of the *Brown v. Board of Education* school desegregation decision, the Lucy case represented southern resistance to the law of the land, and cast the university in an obstructionist, backward, racist role. It threw a pall over Tuscaloosa. The University of Alabama had lost its role as a progressive leader in Alabama and seemed to wander aimlessly in the desert of lost causes. Interim president James H. "Foots" Newman developed a reputation as an ineffectual bean counter, and according to the *Montgomery Advertiser*, thirty or more of the top educators left the university, which seemed to be floundering.[5]

Losing professors was one thing; losing football games was a different matter. Few students at the school or residents of the state noticed that some faculty members had slipped off to greener pastures, but everybody was aware of the slide in the football program. In 1955, J. B. "Ears" Whitworth had taken over the reins of a struggling program and steered it in the direction of total futility. In three years his teams won four, tied two, and lost 24 games. The program had resembled a Keystone Cops movie. Whitworth's boss, Athletic Director Hank Crisp, doubled as the defensive coordinator, undermining any sense of leadership. Whitworth ran practices without any real sense of planning or purpose. His player evaluations were erratic—he even benched Bart Starr. And the players themselves frequently engaged in drunken brawls, occasionally shot guns in their rooms, and at least once started a fire in Friedman Hall.

The program appeared doomed. Finus C. Gaston, the sports information director of the period, later remarked that Whitworth "didn't have a whore's chance" of correcting the ills of the program. Like interim president Newman, his experience and temperament were a poor match for the needs of the University of Alabama.[6]

The year of change came in 1957. In September the university's search for a new president ended with the hiring of Frank Anthony Rose, a tall, handsome, imperiously thin Mississippian. He was a man of a few talents and enormous charm, and on the surface he seemed the very ideal of the New South. Rose was fond of talking about his boyhood when he picked cotton for fifty cents a day and plowed fields to earn money to attend Transylvania College in Lexington, Kentucky. There he excelled in his studies, was elected to Phi Beta Kappa, and graduated with a degree in philosophy and religion. After some additional postgraduate studies he became a professor at Transylvania, an ordained minister in the Disciples of Christ, and, at the age of thirty, without an advanced degree, the president of the Kentucky college. It was nothing less than a meteoric rise, one accomplished seemingly without effort.

His gift, his near nonpareil talent, was talking. Onstage he could silence the birds. A series of speeches before national and regional groups led the National Junior Chamber of Commerce to name him one of the ten outstanding young men in America, an honor he shared with Robert F. Kennedy, among others. But he was even better in one-on-one conversations. Anyone who talked with him departed supremely confident that he or she had found a kindred spirit. In conversation he would smile, laugh lightly, nod his head, and mutter such rejoinders as "I know, I know, you're so right, you're so right." And if he wasn't agreeing with his fellow conversationalist, he was chatting about himself and the great plans he had for the future.

E. Culpepper Clark, a former faculty member and administrator at Alabama, and author of *The Schoolhouse Door: Segregation's Last Stand at the University of Alabama*, called Rose "spiritually impoverished" and totally lacking the "empathy gene." Although there was no denying that he was a captivating man, a quality that made him a first-class fund-raiser, Rose played fast and easy with the truth and creatively invented biographical incidents out of whole cloth. Well dressed in conservative but perfectly fitted suits, and bearing a striking resemblance to Crimson Tide football legend Johnny Mack Brown, Rose cut a dashing figure. No sooner was he in the president's office than he began to talk and raise cash. Between January 1 and March 7, 1958, he delivered fifty-four speeches, speaking earnestly about what was needed to make Alabama a great university. But greatness took money. Job number one, he figured, was to improve faculty salaries, a general line that made him immediately popular on campus.[7]

And he was successful. In the immediate post-Sputnik environment the federal and state governments were shoveling money into education to guarantee America's success in the Cold War. It was the age of the great educational giveaway. Soon faculty salaries shot up like a Soviet rocket, enrollments increased, and new buildings began to sprout on campus, including, Clark noted, "a new administration building named for Rose and a high-rise dormitory named for Rose's equally charming wife, Tommye." People at the University of Alabama were striding forward, and Frank Rose was leading the way.[8]

Still, Cold War manna alone was not enough to succeed at Alabama. Although the state legislature had been notoriously tight-fisted with educational expenditures, raising money was the least of Rose's problems. An astute observer of the Alabama scene, a member of one of the state's leading political families, remarked that for whites in the late 1950s and early 1960s "there were only two topics of conversation: football and niggers." Football and race—they formed the substance of discussions at the country clubs in Birmingham, Montgomery, and Tuscaloosa; at the meetings of the Birmingham Downtown Improvement Association, the Association of Citizens Councils of Alabama, and the Ku Klux Klan; and at every lunch counter, country store, and restaurant in the state. Football and race, race and football—they were what white Alabamians talked about, argued about, and commiserated about. They were what unified a state sharply divided along racial, class, and educational lines—and what any president of the University of Alabama had best be able to handle questions about.

After the settlement of the Montgomery Bus Boycott and Lucy's expulsion from the university, the epicenter of the civil rights debate moved outside of Alabama. In the fall of 1957, Little Rock, Arkansas, occupied the front line of the movement. Governor Orval Faubus's segregation stand and President Dwight D. Eisenhower's defense of federal authority captured the headlines. But the seismic quakes in race relations caused by *Brown v. Board of Education* and the Lucy case had not yet stopped. Little Rock might have pushed the University of Alabama off the front page, but the problems—and the questions—remained. When Rose took office the Board of Trustees wondered: Would he prevent the integration of the university? The faculty asked: Would he facilitate the desegregation of the university?

In typical Rose fashion, he answered both questions in the affirmative. The new president had, Clark believed, "the remarkable ability to convince everyone and anyone, from the staunchest segregationist to the most determined liberal, that he was on their side." Off the record, he expressed a variety of ideas for either "keeping 'Bama white" or "moving 'Bama into the mainstream." On record, he said little and did even less, hoping against hope that the fragile status quo would last forever. It wasn't much of a policy, but for a politically minded president there were not many other options.[9]

Popularity was a fine alternative to policy, Rose must have judged, and the sure way to please everyone at Alabama was to do something about the sorry state of the football team. On November 9, 1957, almost three weeks before going on the university payroll, Rose led a small group of Alabama football supporters on an expedition to Houston, where they had a discussion with Bear Bryant. At that moment Bear was on top of the college coaching world. Under him Texas A&M had gone unbeaten in 18 consecutive games, and on the November 4 football poll the team was ranked number one in the nation. On the afternoon before the meeting, A&M had defeated SMU 19–6, making them 8–0. The team featured running back John David Crow, and only one time in their first eight games had the defense given up more than six points.

No one at the meeting was coy. More than just a great coach, Bryant was an Alabama graduate, a visible link to the school's legendary days of unbeaten seasons and Rose Bowl wins. Alabama, Rose emphasized, more than wanted Bryant, it needed him. Ears Whitworth had already been given his walking papers, so there was no air of conspiracy. Bear's concern, however, was for Athletic Director Hank Crisp, who had recruited him out of Fordyce, Arkansas, to play for the Crimson Tide. Bear had his faults, but a lack of loyalty was not one of them, and he refused to oust Crisp against his will. But there was no way he would accept the position at Alabama without total control of the program; he wanted no buffers between Rose and himself.

Beyond that, he was not entirely sure he wanted to leave A&M, where he had influential friends, a recently signed long-term contract, and prestige. He had been offered the Alabama position in 1947 and again in 1954, and both times he had turned it down. Bear ended the meeting by saying he would give it some thought, eventually suggesting a few coaches who would fit Alabama's demands.[10]

As so often happens at meetings of these sorts, the participants departed with different interpretations of the outcome. Bear later insisted—and there is no reason to doubt him—that he had not agreed to take the job. But others felt that he was leaning in that direction. As usual, Rose had all the right answers. Crisp would—and did—endorse Bryant. A salary, never a sticking point, could be worked out. The meeting ended cordially, if inconclusively, with handshakes. Bryant had only one last demand—he wanted to keep the matter quiet. Regardless of where he coached in 1958, he was still the A&M coach, and his team had a national title in sight.[11]

——

But quiet Rose wasn't. In the week after the meeting he glowed like a man whose proposal had just been accepted by the belle of the ball. During the next week he addressed several groups, reporting unofficially—information just for those special people in the room—that the university would hire as their new coach a man with "a remarkable record in his profession.... We expect to get a man who is a good recruiter, who can recruit the South, and who knows the South, a nationally recognized man." The description sounded to the Alabama faithful like only one man: Paul "Bear" Bryant.[12]

It sounded like that to Texans as well. On November 15 Jack Gallagher of the *Houston Post* broke the story under the headline "Bear Goes to Bama." Though no one involved confirmed the story, Gallagher suggested that the deal was done. Bryant's only recorded reaction was to tell Mickey Herskowitz, his closest friend at the *Post*, to come see him at his suite at the Shamrock Hilton after the Texas A&M–Rice game.[13]

Whether it was Gallagher's report, injury problems on the A&M

team, inspired play by a very respectable Rice squad, or some trick of the football gods—the sort that makes a kicker miss an extra point after an announcer remarks that he has not missed one for three seasons—Texas A&M played its worst game of the year. They fumbled six times and three times missed opportunities to score inside the 20. On the other side of the ball, Rice quarterback King Hill scored on a one-yard sneak, kicked the extra point, intercepted two passes, and, in the final four minutes, punted the ball out-of-bounds on the one-yard line. The final score: Rice 7, Texas A&M 6. A&M fell to fourth in the next poll, effectively ending their run for the national title.

Herskowitz visited Bryant after the game. The mood in the suite was funereal. In the room with Bear were his wife, Mary Harmon, and Bob and Kate Bernath, A&M friends. After some uncomfortable silence the group went downstairs to the Cork Club for dinner. There an Aggie graduate approached Bear, introducing himself, praising the coach, and extending his hand. "Bryant ignored it," Herskowitz wrote, "lifted his glass and took a long, slow drink." After the man departed, Kate Bernath said, "Paul, I believe that was the rudest thing I have ever seen. You made that man feel like a fool."

"Good!" Bear replied. "That's exactly how I wanted him to feel."

As Herskowitz saw it, Bryant was wounded and mad, and in no mood for public niceties. The man should have known better than to approach a wounded bear. Paul Bryant "did not suffer fools gladly. He did not suffer losing gladly. He did not suffer suffering gladly."

Now the news was everywhere. Bear Bryant was going to escape from his long-term contract at A&M and return to Alabama. On November 20, columnist Paul Cox of the *Anniston Star* confidently reported, "Controversial coach Paul (Bear) Bryant will succeed

J. B. Whitworth as head football coach at the University of Alabama and also is expected to replace Hank Crisp as athletic director. While University officials continue to deny that the Crimson Tide has already selected a coach to rebuild its football forces, this corner has learned that Bryant is the only one ever seriously considered." Other papers carried similar stories, none of them with confirmation from Bryant himself. Bear had to prepare his team to play the Texas Longhorns, and all any reporters in Texas and Alabama seemed interested in was where he would coach in 1958.[14]

"Few events have excited the state of Alabama as did the rumored return of Bear Bryant to be the head football coach at The University late in the 1957 season," noted the Tide's radio color man, John Forney. It was a time when wild rumors were accepted as established facts and no piece of unconfirmed trivia was too unimportant to share. Stories often began with something along the lines of, "A friend of mine who knows a friend of Mary Harmon's says…" It was said that Paul and his wife had bought property in Tuscaloosa, or at least that they had agreed to rent a house. It was said that Bear had already signed a contract, or had at least agreed in principle. For the citizens of the state, the most football-obsessed in the nation, November 1957 was a heady time. The thought that Bear was coming to rescue the program lifted the hearts of the Tide faithful and induced hope.[15]

With each new report spinning far out of his control, Bryant's mood darkened. "I wish that talk would die down—it's bad for my football team," he told reporters. Herskowitz encouraged him to take control of the story. Just issue a flat blanket denial. Perhaps he could adopt the tactic of William Tecumseh Sherman: "If chosen, I will not coach. If hired, I will not show up." Bear refused to give a firm denial. "No," he said, "I wouldn't want to say that because I might do it." Rose, reporters, and Alabama supporters had put him in a very uncomfortable position.[16]

His team's performance on the field did nothing to improve matters. On November 28 the Aggies lost to the Longhorns by the score of 9–7. They now had lost two games, an undefeated season, and a national title, by just three points. It was hard for the competitive coach to abide. The night after the game, Bryant received a call from an old Alabama friend. The caller wanted to know if Bear was coming back to the Capstone. The man, as he soon learned, was on another fool's errand. "It's sonsabitches like you who cost me the national championship," Bryant cursed before slamming down the receiver.[17]

By then all he was holding on to was his anger. The decision had been made. Shortly after the Texas game he met with a group of reporters shoehorned into his office so tightly, Herskowitz recalled, "they could identify the brand of deodorant the next guy was wearing, if any." Bryant began to talk, finally and from the heart, about the Alabama job.

There was only one reason he would consider it, he began with slow deliberation. "When you were out playing as a kid, say you heard your mother call you. If you thought she just wanted you to do some chores, you might not answer her. But if you thought she *needed* you, you'd be there in a hurry."[18]

He didn't make a formal announcement. All he said was that "mama called," and there wasn't a man fool enough in the room who couldn't read between the lines. Even if there was, Bear's daughter, Mae Martin, soon ended the speculation entirely. In an interview with a Birmingham reporter, she said, "Mama said I could tell you . . . that we are looking forward to being back home in Alabama soon." With Mary Harmon and Mae Martin on record, it was a done deal.[19]

On December 3, two days after Mae Martin's announcement, Bryant signed a ten-year contract to be Alabama's coach and athletic director. President-elect Rose announced that Bear would receive $17,500 a year. "I am happy to come home," Bryant said, "and will give my dead-level best to help build a well-rounded athletic program at the university." Of course, when he talked about a "well-rounded athletic program," he really meant a championship football team.[20]

"The first thing a football coach needs when he is starting out is a wife who will put up with a whole lot of neglect," Bryant later said. "The second thing is at least a five-year contract. He needs five years so he can set up his program and surround himself with people who are winners.... And so he can weed out the hangers-on and the politicians who can't help him, the ones who just get in the way." If there was a main thing that Bear Bryant did better than anyone else, it was to keep the main thing the main thing—and the main thing was winning. Anything that interfered with winning he shed like a snake's skin.[21]

In parable form he said as much to his son, Paul Jr., shortly after the family moved back to Tuscaloosa. The poverty of his early years in Moro Bottom drove him to succeed. It was part of who he was, never erased by success and wealth. Once, early in his coaching career, a reporter asked the name of his hometown. "Moro Bottom," Bear growled. "Moro what?" the reporter inquired. "Bottom. Like your ass."

Paul Jr. knew that Moro Bottom gave his father his burning desire to succeed. He recalled a day in 1958 when his mother hauled him to the Indian Hills Country Club. While she took care of an errand, he went to the locker room and watched some older teenage friends play poker. Oddly, his father happened by and noticed his son at the table.

That night, with his son within earshot, Bear began a conversation with Mary Harmon. At first it seemed like idle talk. Both had gone to school at Alabama and had remained in Tuscaloosa while Bear served as an assistant coach between 1936 and 1939, so they knew most of the leading families in the town. Making a sort of inventory of their acquaintances, Bear talked about the progress— or lack of progress—of the sons, most of whom had been part of the card game. One he said didn't have much going for him, and another might have been a fine athlete but didn't seem to have the toughness needed. And a third lacked any grit at all. And so he continued, making harsh observations to Mary Harmon about every boy at the card table.

Finally, to punctuate the message, he looked over at his son. "And we ain't gonna have any country club cowboys in this family, are we?"

"No, Papa," Paul Jr. answered. There would be no Fordyce "city" boys in it. No smug wiseasses. Not in Bear Bryant's household.[22]

Bryant had returned to Tuscaloosa in early January 1958 with a short fuse and a burning desire to succeed. John Forney was with him on several occasions and was struck by his edginess. "Both in private and public gatherings he gave the impression he was not truly happy about having to come back to Alabama; that he was paying back an obligation," the radio announcer for the Crimson Tide observed. "His general mien led me to believe he thought he was missing out on the opportunity to cash big chips—oil chips—in Texas." Forney recalled an incident at an alumni barbecue at the Birmingham State Fairgrounds when Bear mumbled a few brief remarks and said he would answer some questions. A well-intentioned man asked how he would end the epidemic of fumbling by Alabama runners: "Do you make the players carry the ball around the campus and have it stuck to them with glue?" Bear hesitated, shot the man a hard, cold look, and answered, "Well, that certainly is a stupid question. Let's see if I can think of a suitably stupid answer." The remark effectively ended the Q&A portion of the gathering.[23]

Writer Keith Dunnavant recounted a similar episode. Ears Whitworth had kept an open-door policy for former Alabama players and close friends of the program. He had reserved time on Wednesdays, for instance, for games of dominoes. Friends would drop by, play a few games, and offer advice about how to reverse the Crimson Tide's fortunes. Whitworth's record attested to the worthlessness of both the policy and the advice.

Domino Wednesdays ended in January 1958 when Bear moved into the head coach's office. In short order he informed all domino supplicants that he had no time for such tomfoolery, but he would be willing to meet by appointment at five-thirty in the morning with anyone who had legitimate business to discuss. That was it—a clear statement that he was a serious man with no time to waste. "Just wait'll that joker starts losing, and then he'll want our help," one of the men angrily predicted.[24]

There is no doubt that when Bryant, accompanied by Mary Harmon, Paul Jr., and Doc the crippled dachshund, drove his white air-conditioned Cadillac to Tuscaloosa that January he was not the happiest of men. Perhaps, as Forney believed, he was having second thoughts. Unquestionably he was bitter about the ragged end to what had the makings of a glorious season. But the sobering reality was that he faced a daunting challenge. Alabama regarded him as a football messiah, a coach who could turn water into wine. From Whitworth he had inherited "a fat, raggedly bunch," a team that had finished the inglorious 1957 season by getting spanked by rival Auburn 40–0. Once again, he had to prove himself. He had done it at Maryland and Kentucky and Texas A&M. Could he repeat the feat at the place that mattered most?

———

The Crimson Tide that Bear inherited was a loose, undisciplined team with a well-earned reputation for ill-disciplined behavior and play. A few older Korean War veterans set poor examples for the rest, teaching them to sell their books for beer money, set wastebaskets on fire for laughs, and threaten strikes if they didn't get their way. Friedman Hall, nicknamed "ape dorm," was the center of iniquity on campus, a place that coeds rigorously avoided and to which campus police were frequently summoned. Most of the boys liked their football well enough—but not well enough to really care.

As he had when he first went to Texas A&M, as soon as he reached Tuscaloosa Bryant began to separate those who really wanted to play from those who just thought they did. "My plan was to bleed 'em and gut 'em, because I didn't want any well-wishers hanging around," he later said. He was brutally honest with the players. His governing philosophy was, as it had been since his days at Kentucky, "Be Good or Be Gone." He expected everyone to show up on time, listen to what they were told, and give everything they had during every second of practice and every play in a game. All coaches say roughly the same thing. What separated Bryant from most of the others was that he truly demanded it, and woe to the players who didn't reach his level of commitment.[25]

The players witnessed this at their first meeting in the new year. Bryant began the meeting, punctually, by calling a player's name. "Gilmer? Where's Gilmer?" No answer. "Is Jerry Gilmer in this room?" he asked again. Someone said, "Coach, I don't believe he's here." Looking over at Carney Laslie, assistant athletic director and longtime associate, Bryant shouted, "Dammit, Carney, go upstairs and pack his things. He's off scholarship." Jerry Gilmer was a relative of Harry Gilmer, Alabama's legendary quarterback from the 1940s. "God almighty," one player recalled thinking, "if Coach Bryant would shitcan a Gilmer as quick as a heart attack, no one was safe."[26]

He wasn't just building a team; he was instilling a culture. Every player had already heard a few stories about Bryant's toughness. They were the stuff of football horror stories, passed in hushed tones from one player to the next.

Michael Oriard, a player who grew up in the Pacific Northwest, captained Notre Dame, and played for the Kansas City Chiefs in the NFL, recalled hearing Bryant stories as far back as the 1950s. One that chilled him to the bone claimed that while Bear was coaching at Texas A&M he had a "pit" dug in the practice field, where "he sent two competitors for a starting position to take on each other, no holds barred. Whoever emerged from the pit played that week." To Oriard, the story was "a little like the tale, whispered at night around a campfire, about the escaped maniac with a hook instead of a hand who prowled Lover's Leap. Bear Bryant was the boogeyman of my football childhood."[27]

Players at Alabama who had heard similar rumors soon experienced the reality of Bear's methods. The ones he wanted to impress the most were the freshmen and the sophomores, the ones who would be around for two or three years and would acculturate the new recruits. He didn't "give a squat" about the seniors and he said so. At a meeting in early January he bluntly asserted, "I don't care if every senior in this room gets up and walks out. Because for you to play, you're going to have to be twice as good as a junior or sophomore, and I doubt very seriously that any of you are."[28]

And so it started; in the middle of winter more than one hundred players began to learn about their new coach and how he insisted football be played. In the process, they also learned about themselves and, many later claimed, about life. Bryant maintained that football games were won in the fourth quarter by the team that was best prepared, in the best condition, and wanted to win the most. His off-season conditioning drills, spring practices, and summer two-a-days were designed to see who would quit under intense physical and emotional stress. "I'd rather have a player quit on me in practice than in the fourth quarter of an important game," he often said.

Quitting was an important theme in Bryant's lectures. Repeatedly during that first winter he talked to the players about what he required of them. Go to classes, he said, write your mamas and papas, show respect for your classmates, and "demonstrate your class." And don't quit. Quit once and it is liable to become a habit.

Jack Pardee played for Bear on his Texas A&M teams and vividly recalled such talks. "Coach Bryant told us that if you hang in there, something good will happen," the All-American player said. "All these old clichés came true in front of us. The lessons we learned were useful in life, not just on the football field." Bryant's talks had a strong working-class ethos. "One season when things weren't going well," Pardee remembered, "we had a meeting where Coach was urging us to keep at it. He said, 'What's going to happen when you're 35 and you get a pink slip, the kids are hungry and your wife runs off with the shoe salesman? Are you going to quit then?' I was 18 at the time and it was hard to relate, but by the time I was 35, all those things had happened to me, except the shoe salesman part. I even had cancer when I was 28. I had four kids and didn't know if I'd live a year. Coach Bryant taught us to never give up. The things he preached came true."[29]

He addressed the same issue in Alabama. Jerry Duncan, a player from the mid-1960s, recalled the time when one of Bear's assistant coaches told him that the players were tired. He said he was tired too, "tired of putting up with you players who are reading in the newspapers how good you are when, in reality, you aren't good at all." He was laboring to make them good players and they were prattling about being whipped. Duncan remembered Bear saying, "What I want you to know, though, is there'll be times later in your lives when you won't want to work. You might have a wife and three kids. Your wife might be sick and your kids might be sick. You might have hospital bills to pay, and you might think you're too tired to go to work. But you'll have to go to work at that time just to make it."[30]

Quitting was also a major point of conversation among the players once the off-season "voluntary" conditioning drills began. They were held on the third floor of the old gymnasium above the athletic department offices. And they were anything but voluntary, for the players who did not "volunteer" soon had their "plate" taken away—meaning they lost their meals, board, and scholarships. The room was about 75 by 100 feet, too small to accommodate the entire team, so the squad was divided into thirds, and each session lasted forty-five minutes. Only on rare occasions did Bryant attend the drills, which were run by the assistant coaches under the overall control of Jerry Claiborne. There were two doors in and out of the room, and once the sessions began they were shut and locked. For the next forty-five nonstop minutes, with the heat turned up to a devilish temperature, no one got in or out of the room. If a player had to vomit—and almost all of them would—two industrial-sized trash cans were placed next to the doors.[31]

The coaches divided the room into stations, and the players moved from station to station without rests. Jack Rutledge, a sophomore lineman from Birmingham's Woodlawn High School, never forgot the practices. "They had mats where we could wrestle. You wrestled for your life," he said. "They had big weighted bags hanging from the ceiling. They'd pull them back and throw them at you, and you had to stop them with your arms behind your back. That canvas would tear apart your face, drawing blood." Finally, there was the station for calisthenics. "We'd do push-ups and sit-ups 150 at a time, then start again. Your butt would get raw, even start bleeding."[32]

In February the Birmingham newspapers reported that Alabama was in the process of expanding its intercollegiate sports program and was adding a wrestling team to be coached by Pat James. In reality there were no such plans, but assistant football coach James was overseeing the wrestling drills for the football players. James had been a standout player for Bryant at Kentucky and, next to Bear himself, was the most frightening member of the staff. To begin with, he was physically imposing—a big, thick-necked, cauliflower-eared, broken-nosed man with eyes that seemed offset. Added to this, he had no traceable sense of humor—or if he did, a quirky, sadistic one—and seemed to some players to be in training for a guard's position in the state penitentiary. His wrestling drills were cruel, Darwinian contests. Players fought for survival, then crawled off the mats, struggled to their feet, vomited into a trash can, and staggered on to the next station.

Before long, players started quitting. Bryant talked about total commitment, and he totally demanded it. It was not idle chatter or hyperbole. Some players simply would not or could not pay the price he demanded, and he offered very little encouragement to any of them. In later years Bryant's assistant coach Gene Stallings, a veteran of Bear's Junction Station training camp who joined the staff in Tuscaloosa, admitted that there was a method to the madness

Bear brought to Alabama. "We put it on these guys," he said. "We were sent there to run people off." And they did. That winter the "bump-bump-bump" of trunks being dragged down steps late at night echoed through the halls of the athletic dorm, as players, too ashamed to face their friends or Coach Bryant, hightailed it out of Tuscaloosa.[33]

Bryant didn't lose sleep over the victims of his methods, hardly, in fact, even thought of them. To him they were "riffraff," though in later years he tried to smooth the harsh edges of his use of the term. Bert Bank, the producer of Bear's television show, recalled a story that underscored the point. As the two walked into a Tuscaloosa hotel for a cup of coffee, they passed the bellman, a former player who had quit the team. "Hello, Coach. Hello, Mr. Bank," he said. Bank returned the greeting, but Bryant breezed by him without a word or a look. Bank was shocked by Bear's behavior, and said as much. But Bear had his reasons: "He's a quitter. Hell, I wouldn't let him carry my suitcase in here. If I was supposed to be on the fifth floor, he'd be liable to leave it on the second."[34]

The winter conditioning drills drove off some players; spring practice drove off more. During an unusually hot and muggy March and April, the players hit and ran and ran and hit. It was a time when coaches believed that permitting players to drink water during practices smacked of coddling, and excessive mothering was not in Bear's nature. Trainer Jim Goostree gave the players salt and potassium tablets that combated cramps and, incidentally, increased the need for water, but there were no water breaks during practice sessions. The players went to about any length to get some liquid into their mouths, including sucking on sweaty towels, and once in the showers they tilted back their heads, opened their mouths, and drank until they were virtually waterlogged.

By spring practice most of the players were so frightened of Bryant that they would do anything to please him—or at least avoid his wrath. One player became sick running wind sprints but refused to stop. "All of a sudden I started to vomit," he said, "but I kept running...and barfing over my shoulder...and I could hear the coaches, 'There's a man that wants to play, there's a man that wants to play.'"[35]

To Bear's way of thinking, a real football player played sick—and hurt. Whenever a player suffered an injury that was not immediately debilitating, Bryant remarked, "Football players are always hurt, you've got to play with the hurt." Certainly he had played with the hurt. During his Alabama days he had had a cast removed and had taken the field against Tennessee with a broken leg. And if he had done it, his players could do it.

Don Cochran learned this before the first game of the season. The week before the contest against LSU, Cochran badly dislocated his elbow. X-rays were taken and it looked bad. On Sunday Bryant accompanied Cochran on a visit to Dr. John Sherrill. As Cochran recalled the meeting, "Coach Bryant says, 'Doc, how long's it gonna be before he's ready to play?' And Dr. Sherrill said, 'About a month.' And Coach Bryant said, 'Sheeit.' He turned around and put his arm on my shoulder, the one that was bad, and he said, 'Don, you be ready for practice by Tuesday?' And I said, 'Yessir, Tuesday.'"[36]

A few years later another player collapsed in practice gripping his chest. "I think I'm having a heart attack!" he screamed. "God, I think I really am!" Jim Goostree, a disciple of the Bryant school of compassionate care, walked over to the player and said, "You've got to suck up them heart attacks, boy!" Eventually the player quit, but upon entering the Army he received a full medical examination and tests, which revealed that he had indeed suffered a heart attack on the practice field that day. He *had*, in fact, sucked it up pretty well.[37]

So it continued throughout spring practice and into summer two-a-days before the school and regular season started. Players went without water, vomited during conditioning drills, played hurt, and, if necessary, sucked up heart attacks. Or they quit. It was that simple. They bought fully into the program or they were long gone. The most famous defection was center Eugene Harris, who reached his limit one hot day in spring practice. On his final play at the University of Alabama he snapped the ball, brushed past the noseguard, sprinted past the linebackers and defensive backs, took the most direct route toward the chainlink fence that stood between him and freedom, and leaped at the fence, hitting it about four feet high and neatly vaulting over it. It was said that Harris continued to sprint toward the locker room, shedding jersey, pants, shoulder pads, hip pads, and the rest of his equipment as he ran. According to witnesses, Eugene Harris, by the time he arrived at the locker room, was wearing only a jockstrap. By the time practice had ended and the other exhausted players slumped into the locker room, Harris was gone, never to be seen or heard from again.

The legend maintains that Bryant's only comment was, "Manager, if any of these other turds want to quit, open the gate for them."[38]

The legend of Eugene Harris, like all good legends, contained an important message. It was told and retold over the years, undoubtedly with some embellishment, to define what it took to play football for Paul "Bear" Bryant. You either had to give yourself to him body and soul or run like you'd stolen something. The players who remained at the end of the season were Bryant players—and many others would follow. As a whole, they tended to be smaller and quicker than the players they would compete against. They were also more disciplined and had higher football intelligence. And without question they were far better conditioned and meaner. The vast majority were southern boys who took on the personality of the coach they generally feared, often cussed, sometimes loved, and always respected. They became Bryant's Boys. And over time they developed an intangible aura.

Bear Bryant and his Alabama team played in the inaugural Liberty Bowl of 1959 in Philadelphia. Although Alabama lost 7–0 to Penn State, the game began a streak of bowl appearances by the Crimson Tide that lasted until Bryant's retirement after the 1982 season. Photographs of the players showed folks back in Alabama that Bear knew how to dress his boys up right and take them to town. (Bryant Museum)

2

"Dixie's Pride, Crimson Tide"

The main thing I admired was this: When he walked on the field with his slow, big-cat amble, eyes squinted against the sun, the skin of his face as corrugated as a mountain range, you knew one thing. You knew that win, lose or draw, football would be played there that day.

—Howell Raines

I AIN'T NEVER been nothin' but a winner," Paul Bryant was fond of saying. It wasn't an opinion. It was proven fact. He won as a player at Fordyce and Alabama, and as a coach at Maryland, Kentucky, and Texas A&M. Time and again he had accomplished more with less than arguably any coach in the country. And at the University of Alabama—a school that had won only four of 30 games during the three seasons before his arrival—he turned the program around with remarkable speed. In 1958 Alabama lost its first game 13–3 to LSU, the year's national champion, and finished the season 5–4–1. They improved to 7–2–2 in 1959 and 8–1–2 in 1960, finishing with national rankings of ten and nine, respectively. Bryant won with undersized, stunningly conditioned players, a group of "mean little guys" who were to a man more afraid of their coach than any opponent they faced on the field.

President Frank Rose had hired Bear to restore the glory of Alabama football, and he was on track to do it. And for Alabamians and southerners more generally, "glory" was not an ideal word. By the 1960s the Deep South had embraced football with a passion and meaning unrivaled in the rest of the country. The schedules of the Tigers, Rebs, Bulldogs, and Tide formed the rigid spine of autumn social calendars in Louisiana, Mississippi, Georgia, and Alabama. Each team seemed vital to the health and well-being of the state. But even in this atmosphere of heightened fanaticism Alabama stood out, for the Crimson Tide was not just Alabama's team. It was at a more fundamental level the pride of all Dixie.

———

American football began in the Ivy League while the South was painfully coming to terms with the realities of Reconstruction. In 1869 Rutgers defeated Princeton in the first intercollegiate "football" game, a contest that allowed no running with the ball or tackling, one resembling soccer more than football today. In the 1870s football followed the style of Harvard's Boston Game, which in turn had more in common with rugby than soccer and permitted running with the ball and, under certain conditions, passing. By 1876, the final year of Reconstruction, Yale and Princeton had adopted the Harvard game, and America's three most exclusive colleges formed the Intercollegiate Football Association to codify the rules of the sport.

During the next half dozen years rule changes Americanized football, including the legalization of blocking, the creation of the line of scrimmage, the adoption of a downs system to govern the transference of the ball from one team to the other, and a new system of scoring. Walter Camp, Yale's captain and later coach, was the driving force for most of the changes during the next generation, and under his guidance and promotion football became the premier college sport. By the 1890s homecoming games, and especially the New York City Thanksgiving Day game, drew thousands of spectators, hundreds of thousands of dollars, and were covered in the society and sports pages of newspapers and magazines. By the turn of the century gamblers bet millions on football games and colleges competed for the top recruits. The game, in short, had become modern—overemphasized, dangerously violent, rabidly followed, the source of student and alumni pride, and riddled with scandals.

But during the 1890s football became something more than just a sport: Writers, coaches, and politicians transformed it into an ethos. Unlike baseball, whose ideology emphasized democracy and America's rural heritage, football was unabashedly elitist and aggressively modern. It was the sport of the most privileged colleges, played by sons of Theodore Roosevelt and other American leaders. It was violent, yes, but it was also a manly testing ground, a harsh laboratory for the next generation of leaders. The ideology of football echoed Roosevelt's call for the "strenuous life" and John Philip Sousa's stirring marches. It was the sporting equivalent of Owen Wister's *The Virginian* and Jack London's *Call of the Wild*. Football was the visible expression of manly power at a time when the United States was competing for a world empire in the Caribbean and the Pacific. Of course it was the sport of the elite—it showcased their values. "In life, as in a football game," Theodore Roosevelt counseled the American boy, "the principle to follow is: Hit the line hard; don't foul and don't shirk, but hit the line hard."[1]

Yale was the greatest team of the late nineteenth and early

twentieth centuries, averaging less than one loss a year for its first forty years in the sport, and during the era a group of latter-day Johnny Appleseeds carried the highly regimented, scientifically managed Yale system west. In 1892, Amos Alonzo Stagg, a member of Skull and Bones at Yale and a selection on Camp's first All-American football team, accepted a position as head football coach at the University of Chicago. There he built one of the strongest programs in the Midwest. Others followed Stagg's meanderings. Fielding Yost gained fame at the University of Michigan, and during World War I and the 1920s others, such as Robert Zuppke at Illinois, James Michael Phelan at Purdue, and Knute Rockne at Notre Dame, did the same. The formation of the Western Conference (later known as the Big Ten) attested to the flowering of the sport in the Midwest.

Football also traveled south, and although it discovered pockets of interest, the soil was not as fertile as in the Midwest. Few high schools had budgets to support football programs, and even if they did, southern public education lagged woefully behind the North. Most students dropped out of school long before the sixth grade and went to work in the cotton plantations, lumber mills, and farms that fueled the southern economy. Furthermore, public and private southern colleges normally lacked the student population or funding to compete in the sport. The sons of the elite who went to regional institutions understood football in the same way they understood medieval jousting. For jousting they read Sir Walter Scott; for football they read articles in *The Century, Collier's, Harper's Weekly, Outing, Outlook, Independent,* and other popular magazines. Some even attended Princeton or Yale, learning the basics of football and returning home with an enthusiasm for the sport.

Yet for more than a generation the South lagged behind the North in football. As in so many measurable areas of life—such as education and health standards—the South seemed to conform to the North's image of the "Benighted South," a cultural desert of illiteracy, hookworm, and racism, where the Ku Klux Klan reigned supreme and "natural" leaders wallowed in the memory of the Lost Cause. In this context, intersectional games became jokes. For example, in 1890, Virginia, one of the best teams in the South, ventured north to play two Ivy League colleges. On October 31 they were pummeled by Pennsylvania 72–0, and the next day they were humiliated by Princeton 115–0. As a point of comparison, the following week Virginia played Randolph-Macon, another southern school, and won 136–0, and Penn was later soundly beaten by Yale 32–0.[2]

Most northern schools scheduled intersectional games against southern teams early in the season. They were warm-up games, intended as easy wins and confidence builders. The contests were almost always played in the North. Southern teams boarded trains like sacrificial sheep, with little hope of keeping the game close, let alone of winning. Southern newspapers reported the dismal outcomes as they had General Lee's move into Pennsylvania—a valiant effort but in the end a disastrous defeat. The exception that proved the rule took place in 1905 when Vanderbilt, probably the finest squad in the South, visited Ann Arbor to play a mighty Michigan team. The final score: Michigan 18, Vanderbilt 0. But the Nashville press treated the outcome like a singular victory. The *Nashville American* proclaimed it Vanderbilt's "greatest triumph since the team was organized."[3]

Football came to Tuscaloosa during these hard years. In 1892 a round-jawed, pugnaciously defiant, pudgy boy named William G. Little arrived on the Alabama campus. He was a native of Alabama but had spent some time at Phillips Exeter Academy in Exeter, New Hampshire, and hoped to attend an Ivy League college. But the death of a brother brought him home and landed him at the University of Alabama.

In prep school Little had gained a basic familiarity with football, and he arrived in Tuscaloosa with a pair of cleats, a battered leather ball, and stories about the thrilling game that had become a passion in the Northeast. Surely, he thought, Alabama would want to field a team. After all, Auburn had done so the year before. And so it happened—Little organized a student-run, student-financed team at Alabama. That first season they won two of three games against Birmingham high school and athletic club teams, and lost a game against Auburn by the score of 32–22. It was an inauspicious beginning—but it was a beginning.

During the next twenty-five years or so, Alabama football prospered. Although the team never traveled north to play a national power, it won more than it lost against Southern Conference schools. Like other southern colleges, it developed colorful traditions that harkened back to the South's Cavalier and Lost Cause mythology. Southern sportswriters continually referred to the chivalric and martial spirit of regional players, and in the 1890s the singing of "Dixie" at the contests became a staple. Auburn waved "The Bonnie Blue Flag" during games; defensive stands reminded journalists of the heroics of General Stonewall Jackson; and sportswriters struggled to get through a paragraph without employing some knightly image. By the turn of the century, southerners had transformed the game into something noble, courteous, and manly.[4]

Until the mid-1920s Alabama enjoyed only moderate success in the Southern Conference, and almost none at all in important intersectional games. Sewanee—which in 1899 went 12–0 and outscored opponents 322 to 10—and Vanderbilt were the class of the South. But the Crimson Tide's fortunes changed quickly after the Great War when Xen Scott became head coach. A former horse-racing writer, the hatchet-faced, chilly-eyed Scott compiled a four-season record of 29–9–3 and elevated the program above the also-ran level. But in 1922 mouth and tongue cancer forced him to leave coaching.

Wallace Wade replaced Scott. It was said that Wade lost weight when he coached football, and it may have been true. Certainly he was an intense coach, totally devoted to his job, prickly about the slightest interference, and absolutely assured that he knew the right way to teach the game. A native of Tennessee and a graduate of Brown, Wade had served in the war and brought a military discipline to coaching. The game, he preached, was simply a matter of execution. Blocking, tackling, and running—the team that executed those three basic skills the best usually won. So Wade drilled his players, laboring over technique and timing until he was satisfied that it was nearly perfect.

To reinforce the idea of perfection, line coach Henry "Hank" Crisp developed his own methods. As a young boy Hank had lost a hand in a farming accident, and he wore a stiff leather sleeve over the stump. In practices, Winston Groom wrote, "Crisp would squat behind [the players], one by one, the leather stump between their legs, counting '1-2-3'…and if the snap was '3,' they had best be off and running." The absence of perfection came with a painful price tag.[5]

The Crimson Tide achieved greatness in 1925, finishing the regular season 10–0 and outscoring their opponents 277 to 7. In successive games they shut out LSU, Sewanee, Georgia Tech, Mississippi State, Kentucky, Florida, and Georgia. Led by quarterback and defense stalwart Pooley Hubert, stolid end Wu Winslett, and halfback Johnny Mack Brown, a handsome, swift, and irrepressible runner, Alabama was the finest team in Dixie.

But Dixie, after all, was still only Dixie. National attention focused elsewhere. Nineteen twenty-five was Red Grange's final year at the University of Illinois. The year before, in the inaugural game for the new Memorial Stadium at Illinois, Grange had become a legend when he returned Michigan's opening kickoff for a 95-yard touchdown. Before the quarter was completed, he had scored three more times on runs of 67, 56, and 44 yards. After Illinois's one-sided victory ended Michigan's 20-game unbeaten streak, famed sportswriter Grantland Rice had rhapsodized:

> *A streak of fire, a breath of flame*
> *Eluding all who reach and clutch;*
> *A gray ghost thrown into the game*
> *That rival hands may never touch;*
> *A rubber bounding, blasting soul*
> *Whose destination is the goal—Red Grange of Illinois!*

The story of the "Galloping Ghost" was born.

If wherever Grange was playing was the hottest ticket in 1925, other players and teams attracted the attention of the national press. Ernie Nevers at Stanford, George Wilson at Washington, Andy Oberlander at Dartmouth—they were the stars of 1925. The South's position in the sporting firmament was underscored by the year's consensus All-American list. Twelve players—not one from Dixie. As far as the rest of the nation was concerned, Alabama might as well have played their games in the dark.

But 1925 was also one of the periodic tipping points in the history of intercollegiate athletics. There were several indications that football was running amok and that the ideal of the student-athlete was not ideal. The Galloping Ghost was one. On November 21, before more than 85,000 spectators in Columbus, Grange led the Illini to a 14–9 victory over Ohio State. Five minutes after the game ended he told a group of reporters in the locker room that he planned to drop out of college to play professional football. The next day he signed an NFL contract with the Chicago Bears. Between his salary and share of gate receipts, he earned more than $100,000 for a nineteen-game barnstorming tour. That he had cashed in on his fame faster than he could snake his way to a touchdown struck many observers as crassly materialistic and gave them second thoughts about the state of college football.

A *Peoria Journal* editor thought that Grange's decision to desert Illinois for money "must be distinctly harmful to any institution in that it confirms critics who contend colleges have gone daft on interscholastic athletic contests and that education has been lost in the shuffle." And a *Christian Science Monitor* writer mockingly suggested, "James Russell Lowell once wrote that a university was a place where nothing useful was taught. How admirably Illinois has answered this slur by so instructing an undergraduate that he could earn a million dollars without even the formality of graduating!" And so it went in papers and magazines across the nation— college football had lost its sense of direction, betrayed the values of Teddy Roosevelt, and become a symptom of what was wrong with America, not what was right about it.[6]

At about the same time, Howard Savage, a staff member of the prestigious Carnegie Foundation for the Advancement of Teaching, issued a study entitled the "Twenty College Report," a preliminary statement for a much fuller report released in 1929. Savage's paper criticized the overcommercialization and educational abuses of intercollegiate sports, especially football. Cheating scandals, tramp players, financial irregularities—the list was long, specific, and unseemly. And who was to blame? The search for responsibility for the sad situation ended "at the door of the college president."

As Shakespeare's Cassius said, "The fault, dear Brutus, is not in our stars, / But in ourselves, that we are underlings."[7]

Grange's bolt for the pros and the "Twenty College Report" had nothing and everything to do with Alabama football. The nice thing about existing outside of the mainstream is that you are outside of the mainstream—the events that piqued moral outrage in the Harvard and Yale presidents' offices and the *New York Times* editorial room sent few ripples as far away as Tuscaloosa. But the splash was greater in the East and the Midwest, where presidents puffed with moral outrage said that college football really had become a nasty, commercialized business. As historian Andrew Doyle observed, after l'affaire Grange and the Savage Report, college administrators "embarked on one of [their] periodic episodes of soul-searching and self-flagellation over the inherent contradiction between the big-money entertainment spectacle of college football and the educational mission of the university." Something had to be done, even if that something was small and symbolic.[8]

Their symbolic target was the Rose Bowl, college football's oldest bowl game, and in 1925 its only bowl game. It was a commercialized extravaganza, a boondoggle trip that took student-athletes away from their classes, mixed the young innocents with unsavory Hollywood types, and served as a shameless publicity advertisement for sunny Southern California. As the snow began to cover the Northeast and Midwest, the best teams in the regions indicated that they planned to celebrate the new year at home. Three top eastern independents, Dartmouth (8–0), Colgate (7–0–2), and Princeton (5–1–1), turned away Rose Bowl representatives. So did Michigan (7–1), the winner of the Western Conference. Even in the West, Washington, 10–1–1 and the class of the Pacific, was not sure it wanted to travel down the coast, though the school's president eventually decided to accept the Rose Bowl invitation.

But Washington still needed an opponent. Ranked number four in the country, Alabama, like the last kid selected in a pickup game, suffered the humiliation of the wait. As far as members of the Rose Bowl selection committee were concerned, it was as if Alabama were playing some sport other than football. An official in charge of finding an opponent for Washington commented, "I've never heard of Alabama as a football team, and I can't take a chance on mixing a lemon with a rose."[9]

Four weeks before the game the Rose Bowl committee reluctantly made an offer to the Crimson Tide. Of course, the entire process had been humiliating for the "pride of the South." Alabama's president, George Denny, and coach, Wallace Wade, demonstrated their pique by sitting on the offer a few days, pretending that they were unsure of their final decision. It was all a show. The truth was that they probably would have marched their players to Pasadena on foot for a chance to play in the game.

The 1926 Rose Bowl game was a rare opportunity for Alabama—and the South—to shine on a national stage. Commentators in the 1920s chastised the South for its religious bigotry, political corruption, and educational malfeasance, characterizing the region as America's great cultural wasteland. Baltimore journalist H. L. Mencken led the attack against the South's peculiar ways. In his 1920 essay "The Sahara of the Bozart," he sniffed, "Down there, a poet is now almost as rare as an oboe-player, a dry-point etcher or a metaphysician." And it was not just poets the South lacked. Mencken charged, "Critics, musical composers, painters, sculptors, architects…there is not even a bad one between the Potomac mudflats and the Gulf. Nor a historian…sociologist…philosopher… theologian [or] scientist. In all these fields the South is an awe-inspiring blank—a brother of Portugal, Serbia, and Albania."[10]

Above the Mason-Dixon Line, the 1925 Scopes Trial reinforced

Mencken's view of the South. Dubbed the Great Monkey Trial, it focused national attention on a Tennessee law that forbade the teaching of the theory of evolution in the state's public schools. Featuring the clash between Bible-wielding William Jennings Bryan and agnostic Clarence Darrow, the trial underscored the social and cultural gulf between the relatively scientifically progressive and prosperous North and the religiously fundamentalist and economically hard-pressed South. The Scopes Trial, combined with the cross burnings of the Ku Klux Klan, the corruption and sufferings of the convict lease system, and reports about the region's scourge of pellagra and hookworm, badly lowered the image of the South in the rest of the country, and it was never high to begin with.

It was in this context that the 1926 Rose Bowl was contested. Regardless of its stellar record, Alabama was given no chance. They may have been undefeated, but they had played only other southern teams, or, as it was understood nationally, a string of palookas. Even southern commentators disparaged Alabama's chances of defeating a Washington squad that had rolled over opponents by such scores as 56–0, 59–0, 64–2, 80–7, and 108–0. The head of the Southern Conference claimed that the Crimson Tide "would offer no more opposition than could be furnished by any California high school team." And an Atlanta sportswriter believed that "Alabama would travel all the way out there, get spanked, and come home with a good record dented."[11]

On January 1 Alabamians gathered in theaters and other public places to follow the game's play-by-play over the Associated Press wire. In Birmingham, Eugene "Bull" Connor provided the play-by-play voice-over. Other citizens braved the chilly temperatures and stood, hands in pockets and coat collars turned up, on town streets outside telegraph stations to follow the progress of the game. They fidgeted, talked nervously, hoping that their team would show well but fearful of another painful humiliation. Historian Andy Doyle argued that these communal gatherings to follow the action on the West Coast were similar to the people who huddled together in telegraph offices in 1863 "to await news of Lee's fate at Gettysburg."[12]

Nothing in the opening minutes of the game challenged opinions that the Crimson Tide would suffer a crushing defeat, or gave solace to the Alabamians following the wire reports. On Alabama's first possession, Washington's All-American back George "Wildcat" Wilson intercepted a pass, then led his team 75 yards for the game's first touchdown. Many spectators had barely reached their seats and the score was Washington 6, Alabama 0. Early in the second quarter Wilson took his team on another stunning drive, escaping for long runs and finishing it off with a touchdown pass. In ten previous games the Tide had yielded only seven points, but in just over a quarter of action Washington had scored 12. At the half, with Alabama trailing 12–0, a sectional humiliation looked like a lock.[13]

Coach Wade said little during halftime, but what he said cut deep. "They told me boys from the South would fight," he said as he looked from player to player. With that he departed the locker room.

Alabama turned the tide in the third quarter. With Wildcat Wilson benched with injured ribs, the Crimson Tide rallied. On one drive Pooley Hubert pounded into the line five straight times for 42 yards, finally scoring on a one-yard dive. The next time Alabama got the ball, Johnny Mack Brown scored on a 63-yard reception. A short time later Brown caught a Hubert pass and wriggled around and through Washington defenders for another score. In seven minutes Alabama had tallied three touchdowns. The Tide led 20–12.

By then it was evening in Tuscaloosa, Birmingham, Montgomery, and the other towns in Alabama. The streets were dark, and the chilly night bit into anyone out of doors. But in the theaters and auditoriums where people had congregated to follow the game it seemed like springtime. People smiled and cheered and seemed to hold their breath forever.

Washington came back, scoring in the fourth quarter to cut Alabama's lead to 20–19. Late in the game the Huskies mounted another drive. On the key play, Wilson broke loose and headed toward the goal line, but Brown made a game-saving tackle. With little time left, Alabama once again gained possession and ran out the clock, securing a victory that legendary coach Pop Warner called "a shock to everybody."

In Pasadena, the Alabama players celebrated, hardly noticing that Washington coach Enoch Bagshaw huffed off the field without shaking Wade's hand. In a year when critics had excoriated football coaches for misplaced priorities, it was the season's final graceless act.

Across the country the two words "Alabama Wins" came off the AP wire. Throughout the state of Alabama, men, women, and children exhaled. Then they went wild with joy, celebrating the most significant sporting contest in the history of the South. Sportswriters and editorialists called the game a "miracle" and a "divine gift." Vanderbilt's coach Dan McGugin later remarked, "Alabama was our representative in fighting for us against the world. I fought, bled, died and was resurrected with the Crimson Tide."[14]

"Us" was not Alabamians. "Us" was every white person born and bred in Dixie. Striking among the newspaper accounts of the game and its results was the transformation of the Crimson Tide into Dixie's team. "South Wins West Coast Grid Classic," read the front-page banner headline of the *Pensacola Journal*. "Dixie Acclaims Her Heroes," echoed a headline in the *Atlanta Journal*. "An impressive victory for the entire South," asserted an editorial in the *Birmingham Age-Herald*. Alabama's victory was the South's victory—a triumph over wiseasses like Mencken, and smug literary types, and all those other critics who rendered second-class citizenships on southerners. Alabama's surprising accomplishment was the critics' comeuppance.

It was something, noted a journalist, to be painted on "a ten-league canvas with brushes of comet's hair."[15]

The team returned home like a Roman legion after a dazzling foreign campaign. Southerners hailed their train as it clanked toward Alabama. They were celebrated in New Orleans, cheered in small towns and hamlets, and when they reached Tuscaloosa, they were met at the railway station, transferred to open wagons, and drawn through the streets by teams of Alabama freshmen. A band played "Dixie," and orators reached for the stars. "When the band plays 'Dixie,' over this team," said one, "it can whip eleven Red Granges."

After defeating the University of Washington 20–19 in the 1926 Rose Bowl, Alabama returned to the Tuscaloosa train depot to a frenzied crowd of supporters. Local fans commented that "Washington crossed the Delaware, but couldn't wade the Tide." (Bryant Museum)

"We did it for the Anglo-Saxon race," said Alabama's president Denny. The game on January 1, 1926, he proclaimed, "was a great victory for Alabama and the South." The president of the Southern Conference added that Alabama "upheld the traditions and fighting spirit of the Old South."[16]

The 1926 Rose Bowl was unique in that it lifted the spirit of an entire section of the country and conferred a regional mantle on a state team. "No victory in football ever changed the destiny of one section of the country like Alabama's furious seven-minute comeback against...Washington," wrote Birmingham sportswriter Zip Newman in the 1960s. The game transformed the Crimson Tide into Dixie's Pride as surely as First Manassas changed Thomas Jonathan Jackson into "Stonewall," totem of southern resistance and bravery. Recognizing this point, and comparing Alabama's football team with the carvings of Robert E. Lee, Jefferson Davis, and Jackson on Stone Mountain, a writer in the *Atlanta Journal* commented, "The Crimson Tide no longer belongs exclusively to Tuscaloosa and the state of Alabama. It belongs to the whole South just like the Stone Mountain Memorial."[17]

Over the next two decades Alabama chiseled in stone its standing as Dixie's Pride. They returned to the Rose Bowl five more times, winning three, losing one, and tying one. In the 1935 Rose Bowl the undefeated Crimson Tide played the unbeaten Stanford Indians. Alabama featured the passing combination of Dixie Howell to end Don Hutson. Playing the other end, the one with his nose in the middle of a block or tackle and not with his hands reaching toward the clouds, was Paul "Bear" Bryant. Recruited by the crusty and profane Hank Crisp, Bryant cherished the memories of the season and the Rose Bowl—the Alabama band playing "California Here I Come" during the final regular-season game, the free food on the long train ride west, meeting Mickey Rooney and having his picture taken with Arkansas native Dick Powell, and beating Stanford 29–13.[18]

One play stuck with him all his life. It was toward the end of the contest and Alabama had the game won. "When they were back in the huddle," Bear recalled, "I looked down on the ground, and there was a bunch of money. I mean, it was a bunch to me. There was a silver dollar, two or three half dollars and some quarters. There must have been between $3 and $4. So I picked it up real fast and had it in my hand. I was planning on running to the sidelines on the next play and giving it to somebody on our bench to keep for me." But on the next play Washington's All-American back carried the ball toward Bryant's end, and Bear had to make a hard choice: Hold on to the money or make the tackle. He lost the coins—but he made the play.

It was the right decision. The money probably would not have made it back to Alabama, but the memories of the victory and the national championship lasted a lifetime. And not just Bryant's lifetime. Alabama's 1935 Rose Bowl triumph, like its 1931 victory, bolstered southern confidence during the bleak years of the Great Depression, providing not money or relief but a sense of hope. "You got to keep from losing before you can win," Bear liked to say. Alabama's victories helped the South keep from losing during a dreary, hard time. During the 1920s and 1930s, years of economic hardship in and cultural criticism of the South, Alabama football provided a singular example of excellence. They played a game originated and codified in the North, and during many years played it better than any other school in the nation.[19]

Writing in the midst of World War II, journalist John Temple Graves dissected the origins of the South's fighting spirit, searching for the reasons his section of the nation was more motivated to go to war than the rest of the country. The hunt took him back to the football fields of the prewar decades. "For all the last stands, all the lost causes and sacrificing in vain, the South had a heart. And a tradition," he wrote. "But the South had a new tradition for something else. It was for survival, and for victory. It had come from the football fields. It had come from those mighty afternoons in the Rose Bowl at Pasadena, when Alabama's Crimson Tide had rolled to glory.... The South had come by way of football to think at last in terms of causes won, not lost."[20]

For Graves, writing during those wretched days after the fall of Corregidor, Alabama football had become a crucial factor in southern history.

———

But in the South there was no escape from history. From almost the earliest days of settlement, through the boom years of King Cotton, and into the midcentury, race had defined the region. In Tuscaloosa, Bryant single-mindedly labored to build the Crimson Tide into a national championship team. He thought about players and formations and training schedules, obsessed over the smallest details that often made the difference between winning and losing, and even mulled over an investment idea or two, but he did not dwell on the one subject that ignited even more discussion than his team. Racial matters rarely occupied his mind—football did.

Bryant viewed race in the context of football. For instance, occasionally when he became aware of a talented southern black player, he passed it along to one of his coaching friends in the North. Hugh "Duffy" Daugherty at Michigan State benefited the most from this informal bird-dogging. Daugherty was one of the first major-college coaches to vigorously and systematically recruit southern black players. In 1955 Michigan State went 9–1, finishing the season ranked number two in the country and defeating UCLA 17–14 in the Rose Bowl. By then only Indiana and Illinois had more black players than MSU.[21]

In the late 1950s and early 1960s Bear and Duffy continued their informal exchange, Bryant sending names of southern black prospects who might want to head north and Daugherty doing the same with northern white recruits who might be a better fit in the South. Duffy, a Pennsylvanian, had close ties to the western half of the state, the same area Bear had recruited heavily when coaching at Kentucky. In early 1961, Bryant told Daugherty about a fine black quarterback in Virginia. Duffy returned the favor by mentioning Joe Namath to

Bear. By then it was clear that Duffy would get Tom Krzemienski from Beaver Falls but not Namath, and given that fact, he hoped that Namath would get out of the entire region. The "you scratch my back, I'll scratch yours" relationship continued. In 1962 Bryant gave a talk to the Roanoke Touchdown Club awards banquet and learned about Charles Thornhill, perhaps the finest running back in Virginia. He called Daugherty after the talk, and even helped recruit Thornhill for MSU. "When Bear spoke to you, it was like God speaking," Thornhill recalled. "You did what he said." Bryant had nothing to lose. Given the realities of race in America, there was little chance that MSU and Alabama would suit up against each other.[22]

By the early 1960s MSU had even more black players, and at the midpoint of the 1961 season the team was undefeated. In the October 15 national poll MSU jumped past the unbeaten Ole Miss to claim the number one ranking. An editor for the Ole Miss newspaper, the *Mississippian*, bemoaned the snub to his school's all-white team, commenting that they would welcome the chance to play against MSU and other Big Ten squads. But, he lamented, "the archaic thinking which prevails in our capital city makes this impossible." The bottom line: "We can't play any teams which have Negro players."[23]

The racial barriers were not quite as unforgiving across the state line in Alabama. In 1959, after finishing the regular season 7–1–2, Alabama received an invitation to play Penn State in the inaugural Liberty Bowl in Philadelphia. Six seasons had passed since the Tide's last bowl appearance, and the team had not traveled above the Mason-Dixon Line since 1946. Across the campus, students hailed the opportunity to play an important intersectional game. "An excellent chance," commented a *Tuscaloosa News* reporter, "to regain much of the prestige that was lost in recent years by showing the East what kind of football is played in the South—and by this Alabama team in particular."[24]

The problem for some Alabamians was that one of the Nittany Lions was black, and the Crimson Tide had never participated in an interracial contest. The player, a large second-team All-American named Charlie Janerette, was from Philadelphia, where he had been a close friend and high school teammate of Bill Cosby's, and was probably the inspiration for the Fat Albert character. Returning to Philly for the Liberty Bowl gave him a chance of playing in front of hometown fans. The distinction of Janerette's race did not trouble Bryant an iota, nor his players for that matter.[25]

Some of the seniors on his team, however, were exhausted from the season and did not relish the thought of another three weeks of practice to play in a second-tier game in the frozen industrial city. "How far is Philadelphia from Canada?" one asked a teammate. Even Bryant admitted to a reporter that a couple of players "told me that they had never been north of Gadsden." But Bear put the matter to rest. "I know you don't want to go," he announced in a 7 a.m. meeting with his seniors, "but the school needs it, our recruiting program needs it, so we're going up north; we're going to play the Yankees, they're big, they're slow and they don't like to hit."[26]

Once he had decided to take his team to Philadelphia, Bryant put his uncanny political skills to work. He confronted no opposition at the university. "I don't think Bryant had to lift a finger more than to say 'I think it will be good for the program,'" commented a former university professor and administrator. "The university made a decision and the decision had to be made, even if it was a shrug." President Rose supported him, and if a few members of the Board of Trustees harbored objections, they kept a public silence. The only request the recalcitrant trustees made was for Alabama's Million Dollar Band to play "Dixie" a few times during the contest.[27]

The recently elected governor, John Patterson, a young, handsome, ambitious political operator, posed more of a problem. The assassination of his father, who was running for attorney general as an anticrime and anticorruption candidate, had thrust Patterson into politics. Moving forward with his father's plans, he became attorney general in 1955, and won the gubernatorial race in 1958. Politically he leaned toward a reforming brand of populism, convinced that the state's property tax system and education badly needed change. But he was utterly convinced that *Brown v. Board of Education* was a tragic mistake and that Alabama and the other southern states should delay its implementation for as long as possible. In his successful 1958 campaign he won the support of the Ku Klux Klan, the Citizens Council, and other opponents of desegregation; he spoke at political rallies in front of a sign that read REMEMBER LITTLE ROCK; and he made his chief rival, George Wallace, look like a card-carrying member of the NAACP.

Bear approached Patterson directly, friend to friend. He picked up the phone, dialed the governor's number, and spoke his mind, pointing out that the contest would be integrated. "Bryant called me and we concluded it was best to try to go ahead with [the game]," Patterson recalled. "There were some legislators that had complained to me that Penn State had a black player, but I didn't have that much to say about it." Patterson agreed that there was no need to make a fuss over the color of one player. As Bear recalled the conversation, Patterson said, "Shoot, Bear, I'm just trying to get some votes. Go on up there and play 'em."[28]

Patterson even recalled that after the Penn State business was taken care of, Bryant said, "You realize we are going to have to start recruiting some of those blacks pretty soon." "I told him I was all for it," Patterson replied, though given that he opposed the integration of the University of Alabama and was using every means at his disposal to delay implementing the *Brown* decision, his response may have been less than heartfelt.[29]

A short time later Patterson gave his blessing publicly in a brief press release: "I congratulate the Crimson Tide on its invitation to play in the Liberty Bowl which brings Alabama back into national football prominence. I commend the Alabama team on its excellent record and spirit, and I wish for a great victory at Philadelphia. I am glad to see Alabama back in the bowls." He decided that it was not the place to mention Charlie Janerette, to say nothing of Bear's recruiting predictions.

In a letter to Patterson, Bryant, and the school's administrators, the Dallas Citizens Council expressed their displeasure about the planned integrated game, but understood that it was probably too late to cancel it. They closed their letter by adding, "We sincerely hope that never again will a team representing the people of Alabama participate in an integrated sport involving physical contact, direct or indirect, with a negro." Furthermore, *Montgomery Advertiser-Journal* columnist William J. Mahoney Jr. thought that the decision to play Penn State was founded on "callous cynicism." "If racial segregation is right and the fight to maintain it in the South is wise and proper," he wrote, "then the invitation to match a white Southern football team against an integrated squad is wrong."[30]

But the protests were few. An editorial in the *Montgomery Advertiser* noted that there had been "some disgruntled mumbling" over the racial composition of Penn State, but reminded readers that total segregation was an impossibility. Alabamians Dusty Rhodes in professional baseball and Bart Starr in professional football played against black opponents, and residents of the state rode on integrated planes and trains. "Southerners contradict themselves frequently on matters of race," he concluded. "Especially is this true in sports." The editor thought the best course of action in this particular case was to enjoy the game. Others agreed. On the whole, football seemed to have trumped race.[31]

Alabama met Penn State on a windswept field in front of an announced attendance of 36,211. In a stadium that could hold 100,000, the clumps of sports fans looked like divots on a fairway. Spectators shivered, stamped their feet to keep up their circulation, and drank anything hot, preferably with a shot of something strong. A few weeks earlier Bryant had downplayed the effect the cold would have on his players, remarking that "some of the boys have gotten pretty cold possum-hunting." He had promised, "We'll just put on our long drawers and go out there and scuffle." Tide players did wear long johns under their uniforms, but the wind howling into the horseshoe-shaped Municipal Stadium was bone-chilling, and many of his players were now having third thoughts about a game for which they had already entertained second thoughts. It was too cold to give much consideration to the racial significance of the game, too icy for the quarterbacks to get a good grip on the ball, and far too windy to pass anyway. From the opening kickoff a defensive struggle was ordained.[32]

And defense it was. Defense and punt. The only break in the rhythm of the contest came toward the end of the first half when a strong breeze seemed to block an Alabama punt somewhere high above the frozen field. Rather than continue on its parabolic course, it hit an invisible wall and dropped like a rock, drifting a touch backward. When it was finally downed, the punt had traveled only three yards, and Penn State had the ball on the Alabama 25. They ran a play that gained five yards, then with time running out lined up to kick a field goal. The holder, Galen Hall, took the snap, sprang to his feet, rolled to his right, and threw a screen pass to Roger Kochman, who followed his blockers for about 10 yards then bolted toward the end zone, weaving "through friend and foe." The extra point made it 7–0—a score that did not change in the second half.[33]

At a postgame party Janerette shook Bryant's hand, saying, "Coach, that's one of the nicest bunch of sportsmen I have ever played against." Bear replied, "Charlie, I don't know how to take that. I think I'd rather you told me they were mean and ugly. Maybe we'da won."[34]

Race did not figure prominently in the action on the field or how it was covered by sportswriters. The *New York Times* reporter at the game misidentified Charlie Janerette as "Chuck Janerette" and mentioned his "pile-driving straight ahead blocking," but not his color. Nor did the Alabama newspapers devote much attention to the race story. But in that regard the 1959 Liberty Bowl was more of an end than a beginning. Rather than being the start of a process that culminated in the integration of the University of Alabama and its football team, it was a final blow to the notion that Bryant's program could magically avoid the roiling debate over civil rights that would soon place Alabama in the center of the national consciousness.

———

The modern direct-action civil rights movement began on December 1, 1955, in Montgomery, Alabama, when Rosa Parks, a few Christmas presents in her hands, boarded a city bus and took a seat in the middle section where blacks could sit so long as no white person was left standing. At the next stop a few whites got on the bus, and one was left without a seat. The driver told the four blacks in the fifth row to surrender their seats. Slowly and reluctantly, three did. Parks stayed put. When the driver asked if she was going to stand, she answered, "No, I'm not." Angered, the driver threatened to have her arrested. "You may do that," she said.

Rosa Parks was arrested, but the incident did not end there. Parks's arrest led directly to the Montgomery Bus Boycott, the 382-day nonviolent protest by blacks in the city to desegregate the capital's bus system. Before the boycott, the civil rights movement was largely in the hands of black politicians and NAACP lawyers. What happened in Montgomery was different—a spontaneous movement of, for, and by the people, designed to improve and give dignity to the lives of the vast majority of blacks. The boycott witnessed the emergence of Martin Luther King Jr. as the movement's dynamic, eloquent leader. But more importantly, it gave birth to a new form of mass protest.

A month and a half after the Liberty Bowl game the Montgomery strategy was turned on its head. In Montgomery, the protest took the form of not riding the city's buses. In Greensboro, North Carolina, a group of black college students protested the refusal of service at a Woolworth's lunch counter by refusing to give up their seats. Reporters labeled their protests "sit-ins," and as nightly network news gave them limited airtime they began to spread across the South, from the upper southern states of North Carolina, Virginia, Tennessee, and Kentucky to the Deep South states of Louisiana, South Carolina, Florida, Arkansas, Texas, Georgia, and even occasionally Mississippi and Alabama. Before they ended more than 70,000 people had participated in sit-ins, and more than 3,000 had been arrested. And they gave birth to other "-ins" at other segregated facilities—sleep-ins at segregated motel lobbies, wade-ins at segregated beaches, swim-ins at segregated swimming pools, kneel-ins at segregated churches, read-ins at segregated libraries, play-ins at segregated parks, and watch-ins at segregated movie theaters.

The protests were nonviolent but not nonconfrontational. They were intended to provoke a response, and they did. Describing a Virginia sit-in, a *Richmond News Leader* reporter wrote, "Here were the colored students, in coats, white shirts, ties, and one of them was reading Goethe, and one was taking notes from a biology text.

And here, on the sidewalk outside, was a gang of white boys come to heckle, a ragtail rabble, slack-jawed, black-jacketed, grinning fit to kill, and some of them...were waving the proud and honored flag of the Southern States in the last war fought by gentlemen." The clashes between mostly black protesters and mobs of angry whites became the fodder for newspaper photographers and television cameramen. Racism and more subtle forms of segregation were common in both the North and the South, but in the early 1960s the press stigmatized the South.[35]

Governor Patterson of Alabama steered a more confrontational course than most of his southern counterparts. In late February 1960, thirty-five Alabama State students walked into a cafeteria at the state capital and asked for service. Refused, they walked quietly out. Tame by the standards of the border South, it was more than Patterson would tolerate. He summoned the Alabama State president, H. Councill Trenholm, and insisted that such demonstrations cease immediately and that the students involved be expelled. Otherwise he would take a hard look at the school's state funding. "The citizens of this state do not intend to spend their tax money to educate law violators and race agitators," he told Trenholm, "and if you do not put a stop to it, you might well find yourself out of public funds." A short time later the Alabama State Board of Education expelled nine of the "ringleaders" of a demonstration so peaceful that it hardly rose to the level of a public display.[36]

Patterson's implacable stance, and the protests and violence it spawned, framed the story nationally. Many northerners regarded Alabama and Mississippi as intransigent states bound by racism and the Lost Cause, locked in a shadowy past of lynching, cross burnings, and night riders. Thoughts of Scottsboro and other miscarriages of justice came readily to mind. And in this narrative the heart of darkness of this uncompromising South was Birmingham, the smoldering steel town overlooked by a fifty-six-foot cast-iron statue of Vulcan and run by a small group of influential patriarchs known as the Big Mules.

In early April famed *New York Times* foreign correspondent Harrison Salisbury dropped down into Birmingham like he was parachuting into some remote, dangerous location behind the Iron Curtain. Wearing wire-rimmed glasses and a conservative summer suit, his hair brushed to the side and back and his mustache trimmed neatly, he looked like Dean Acheson's right-hand man, as out of place in Birmingham as he would have been in Kathmandu. But Harrison had made a Pulitzer Prize–winning career of looking hard, asking the right questions, learning fast, and getting the story. The story—aimed at *Times* readers—asked: What's the matter with Birmingham?[37]

"Fear and Hatred Grip Birmingham," Salisbury's March 12, 1960, front-page article, made an Alabama city, not the sit-ins or the civil rights struggle, the new story. Virulent racism now had a location. "The difference between Johannesburg and Birmingham," a black man told Salisbury, "is that here they have not yet opened fire with the tanks and the big guns." Whites and blacks might walk the same streets, but except for the water supply and the sewer system they shared no other public facilities. "Ball parks and taxicabs are segregated," he wrote. "So are libraries. A book featuring black rabbits and white rabbits was banned. A drive is on to forbid 'Negro music' on 'white' radio stations."[38]

Salisbury wrote that decent whites expressed discomfort with police-state oppression but were afraid to act. What could they do? What could anyone do? "Every channel of communication, every medium of mutual interest, every reasoned approach, every inch of the middle ground," the writer concluded, "has been fragmented by the emotional dynamite of racism, reinforced by the whip, the razor, the gun, the bomb, the torch, the club, the knife, the mob, the police and many branches of the state's apparatus."

Virulent racism also had a face. Eugene "Bull" Connor, the loud, outspoken commissioner of public safety, had a ready smile when he was in a good mood, and a penchant for aphorisms. "Damn the law—down here we make our own law," he said, and "White and Negro are not to segregate together." The sentiments may have been badly put, Harrison inferred, but everybody knew what Ole Bull meant. Together, Bull Connor and Governor Patterson implied that it would be best not to mess with Alabama.

Patterson's and Connor's message was clear: White Alabamians, the people they represented, did not truck with the civil rights movement. What might be tolerated in Greensboro or Nashville, cities that practiced near "border-state flexibility," would not play in Montgomery or Birmingham—or even Anniston.[39]

That became clear in the next scarred battle line of the civil rights campaign—the route of the Freedom Riders. Initiatives of the Congress of Racial Equality (CORE), the Freedom Rides were designed to test a recent Supreme Court decision that required desegregation of seating and terminal stations on interstate bus lines. The plan was simple: Two groups of six riders (three whites and three blacks) would take an interstate bus trip between May 4 and 17 from Washington, D.C., to New Orleans. One group would travel on a Greyhound bus, the other on a Trailways bus. During the trip, two blacks would sit toward the front, two whites near the rear, and a black and white couple would sit together. Similarly, the groups would test the segregated restroom facilities and food service in the terminals. The most audacious and risky aspect of the rides was the route—down through Richmond and Lynchburg in Virginia; Greensboro and Charlotte in North Carolina; Rock Hill and Columbia in South Carolina; Augusta and Atlanta in Georgia; Birmingham and Montgomery in Alabama; Jackson in Mississippi; and on to New Orleans in Louisiana. Against the advice of many in the civil rights movement, the Freedom Riders planned a dangerous, nonviolent assault into the heart of Dixie.[40]

The Riders confronted silent hostility in the Upper South, and some violence in Rock Hill, where native Alabamian and future U.S. congressman John Lewis was beaten by a small group of young white men sporting ducktail haircuts and black leather jackets when he attempted to enter a "whites only" men's room. Swinging west through Georgia, they arrived in Atlanta on May 13 and enjoyed dinner with Martin Luther King at a popular black-owned restaurant. A cheerful mood animated the meal. It had been ten days since they had eaten in a restaurant, the trip was going even better than expected, and there were high hopes that King would pick up the check. The reverend praised the Riders' commitment to nonviolence and social justice, listened attentively to their personal stories, and then left without paying for dinner. It might have been an omen.

A few of the Riders thought that King might join their sojourn, but such an option was the farthest thing from his mind. He had learned through inside sources that the trip would soon take an ugly turn. "You will never make it through Alabama," he told a journalist covering the Freedom Riders.[41]

About one o'clock on May 14 the Greyhound bus crossed the Alabama state line, heading for Anniston. An army town, home of Fort McClellan, Anniston was known for its ordnance depot and aggressive Klan. The streets were lined with gawking townspeople, and an agitated mob waited at the bus depot. Men threw rocks at the bus and slashed its tires, shouting racial slurs and trying but failing to get inside the vehicle. After some minutes the police arrived and escorted the bus to the city limits, where it was trailed by cars and pickup trucks driven by members of the mob. Eventually the attackers forced the bus off the road, and with the passengers trapped inside, one of the assailants threw an incendiary bomb through a window. As the Freedom Riders escaped the smoke and flames, they were clubbed and beaten until the police arrived and halted the violence.

In 1961, civil rights activists conducted Freedom Rides throughout the South to protest the region's nonenforcement of federal legislation against Jim Crow segregation. They faced violence from much of the southern population, including attacks of bricks and firebombs, as shown above in Anniston, Alabama. (Library of Congress)

The attacks on the Freedom Riders were only beginning. The next day Klansmen waited in Birmingham for the Trailways bus. Once again, there were no police around to protect the Riders. Brandishing baseball bats, pipes, and chains, men attacked the Riders, beating several seriously. Bull Connor had told the Klansmen that the police would give them fifteen minutes before showing up, and he kept his word. The mob had its fifteen-minute spree.

Later another group of Freedom Riders was assaulted in Montgomery. Department of Justice official John Seigenthaler, who had tried to broker a deal with Governor Patterson to avoid further violence, was aboard the bus and was beaten unconscious when he got out. Throughout the days of rage Patterson insisted that the Freedom Riders had brought the violence on themselves, that their insistence on challenging the customs and traditions of Alabama created a mood in the people that was uncontrollable and ungovernable.

The original Freedom Riders never made it to New Orleans for the May 17 celebration of the anniversary of the *Brown* decision. And most of the riders who followed in their footsteps in the next weeks and months ended up in Mississippi's notorious Parchman prison. But the Freedom Riders did force the Kennedy administration to act, however reluctantly, on their behalf. Almost equally important, however, the ordeal of the Freedom Riders and the newspaper and television coverage it attracted hardened a belief north of the Mason-Dixon Line that the South was a violent, benighted land, a place that time seemed to have forgotten and where "strange fruit" hung like Spanish moss from trees. Yes, northerners read in their newspapers, the South was backward and terrible. And Mississippi and Alabama were the worst states of them all.

———

Bear Bryant and his Crimson Tide team played no part in the violent episodes in Anniston, Birmingham, and Montgomery. Bryant was not a politician, and he was not even much of a political man. He was a football coach; the boys on his team were football players. They didn't strive to be symbols of Alabama's white power structure, or emblematic of the values of the Old South. But that didn't matter. For Bear Bryant history was fast becoming an inescapable burden.

One link in the unbroken chain of industrial towns along the Beaver and Ohio Rivers, Beaver Falls owed its existence to the production of steel—a life's work Namath hoped to avoid. (Beaver Falls Historical Society)

(Beaver Falls Historical Society)

3
The River

Day turn or night turn he left home at five-thirty. All over the First Ward, all over Braddock and in every steel town in the valley, men were putting on their coats and picking up their lunch buckets and going off to work—out of the houses, down through the mean streets and alleys to the mill. Twice a day, morning and evening, the First Ward was lively with men going to work or coming home. To that rhythm the life of the steel towns was set.

—Thomas Bell, *Out of This Furnace*

N AMATH WAS HURT. He had taken the snap, moved to his right, stuck the ball into his fullback's belly, then pulled it back and slid down the line, forcing the outside linebacker to make a choice. Square up to hit him, and Joe would pitch to his halfback swinging wide. Move outside to stop the pitch, and Joe would turn up in the vacated hole at the end of the line. The linebacker could take his pick. He lost either way.

But the defensive end had played through the tackle's block and dove at Namath's ankle, grabbing it just as the linebacker hit Joe high and drove him into the ground, right shoulder first. Before he even got off the turf Coach Larry Bruno knew his quarterback was injured. Joe's right arm hung at his side. Pain distorted his face. He moved toward the Beaver Falls sideline.

Across the field the Ambridge stands exploded with cheering. "The band beat the drums and went into ecstasy," wrote Joe Tronzo of the *Beaver Falls News-Tribune.* "On the field, the Ambridge players were all happy and showed it with a burst of enthusiasm.... Here were members of the race sent into realms of the greatest happiness because a 17-year-old boy was down on the field with an injury."[1]

At the moment Namath went down, Ambridge led the clash of these two unbeaten western Pennsylvania high school teams 6–0 late in the second quarter. They had been pounding the Beaver Falls Tigers since the opening kickoff, gang tackling, throwing punches, hitting late. One of the Ambridge Bridgers had hit all-state candidate Tommy Krzemienski in the groin, sending him to the ground in pain. They played no-prisoners football, steel-town, win-at-any-cost football. And now Namath was slumping toward the sideline.[2]

Ambridge was one of the river teams. In the fall of 1960 the river still meant something. The rivers of the Ohio Valley burned twenty-four hours a day, every day, with the great business of America—steel. It had made Andrew Carnegie the second-richest man in the country, had drawn more than a million Poles, Hungarians, Czechs, and other Eastern Europeans to the United States, and decided the fate of nations in the Second World War. Steel. The spokes of the factories radiated out from Pittsburgh on the river networks of the Allegheny, the Monongahela, and the Ohio.

Ambridge was one of the steel towns that lined the Ohio and Beaver Rivers northwest of Pittsburgh. Some of the towns had names that sounded like charming New England resorts—Beaver Falls, Midland, New Castle, and New Brighton. The names conjured Dickensian England, nineteenth-century Christmastime celebrations. Other towns sounded like they came from the pages of James Fenimore Cooper's Leatherstocking tales—Aliquippa, Mohawk, Hopewell, and Freedom. But there was nothing bucolic or delightful about any of the places. Long ago they had been transformed into towns driven by one single impulse—steelmaking. For thirty-five miles on the Ohio River and twenty miles on the Beaver River, the brown, almost toothpaste-thick water flowed past factory after factory, forty-five in all.

Some of the plants were enormous. Four of them—two branches of the Jones & Laughlin Steel Corporation, North Star Transfer Coal Company (owned by J&L), and Dravo Corporation—stood side by side in Aliquippa. Along the river, they shipped steel, tar, and ammonium sulfate; received sand, gravel, and coal; and had direct links to at least one major rail line each. North Star operated a twenty-ton electric stiffleg derrick; Dravo maintained mooring clusters of steel sheet piling at 280-foot intervals; and the second J&L plant had acid storage tanks with an 80,000-gallon capacity taking up approximately three miles of riverfront property.[3]

None of these facts conveyed the enormity of the sight of the four mills sitting on the left bank of the Ohio River in full operation day and night. A person needs to stand under a twenty-ton derrick to fully grasp its size, or then to see it against the backdrop of a three-mile mill to understand how tiny it might seem. The mills simply defined everything else, from the gray-sweatshirt-colored sky to the sluggish water to the noxious-smelling air. It was the sight, sound, and smell of industrial America in its last Indian summer.

Ambridge did not hide its function behind a quaint name. Its name was an abbreviation of the American Bridge Company, a factory that specialized in heavy industry. Its high school team's nickname was equally unimaginative—the Bridgers. The town and the high school were all about getting the job done. The truth was that Ambridge and Beaver Falls shared the same ethic. What one saw as a "dirty play" and a "lack of sportsmanship," the other interpreted as "toughness" and "team spirit."

Namath made his way to the sideline, breathing hard and grimacing in pain. "Coach, my shoulder really hurts," he told Bruno.

The first half was almost over, and Bruno decided to play it safe and not press his quarterback to return to the game. "Okay, Joe, you better take it easy. Don't go back in."

"No, no, it's not that bad," Namath responded. "I think I can go back in." More than just a football thing, it was a mill town thing. The boys on both teams were steelworker kids. They played through pain, played with broken fingers, torn ligaments, and assorted other injuries. Putting his helmet back on, he trotted back onto the field, his arm still limp at his side.

With the ball on the Beaver Falls 46, Namath called a pass play. He dropped back and threw, still favoring his right arm. The pass dropped to the ground yards away from the receiver. He called another pass play and once again missed his target—"missed by a mile." For an athlete who could hit a stop sign with a rock from thirty-five yards away, his inaccuracy was alarming.[4]

His shoulder hurt, but he decided that if his arm was going to fall off, it might as well be on a big one. In the huddle he called, "Z-out; Roll-Right; Transcontinental; On One"—a long roll-out pass to a receiver streaking down the other side of the field.[5]

He took his position behind the center, his hunched shoulders giving him the look of a question mark awaiting a sentence. "Green Thirty-Two! Hut One! Hut!" He took the ball, quick-stepped back into the pocket, and began to roll to his right, moving closer and closer to the sideline. At the same time, Krzemienski took off down the left sideline, racing toward the flag on the goal line. Covered by Freddy Kleges—an outstanding three-sport athlete and a future professional baseball player—he moved past the 30, the 20, and the 15-yard line. By this time Kleges was letting Krzemienski run uncovered, knowing that he was out of reach of a pass. More than 60 yards separated Namath and his receiver.

Then it happened. Namath released the ball, and it spiraled with a flat, graceful arc over Kleges's head toward Krzemienski's outstretched hands. Perfect. A 54-yard touchdown—but from where Namath released the ball to where Krzemienski caught it the distance was closer to 70 yards. Just like that, at 8:39 on the night of September 30, 1960, a star was born. When his team needed it most, Joe Namath had tossed a magnificent pass—one that perhaps only a few professionals could have thrown—to completely alter the course of the game. Beaver Falls defeated Ambridge 25–13. Namath became a steel-town high school legend.

Namath was born close to the river, not far from the tracks, a son of immigrants born into a city populated by sons of immigrants. His people came from Hungary in the early 1920s, searching for a better life and ready to work hard to achieve it. His father, Janos (John), was brought to America by his own father, Andras (Andy), who had already settled in Beaver Falls, one of Pennsylvania's steel-mill locations. Andy told John to be an American—forget about returning to Hungary, learn and speak English, and get a job in the mills. John listened. He became a hardworking American, sweating out a livelihood in the Moltrup Steel Company, getting drunk at Aquino's Bar, fighting when the occasion demanded, and dressing like a slick Chicago gangster.

In 1931, he married a sweet, hardworking Hungarian American girl named Rose Juhasz in St. Ladislaus, the Hungarian Catholic church at the top of the 9th Street hill. Exactly eight and one half months later they had their first son, John Alexander, who went by Sonny. Robert (Bobby) followed in 1934, Franklin (Frank) and Rita in 1938, and their last, Joseph William (Joe), on May 31, 1943. Rose was sure that her last child would be a girl, and the local doctor agreed, an opinion with no medical foundation. When Rose first laid eyes on Joe she said, "Oh, no, this couldn't be mine." The baby was not female, he was darker than the others, more Mediterranean-looking than central European. He was different.

Even with a family to support, John's Moltrup job paid the bills with room to spare, and during World War II things only got better for a steelworker in the midst of America's "Arsenal of Democracy." Providing the materiel to fight against Germany in Europe and Japan in the Pacific demanded three shifts a day—7 a.m. to 3 p.m., 3 p.m. to 11 p.m., and 11 p.m. to 7 a.m.—and more workers to fill them. The best shift was 3 to 11. A man could finish his shift, go straight to a bar, drink into the early morning, and sleep into the afternoon before heading back to the mill. It wasn't a bad life. Working in a draft-exempt industry and making good money, John lived better than he ever had.

As straightforward as the wartime effort was, the town itself could be a confusing place. Driving around a mill town like Beaver Falls was especially strange. Within the confines of Beaver Falls, for example, the road system seemed like a maze. It started off simply enough on the streets and avenues within the central city—lined with churches, schools, restaurants, gas stations, shops, and other places of business—where there was a logical grid pattern. The town's main drag, 7th Avenue, accepted thirty-seven separate side streets with perpendicular regularity, like any well-designed city. But then the order ended and a dizzying array of seemingly random streets shot off in wild directions—streets dead-ended into buildings, hairpinned around factories, or meandered for a while before deciding to make an abrupt left or right across the Beaver River into New Brighton or Fallston, where the confusion began anew.[6]

What a motorist failed to see was that the street system of Beaver Falls was an afterthought, a minor consideration developed only after the steel mills were in place. The real thoroughfare was the river, and when a motorist traded an automobile for a boat, the water proved an incredibly organized pathway. Up and down the Beaver River, industrial plants sat shoulder to shoulder like close-set houses on a very dirty country lane, where barges dropped off coal and took away steel.

For workers like John Namath, the river was a back door not taken—his life's work began and ended at the foot of one of the labyrinthine streets leading to the front doors of Moltrup's. And that muddle, the confusing streets and avenues webbing off of the river, held a human dimension as well. Beaver Falls was a trap, a town that lured immigrants with the promise of good jobs. Immigrants like Joe's Hungarian grandparents came, got lost, found employment in the mills, and stayed. And over the years it became increasingly difficult for their sons and grandsons to escape. Working in a steel mill provided a good life for a man and his family, but not an easy one—the shifts, the heat and pollutants, the very work itself wore men down and often into the ground at an early age. Entering a mill for a life of work was not a decision to enter into lightly, and everyone who worked there understood one very important fact—few who went into the mill ever came out. It was a lifetime commitment.

The livelihood provided by the steel mills stood as a birthright to all of the young men of western Pennsylvania, and well-trod paths lay from Beaver Falls High School to every one of the factories. Perhaps John Namath recognized in his young son an inability to live out a life as a worker in one of the steel mills, perhaps he wanted to warn Joe away from the trap of the mill life, or perhaps he simply wanted to show him where he spent the better part of his days—whatever the reason, when John Namath took his young son on a visit to the mill when Joe was ten years old, the memory of that day would remain seared into the boy's mind.

Outside Moltrup's, Joe walked toward the entrance with his father amid a stream of workers who jostled each other, kidded John, and tousled Joe's hair. But for their lunch pails, it might have been the line on Ellis Island fifty years earlier, as all of the brands of wretched refuse welcomed by the Statue of Liberty seemed to be on hand—Dagos and Hunkies, Litvaks and Polacks, Micks and Hebes, Russkies and Cheskeys, Huns and Negroes—all of them making their way side by side into the mouth of the factory. The mill was the perfect embodiment of Israel Zangwill's "great Melting-Pot," the American democratic ideal. It took all men and turned them into equals putting in a good day's work. Work trumped race and ethnicity. It signified membership in the fraternity of the steel town. There was racism to be sure, but it remained a hidden belief practiced mostly by those who never set foot in a mill. "Nigger" was as bad a swearword as any child could utter, the kind that would get his head smacked by any bystander, family or not. It, moreover, was precisely the kind of term that every white immigrant in the area understood all too well—in a sense, they were all outsiders.

When they entered Moltrup's, the men went off to the factory's version of a locker room to get ready for their shift, while Joe and John walked along the outskirts of the mill floor. Every one of Joe's senses was immediately assaulted. What struck him first was the noise. He and Linwood Alford, his black neighbor and best childhood friend, once got caught on a trestle when a train came, and the two had to hang from a railing a hundred feet off the ground while the train passed just a few feet overhead. The noise in the mill made that passing train seem like nothing more than a car with a bad muffler. He wanted to cover his ears, but that would mean letting go of John's hand as well as admitting that he was frightened. The cacophony was myriad and overwhelming—whirring sounds from the massive conveyors taking hot metals from one end of the room to the other, hammering, forging, or banging, and a constant scream in the background that, had he not seen everyone remaining calm and in place, he would have assumed was a fire whistle alerting everyone to run for their lives.

The rotten-egg smell of sulfur was there, but it was not as overwhelming as the smell of the cold metal of the machinery. It was crisp, almost clean, but somehow *wrong*—too cold, with a chemical tartness that hit his senses with the same kind of bizarre feeling he got from chewing on aluminum foil. Only after absorbing all of this could Joe actually take in what was going on. What was most amazing was that in the midst of all this confusion, the workers did not seem the least bit concerned. They moved easily from one place to another, sometimes even playfully bumping into one another the way Joe and his friends did in the hallways of school, while wearing long johns and protective gear in the 130-degree heat. They wandered from station to station, seemingly unaware that a giant pot of molten steel sat bubbling like a captured volcano no more than ten feet from them. When he looked closer at that pot, Joe noticed that there were men working with it—as if it were no more dangerous than a piece of paper or pencil would be to a schoolteacher.[7]

Could this really be where his father went every day to work? It was one thing to go into the mill, but it was another thing entirely to go *back*.

John Namath had anticipated what impact a trip to Moltrup's would have on his youngest son, and it worked. Joe decided right then and there that he would never reenter this hell on earth no matter what happened.

There were a couple of ways to wash the taste of the mills out of the mouth. Literally, and most often immediately after a shift, the mill workers headed to a bar. That much of its social life revolved around alcohol appeared quite clearly with a quick look at the Beaver Falls bus lines. Since steelworkers tended to use public transportation more than their own cars, a bar stood at every bus stop in hopes of intercepting them on their way home from—and occasionally to—work in the mills. Aquino's Bar catered to the Moltrup's and Mayer China crowd; the Corner Tavern, Millgate Inn, and Ernie's Bar surrounded Babcock & Wilcox; the Uptown Inn, Danny's, Patsy's, Joe's Café, Boulevard, Tress's Annex, the Evergreen, Domino's, D&J Bar, Loghouse, and Rio Grill dotted the central city; the Redline Inn served the black community on Mount Washington; and the Sportsman Bar provided after-hours entertainment for its members. Add to these and the other public houses the various private clubs, like the American Legion, Owls, Elks, and Knights of Columbus, and the ratio of bars to population was as high as anywhere in the nation. It did not take long for someone growing up in Beaver Falls to recognize what people did for fun and escape.

The other way out of the mills was through sports. Each of the mills linked itself to sports by maintaining recreation leagues for its employees and building facilities near its plants. Moltrup's opened the town's first fully equipped playground in 1919 next to its plant, then turned it over to the city in 1940, but it was the youth leagues affiliated with the steel industry that really thrived. Local 1082, the steelworkers union, ran a variety of basketball and baseball leagues for the children of its members, including the Namaths. Golf outings also brought workers together outside the hot mills, and the prizes for long drive and closest to the pin reflected the prosperous status of the industry. Basketball, golf, and baseball were sports to play and watch—football, though, was a sport to live. And no sport matched the nature of steel production quite as well as football. Steelwork and football were filled with tough men working as teams in dangerous environments, creating a communal atmosphere and accepting that they were small parts in a larger machine. Perhaps a local advertisement for a game summed up the combination best—"A tough sport for a strong people."[8]

Most importantly, football became at least a temporary way out of the mills. Saturday and Sunday games offered an escape, but the real passion was for Friday night. That was when the high schools played and when the millworkers reminisced about their own playing days. Tales of great victories snatched from defeat, while playing with broken bones, mixed with the smoke in the bars across the street from the American Bridge Company in Ambridge and up the street from Jones & Laughlin in Aliquippa. Stories of stopping Joe Walton one Friday night a decade ago or leveling Mike Ditka in practice only a few years before were told with the clink of beer bottles and shot glasses as the late Friday night sound track.

More than any other bar and grill in Beaver Falls, the Corner Tavern embodied the region's personality. Aloof, it sat halfway up a hill leading out of the central city in a borough called West Mayfield alongside the massive main plant of B&W. Inside, none of the wooden and metal tables had four equal legs and the booths were well worn and dirty from constant use. At about 6 p.m. on Friday nights the place was full with men drinking Iron City, Schmidt's, or Pabst Blue Ribbon and Imperial brand whiskey. Some ate meatball sandwiches, but more ate fish since it was a Friday, and almost all of them smoked foul-smelling Camel filterless cigarettes or, worse, Swisher Sweets cigars, knocking their ashes onto discarded peanut shells on the checkerboard floors. Then it was time to walk down College Hill to Reeves Stadium on the campus of Geneva College—a little Calvinist school in the midst of Roman Catholic Beaver Falls—to watch the Tigers. At the stadium they met up with other fans working their way up the hill from downtown, and soon the stands were full.

That football might serve as a profession and therefore offer a way out of the mills permanently was a concept born in the region. In

1895, John K. Brailler of Latrobe, Pennsylvania, was credited as the first professional football player when he received ten dollars to play in a game against Jeanette. Residents of Greensburg, Pennsylvania— a Latrobe rival—challenged the Brailler story, claiming that in fact Lawson Fiscus received twenty dollars per game during the 1893 season, making him the first professional. Scooping both Brailler and Fiscus, however, was William W. "Pudge" Heffelfinger, who received money to play as one of the Allegheny Athletic Association's ringers in 1892. (The Heffelfinger claim seems the most authentic.) At any rate, all of the contending players—Brailler, Fiscus, and Heffelfinger—played for pay in western Pennsylvania.[9]

But Namath need not look to the nineteenth century for proof that football might pay the bills—a professional team played just up the river in Pittsburgh. The Pittsburgh franchise was not only a member of the National Football League, but also served as a symbol of the inextricable link between football and steel. In 1940, Art Rooney married the region's two great obsessions. A little over two decades later, he consummated the relationship when he accepted an offer from the head of Republic Steel to put the logo—a circle with three hypocycloids and the word "Steel"—of the U.S. Steel Corporation on the team's helmets. A couple of years after that, Rooney changed the logo's text from "Steel" to "Steelers" and the uniform and family of football and steel were complete.[10]

Professional football was not a realistic goal for Namath and other good players in western Pennsylvania trying to escape the mill life, but a college scholarship was. A scholarship meant an education and a degree, and a degree was the way to a white-collar profession. For the Namaths, a scholarship was not an abstract idea, as Frank had already received one. When Frank graduated in 1955, he had no intention of continuing his football career. He was an excellent player, built like an ice deliveryman who might be slowed down by a couple of blows from a sledgehammer. He did not lack intelligence—he was as smart as most of the football players—but he was completely devoid of preparation. He had taken no preparatory courses and none of the entrance exams required for college acceptance. So when he arrived home from a baseball game—Frank was an excellent catcher—on a hot afternoon in August, he was thoroughly shocked to see a suitcase sitting by the front door and a University of Kentucky assistant coach speaking with his father. "Frank," his father shouted at him, "you're going to Kentucky… now!" And that was that. Only later did Frank learn that he had received an offer to play professional baseball, but that his father and mother had decided that college was a better option. That day, without so much as a shower, Frank put his suitcase in the assistant coach's car and rode to Lexington, Kentucky, where he first became a member of the Wildcat football team, and only then took an entrance exam.[11]

Frank Namath's matriculation into an esteemed university sent a message to Joe—even the most unprepared student could continue to play football in college if he was good enough. Frank's positive example, combined with the negative image Joe took away from his visit to Moltrup's, solidified his decision—Joe Namath was getting out of Beaver County one way or another. His future lay somewhere other than in a steel mill. Whether he took Frank's college way out or his eldest brother Sonny and sister Rita's military way out, he decided that he would never again set foot in that cacophonous hell called a factory. It was a promise to himself that he never forgot or reneged on.[12]

———

Unfortunately for Rose, the kids were not the only Namaths playing around Beaver Falls in the 1950s. John Namath had few serious vices. He did not abuse his children, never gambled away the grocery money, and kept his drinking to a manageable limit—although citizens of a steel town like Beaver Falls defined "problem drinking" loosely. Their attitudes resembled the old joke about the Irishman who stated with seriousness, "It was too early in the morning to drink, so I just had beer." Still, John Namath spent his life well within the town's rather liberal boundaries. He did, however, have a wandering eye and a casual attitude about family commitments. It was not unusual to see him out on the town dressed in a white suit, two-tone shoes, and a stickpin in his tie, looking for a good time.

Rose confronted John on several occasions about his infidelity, including one particularly boisterous episode, the memory of which remained with Joe throughout his life. Standing at the top of the stairs in their Bridge Street home, Joe witnessed his parents in a heated argument. As they yelled at each other in a mixture of English and Hungarian, the ten-year-old boy felt a pain inside that he remembered forever afterward as the worst feeling of his life.

By 1955 Rose had had enough and filed for divorce. She and Joe moved out of the Bridge Street house and lived in a series of small apartments for the next several years. In one stroke, Joe lost his father as well as the close proximity of his best friend, Linwood Alford. Joe's devotion to his mother grew during their years alone together, and by the time he left Beaver Falls his regard for Rose bordered on religious adulation.

While John's infidelity was odd but not unheard of in Beaver Falls, Rose's response to her husband's indiscretions was unique. Rumors swirled after the divorce. Beaver Falls residents knew of John's behavior and firmly supported Rose. Since there was child support but no alimony in Pennsylvania, Rose would raise her youngest son without the benefit of a high-paying job in the mill. Sonny, Bobby, Frank, and Rita, though, helped their mother and young brother financially as well as emotionally. For them, there was no debate over who was to blame, and they largely broke off their relationships with John. Joe, on the other hand, managed to remain close to both his parents, but even so his relationship with John was more contentious than with Rose. Once, for instance, the two fought openly at a baseball game. John, who served as business manager for the Little League team, yelled at one of the players for a mistake he made. Joe came to his teammate's defense. "Don't yell at him. He's trying. You're not the coach." "Don't you talk back to me." "Well, leave him alone. You're not the coach." Thinking the other might strike a blow, both Joe and John put up their hands in defense. They did not speak for more than a month after the altercation. So there was real tension between father and son—a condition that *never* occurred with Rose—but, unlike his brothers, Joe's distaste remained manageable and he stayed close to his father for the rest of John's life.[13]

After the divorce, Joe's siblings quite naturally stood by his side at all stages of his development, teaching him, supporting him, encouraging him. Bobby taught him to "throw from the ear," an indispensable aspect of Namath's football ability; and Sonny, the eldest Namath and absent for most of Joe's youth, witnessed the intensity of his youngest brother's love of sport. On one occasion while Joe was in junior high school, Sonny invited Joe to join him and his wife on a trip to Washington, D.C. In the midst of a recreational basketball league run by the steelworkers union Local 1082, Joe rejected the offer. "I'd really love to, Sonny," he concluded. "But I just can't miss the game." It was not an uncommon response for kids in the region, and rather than being disappointed or even surprised, Sonny respected his young brother's dedication.[14]

More than anyone, Frank stood closest to Joe, not only in teaching his younger brother but also in shielding him from much of the unnecessary confusion confronting a young athlete in the sports-mad town. Once, during Joe's senior year, Nate Lippe, the Beaver Falls basketball coach, came to the Namath house to see Joe. "Is Joe here?" Lippe asked Frank. "I brought him a basketball." It being an autumn afternoon, a few months before basketball season, Frank wondered why. "Well," Lippe continued, "I just wanted him to get the feel of the ball, start practicing with it, you know?" Frank immediately recognized the request as an intrusion on Joe's football season, a failure by Lippe to acknowledge the immutable order of the athletic calendar. Beaver Falls chain-smoked its sports, lighting basketball season with the glowing end of football and beginning baseball with the final spark of basketball, then beginning the cycle anew at the end of summer for football season. "Coach," Frank said, barely hiding his disgust for such a neophyte to the local sporting etiquette, "this is football season. He's not going to pick that basketball up until football season's over. Then he's not going to pick up a baseball until basketball season's over. You get it? You're wasting your time."[5]

While his brothers sought to teach and protect him, Joe's mother sought only to comfort her youngest child. After her divorce from Joe's father, the two lived together, with Rose doting on "the baby." Sometimes her affection caused problems. For instance, she often allowed her son to sleep in on school days. Truancy notwithstanding, when this happened on Fridays during football season it threatened Namath's eligibility for that night's game. A couple of times during the 1960 season, Coach Bruno received word from an assistant coach that Namath was not in homeroom. Bruno would then rush out, speeding off in his 1939 Chevrolet to pick up his quarterback and ferry him to the school. "Mrs. Namath," he would plead, "you've got to make sure he comes to school on game days. If he's marked absent, he can't play." As Joe threw on a pair of chinos and his game jersey (worn to school the day of games), Rose smiled and explained. "He was out late last night, Coach," she began. "He's tired."[6]

———

After the Ambridge game, the Tigers faced no real challenges on the field. The next week they traveled to Butler and won 26–6, and two weeks after that, they returned to Reeves Stadium and beat Farrell 33–18. Their last game that October came against Mike

Ditka's alma mater, Aliquippa High School. But Ditka was no longer there and Beaver Falls won 34–7.[17]

They finished up their perfect season in the first two weeks of November with a 26–0 victory over Ellwood City and a 40–6 win over archrival New Brighton. Combined with the defeat of Monessen High School, the only other undefeated double-A team up to that point, the victory over Ellwood City sealed the double-A state championship for Beaver Falls. They ended the season with a combined total of 305 points; their opponents managed only 72. Namath finished the season completing 85 of 124 passes for 1,511 yards with only three interceptions. He threw 10 touchdown passes to Krzemienski alone.[18]

By the end of his senior football season, Namath appeared to be a new cast from the old Ohio Valley football mold. He was talented.

The Beaver Falls Tigers celebrate an end to their perfect season of 1960. Head Coach Larry Bruno appears at back right wearing a tie, and Joe Tronzo of the *Beaver Falls News-Tribune* stands in the front left with his hand on his ever-present hat. (Beaver Falls High School Yearbook, 1961; Krzemienski Collection)

Moreover, he could run the ball as well as anybody in recent memory. Namath possessed strong knees and ran the option as well as he passed the football. Other sportswriters emphasized his raw physical ability, stressing his "sling-shot arm and slippery hips," and referred to him as Namath "the nimble" and an offensive "triple-threat." Most memorably, on the second play from scrimmage against Midland, he rolled out to the right, cut back against the pursuing defenders, and sprinted 60 yards for a touchdown. Local sportswriters described Namath as a "sleight-of-hand magician." This description seemed particularly accurate since on four separate occasions during the course of his senior season, Namath's play-action fake handoffs were so convincing that the referees stopped the play when the decoy running back was tackled, then had to decide what to do when the Beaver Falls quarterback showed them the ball still in his hand. On all four of these occasions, the referees marked the play where the running back was tackled—without his ever having touched the ball. It also spoke to the fact that Bruno was an amateur magician himself.[19]

But a quarterback needs to be able to throw a football, and Namath was better than anyone at that. No one ever threw a football better than him, not even Babe Parilli, who currently played with the Colts; even Johnny Unitas—Namath's idol and the reason he chose the number 19—did not throw a prettier pass. Joe Tronzo referred to him as the "Hungarian Howitzer," a quarterback who could throw a football as far as any high school player he remembered seeing. Namath's ability to throw a football came from a classic combination of nature and nurture. His large hands made things a lot easier for him, as he could control the ball better. While many quarterbacks—even many good ones—had smallish hands, Namath could palm a basketball easily while still in high school. That meant when he held a football, the pinkie, ring, and middle fingers of his right hand spread easily across the laces of the ball, while his index finger sat back almost to the ball's point. More importantly, his large hand meant that his thumb could be positioned loosely underneath the ball with no real danger of his losing control. This "loose" hold gave Namath much greater control than a quarterback who needed to "choke" a football in order to maintain his grip. Namath's loose grip enabled him to use his wrist when throwing the ball. Specifically, he was able to "snap" the ball off his fingers, much like a baseball, rather than force it off with his entire hand or, worse, shot-put it with his entire arm.

Namath's natural gifts could take him only so far—many people with large hands still throw a football that flies like a wounded duck. As a youngster, Namath learned one of the most important lessons for a quarterback when his brother Bobby continuously coached him to "throw from the ear." Releasing the ball from beside his right ear did several things. It allowed the ball to travel at the proper trajectory from the quarterback to his receiver—that is, it allowed for an easier pathway over defenders while providing enough room for an arcing path to the receiver. Even more important than the pathway, throwing from the ear established good mechanics, emphasizing the wrist as the "hinge" of release rather than the "catapult" of the arm. Flicking the wrist was a tougher way to throw the ball when a quarterback was young—even with a smaller leather football, which was generally unavailable in the 1940s and 1950s—but it created a template for how the ball should be thrown. It was frustrating in the same way that a seven-year-old would be frustrated trying to use proper shooting form with an adult-sized basketball at a ten-foot rim.

As frustrating as it may have been at times, Namath practiced throwing a football properly—snapping his wrist at the ear—at a very young age, and therefore established what amounted to perfect mechanics. From the ear, he perfected his follow-through. The adage for follow-through was that a right-handed quarterback should release the ball, then move his arm as if to put his right hand into his left front pocket—a motion that was often referred to as "picking a dollar bill out of the pocket." Of all the mechanical moves, the follow-through was the easiest, provided the quarterback had already mastered throwing from the ear. With Namath's release, the proper follow-through was a veritable fait accompli.

By the time he became a high school quarterback, Joe Namath had already achieved mastery in throwing the football through untold hours of practice. As his body grew, his arm grew stronger to match his perfect mechanics. The result was a pass that left at the proper trajectory, very quickly from the fingertips, and, finally, with an exceedingly high rotation. The rotation of the ball made it fly farther—not like the knuckleball floating in the air from a "flat" pass—but also better. Namath's passes traveled through the air with almost no lateral deviation from their pathway. Combined with the fact that his release kept the front tip of the ball "up," Namath's passes were relatively easy to catch—easy to track because of their straight-line accuracy, but also easy on a receiver's hands.

What Namath brought to the field in terms of physical ability, Head Coach Larry Bruno soon helped perfect. Bruno taught Namath to point his feet (sometimes even his toes) in the proper direction. It was not simply a matter of stepping into a *throw*, although that was certainly important, it was more a matter of stepping into a *pass*. To some the difference might seem insignificant, but to a receiver tracking an airborne football across the middle of the field, it meant a lot. From Bruno, Namath learned to perfect not only the speed and trajectory of his passes, but also the proper location in the route. He learned the very difficult art of "throwing a receiver open," where he not only hoped to complete a pass but also to help his receivers live to tell about it. With Namath, receivers always knew that if a ball came in "hot," there was a good chance that a defender was waiting to deliver a big hit.

Namath's ability to pass the football rather than simply throw it led him to his next stage of development—the intellectual side. He became a disciplined on-field leader. He learned to audible— change plays at the line of scrimmage—if he saw a defense lined up in a way that he might exploit. If the safeties crowded the line of scrimmage, for instance, and a running play had been called, he would change the play to a pass that would send his receiver deep. If, on the other hand, the safeties lined up very deep, he might call a quick run up the middle or even a crossing pattern "underneath" the coverage. It was by no means complicated by professional standards, but Namath's ability to audible at the high school level put him well ahead of just about any other teenager in the nation.

Namath was, in fact, totally committed to winning, body and soul. He was a disciplined and intelligent athlete. He once removed one of his receivers, Tony Golmont, from the lineup for an entire half for breaching Namath's authority by talking in the huddle. He was also physically tough. He played the New Castle game with a severely twisted ankle and the Midland game with pleurisy. Most amazing of all, he finished the Ambridge game with a separated shoulder, then played the remainder of the season with only a small rubber doughnut as added protection. Had the injury not been so painful, the tiny makeshift shoulder guard would have been hilarious.[20]

Namath's athleticism, knowledge of the game, fierce dedication, and threshold for pain put him in the immediate company of Bucky Mutscheller, Joe Walton, and Mike Ditka. Off the field, though, Namath was not the kind of young man the town embraced wholeheartedly, and his antics became enough to turn a good portion of the town against him. Namath's behavior was simply ever so slightly outside the steel-town boundaries of acceptable.

In truth, though, the entire Namath family was considered a little offbeat. The Namath kids had a reputation for derring-do. Sonny occasionally frightened pedestrians by driving his car on the sidewalk. Bobby urinated away the evening's beer on the street. Frank took his teeth out before beating up anyone who looked cross-eyed at him or called him a Hunkie. Even Rita, the only girl in the clan, once stole a policeman's lantern and led him on a five-block chase before discarding it. The kids were rascals. They smoked cigarettes (Rita, cigars), stayed out at night later than others their age, put stray cats in parked cars, then got up the next morning and started all over again. The Namath family motto was that anything fun was worth the effort. To the town's more upstanding citizens, these adventures seemed like harbingers of a lifetime of crime, but in reality nothing ever came of it.[21]

Growing up in a broken home gave the youngest Namath more independence than his siblings had. Since Rose worked at W. T. Grant's, a five-and-dime-type store, Joe spent a great deal of his youth unsupervised. Often he would be out on the streets of Beaver Falls well after midnight even though Coach Bruno enforced a curfew. Sometimes he met Joe Tronzo coming out of the *News-Tribune* offices and joined him at the Sandwich Shoppe. To Tronzo's dismay, Namath always ordered beer even though he knew he would not get served. As the baby of the Namath family Joe was spoiled as well. With older siblings who were financially independent by the time he reached high school, he was considered rich by Beaver Falls standards. He always seemed to have cash in his pocket, decent clothes, and his own automobile. He drove a 1955 Ford that he began to paint but never finished, so it had a green roof and a primed body. The car might have been ugly, but a high school senior with his own car in 1960 Beaver Falls was akin to a bachelor in New York with a llama rug.[22]

Namath's behavior often seemed to be a direct insult to the community's steel-mill values of hard work, respect, and modesty. He said and did what he felt, and people disliked him for a variety of reasons—some valid, others not. Once, after finally getting to dress in his sophomore season, he accosted *News-Tribune* photographer Pete Pavlovic on the sidelines, yelling, "Hey you, get your Brownie and get the hell out of the way! I want to see the game!" Another time, after getting an ice cream cone at Hank's Frozen Custard, he took an unattended school bus and, cone in hand, drove it around a bit before returning it to the parking lot. On another occasion, he saw a schoolmate working on the brake lines of his car and took the loose wheels and rolled them down the road. He fought at dances in New Brighton, smoked cigarettes in school, shouted at people while hanging out on 15th Street, and was a regular at the Blue Room pool hall where he played a pool game called cribbage for money with men years older than himself. Even in celebration he seemed on the verge of criminality. After the team won its final game, Namath led an attempt to steal a balloon from the roof of Sahli Motor, a local car dealership. He intended to put the balloon on top of the high school. Namath and his pack were caught by the police in the act, but at the genuine indifference of Ed Sahli, the owner of the dealership, they were let off with a relatively mild warning. Put together, all of the indiscretions in Namath's life seemed like a cavalcade of minor pranks bordering on rebellion.[23]

One of Namath's major partners in crime was Whitey Harris. The two knew each other from Little League baseball, and by high school they had become inseparable friends. Both wanted to be the center of attention and to have as much fun as possible. Whitey tended toward outrageous behavior—he once allowed everyone in a class to hit him in the head with a textbook just to show off the hardness of his skull.

Joe Ursida found out the hard way about Joe's and Whitey's mischievousness. In 1960, Ursida was a freshman at Beaver Falls, and one day during practice a coach asked him to get a key for him. Entering the varsity locker room, Ursida ran into Joe and Whitey. "Hey freshman," Namath said, "what are you doing coming in here with those shoes on? Take 'em off!" Ursida took off his shoes and started to walk through the room in his socks. "Hey freshman, what are you doing in here with those socks on? Take 'em off!" He did that as well, and began to cross the room in bare feet. "Hey freshman, what are you doing *walking* in here? Crawl!" As he crawled across the floor, Namath and Harris hit him over the head with their jockstraps, dirty from the day's practice. Fortunately for Ursida, Krzemienski heard the commotion, looked around the corner, and said, "Knock it off." Joe and Whitey did, adding, "Okay, freshman, it's your lucky day. Get what you need and get out."[24]

Along with abusing freshmen, finding beer was a constant quest in Joe and Whitey's friendship. That Pennsylvania's drinking age was twenty-one made drinking merely inconvenient for high school students. Taking turns driving, Namath and Harris traveled west from Beaver Falls, passed close to Whitey's suburban home, then headed down a rural road for ten miles across the state line into Ohio. There the drinking age was nineteen, an age each could pass for. In Negley, the closest border town, bars like the Stateline Tavern, the Rye Bar, Pappy's Bar, and an unmarked building known by generations simply as "The Valley" served Pennsylvania teenagers. Whitey, Namath, and whoever might accompany them drank pitchers of Genesee beer off wobbly tables, smoked cigarettes, and shot pool while an owner pretended to believe they were of age. On one occasion, the two even got served before a game. While they were supposed to be "getting mentally prepared" before the Butler game, they went into a bar and ordered two beers. More surprised than happy at being served the alcohol, neither finished his drink before returning to the locker room.[25]

That the Namath family and Coach Bruno overlooked Joe's indiscretions made perfect sense. What Joe Tronzo of the *Beaver Falls*

News-Tribune did for Namath and his reputation was above and beyond the call of duty.

Tronzo was an old-style journalist who looked the part. Short, hunched, and thin, with gray hair partially covered by a hat his ancestors might have worn on their way to America in the mid-nineteenth century, Tronzo was only thirty in 1960 but already looked like an old man. He smoked a particularly malodorous brand of Marsh Wheeling cigars and composed his stories on a dated Royal typewriter well past midnight at the *News-Tribune* building. He was opinionated, his demeanor matching his grizzled appearance. During World War II, he was a legman for *Stars and Stripes* during the Nuremberg Trials and came away from the experience disillusioned, finding the prosecution of a military after a war a farce. In addition to cynicism, Tronzo emerged from World War II with a love of history. Specifically, he loved the idea of a past filled with heroes, and he approached his sportswriting with this sense of historical iconography in mind, especially with regard to the young athletes he covered.

From September through November, Tronzo focused on Beaver Falls High School football. He met regularly with Coach Bruno to discuss strategy and results, with each understanding that coaching was Bruno's domain and writing was Tronzo's. He took players out to dinner when possible and always kept his personal comments on each player completely positive, managing to compliment every player who had even a tangential role in the team's success.[26]

Tronzo's favoritism served a purpose beyond simple Saturday morning accolades. He hoped to get each of the Beaver Falls players enough attention to secure them football scholarships. The simple fact of the matter was that most of the high school students from Beaver Falls were not going to college without some sort of financial assistance, and success on the football field was the most likely way to get it. In 1960,

Tronzo helped more players than ever—Bill Heistand and Ernie Pelaia attended Western State College in Colorado, Jimmy Seaburn played for Army at West Point, Terry Krivak went to Baldwin Wallace, Larry Patterson played at West Texas State, Harry James and Tony Jackson went to Westminster, and Stan Kondracki played for Denison. Even Whitey Harris, an undersized linebacker at five feet seven inches and 150 pounds, received a scholarship offer from Youngstown State.[27]

In Namath's case, Tronzo attempted not only to accentuate the positive, but also to eliminate the negative. On one notable occasion, he unofficially expunged Namath's public record. Only once in his mischievous youth was Joe Namath arrested. It occurred when he was caught inside the Beaver Falls High School gymnasium with some friends playing basketball while the school was closed. Technically this gave Namath a breaking-and-entering record, a not-so-minor-sounding charge that brought to mind images of armed jewel thieves and petty thugs. In reality, he had sought to steal nothing but practice time on a basketball court. Tronzo realized that the report might hurt Namath's chances for a scholarship to college and decided that this young man's life should not be determined by such a small indiscretion. So he went to the Beaver Falls police headquarters, snuck into the records room, and removed the Namath file. Now whatever rumors recruiters might hear about Joe's off-field behavior would not have the potentially damning support of a police record with a serious but silly charge.[28]

Publicly, the backlash against Namath's off-field personality became noticeable enough for Tronzo to address it in an article for the *News-Tribune*. On November 15, 1960, four days after the Tigers won their ninth and final game, Tronzo offered up his official position on Namath:

Probably more rumors have cropped up about Joe Namath than any other high school kid since I have been covering sports. To hear people talk it would be hard to determine whether he played for Beaver Falls or Morganza [a Pennsylvania reform school].

Among the stories are that he sawed a cow in half in the auditorium of the high school, punched a pregnant woman, punched a school administrator, bombed school board members['] houses, poured gasoline on a fifth grader and set him afire, threw eggs at Richard Nixon, kidnapped Kay Neumann and sundry other things.

There are some people who have said that I have made a hero out of the worst juvenile since Cain took the sling to Abel.

Actually even if Joe did all the above plus a few others, I would write him up in the same way. I am not interested in what a kid does off the field.

I mean that my primary job is to report what goes on in the sport scene. If he is a hero on the field he is a hero on the sport page.

If a kid has bad habits that is up to his parents, teachers and preachers to correct. Certainly it is not our job. It must be remembered that in Beaver Falls there are more parents, teachers and preachers than there are sports writers.[29]

Although Tronzo claimed no interest "in what a kid does off the field," he described Namath's intellect as high but his study habits as lazy, and, most importantly, explained that Namath's position on the football field necessitated confidence. He thought that Namath had "more nerve than a raw tooth," a potentially troublesome attribute off the field, but something necessary for on-field success. No different than his "natural" throwing, faking, and running talent, confidence enhanced Namath's ability to run Bruno's offensive scheme. For Tronzo, to deride Namath as "cocky" and simultaneously praise him as a great quarterback was hypocritical.[30]

After their senior season at Beaver Falls, Namath and his receiver Tom Krzemienski became two of the most sought-after players in the nation. Although not a "package deal" to recruiters, they visited prospective colleges together. (Krzemienski Collection)

4

The Privileged Son

You know, he really was a PIA—a pain in the ass.

—Rita (Namath) Sims

Even without Tronzo and the *News-Tribune*, Namath, Krzemienski, and Golmont—as well as Butch Ryan one year later—would have received offers from major colleges and universities to play football. Golmont ended up at North Carolina State and Ryan at the University of Iowa. Although Namath and Krzemienski visited prospective colleges together, early in the recruitment process they decided not to present themselves as a package deal. If one wanted to go to a particular school, he would make the decision independent of the other.[1]

Namath's first campus visit was to Notre Dame. Bruno and Bill Ross drove Namath, Krzemienski, and Golmont the 400 miles to South Bend in a station wagon. The three teenagers sat in the unseated back section while the coaches sat in front. Somewhere in Ohio, Namath decided to entertain his teammates. Using a lighter he carried for his periodic smoking habit, he began igniting his farts. It was of course nothing more than silly teenage behavior, but it spoke to the fact that Namath was different from even his closest fellow recruits. Golmont was one of the few players on the team with a steady girlfriend and seldom ventured onto the Beaver Falls scene, however small that was, without her. Krzemienski came from a family of seventeen children and a widowed mother, who ran a general store in the back of their home. His life was sheltered and defined by family responsibilities.[2]

But there they sat: the henpecked Golmont and mama's boy Krzemienski, watching their quarterback ignite bombs of gas in the back of a station wagon on their way to the cathedral of college football. All three of them were still kids, but one was a lot less shy and even more uncouth.

Because of its reputation, Notre Dame recruited itself. The service academies still competed at a high level, but no longer represented the pinnacle of college football, especially for those recruits not willing to commit to the military with their scholarships. In the pure world of football unencumbered by civic duty, Notre Dame constituted the postwar standard. Being tied to the Roman Catholic Church did not hurt either. Although Namath was Hungarian, and decidedly not Irish, he was still an active member of St. Mary's Catholic Church, where he attended school from the first through the eighth grades. Not quite an avowed altar boy, he never looked upon Notre Dame's Catholicism as an actual factor in his decision, but Rose brightened at the idea of her youngest child attending the ideal school for combining education, religion, and athletics. Notre Dame, moreover, was relatively close to Beaver Falls, which meant that his family could visit the campus and see the games. Finally, Notre Dame was the alma mater of a recent Beaver Falls hero, Jim "Bucky" Mutscheller, who starred at Notre Dame then went on to play for the Baltimore

Colts. As the Colts' tight end, Mutscheller played a pivotal role in the 1958 NFL Championship Game when he caught a pass from Johnny Unitas to take the ball to the one-yard line on the play preceding Alan Ameche's famous game-winning score. None of this was lost on Joe, who followed Mutscheller closely and idolized Unitas.

Despite its advantages, Notre Dame had its problems as well. For all of the Knute Rockne/Four Horsemen/Wake Up the Echoes aura, the 1960 team was terrible. On the eve of Namath's visit to South Bend, the Fighting Irish were 1–7 and in the midst of the worst coaching performance in the school's lengthy history. Joe Kuharich, born in South Bend and a star for the Irish in the glory days of the mid-1930s, had appeared to be the perfect fit as head coach for the Irish. But it turned out that he was neither a good coach nor a good recruiter, as Namath got to witness firsthand. When the coaches and players arrived, Notre Dame sent no one to meet them, leaving the recruits outside the stadium without escorts or tickets. As they waited, an assistant from the Iowa Hawkeyes, Notre Dame's opponent that day, recognized Bruno and asked him what had happened. Upon hearing the story, he invited the five from Beaver Falls to join him on the Iowa sideline. So Namath watched Notre Dame lose to Iowa 28–0, surrounded by Hawkeye players, during his recruitment to play for the Fighting Irish.

The other major problem with Notre Dame was not Kuharich's fault. On a follow-up visit to the school, Namath saw something he could not during the Iowa game. Walking across campus with his brother Bobby and absolutely in awe of the grounds, he noticed something for the first time. "Bob," he asked, "where are all the girls?" "There aren't any," Bobby Namath replied. Pointing across the campus, he said, "All the coeds are over there at St. Mary's." Namath looked at the school his brother pointed to, saw that a lake stood between him and it, and contemplated the obstacle. In order to get to any women, he would have to become a much better swimmer. For Joe, that seemed a bit much even for the honor of playing for the Fighting Irish.

Although Notre Dame's lack of coeds did not cement Namath's final decision against South Bend, it pointed to another important factor in the recruitment process. How much fun was the visit? The atmosphere of freedom and good times of a college campus meant as much to Namath as the football team's success or failure. Quite simply, what the campus looked like and how much entertainment the campus guides provided was an obvious focal point for a seventeen-year-old kid. And every recruiter knew it.

In the end, he thought at least enough about Notre Dame to sign a letter of intent to play for the Fighting Irish. It was not, however, a final decision. Being independent meant that Notre Dame could sign as many players as they wanted without having to abide by an NCAA rule that allowed players to sign with only one team per conference. For players like Namath, this had the flip-side advantage of his being able to sign for multiple teams—one per conference—which he did.

Other schools without the bona fides of Notre Dame were simply cursed when it came to year-end recruitment. In December, for instance, Namath and Krzemienski flew out of Pittsburgh in the midst of an intense snowstorm. Hoping for a respite from the weather, Namath was sorely disappointed, if not really surprised, when the plane landed in Minneapolis. The University of Minnesota Gophers had just won a share of the Big Ten Championship, a national championship, and were preparing for the Rose Bowl under the leadership of Murray Warmath, undoubtedly one of the top coaches in the country. What Namath came away with, though, was a typical case of snow blindness. No matter how good the facilities, how successful the team, and how persuasive the coach—all first-rate in Minnesota's case—Namath retained only memories of a frozen prairie where the students wore so many layers of clothes that he could not decipher their gender. At least Notre Dame's coeds were identifiable in their sequestered home; and if the lake were frozen, that meant Namath could at least walk to St. Mary's.

The next visit gave Namath and Krzemienski an opportunity to thaw out. The University of Miami had the best combination for a Beaver Falls recruit. Not only did it provide the best weather the two had seen since August, but their ex-teammate Rich Niedbala played for the Hurricanes and entertained them for a three-day weekend. In South Florida, Namath enjoyed a round-the-clock party, with free drinks and dress codes that left no doubt as to the gender of the students. He basked in the sun and fell in love with the climate as the memory of his frozen trip to Minnesota melted away. For Niedbala, though, the visit was tense. Namath and Krzemienski constituted polar opposites in terms of personality. Krzemienski was looking for wholesome fun, Namath for action. So Niedbala enjoyed the simultaneous comfort of introducing the perfect combination of athletic ability and manners in Krzemienski, while waiting for the inevitable explosion of the time bomb of misbehavior that was Namath.

Adding to Niedbala's anxiety was that Miami's head coach, Andy Gustafson, was as straitlaced as anyone in the game, and he had a football ancestry to prove it. At the University of Pittsburgh, Gustafson starred in the mid-1920s for Jock Sutherland, who had played for the most influential coach in the early history of the game, Pop Warner. As if that were not enough, Gustafson went on to serve as an assistant coach for Earl "Red" Blaik from 1934 to 1947, first at Dartmouth and then as part of the miraculous rebirth of Army as a football power. At the time of Namath's visit, "Coach Gust" had just finished his thirteenth season coaching the Hurricanes.

Gustafson was a strict disciplinarian who demanded that players work hard, go to class, and shave off all excess facial hair. To the horror of Niedbala, Namath appeared in South Florida with several scraggly hairs hanging on to his chin—the kind of "beard" that only a seventeen-year-old would find worth keeping. "Joe," Niedbala told Namath, "Coach Gust hates that kind of shit. Make sure you shave it off before you meet him." Namath said he would, but never did. "I want to tell you two boys," Gustafson said at the official meeting with the Beaver Falls players, "you've both got the kind of ability we like here. We'd love to have you down to play for us." Then, hesitatingly, he added, speaking directly to Namath, "But I've got to ask, what's that stuff going on with your chin?" Niedbala cringed, but Namath did not miss a beat. "Oh, this?" he said, rubbing his chin. "Yeah, I'm playing Joseph in the school Christmas play." The answer delighted Coach Gust, and Niedbala breathed once more.[3]

On the way home from the Pittsburgh airport the newly adopted father of Jesus bragged about all of the towels he had stolen from the hotel.

Despite the weather and the beaches, Miami simply was not yet the type of school highly recruited northern football players attended. Colleges in the early 1960s drew the vast majority of their football players from within their own region, and Pennsylvania football players tended to stay close to home. In-state schools Penn State and the University of Pittsburgh filled out their rosters mostly with Pennsylvanians and looked like logical choices for Namath. But the Pitt campus looked too much like a larger version of Beaver Falls with no real greenery, and Penn State head coach Rip Engle showed no interest in Namath.

Geographically, then, along with Notre Dame and the frozen tundra that was Minnesota, that left the rest of the teams of the Big Ten Conference for Namath to consider. Namath visited several schools, including Indiana, Purdue, and, particularly memorably, Michigan State. When motivated, few coaches recruited as well and as doggedly as Duffy Daugherty of MSU. He built a powerhouse with southern blacks who could not yet play in the SEC or ACC, but still maintained a strong presence in Pennsylvania and Ohio. So Namath and Krzemienski were natural targets.

Namath's trip to Michigan State was unsettling. After they visited the East Lansing campus, Daugherty took the recruits to one of the state's premier restaurants, Schuler's in Marshall. Taken over by its founder's oldest son, Winston Schuler, in 1934, Schuler's reflected its manager's passion for Old English inns, with a décor heavy on British relics and a menu rich in red meat. Win Schuler also believed in the English tradition of patronage, and after the two recruits finished off their slabs of roast beef, he invited them to his rather extravagant home. There, he took Namath and Krzemienski to his bedroom and opened his closet. "Here you go, boys," he said as he pointed to the hundreds of ties hanging on the wall. "Pick out any one you like and it's yours!" It was an odd bit of boosterism and not all that impressive to the Beaver Falls visitors. They kept the ties, but the meal made the bigger impression.

In the end, though, it was not neckties that led Namath away from Michigan State, but Daugherty's general indifference toward him. Known as a "three clouds of dust" ground game coach, Daugherty may not have seen the benefit of a passer like Namath. Whatever the reason, he let the pursuit of the quarterback end with the strange gift-giving ceremony in Schuler's bedroom. On the other hand, he continued his recruitment of Krzemienski in earnest, eventually landing the end for his team.

Stolen towels and gifted ties notwithstanding, Namath got his first real taste of what a college scholarship might mean in terms of individual gain when he visited Iowa. Upon arrival on campus, Namath and Krzemienski sat and watched the Iowa basketball team practice and were asked if they would like to join in a scrimmage.

Outfitted with Iowa practice jerseys and borrowed shoes, the two football recruits played alongside Hawkeye star Don Nelson and did well enough that Iowa's new head football coach, Jerry Burns, suggested that the boys play basketball as well as football when they came to the school. To help them remember the day, the coach let the two recruits keep their basketball warm-ups as souvenirs.

The next stop was not so spontaneous, as the two were taken to a plumbing supply shop and led into the back room to meet the owner. "Anything you boys ever need," the owner told them, "you come and see me." The message became clearer when he later visited them in Pittsburgh and took them out for a steak dinner. "Okay," he began, "what's it going to take to get you two to Iowa?"

Namath caught the drift. "We want a thousand dollars," Namath began, speaking for the wide-eyed Krzemienski, "and a brand-new car...each." Iowa's moneyman said okay, paid the dinner check, and headed off to Iowa to prepare the final "contract." Namath signed his second letter of intent with the Hawkeyes.

By the first few months of 1961, Namath was no longer a neophyte to the ways of recruitment. He was a commodity and he knew his price could very well be high. Sometimes it was good to string the recruiter along and negotiate to the highest possible price. Other times the negotiations ended abruptly.

At Arizona State University, Namath met head coach Frank Kush, one of the more straightforward recruiters. Kush had put together several excellent years, including a 10–1 record in 1959 and a 7–3 record the year Namath visited. But Tempe was not exactly South Bend when it came to football pedigree. The school's regular rivals included New Mexico A&M, Hardin-Simmons, West Texas State Teachers College, and Texas Mines. Born in Windber, Pennsylvania, about seventy miles east of Pittsburgh, and having led Biggie Munn's 1952 Michigan

State Spartans to a national championship, Kush had no intention of remaining hidden in the Border Intercollegiate Athletic Association for long. He needed big-time players and intended on getting them. So after Namath's initial visit, he followed him back to Beaver Falls for some serious one-on-one discussions. In a final push, Kush took Namath and Coach Bruno for a drive one night. Parking the car, with Namath in the passenger seat and Bruno in the back, Kush laid it out: "Okay Joe, let's quit shitting around. Do you want a brand-new car or two hundred dollars a month?" As Bruno contemplated plugging his ears or climbing out the window to avoid witnessing the ongoing violation, Namath replied, "I want to go to Maryland."[4]

And there it was—the wild card in the recruitment battle, the University of Maryland, a team from the Atlantic Coast Conference that only technically seemed to reside in the South. Even during the most tumultuous time in American history, Maryland had refused to secede, making it a slave state still loyal to the Union. More than a century later, it was the only state in the original 1953 ACC not to have been a part of the Confederacy. More than just a crossroads of the American Civil War, it was also an excellent football institution. Although the Maryland Terrapins finished the 1960 season unranked, it was a strong program, having won the national championship in 1953 and keeping a regular contingent of Pennsylvanians on the roster. Most importantly, though, Maryland had a secret weapon—a team manager named Al Hassan.

Albert Hassan was better known as "Hatchet," a childhood nickname given him because of his sharp nose. He grew up on the south side of New Castle, Pennsylvania, about twenty miles due north of Beaver Falls. At seventeen Hassan joined the Navy with six friends from high school, serving from 1954 to 1957. Upon his discharge, he went to visit his brother Jan in northern Maryland. When Jan suggested that Al apply to college, Hatchet, referring to

From nearby New Castle, Al "Hatchet" Hassan spent the summer of 1961 in Beaver Falls helping Namath prepare for the Scholastic Aptitude Test and recruiting him to the University of Maryland. (Hassan Collection)

his poor academics, replied, "I couldn't get in with a machine gun!" Still, he humored his brother, allowing him to send letters on his behalf to Grove City College in Pennsylvania and the University of Maryland. To his amazement, Al Hassan received notice from Maryland that he had been accepted as a student.

Coming from New Castle, a miniature version of filthy industrial Youngstown to the west, Hatchet thought the campus of Maryland was a dreamland of ivory towers, pillared halls, and open, manicured lawns. He had no money and stood out as an interloper even in the relatively mild form of class warfare practiced at a public institution with plenty of poor students. So he hustled. He began with the football program, arranging a meeting with head coach Tom Nugent and assistant coach Bernie Reid. Impressed by Hassan, Reid offered him a position as a student manager for the football team. This position offered Hatchet a double victory. On the one hand, he received regular compensation for his duties, money that he desperately needed. On the other, though, he received benefits beyond his normal job description. For instance, he ate at the athletic dining hall as much and as often as possible for free—a considerable windfall for any college student in a financial crunch.

It was apparent to the coaches that Hassan had the potential to provide them with something much more valuable than the food he ate in the athletic cafeteria. Hassan was a student with important ties. He may have matriculated to Maryland from his brother's in-state home, but he actually grew up in perhaps the most fertile bed of football talent in the nation.

New Castle High School, or, as the locals called it, NEC-High—pronounced *Neek*-High—was on a regular schedule with the Beaver Falls Tigers in just about every sport, including football. Over the holiday break between 1960 and 1961, Hassan sat with his buddies Lefty Rich and Fritzu Joseph at the New Life, a New Castle diner on the south side of town. In New Castle, like every other town in the region, football was part of virtually every conversation, and the story of the year was the juggernaut called the Beaver Falls Tigers. Beaver Falls, Hatchet heard, had not only beaten New Castle in the third game of the season, they had absolutely destroyed them, 39–0. What had been hailed as a clash of powers ended up being a rout in front of 20,000 New Castle fans, with a young quarterback named Namath leading the slaughter.

When Hatchet returned to College Park, he met with Roland Arrigoni, Maryland's assistant coach in charge of recruiting the Ohio River valley. Knowing that Hatchet had just been back in western Pennsylvania, Arrigoni asked if he had ever heard of this quarterback who had set the region on fire. "Yeah," Hatchet told him. "He beat the crap out of my high school early in the season."

Arrigoni's eyes lit up. "You *know* Namath?" It was technically a question, but it came out more like a whispered celebration. In truth, Hassan knew Namath no better than Arrigoni did. Recognizing the excitement in the air and the potential to better his standing with the team, he bluffed. "Sure, I know him." And at that moment, Al "Hatchet" Hassan began his brief but intense career as a specialized recruiter for the Maryland Terrapins football team.

On January 20, 1961, Hatchet stood inside the terminal at the National Airport in Washington, D.C., awaiting the two recruits from Beaver Falls. Hassan's father had died just a week before Namath and Krzemienski visited Maryland, but that did not slow the recruitment festivities. He took the two to a fraternity party where he played a prank. "You see those guys over there," he said, pointing to a group of about seven members of the fraternity. "If I spill my drink, that means it's on!" The idea of getting into a fight on the first night's visit was unthinkable for the recruits. What would happen to their scholarship offers? What would happen to the *other* scholarship offers they had already received? They were not sure, but fighting a group of frat brothers on a recruitment trip had to constitute some sort of NCAA violation. And then there was the matter of their clothes. They were, each of them, wearing the only suits they owned. If they fought, they would inevitably ruin them and have nothing to wear on the next trip.

Hatchet never spilled his drink, never intended to, but was just "busting on" the new guys. It was a good ploy to get the attention of Namath, who preferred the company of someone who would plan such a prank. Namath fell in love with the school as he had none of the others. Notre Dame remained a viable option, but Maryland became his new number one choice and the third to receive his signature on a letter of intent.

It was not that Maryland was better than Iowa or Notre Dame. Clearly, each school had advantages and disadvantages. But only Maryland had Hatchet, and through him the Terrapin coaches stayed close to Joe.

Since Hatchet lived only a short drive from Beaver Falls, he spent most of the summer of 1961 in Namath's company. He followed Namath's summertime baseball games and, for his part, got to see a lot of good ball, as Namath and Krzemienski led their American Legion team to a championship series. He also got to hang out with Namath at such local spots as the Blue Room pool hall. The two drank beer at night and enjoyed the vacation from commitments and worries. More than just a friend, Hatchet was also a classic "fixer" with extensive connections. Over the summer, Namath's car—an ancient Ford that, according to Hatchet, "couldn't pass an inspection from Helen Keller"—became a cause for concern as it came due for its annual service check. As Namath worried about losing his wheels, Hatchet asked a mechanic friend for a favor. Five dollars later, Hatchet presented Namath with a new sticker for his windshield, verifying his car's legality. Namath smiled like a child at the sight of the inspection sticker. For Hatchet, it was but a small bit of manipulation, but for Namath it literally guaranteed his freedom until the car broke down of its own accord.

But Hassan also had a more serious task. He spent the summer with Namath attempting to help his friend and recruit prepare for his college entrance examination. This was not a mere formality, since the Atlantic Coast Conference had recently made it mandatory for every student-athlete to score a minimum of 750 points on the Scholastic Aptitude Test in order to be eligible for a scholarship. So Hatchet and Namath took some time out from their very busy social calendar to brush up on vocabulary and mathematics. They would, as Hatchet put it, study a bit and then get bored and turn their attention to the evening out. Night after night they returned to the Blue Room, beer, and anything else that would keep their minds off of SAT preparations.[5]

In the winter, still wavering between attending College Park and South Bend, Namath abruptly ended his high school basketball career when he and the only other senior on the team, Benny Singleton, another black friend, walked out of a game. The problem for the seniors, and the rest of the team for that matter, was the head coach, Nate Lippe. Lippe was a legend in the annals of local basketball and came out of retirement to coach the team. Unfortunately, he brought with him out of retirement the style of play he employed in the 1930s. Everything, according to Lippe, needed to be structured: Pass right, cut left was pretty much his entire offensive strategy. A great athlete who could dunk two-handed behind his head from a standstill under the basket and palm a basketball like it was a softball, Namath might have had a future playing basketball as a guard at a major college program. Coming immediately from a coach who was twenty years *ahead* of his time on the football field to Coach Lippe was not a transition Namath was able to make. Moreover, Lippe was troubled by Namath's independent behavior. Namath sometimes practiced while wearing a hat or with a lollipop in his mouth. At one point Lippe dismissed him from the team, but brought him back after a short suspension. Finally, frustrated with the archaic style of play, Namath palmed the ball off his dribble, feigned a throw at his opponent, then took an uncontested shot while the defender covered his face. Removed from the game for the Harlem Globetrotter play, Namath walked out of the gym for good, along with Singleton. It was, after all, their senior year, and if there was one thing Namath knew, it was that seniors were supposed to enjoy themselves to the fullest.[6]

If Namath saw basketball as an expendable sport with regard to his athletic future, he still held out hope for baseball. In a decision that harkened back to his Local 1082 basketball days and Sonny's offer of a trip to Washington, D.C., he bypassed Pennsylvania's prestigious Big 33 all-star football game so that he would not miss an American Legion play-off game. The Chicago Cubs made the strongest bid for Joe's baseball services. In 1961, they sent Patrick Joseph Mullin to Beaver Falls to woo him. Born in Trotter, Pennsylvania, Pat Mullin was familiar with the region. He had a long career with the Detroit Tigers, earning a respectable lifetime batting average of .271. Mullin's annual statistics, however, told a more revealing story. In 1941, for instance, he batted .345, but was ineligible for the batting title because he played in only 54 games. In fact, in his fourteen-year career with the Tigers, Mullin averaged only 62 games per year. So he knew not only how difficult it was to break into the major leagues, but also that being there was no guarantee of stardom. He understood that more than just about any other sport, baseball was a career of attrition.[7]

As the summer wore on, the Tronzo house became an unofficial meeting place for Namath and his suitors. Tronzo's role in the courting of Namath the baseball player, however, remained little more than housekeeping. "He never asked me for advice," Tronzo remembered. "I don't think he ever asked anyone for advice. He made up his own mind." This time Namath got the advice he never asked for. Unfortunately for the Cubs, Mullin was honest. Perhaps it was because he remembered his own struggle to get to the major leagues and his subsequent mediocre career with the Tigers and saw that same future in his recruit. Perhaps it was because he was aware of Namath's superior football ability and realized the futility of trying to get a football superstar to choose baseball. Or perhaps it was because he just liked the kid and did not want to mislead him. Whatever the reason, on a summer day in 1961 at the Tronzos' dining room table, Mullin terminated the baseball recruitment of Joe Namath. "Joe, I want you badly. I've been told my job depends on it. But your future's in football."[8]

Although he continued to keep the Air Force in the back of his mind, it seemed that despite quitting the basketball team and declining an offer to play baseball in the major leagues, by August 1961 an athletic future still looked pretty well guaranteed for Namath.

———

Namath's scores arrived at the University of Maryland before they reached the Namath household, so Hatchet called. "We didn't make it," Hatchet said. "Seven forty-eight. Missed by two." Maryland, Notre Dame, and Iowa, each bound by the 750 standard, pulled their scholarship offers.[9]

When his test scores came up short, Joe Namath was completely unprepared. Since he had no initial strategy, let alone a backup plan, it looked as if his football career were over. But as the summer of 1961 came to an end, once again—along with his mother, siblings, coach, local sportswriter, and transplanted friend from New Castle—someone was watching out for Namath.

After winning the national championship in 1961, Bear Bryant and senior quarterback Pat Trammell (between Bryant and JFK) met with President Kennedy. A little over a year later, Kennedy led the advance to desegregate the university. (Bryant Museum)

5

Playing Defense

My view was, regardless of its ability, if a team wallows around all week playing drop-the-handkerchief and the players don't think tough or live tough, how can they be tough on Saturday?

—Paul "Bear" Bryant

THE 1961 SEASON had not yet begun, but John Forney was already in a good mood. He had been replaced the year before as host on *The Bear Bryant Show* after his advertising agency had lost the account, but he remained close friends with "Preacher" Franklin, the representative of the program's leading sponsor, the Coca-Cola Company. Preacher told him he felt bad about what had happened and promised to get him back. Before the 1961 season, Preacher did just that, announcing that because of Maury Farrell's slight connection to RC Cola, he was replacing him with Forney as Bryant's sideman.[1]

From the first season of the show it had been delightfully apparent that the host's job was virtually irrelevant. All he had to do was get the show started on time, roll the game film, ask Bear an initial innocuous question, and then just make sure that the commercials got in and the show ended on schedule. Bear was a natural talker—or more precisely a grumbler—who never said anything truly insightful, and depending on how late he got to bed the night before, his voice could get so low that the listener could almost count the decibels on the fingers of his two hands. But that hardly mattered to Alabamians, who made *The Bear Bryant Show* the most important Sunday activity after church and lunch, and for some it rated above their salvation and stomachs. They just loved the soft sound of his voice and the predictable pattern of his comments: "Now that's Pat Trammell rolling out with the ball. He's a fine runner. Came to us from Scottsboro. Scottsboro's a fine town. I have a load of friends in Scottsboro. Pat's got a fine mama and daddy. Fine folks, like all of them in Scottsboro." Always the same—he mentioned the player, his hometown, and his parents, and if Alabama won, which by 1961 they did on a regular basis, he employed the word "fine" multiple times. For Alabamians, watching Bear Bryant was a civic experience.

Changing the show's host, therefore, was not crucial to its success, but it was meaningful to Bear. He liked working with Forney, but he was an intensely loyal man who was bothered by the dismissal of Farrell. He knew only one way to deal with the issue—directly. He had a private conversation with the two men. "Maury, I'm real disappointed you're not going to be doing the show with me," he began. "I've been comfortable with you and I think you've done a good job. However, if you've got connections with RC I can see how Coke feels about that." Turning to Forney, he added, "John, I don't have anything against you doing the show, but I wanted you to know that I'm disappointed Maury will not be here. I did not want any misunderstanding on this, and I did not want Maury to feel I had asked for a change."

The conversation was the essence of Bryant's style—face-to-face, man-to-man, all the cards on the table. Forney and Farrell knew just where they stood. Then it was behind them, and the three moved forward and worked together for years.

Forney's new role came at a propitious moment. After watching the Tide during spring practice, he expected good things out of the 1961 team. But at the Masters golf tournament he encountered Bob Ford, a former member of Coach Bryant's staff who had gone on to coach at another school. "John," Ford said, "Alabama is going to be great. I don't think anybody realizes what a tremendous football team they are going to have over there."

The core of the team was Bryant's first recruiting class, and he had shaped them in his own image. Even though the Crimson Tide had been doormats in the years before his arrival, he had promised the younger players that if they did what he said and committed fully to the program, they would win a national title before they graduated. And he expected them all to graduate. Bryant's speech brought tears to the eyes of freshman Billy Neighbors, and he and his teammates accepted Bryant's challenge. They were led by winners. Pat Trammell at quarterback and Lee Roy Jordan at center and linebacker were not only outstanding players, they were inspirational. Bryant talked endlessly about having class and playing with class. Trammell and Jordan were his poster boys.

And there was promise of even better to come. Just before the first game Forney bumped into a close friend of Bryant's in a liquor store, and given the time of the year they began to talk about football. "John," he said, "take a look out there in my car." Forney saw a young man sitting in the front seat wearing a porkpie hat and chewing on a toothpick angling out the side of his mouth. He said the boy's name was Joe Ne-MATH, and he came from Pennsylvania. "The coach thinks he can be a great one."

———

It was the year of the two quarterbacks, one indomitable, on the field every Saturday, driving, pushing, willing the Tide to victory; the other the brash kid from the North, unproven and untested, yet confident, and by the standards of his teammates "something out of somewhere else." Pat Trammell was the team's unquestioned leader, "the bell cow of the whole outfit," commented Bryant. Joe Namath was the carpetbagger wunderkind, uncomfortable in his new surroundings but supremely gifted on a football field—"the best athlete I had ever seen," Bryant later wrote. In 1961 Trammell was determined to give substance to Bryant's bold 1958 prediction. For Namath, a freshman and therefore ineligible to play on the varsity team, 1961 was a time to watch and learn, on the football field and off.[2]

Trammell came from Scottsboro, a town in the mountains of northeast Alabama. Son of a gentle, good-hearted community doctor and a determined, outspoken mother, Pat grew up like other boys in the rugged area. He showed respect and was an excellent student, but he also was quick to speak his mind and not adverse to a good scrap. People later talked about the domineering Trammell gene, but Pat was very much his mother's son. She was "a force of nature," Pat Trammell Jr. recalled, and her son carried on the family tradition. An all-state football and basketball player, he had committed to play basketball and study engineering at Georgia Tech. But in early 1958 Bryant and Gene "Bebes" Stallings convinced him to come to Alabama.[3]

He was a big, handsome quarterback and, it soon became

apparent, had a large, striking personality. Playing on an under-sized team, his size—around six foot two and a shade over 200 pounds—made him look more like a lineman than a quarterback. But no tackle or guard ever ran a team like Trammell. From his first days in the program he let it be known that he was in charge. The legend of Pat Trammell began early when he intimidated the other freshmen, especially the sizable group of quarterback recruits. Bill Oliver, a teammate, recalled that one day some of Pat's rivals were sitting around a table talking about the team when Trammell barged into the room. He snapped open a knife, threw it into the tabletop, and while it was still quivering announced that he would be the quarterback. No one uttered a word, recalled Oliver. "Right then they all became halfbacks."[4]

Even if the story has been embellished over the years—after all, Bryant, not Trammell, would choose his quarterback—it illustrates a crucial aspect of Pat's character. Like Bryant, he was physically intimidating. If he thought a player wasn't putting out in practice or a game like he should, he would really get in his face. "He'd slap the boy hard, real hard, or tell him to get the hell off the field," commented a journalist. He terrorized some of his teammates, but they respected him. Bryant said that more than respecting Trammell, his teammates "rallied around him like little puppies. He could make them jump out a window to win. We didn't have any bad practices when he was there because he wouldn't let it happen."[5]

And no one intimidated him—not teammates, not opponents, not even Bryant himself. His confidence was unshakable. Although most of the players—and coaches—kept a respectful distance from Bryant, Trammell cultivated a sort of friendship with his coach. Often he arrived early for practice and dropped by Bryant's office for a chat. They would sit and talk—sometimes about football, but more often about life. "I just loved that," Bear wrote.[6]

Other times Bryant approached Trammell. A telling staple of the Trammell legend concerned the day Pat was eating lunch and Bear sat beside him, a new play diagrammed on a paper napkin, and said, "I was thinking about going over this play in practice. Maybe trying to work it into this week's game. Why don't you take a look at it?" Trammell kept eating as he glanced at the play, considered it, and replied, "Coach, I think it's crap. It'll never work."[7]

Most of Bryant's best recruits were southern boys from humble families who needed a football scholarship to attend college and escape the hardscrabble life of their parents. Trammell, of course, was a superb student who came from the more affluent side of the tracks. And at Alabama he continued his success in football and academics, majoring in physical chemistry in the department of chemical engineering and graduating magna cum laude and first in his class. Like his father and two brothers, he too became a doctor.

But Trammell and Bryant were more alike than their childhood experiences suggest. The need to win drove both of them. Bear never had to motivate Pat, and he seldom needed to push the team when Pat was around. Trammell became Bryant's alter ego. Bill Lumpkin, the sports editor for the *Birmingham Post-Herald*, showed how the Trammell-Bryant relationship worked. It was raining one day before practice, he recalled, and the sky was darkly threatening worse. The players were gathered outside the old athletic department, many hoping that Bryant would call off practice. Trammell arrived and told them to stop their wishful thinking. "You know that's impossible," he said. "As soon as The Man comes out, the rain will stop."[8]

Only one characteristic about Trammell bothered Bryant—his

foul mouth. Bear said his language was salty, but in fact it was much spicier. In an effort to clean it up, Bryant tried talking to him, making him run in the mornings, and even threatening to keep him from playing. Nothing worked. Finally Bear decided to appeal to a higher authority. When Bebes Stallings mentioned that Pat's mother was coming to Tuscaloosa for a game, Bear said, "Great, bring her around to my office so I can talk to her about Pat's cussing." Pat's mother really liked Bryant and spontaneously demonstrated her pleasure when she walked into his office. "God damn, Bear. It sure the hell's good to see you!" she said. As they hugged, Bryant looked at Stallings and mouthed, "Don't say anything about the cussing! Don't say anything about the cussing!"[9]

But Bear liked everything else about his quarterback. Trammell, like Bryant, was a planner and a doer, not a hoper. He was an all-state football and basketball player, finely coordinated, and intelligent. But his drive to succeed—to win at everything he tried—separated him from the pack. Bryant wrote, "He was not a great runner, but he scored touchdowns. He didn't pass with great style, but he completed them." Billy Neighbors, the All-American tackle who played on the same teams as Trammell, said that Pat was "the smartest football player" he had ever known. "It was just the way he ran the team." Both coach and teammate were trying to describe Trammell's intangible quality, which was quite simply that he had the uncanny knack for doing what was required to win.[10]

———

Trammell expected greatness in 1961. Like the other players Bryant had recruited in 1958, he had been promised that if he and his teammates bought into the program they would win a national title before they graduated from Alabama. If the idea seemed far-fetched in 1958 and 1959, by 1960 it had become a tangible goal. In the first four games that season, the Crimson Tide defeated Georgia and Vanderbilt, tied Tulane, and lost to Tennessee. It was a decent start, but hardly remarkable. At midseason the team reached its stride, winning its last six regular-season games and tying Texas 3–3 in the Bluebonnet Bowl. Alabama finished the season ranked in the top ten.

Preseason football magazines predicted that Alabama would enjoy a solid 1961 season, but by no means ranked them to win the powerful, twelve-team Southeastern Conference. The year before, Ole Miss had finished the regular season undefeated, beating Rice in the Sugar Bowl, completing the season ranked second in the nation (behind Minnesota, which had lost a game during the regular season and been beaten by Washington in the Rose Bowl). Veteran sportswriter Bill Keefe of the *New Orleans Times-Picayune* predicted that the Rebels would be even stronger in 1961. But he granted Alabama "Dark Horse" status.[11]

On a brutally hot afternoon between the hedges in Sanford Stadium, the Tide opened their season against Georgia. It was Johnny Griffith's debut as head coach. Twelve years earlier he was playing halfback for Georgia, but when Wally Butts was forced out as head coach, Griffith was promoted from his position as freshman coach. If he lacked experience, his team didn't, and sportswriters thought the Bulldogs would give the Tide a game.

They didn't. Alabama dominated both sides of the ball. Halfback Mike Fracchia, the finest open-field runner on the team, scored the Tide's first touchdown of the season in the second quarter, and Tim Davis kicked a field goal to give Alabama a 10–0 lead at half. In the second half the Crimson Tide stretched out their lead to 32–0 before Georgia scored on the last play of the game. The final score: Alabama 32, Georgia 6.[12]

The Georgia contest set a pattern. Defense had always been the hallmark of Bryant's teams, but the 1961 squad elevated it into a wolfpack art form. Linebackers Lee Roy Jordan and Darwin Holt led the defense. Born the fifth of seven children to industrious Christian parents, Jordan had been raised on a farm outside Excel, a small Alabama town of about 250 people located between Montgomery and Mobile. Lee Roy learned the meaning of hard work at a young age. "On our five-or-so-hundred-acre farm we grew cotton, peanut, corn, cantaloupe, watermelon, vegetables—actually about anything you could grow or eat." Picking cotton was the most exhausting chore. "Seems like I dropped more on the ground than I got in the sack, but my father wasn't a man to waste anything, so I picked it up." Dragging a sixty- or eighty-pound sack through rows of cotton, lifting and hauling cotton and hay bales, tending to cattle and horses, Jordan developed "natural country muscle." And like strong boys across the state, he put it to good use on the football field.[13]

Auburn, Southern Mississippi, and Alabama recruited Jordan in 1958 during his senior year. "Auburn had won the national title in 1957 and offered me a scholarship, but they withdrew it after I got married. But that didn't matter. I wanted to attend Alabama from the get-go." He met Bryant for the first time on a recruiting visit to Tuscaloosa. "All I said was 'Yes, sir' and 'No, sir' until Coach Bryant got me into his office. I sat on that old couch of his. I think the springs had been removed and the legs amputated, because all I remember is looking up at him sitting behind his desk, which I think was on a two-foot pedestal. I looked up at him and he looked down on me." Finally, Bear said he wanted Lee Roy to play for his team. Suddenly talkative, Lee Roy answered, "Yes, sir. That's exactly what I want to do."

Jordan was part of Bryant's second recruiting class, and although practices were no day at the Gulf Coast beach, they were not as bad as the year before when Bear was testing the resolve of his inherited players. From the first, Bryant liked Jordan. "I think he thought that I was about as country as he had been when he arrived at Alabama," Jordan said. "Coach Bryant used to tell me stories about his youth in Arkansas, when he sold eggs and chickens and whatever his mother had grown." "Yep, Lee Roy and I have a lot in common," Bear told reporters after he and his linebacker had had a good talk about the year's peanut crop.[14]

Bryant also knew how to motivate Lee Roy. A teammate recalled that Jordan "was the only man who ever practiced too hard for Coach Bryant." Bear told his players, "Every play is a personal challenge," and Jordan took him at his word. It was like he was working on his daddy's farm. He didn't leave any cotton on the ground. Bryant couldn't and didn't ask for more. "I don't recall him ever yelling at me—and if he had, I would remember it," Lee Roy said. "All he had to do is to come over to me, put one of those big hands on my shoulder, and say, 'Lee Roy, I appreciate everything you've done for us, now go out there and do your job.'" And Jordan, a junior in 1961, did his job with All-American competency during the season.[15]

Backing up the line on defense beside Jordan was Darwin Holt. In an era when most players went both ways, Holt was a defensive specialist. He generally replaced Pat Trammell when Alabama was on defense, but occasionally during particularly crucial series Bryant left Pat in as safety. Of the "quick little boys" who played on the 1961 squad, Holt might not have been the quickest, but he was certainly one of the littlest. Bear had first seen Darwin back in Texas when he was recruiting his brother Jack. Watching game film of a contest played on a muddy field that ended 2–0, Bryant was unimpressed by Jack Holt but was struck by Darwin, a small underclassman who battled every play like his life was on the line. Seeing him fight for a loose ball, Bear, pointing at the screen, said, "I want that 'un. That little bitty number 64. He's a battler!"[16]

Bear got Darwin. In 1957 the "little bitty" went to Texas A&M, and then in 1959 followed Bryant to Alabama. He was still dramatically undersized—about five-eight and 160 or so. Bear claimed that "Darwin wasn't any bigger than a minute, except in the heart." Like Jordan, Holt played with a ferocious intensity, an all-out reckless abandon that pleased his coach. It was almost as if Holt didn't realize he was too small and untalented to make an impact on a game. Self-assured, with a cocky edge, he thought he belonged on the field every play. And when, after sitting in storage for a few years, he got his chance to play he made the most of it. During the 1961 season Holt always seemed to be in a crucial defensive play—at the bottom of a pile scrambling for a loose ball, the first man to reach a screen play, or the second hitter on about any run. He was not as talented as Jordan or All-American tackle Billy Neighbors, but like the scrappy tackle Charley Pell, Darwin gave Bear every little bit of talent he possessed, and then some.[17]

In 1961 the Tide's defense was so superior that the offense seldom had to take any risks. In one late-season game Trammell called for a quick kick with the ball near midfield. It was an odd call, to say the least, and Bear questioned it when Pat reached the sideline. "Those——," Bryant recalled that Trammell said. "They aren't blocking anybody, so I thought we might as well see if they could play defense." They were words of a cocksure quarterback—confident in himself, his teammates, and the team's defense. And Trammell knew that it was exactly the sort of backhanded statement that Bear himself might have uttered.[18]

By then the Tide was rolling on a crest of success. After the

Georgia victory, Alabama defeated Tulane 9–0, Vanderbilt 35–6, North Carolina State 26–7, Tennessee 34–3, Houston 17–0, Mississippi State 24–0, and Richmond 66–0. Going into the Georgia Tech game, Jordan and his teammates had yielded only 22 points to the opposition, less than three points per game. No modern college football team has since matched Alabama's record for defensive excellence. Playing basically one-platoon football, they outquicked, outmeaned, outhit, and outlasted their opponents. "We didn't like to be scored on," Lee Roy Jordan remembered. "We took it real personal."[19]

Played before a full house in Legion Field, the Georgia Tech game looked like another win for the defense. And in some ways, it was. The game was scoreless at the end of the first quarter, but in the second Mike Fracchia scored on a 16-yard end run. In the third quarter Tim Davis added a field goal to give the Tide a 10–0 lead. It was more than enough. In the entire game Tech made only six first downs, rushed for 30 yards, and passed for 66 yards. Alabama won 10–0, increasing their shutout streak to four. But a play toward the end of the game made the contest notorious.

In the fourth quarter Georgia Tech lined up to punt the ball, something they did nine times in the game. Punt returner Billy Richardson, flanked by blockers on either side, dropped back to field the kick. It was a weak punt, a semi-shank that forced Richardson to run forward and signal for a fair catch. Unaware of either the quality of the punt or Richardson's signal, Darwin Holt prepared to block Tech's outside coverage man streaking down the field.

What happened next was obvious. Holt had his eyes riveted on Chick Graning, watching for him to veer right toward Richardson. When Graning broke right, Holt, slightly out of position because of the shank, lunged sideways, hitting Chick high with his forearm and elbow. Holt's forearm connected with Graning's face under his single-bar facemask, fracturing his jaw, knocking out three teeth, and giving him a concussion. "His face just exploded," Holt recalled. "Broke his upper and lower jaw. And his teeth were lying on the ground. That's what I saw. His face looked like a medicine ball."[20]

Why it happened was less obvious and subject to interpretation. Holt later claimed that he intended to hit Graning in the chest, "and that's exactly where I would have hit him if he hadn't started to duck and come down low." In any case, he insisted, it was a legal block, pointing out that the referee was looking right at him and did not throw a flag. Graning said that he had not begun to duck, and that the hit was a cheap shot. "There is absolutely nothing wrong with good, clean, hard football, but I believe Darwin crossed the line," he insisted.[21]

Game films are inconclusive and certainly cannot answer the question of intent. They do show that the hit was not late. Holt blocked Graning at almost the exact moment that Richardson fielded the ball. Perhaps Graning had seen Richardson's fair catch signal and relaxed, but Holt was doing his job and looking the other way. But it does not appear that Graning ducked. Holt aimed high and hit high. Unquestionably he was a hard-nosed player—"as mean as a snake," one of his teammates said—and if he got a chance to hit someone during a play, he did. Yet it is doubtful he intended any real harm. Like several other notorious hits that resulted in serious injuries, it was more an accident of timing and physics than the planned result of a dirty play. It was a freak play that happened in the blink of an eye.[22]

The hit knocked Graning out of the game, but spectators at the contest were not aware of his injuries and he was not taken to a Birmingham hospital. Only on Sunday, back in Atlanta, would he be admitted to the hospital—and only then would the terrible seriousness of his injuries be reported. The Sunday newspaper coverage of the game hardly mentioned the play, and Bryant did not know the extent of the damage. It was not until Monday, November 20, that the play assumed ominous, even conspiratorial dimensions.[23]

In the incident *Atlanta Journal* sports columnist Furman Bisher glimpsed a nefarious pattern of behavior. Never on good terms with Bryant, he attacked with the full force of his typewriter in an article entitled "The New Darwin Theory." From the beginning his assault was personal. Bryant lectured his players endlessly about demonstrating class. Partially, Bear's idea of class entailed doing the right thing—writing home to their parents regularly, speaking respectfully to adults, going to class, representing their school and hometowns properly. But it also meant looking a certain way. Alabama players wore coats and ties to their games, khakis and button-down shirts around campus. The look was a direct refutation to everyone who thought Alabamians were all redneck hicks in white T-shirts and blue jeans, the sort of characters that appeared heckling blacks at sit-ins and applauded the rants of Bull Connor. Bryant's players represented a different Alabama, one with character and restraint. It was powerful symbolism for Alabamians who cringed at how their state was portrayed in the national media.

Bisher, however, said it was all an act of deception. He charged that Bryant and his team had no class, unless one was liberal with the definition of the word. "You have heard of the rather uncouth fellow, pointing lustily at a member of the opposite sex, say, 'There goes a broad wit' real class,'" he wrote. "This is, it seems, the definition of class that Bryant had in mind, the slang for excellence or style." Or perhaps the coach used another dictionary definition of the word: "Group of animals or plants ranking below a phylum or subkingdom and above an order."[24]

Gradually Bisher moved from a blitzkrieg assault against Bryant to an equally violent campaign against his players, particularly Darwin Holt. Labeling Holt "bestial," and charging that he bit a Tech player in the 1960 contest, the Atlanta sportswriter called on the University of Alabama and the Southeastern Conference to throw Holt off the team. "I surely would expect no less of Georgia Tech," Bisher concluded.

The column lit a firestorm of accusations. During the week the *Atlanta Journal* printed daily letters condemning Bryant and Holt. "With players like Darwin Holt as living testimonials to your teaching results, I fear that you, after all, will not go down in sports history as one of the South's great football coaches," began sports columnist Ed Miles in an open letter addressed to "Cousin Paul." He went on to present Holt with the "Unsportsmanlike Award of All Time." Another letter congratulated Bisher and said it was time "to put a stop to the Bryants and Darwin Holts of collegiate football." And in yet another, two Alabama alumnae fretted, "A 'victory' that can cause such serious injuries to two young men, one in a physical way and the other in a spiritual way, is a defeat."[25]

The criticism prompted SEC commissioner Bernie Moore to run for cover. Initially he had stood behind the referee's decision. No penalty had been called, he emphasized, and that was that— but he did plan to review the game films. After that mild statement, he kept out of sight, and it was never reported what he saw in the films. Not until the following season did he comment that the rules did need to be "tightened up." He instructed league officials to pay more attention to "striking with the forearm and piling on the ball carrier after the ball is dead."[26]

While Atlanta raged and Moore hid, Alabama defended their coach and players. John Forney later commented that Holt was guilty of teeing off on Graning, but the Atlanta media "chose to blow the matter way out of proportion." Bisher and Miles were less concerned with Graning's injuries and Holt's offense than with Bryant, "who was moving Southern football dominance west, from Atlanta and Knoxville to Tuscaloosa."[27]

Birmingham News columnist Benny Marshall agreed, admitting that there was no defense for Holt's hit. "None has been offered here. None. None." But he immediately added, "There is even less defense for last week's hysterical *Atlanta Journal* orgy led by men with jaws a-drool, hungry for a kill." Reflecting on the history of journalism, he added, "It was infamous, disgraceful, indecent, unworthy of the newspaper profession." Sounding like a lawyer during closing arguments of a libel case, he asked, "Is Darwin Holt a monster? A beast? A gangster? A ruffian? He was called these things, and more, in *The Atlanta Journal* last week, wherein he received more attention than a murder on Peachtree might have provoked." It was nothing short of the worst screed of "yellow journalism at its rankest." "Inch after inch of *Journal* space has been filled with statements which could not be substantiated in any way, with innuendo, with inhuman intensity aimed at Holt, and Alabama and Bryant, who teaches hard-hitting, not dirty, football." He concluded that Chick Graning's injuries would heal. "I don't know about those that Furman Bisher and Ed Miles have inflicted on Darwin Holt." Bisher's and Miles's attacks, Marshall thought, were the most "vicious."[28]

Coaches Bear Bryant and Bobby Dodd also waded into the

roiling waters of debate. They had been longtime friends, but that relationship ended with Holt's hit. After the game Dodd told Bisher that he planned to write Bryant and President Rose "telling them exactly what Georgia Tech thinks about the incident. I will also point out that this is not the first time in which Darwin Holt has been involved in such uncalled-for attempts at illegal play."[29]

Dodd was blunt in his letter to Bryant, pointing out that the unfortunate play was "not the first, nor the fifth, nor the tenth time that Holt has played this type of football." He described how Holt had bit and kicked players in past games, lecturing Bear that his player "should be barred from competition." And if Bryant kept Holt on the field, it showed he condoned and approved such behavior. Dodd concluded on an informal note: "Knowing you as I do, Bear, if Graning were your son and in the condition he is now in at the hospital, you would personally be searching out Holt in order to get revenge."[30]

Later in the week, after he had watched the game films, Dodd expanded his list of grievances, suggesting that there were scores of other questionable hits in the game. All things considered, he thought a careful reconsideration of the Georgia Tech–Alabama series was in order.[31]

Years later, Bryant said he had no doubt that Holt had fouled Graning, "and the officials should have penalized us." "I probably would have disciplined him my own way if those Atlanta sportswriters hadn't set out to crucify him. A penalty is one thing, a crucifixion is another. After that I wouldn't have done anything if [he] had burned the university down," he said.[32]

In the week after the game, however, he defended his team, their play, and his methods. Certainly he taught gang tackling and physical play, continually emphasizing the need to "out-mean" the opposition. His pregame talks almost always included the need to "physically beat" the other team. But he emphatically did not teach dirty play, and players who received penalties for piling on or late hits soon found a seat on the bench. Winning was his objective, and excessive penalties were indicative of losing teams.

Bryant did not handle the media attack well, especially given that Chick Graning was suffering in an Atlanta hospital. Instead of swallowing hard, accepting some unwarranted criticism, and expressing sympathy for Graning, he stiffened his back and went on the offensive, pointing out the rough play of the Yellow Jacket players. He then had an assistant run the game films for Alabama sportswriters to show Tech's numerous violations. "It was a small thing and showed no class," he later realized. "If I had it to do over, I wouldn't, but our people thought the Atlanta writers were trying to destroy me. Or were using the player's mistake to get at me."[33]

Some journalists even used the incident to frame a larger accusation against Bryant and the state of Alabama. Marion E. Jackson, a sports columnist for the *Atlanta Daily World*, drew a line between Alabama's violence on the football field and its racial bigotry. "Should it be surprising that brutal excesses are matter of fact at University of Alabama which drove Authurine [*sic*] Lucy from its campus, defied the federal courts with campus riots,...and stormed in fury through Tuscaloosa streets," he wrote. Jackson found the outpouring of concern for Graning and outrage against Holt ironic. Newspaper reporters and radio commentators filled columns and the airways with chatter about the Holt-Graning episode, yet the same journalists had maintained a silent indifference to the suffering of Lucy. "Yet, the shoe of intolerance fits on any foot whether that of Chik [*sic*] Graning or Authurine [*sic*] Lucy, and the indignities of misconduct are the same regardless of race, color or creed."[34]

Jackson's column was published on November 25. By then the Holt-Graning affair was giving way to another controversy, one with race at its heart.

———

A soft rain was falling on the streets of Birmingham on November 19, 1961, the day the Crimson Tide jumped past the University of Texas Longhorns as the top college football team in the country. Furman Bisher's incendiary column would not appear until the next day, and the glow of Alabama's victory over Georgia Tech seemed to linger in the air as Bryant hosted a group of sportswriters in the Tallulah Suite of the fashionable Bankhead Hotel. The ice clinking against the crystal glasses full of bourbon created a convivial mood. Bryant mentioned that Rose Bowl officials had approached him about playing in Pasadena on January 1, and most of the sportswriters in the room assumed that Alabama was a lock to play UCLA.[35]

Sitting back against his bed with his thick hands clasped behind his head, Bryant was a very contented man. He had scratched and fought his way from the abject poverty of Moro Bottom, Arkansas, to a top coaching job in college football. Although, a writer for *Sports Illustrated* observed, "the mop of dark, wavy hair that once made him look like Gregory Peck on the way to Navarone" had thinned a bit and was streaked with gray, he was still a strikingly handsome man, a man's man, "with a strong chin and icy green eyes." And his voice was the envy of everyone in his profession, "soft and low, full of corn pone," and impossible to resist. "He can charm a possum out of a tree," the *SI* reporter claimed. Put bluntly, at that moment Bear was famous, and well on his way to becoming very wealthy.[36]

The mood changed in an instant when a reporter with thick, bookish black glasses spit out a question. "Coach Bryant," he began politely, "what did you think of the announcement out of UCLA that the colored players would not take the field against your team if it got to the Rose Bowl?"

Silence followed. The ice in the glasses seemed to melt quietly into the Jack Daniel's. All the inquisitive reporter, Jim Murray of the *Los Angeles Times*, heard was the noise from outside the window—a car screeching to a stop, a drunk shouting, "Go, Tide, Roll!" For several uncomfortable seconds Bryant just stared hard, his cold blue-green eyes fixing the West Coast reporter like he was looking at him through the scope of a rifle.

Then he said, "Oh, I would have nothing to say about that. Neither will the university I am sure."

One southern reporter, beet red with anger, glared at Murray and added, "Tell them West Coast Nigger-lovers to go lick your boots, Bear." Other southern reporters quietly moved closer to Murray and whispered, "Forget the remark of that knot-head. That's not the attitude."[37]

Everything Jim Murray had seen and heard in recent days confirmed his belief that Birmingham was the "gateway to the Ku Klux Klan," the city where "Evening Dress" meant "a bed sheet with eyeholes. And bring your own matches. We're lighting a cross." Murray, like Jackson, was one of a new breed of sportswriters who discerned a link between the segregation and violence in Birmingham, Montgomery, and the rest of Alabama and the all-white, brutally competitive Alabama football team.

Sport, he insisted, was not a world apart; it reflected social and political realities. He claimed that he had traveled to Birmingham "not to find social injustice but to cover a football game. But the crosscurrents of our times are such that the two are intertwined." Murray's claims for going to Birmingham were undoubtedly disingenuous. He was a confirmed and accomplished big league pot stirrer, and a minor league social crusader. The young and crusading Otis Chandler, the *Los Angeles Times*' publisher, had snatched Murray from *Sports Illustrated* to pop the balloon of rah-rah sports. In truth, Murray had flown to Birmingham courting controversy. He didn't have a shred of interest in the Alabama–Georgia Tech game. He planned to find and write about social injustice, and to connect the dots between the Ku Klux Klan and the Crimson Tide football team. Just as the Klan had no place in an enlightened land, he wrote, "an all-white team has no business being No. 1." It was "a denial of democracy."

Murray shivered at the thought of Alabama in the Rose Bowl, regardless of the teams they beat or the national ranking they attained. The notion of Alabama running onto the field in Pasadena was akin to the idea of shifting the nation's capital to Birmingham. For him, the team represented a way of life. He preferred the bowl people to pack the Tide off to the Sugar Bowl in New Orleans where they could battle another all-white southern team. "To a charade—a mummers' parade. A toast to a dead Empire. Lift a glass to a world that no longer exists. Pretend the unreal is real. They're not there, those 25 million non-people. The world is a cotillion, not a deadly, desperate struggle for survival."

The columnist's diatribe against Alabama, coming only a day after his attacks on Bryant, signaled a significant change in sports journalism. College football had traditionally been about schools battling for local and regional bragging rights. It wasn't concerned with public policy, foreign affairs, or domestic agendas. But Murray's reports from Birmingham, brimming with notions that the hatred and violence of the few had intimidated and silenced the many, echoed precisely Harrison Salisbury's articles on fear and hate in Birmingham. "A writer—even a sportswriter—is supposed to cover the news," Murray wrote. "The real news of the game I covered had very little to do with the score. It had to do with the smell of roses and the color of the players."[38]

That November the basic structure of college football began to crumble. Since its initial agreement in 1946, the champions of the Big Ten and the Athletic Association of Western Universities had met in the Rose Bowl. Increasingly, however, the Big Ten faculties had voiced alarm at the creeping commercialism and open disregard of academic standards and priorities represented by the Rose Bowl extravaganza. In 1961, with the contract recently expired, action replaced words. The faculty of Ohio State, winners of the Big Ten title, voted not to accept the Rose Bowl bid, a decision that set off a media circus and a series of mob demonstrations. Rioters broke windows in the Faculty Club, strung up hastily made effigies of leading OSU officials, and carried signs reading DAMN THE FACULTY. How dare a distinctly "secondary group" at the university like the faculty interfere with the football program? a writer asked the president of Ohio State. "Cannot something be done to see to it these 'little' people cannot" thwart the plans of the football team? inquired another.[39]

The end of the Big Ten–AAWU contract opened the door for the return of a southern team to the Rose Bowl. Going into November, Texas was ranked first in the nation in both polls, but on the eighteenth they were upset by Texas Christian University and dropped behind Alabama, making the Tide the overwhelming choice. Before the 1946 pact, of course, Alabama had been a frequent participant in the Rose Bowl, winning four games, tying one, and losing one. Now it had a chance to go back. It was a heady prospect. "I would just about walk out there for a chance to play in it and I believe my players would, too," Bryant said. Anticipating the game, he told Dude Hennessey, one of his best coaching tacticians, to fly to Los Angeles to scout UCLA. It seemed as if everyone in the state was eager for the contest. Throughout Alabama and the South, sportswriters filled their columns with talk of the Tide's opportunity to return to glory in the golden West. "Visions of Pasadena on New Year's Day danced in the heads of Alabama faithful," wrote a local reporter.[40]

On the West Coast during the second week of November, Rose Bowl officials and sportswriters praised Alabama, arguing that the Tide would be a better opponent for UCLA than any of the Big Ten teams. An obscure Bruin campus group, calling itself the Negro College Students of Southern California, went against the grain and voiced its opposition to Alabama. Inviting the Crimson Tide to the Rose Bowl, the members argued, "would give financial profit to the university to further its segregation policies." With Freedom Riders still imprisoned in Mississippi and memories of the violence in Alabama fresh, the organization's leadership said they intended to organize a boycott of the Rose Bowl if Alabama played in the game.[41]

The boycott plan gained attraction on West Coast campuses and in African American communities. A group of Berkeley students supported the boycott, and the *California Eagle*, an African American newspaper, applauded the idea, noting that the University of Alabama "is a Jim Crow institution from stem to stern" and would not schedule an integrated game in Denny Stadium. California schools, an editor insisted, "can't afford to play footsie with discriminating southern universities. Let them show their wares in the White Supremacy game at New Orleans' Sugar Bowl."[42]

Then Murray and Melvin Durslag, another Los Angeles

reporter, "pissed in the holiday punch bowl." Durslag railed against the idea of a sacred Rose Bowl bid going to Bryant's team. "Alabama—An Insult to the Bowl," headlined one of his *Los Angeles Examiner* pieces. "At this stage in the sociological revolution, it would be sheer lunacy for people who believe in integrated athletics to mess with a school whose leaders hold firmly to segregation.... It would be a scandalous affront to USC and UCLA...to invite an opponent which wouldn't permit either on its field for reasons of race."[43]

And Murray was even harder on Alabama, adding more volume and mocking humor to his articles. When southerners criticized him for what they interpreted as scandalous, unfair, and just plain "bullshit" attacks, Murray responded that his columns were actually intended as a public service for Alabamians. If they traveled from Tuscaloosa, Birmingham, and Montgomery to Los Angeles for the game, they "had better be prepared to put up with a few inconveniences—like they'd have to take pot luck with the rest of us at the drinking fountain, the water was integrated, that the buses were very careless in their seating and let just ANYBODY sit in the front, and that you might even sit next to a you-know-what at the football game.... Our kids don't even get to go to school with an escort of paratroopers."[44]

Murray took aim at Bryant as well as Alabama, accusing him of recruiting violations, condoning dirty play, and refusing to use his considerable power for social progress. He retold the litany of jokes about Bear, from "Atheism in Alabama is not believing in Bear Bryant" to the time he took his boys to an island on a fishing trip. "Did they row out?" someone asked. "The team did. But 'ol Bear, he just walked on the water." But Murray found nothing amusing in the southern enshrinement of Bryant. For him, Bryant and his "team in blood-colored uniforms" waved the flag of the Old South. He ended his piece "'Bama and Ol' Bear" with a rhetorical question: "If you're from Alabama, you kiss his ring. But what do you do if you're from Pasadena?"[45]

Murray expected a reaction, and he was not disappointed. A California resident and regular reader of the *Los Angeles Times* wrote the newspaper's president: "Murray has been bitter, partisan, crude, and has displayed, for those of us who grew up in and understand the South, a complete lack of understanding of Alabama." What had happened to fairness in journalism? he wondered. In Alabama the backlash was infinitely stronger. One journalist commented that Murray had thrown "a racial spitball." A second called him a dupe for "a small Negro protest." And a third added that his columns read "as if dispatched from the Congo." Immediately it was clear that the public sentiment in the state was swinging away from a trip to California, where only embarrassment and protests awaited.[46]

In less than a week, an Alabama football story—"Where Will the Tide Play on New Year's Day?"—had morphed into an Alabama race story. If Murray had the freedom to stir the pot and throw "racial spitballs," President Rose was forced to make a quick call. He understood the importance of returning to the Rose Bowl. The contests in 1926 and 1927 had made President George Denny an Alabama icon. But Rose was also painfully aware of the national images of the state and the university. He knew that many Alabamians, even some members of the Board of Trustees, still opposed integrated games, and the idea of playing the game and facing a boycott and protests filled him with dread.

What is clear now—but Rose denied then—was that Alabama had received a verbal commitment from the Rose Bowl committee.

Rose, and especially Bryant, wanted to accept it. But within days of the boycott proposal and Murray's first article, Rose started to move sideways, suggesting in private correspondence that he had not received any sort of commitment. On November 22 he wrote a friend in California that the trustees had "decided that it would serve the best interests of the University of Alabama for us to remove our team from any consideration of the Rose Bowl this year." The reason: "We have been assured that we would be picketed and that there would be many embarrassing incidents." Mostly he blamed Murray for whipping up hysterical hatred of Alabama. "I have never known anyone to be so vicious and so prejudiced as he was." But in other correspondence he indicated that the Rose Bowl committee had never seriously considered selecting a southern team, or that the television people had nixed the matchup. But whatever reason he advanced, the result was the same—Alabama would play another southern team in the Sugar Bowl on New Year's Day.[47]

Rose was near tears when he told the team his decision. He spoke only briefly, and only in the most general terms. But he clearly feared any trip out of the South would end in embarrassment. It is difficult to overrate this concern among many, and especially more affluent, southerners. Even before the Civil War southerners traveling north were acutely aware that above the Mason-Dixon Line they were considered backward hicks, defenders of an antiquated social system and branded by their association with "the peculiar institution" of slavery. The brooding sense of inferiority that this engendered did not die with slavery. Sensitivity to public ridicule remained a raw nerve in the South. Mild attacks in *Time* magazine and *Sports Illustrated* on Bryant's coaching methods, concerns about protests at a Rose Bowl game that would be overdramatized in the media, and the already volatile mood in Birmingham convinced

Rose to stay closer to home. Better to lay the blame on the doorstep of Jim Murray and fly down to New Orleans.[48]

Bear was disappointed, but he understood and quietly accepted the decision. In part it was because he was deep in preparation for the season-ending Auburn game. Once again, he kept the main thing the main thing—beating the cross-state rival, finishing the season undefeated, and winning a national championship. Later in his autobiography Bryant claimed that Murray "wrote about segregation and the Alabama Ku Klux Klan and every unrelated scandalous thing he could think of, and we didn't get the invitation." It was not quite that clear cut, but Murray's columns did raise the dreadful specter of embarrassment in Rose's mind. They were enough to thoroughly stir football into America's racial crisis.[49]

Although race had occasionally brushed against football in postwar America, after the Rose Bowl incident it imbued the game. But what exactly did that mean for Bryant and the South? If the Alabama Crimson Tide truly was "Dixie's Football Pride," as its fight song boasted, then which Dixie did it represent? Was it the symbol of a New South struggling with old traditions and attempting to maintain its regional personality? Or was it the emblem of white supremacy, segregation's last standing warriors on the field of battle? Those questions remained to be answered, but that they were asked was an unambiguous sign that football was not just a game, and Bear was not just another coach.

On December 2, after what seemed like a month, Bear finally smiled. It was in the final five minutes of the Auburn game. With Alabama leading 34–0, the Tigers' Bobby Hunt drove his team 65 yards against the Tide's second team for a first down close to the goal. Then, wrote Roy Terrell of *Sports Illustrated*, "Bear Bryant, a man who would rather surrender his left lung than a touchdown, sent in the Alabama first team." Lee Roy Jordan, Darwin Holt, Billy Neighbors, and the other players who had led the team through its remarkable, incomparable season, ran onto Legion Field. Four plays later Auburn had hardly moved a yard closer to the end zone. It was at that moment that The Man briefly smiled.[50]

Asked after the game if Alabama was a great team, Auburn's coach, Shug Jordan, thought for a moment before replying, "I don't know whether that's a great team, but they were great today. I don't guess anybody has ever hit us quite so hard."

It was another reason for Bear to smile. In 10 games his defense had begrudgingly yielded only three touchdowns and 22 points. Alabama had won all 10 of its games, six by shutouts. In Bryant's South, where defense was revered in all things, it was a remarkable performance, one that has not been matched in more than a half century.

On New Year's Day the Crimson Tide played Coach Frank Broyles's Arkansas team in the Sugar Bowl. Broyles had a fine team, certainly much better than the first time he faced Bryant. During Broyles's first year as head coach at Missouri he had played Bryant's powerful Aggie squad. Before the game Bear had draped his arm around the young coach's shoulders and said, "I've been looking over your squad..." As Bear paused, Broyles prepared himself to receive a compliment. Then Bryant finished his thought—"and I don't believe you have a single athlete."[51]

"I thought it was kind of unusual for your opponent to tell you before the game that you don't have a chance of winning," Broyles said. But Bear was just being honest. His team won 28–0 in a contest that could have been much worse.

Broyles brought a better team to New Orleans. They shared the Southwest Conference title with Texas and had a more than respectable 8–2 record. Their two losses were to Texas and Mississippi, both ranked in the top five in the country. And they had the fastest man on the field. Nicknamed Bambi because of his speed and grace, All-American Lance Alworth ran a 9.6 hundred and was an outstanding receiver. Professional scouts considered Alworth an exceptional talent, so much so that the San Diego Chargers would sign him before he reached the locker room after the game.[52]

Arkansas looked like Alabama's mirror image. Their cardinal and white school colors looked like the Tide's crimson and white, they had great team speed, and, as Alabama player Jimmy Wilson recalled, "they were small, quick, and very, very aggressive." The matchup worried Bryant. To keep the team focused on the game and away from Bourbon Street, he quartered his team and practiced in Biloxi, a quieter and more controllable environment.[53]

Rolling into Biloxi the day after Christmas, the team was greeted inhospitably by driving rain and winds and temperatures more suitable to the Northeast. It made no sense to practice outside, so they walked through plays in the ballroom. "Coach Bryant was pacing the floor," said Wilson, "very frustrated about the fact that we couldn't get any outside work in." Finally he told his players to put on tennis shoes and took them to work out on a parking lot.

January 1 was cold and overcast, but the stands in the old Tulane Stadium were packed. It was Alabama's first major bowl under Bryant, and the players were surprised by the floats, pageantry, and bustling activity of the game. Wilson took it all in—the size of the stadium, the cold wind blowing in his face, and the cheerleaders and majorettes "freezing to death" in their skimpy outfits.[54]

Midway through the first quarter, the Tide mounted a drive. Still short of midfield, Pat Trammell sensed the subtle shift in momentum. In the huddle he looked at his teammates and made a promise: "If anybody misses an assignment on this drive, if we don't score, I'm going to call time-out and kick your ass right here on national television." A few plays later Mike Fracchia broke loose on a 43-yard run, reaching the Arkansas 12 before being tripped up by a desperation diving tackle. From there Trammell scored on a play-action roll-out. In the second quarter Tim Davis booted a field goal and the Tide took a 10–0 lead into the locker room at halftime.[55]

It was more than the Tide needed. The previous week's rain had left the field soggy, making it difficult for Alworth to use his speed on end runs. Repeatedly he lost his footing before being hit, although he did make a sensational catch in Alabama territory late in the game. But a fumble ended the drive. In Alabama's regular season the opponents averaged 2.2 points per game. Arkansas exceeded the average by .8. The Tide won 10–3, giving Bryant his first national title.

Like the Rose Bowl game of 1926, the victory was celebrated across the state. There were parades in Tuscaloosa and celebrations in Birmingham and Montgomery, Scottsboro and Excel. U.S. representative from Alabama Frank W. Boykin had watched the game at his hunting lodge in McIntosh with his entire family. They were even joined, Boykin later wrote, by "our colored people that's done such a good job right down through the years." He judged the thrilling contest one of the greatest in the history of the sport, admiring Bryant's men as they "stood like Stonewall Jackson" against the fourth-quarter assaults from Arkansas. After the game he wrote a long letter of praise to Bryant, thanking him for restoring the university's team and bolstering state pride. "This Alabama football team showed the world, the whole wide world, what our men could do," he wrote. "There was so much joy, there was so much pleasure that you gave all of the home folks and people all over the South, and people all over the nation that want us to keep some part of our way of life."[56]

Boykin did not elaborate on what aspect of the southern "way of life" he meant. But one fact was strikingly obvious: Alabama won the national championship in 1961 without competing in a single integrated contest.

Harry Gilmer introduced the "jump pass" to the University of Alabama in the 1940s, but no one executed it better than Namath, whom Bryant described as "the best athlete I have ever seen." (Bryant Museum)

6

Becoming Joe Willie

You know, when a northerner goes south, he'll pick up a
southern accent; but when a southerner comes north, he
never loses his drawl.

—Joe Tronzo

M IDWAY THROUGH JUNE 1962, a large box from the Behrens
Manufacturing Company of Waukesha, Wisconsin, arrived
at the Alabama men's gymnasium. Addressed to assistant athletic director Carney Laslie, the box contained two Portable Water
Bubblers. The accompanying literature pronounced the three-foot,
wheeled five-gallon tanks to be "America's FIRST Sanitary Water
Caddy," patent pending, and described them as ideal for sports,
marching bands, tobacco fields, and fallout shelters. "At last," wrote
Ed Rozy, trainer of the Chicago Bears, "a really new idea has been
developed to help solve one of the most pesky problems in providing
fresh drinking water for the players on the gridiron."[1]

Bryant paid $199 for the tanks, and it was a 180-degree turn regarding the availability of water to his players on the practice field. Throughout Namath's freshman season, Bryant had abided by the standard belief that water caused cramping in overheated players, so in 1961, as Namath attempted to acclimate himself to the Deep South humidity that clung to him like a wet shawl, he received only salt pills. But now, in the summer before his first varsity season, the coaching staff set up the water bubblers and encouraged the players to drink as much as possible without getting waterlogged.[2]

Bryant's decision was significant, as providing water to dehydrated young men was no small matter. The change may have even saved lives, since the previous regimen of no water and a steady diet of salt pills was a recipe for a heart attack. On a broader scale, however, the water bubblers were indicative of Bryant's general approach to the game. He seldom came up with new ideas on his own, but he never let a good one pass him by.

About 140 miles northwest of where the Alabama coaches set up the water bubblers, the University of Mississippi ran a scrimmage. Richard Ross started at center for the Rebels and wore the red jersey that designated his position on the first team. Kenny Dill, playing middle linebacker on the second team, was Ross's backup. On one play, Ross blocked Dill, and in a flash and flurry of blood, Dill threw a vicious forearm that caved in Ross's cheekbone. Johnny Vaught, head coach of the Rebels, responded to the attack by saying simply, "Kenny, get on the red jersey." Then he added as an afterthought, "Fellows, let's keep our hands to ourselves." Practice resumed as if nothing had happened.[3]

As the University of Mississippi prepared to enroll James Meredith as its first African American student, the entire state resembled the Oxford practice field, as citizens "kept their hands to themselves" only after attacking one another. Leading the fight was Governor Ross Barnett. Everywhere he appeared, Barnett took a hard line against the Kennedy administration. "We must either submit to the unlawful dictates of the Federal Government or stand up like men and tell them NEVER!" he ranted to raucous applause. He then concluded, "I have said in every county in Mississippi that no school in our state will be integrated while I am your Governor. I repeat to you tonight—NO SCHOOL WILL BE INTEGRATED IN MISSISSIPPI WHILE I AM YOUR GOVERNOR!"[4]

No school in America matched Barnett's fierce hold to southern tradition as much as the University of Mississippi. All of the school's outward imagery simply oozed the moonlight-and-magnolia legend of the former Confederacy. The football team, called the Rebels in honor of Confederate soldiers, had as its mascot "Colonel Reb," an unmistakable rendition of a plantation owner and Confederate military officer. At games, the band wore Confederate kepi hats and played "Dixie" while rolling out a huge Confederate flag across the field. Outside the stadium, cotillion-garbed students gathered at "the Grove" to drink pregame mint juleps. Even the school's informal name, Ole Miss, recalled the title given to a plantation mistress. Indeed, so southern was the school's image of itself that it could not even be correctly seen as representing the Lost Cause of the Civil War. It was clearly much more comfortable in the perceived glory of an antebellum society.[5]

Joe Namath's first varsity season was played in the shadow of great social change. While Tuscaloosa seemed to most southerners like Martha's Vineyard compared to the scene in Mississippi, to Namath it was still the land of "colored water." Although he was unaware of the overwhelming emphasis on race in the culture of the region when he arrived a year earlier, he received a quick education on the matter during his freshman year. Even on the football field he was reminded that he was a northerner deep in the heart of Dixie.

Clem Gryska, Namath's freshman coach, understood well the problems of entering southern society from the industrial North. In January 1961, along with Dude Hennessey, another assistant coach on the staff, Gryska had traveled to Pittsburgh to attend the NCAA Coaches Convention. From Gryska's hometown of Steubenville en route to Pittsburgh, the coaches stopped in Beaver Falls to see Larry Bruno in an attempt to recruit Namath. Bruno informed them that Namath was out of town and, at any rate, intended to go to Maryland, so they should not waste their time on him. Gryska and Hennessey left, attended the convention, then proceeded eastward to see two other recruits in Philadelphia and New Jersey. On their way, remembering the talk surrounding Namath at the convention, they felt that they had lost a great player without ever having an opportunity to sell him on Alabama. So Gryska was surprised to see Namath on the freshman team in the fall of 1961. Coming from Steubenville, a town similar to Beaver Falls, Gryska kept a close watch for signs that Namath was having trouble adapting to his new southern home. What he saw was a confident, affable eighteen-year-old who made friends as easily as he completed passes. When Bryant approached him and asked how Namath was coming along, Gryska replied, "Oh, there's no trouble there. Even the rednecks from south Alabama respect him."[6]

Most of the players on the team liked Namath, and his talent soon became obvious. He simply looked different on the field. While his teammates sprinted to the line of scrimmage, Namath appeared to stroll from the huddle. When he finally arrived at the line, usually a full second or two behind the rest of the offense, he stooped behind center, bent over more at the waist than at the knees. It gave him a hunchbacked appearance but also the ability to move away from the center a bit quicker, since his legs were already in a position more conducive to running. This position helped, since Alabama ran a down-line option, where Namath was required to sprint parallel to the line of scrimmage and decide whether to throw a pass, pitch the ball to a trailing running back, or keep the ball and run with it himself.[7]

Namath led the freshman team to an undefeated season. His most memorable accomplishment of the season occurred during the game with Mississippi State. With the Alabama freshmen leading by six points late in the contest, he decided to overrule Coach Gryska and called a pass play on fourth down. His reasoning was that since the temperature was in the high nineties and most of the Alabama players played both ways, they could not physically cover the punt and then play adequate defense. Center Gaylon McCollough questioned Namath in the huddle. "Joe," he said, "it is fourth down and I was sent in to snap for a punt." Namath responded, "We can't punt if we are going to win this game. We have got to make a first down." They made the first down and ran out the clock.[8]

Regardless of the success they had competing with other freshman teams throughout the South, Namath and the rest of the football class of 1965 made their biggest mark on the practice field in Tuscaloosa. Players on the undefeated 1961 squad believed their greatest competition that year came on the practice field from the freshman squad. There, Namath and his teammates prepared the varsity, and in the process erased whatever lingering doubts existed among the Alabama coaching staff and players who still questioned Coach Bryant's decision not only to bring Namath to Tuscaloosa at such a late date but to summon him to the tower.

Namath may have won over the rednecks, as Gryska told Bryant, but one thing he never accepted was their brazen use of the word "nigger." What Namath found even more disturbing than the anger behind the word was the nonchalance and wide variety of its usage.

As he sat at the desk in his room one night during his freshman year, one of his teammates pointed at a picture of Namath from his senior prom and asked, "That your girl, Joe?" Without looking up, Namath answered, "Yes," unaware that his friend was pointing at one of the black girls in the picture, not Namath's date. Soon word spread around the team that their new quarterback was a "nigger-lover." Shortened, Namath's nickname became, simply, "Nigger." Never having lost the olive complexion that surprised his mother the first time she saw him, as well as coming from the North and displaying a seemingly stereotypical streetwise attitude, Namath appeared to his new teammates as the epitome of an inner-city African American. The label stuck. It was not a nickname thrown about only in resentment, either. Namath's teammates called him "Nigger" with apparent obliviousness to the discomfort it caused him. One teammate told his parents, "You ought to see this nigger we got playing quarterback. This nigger's somethin' else." The teammate's parents genuinely thought Namath had broken the color barrier at Alabama until they saw him take his helmet off during one game.[9]

During this time, Namath remembered what he had left behind in Beaver Falls. He thought about all of his black friends, who could never truly visit him in his new home, let alone share in his success. He thought about Linwood Alford, his childhood best friend who used to spend nights at the Namath household, then wait alongside the other Namath children for his kiss good-bye from Mr. Namath when he left for Moltrup's. He remembered Benny Singleton, who had walked off the basketball court with him in a show of defiance against the slow play of their coach—an act that now seemed trivial in light of all the injustice he had witnessed in one very intense year. Then there was his former team, now led by another black friend, Butch Ryan. Ryan, Namath's halfback and backup quarterback in the glorious 1960 season, started at quarterback in 1961 and led the Tigers to a second consecutive undefeated season. That Ryan was black—and no one in Beaver Falls seemed to care a bit about that fact—seemed inconceivable in this land where blacks could not even play against whites.[10]

But what could he do? In terms of the racial situation, Namath knew he was profoundly outnumbered in Tuscaloosa. Besides that, he realized that he was there to play football and not as a social crusader. He decided that the situation of his nickname was brought on because "those people were raised one way and I was raised another."[11]

Namath's nickname was a private matter, not the sort that could be used publicly. And one thing that was almost mandatory for an Alabama character was some sort of strange and evocative sobriquet. For Namath, the names of Tuscaloosa's vaunted football past sprang forth onto his northern ears like some sort of frenetic argument overheard at a foreign airport. Bully Van de Graaff, Pooley Hubert, Wu Winslett, Dixie Howell, Tarzan White, Holt Rast, and B'Ho Kirkland were legendary Crimson Tide players. And Bryant's staff offered more of the same. Dude Hennessey, Bebes Stallings, and Jimmy Goostree were on the coaching staff. Then, of course, there was Coach Bryant. (Assistant coach Sam Bailey was the only one ever to call him Paul, and no one ever called him "Bear.") Coach Bryant added another, more personal list of names with which all of the assistants familiarized themselves. This auxiliary list of Crimson Tide historical names popped out of Bryant's own stories, told in so garbled a drawl that only a few of the more specialized southern linguists among his staff ever picked up just exactly who these people were. Most of the time, they nodded at the coach and, like dogs listening to a master telling them a story of squirrels in the bushes and piss on the living room floor, understood only certain names—names familiar from other stories at other times. Preacher Franklin, Dopey Phelps, Smokey Harper, D. X. Bible, Young Boozer, Biggie Munn, Norbie Ronsonet, Tonto Coleman, and Minnie Bell Heep became catchwords the coaches clung to.[12]

Without a similarly acceptable appellation, Namath would never enter the lore of the land. As it stood, he remained rooted north of the Mason-Dixon Line with a steel-town immigrant name.

Bryant solved the problem and eased the transition. Perhaps he saw in Namath a reincarnation of John David Crow, his Heisman Trophy–winning halfback at Texas A&M and one of his favorite players, but he began referring to Namath as "Joe Willie." It was a simple take on his Christian name, Joseph William, and may not have been as evocative as some of the others in Alabama history, but it seemed to fit, lingering on the tongue with a kind of aw-shucks authenticity. It also served as a stop somewhere between carpet-bagger and Confederate, presenting Namath as an adopted son of Dixie. With Bryant's blessings and subtle rechristening, Namath was certainly on the path toward full southern acceptance, whether he felt completely comfortable with it or not.

Sometimes he got the chance to confront the racism directly. As he was standing in the huddle at a freshman practice, a play came in from the sideline. "Nigger right, on two," was the message to Namath. The word hit his ears like a bee sting. Although he had grown inured to the term around town and even on campus, the huddle was a bit too much. In a quick bit of improvisation, he reverted back to his parents' language. "Okay," he told the team, "*fekete* right, on two." *Fekete* was the Hungarian word for "black," but like the German *Schwarzer* or Polish *czarny*, it carried with it the connotation of a dark-skinned or swarthy person. While it fell short of the

Montgomery Bus Boycott in the pantheon of the civil rights movement, "*fekete* right" was not without a bit of disobedient charm.[13]

———

The newly christened Joe Willie prepared for his grand entrance onto the varsity stage, with the full recognition that he was again in the hands of a coach who stood pat only when pat was the proper place to stand. Like Bruno at Beaver Falls, Bryant stressed preparation. His preparation was so complete that the preparation had a preparation. Before the 1962 season began, he gave the team a summary of what was expected of them on the field as members of the Crimson Tide:

HAVE A PLAN—WINNING THEORY
AT ALABAMA 1962

1. Beat your opponent physically
   a. Better Physical Condition
   b. Be aggressive and "out-mean" them
   c. Consistency—110% every play
2. Genuine All-Out Desire for Team Victory
   a. Goal—to win them all
   b. Personal sacrifice instead of personal glorification
   c. What one can contribute, not what one can receive
   d. When you win there is enough glory for everyone
3. Winning Edge
   a. Second and third effort (R[un]. B[eyond]. I[nitial contact].)
   b. No Penalties, broken signals, fumbles, or interceptions
   c. Sudden Change
   d. Something extra when behind, and in the fourth quarter
   e. Know and play zone and field positions

4. Press Kicking game
   a. Type kick for particular zone
   b. Protection
   c. Coverage and defense
   d. Rush
   e. Returns
   f. Field Ball
5. Defense
   a. No long runs
   b. No passes for touchdown
   c. Force mistakes
   d. Score on defense
6. Offense
   a. Never give up ball without a kick
   b. Extras in danger zone
   c. Score—4 down zone
   d. Discipline
   e. Intelligent Recklessness
   f. It takes eleven to move the ball[14]

On Friday, September 21, at 1 p.m., the team, coaches, security, and some faculty members climbed into two Greyhound buses in Tuscaloosa for the ride along Route 11 to Birmingham. They checked into the Bankhead Hotel in downtown Birmingham, then went to Legion Field in their sweats for a brief practice from 2:30 to 3:00. At 5 p.m., the team ate dinner together at the Bankhead, with Catholic players given the choice of ordering fish since it was Friday. (When the Second Vatican Council ruled in 1965 that Catholics need abstain from meat on Fridays during Lent only, a joke spread that it was because Coach Bryant, an owner of Zeigler's meatpacking plant in Tuscaloosa, had made a deal with the pope in which he promised, "If you let my Catholic boys eat meat on the days before the games, I'll never beat Notre Dame.")

The rest of the night was casual. The team had to remain inside the hotel, but Coach Laslie obtained a movie for the team to watch. This night it was *Machine Gun Kelly*, a gangster film in which the star, Charles Bronson, hid his machine gun inside a violin case before blasting away at his enemies. When Kelly first produced the gun in a hail of bullets, Laslie shouted to the team, "I wish I had eleven like that!" After the movie, the players ate some fruit, then went to bed. The next day passed with the speed of drying paint. The team ate breakfast at about 10 a.m., then returned to their rooms. Namath watched television, but by 1 p.m. he grew antsy and was ready to play. At 3 p.m., he sat down to a meal of steak, English peas, and honey toast, then took a walk with Coach Bryant to go over the game plan one more time.[15]

Prior to the Georgia game, Namath was under more pressure than any sophomore in Alabama history. As defending national champions, the Crimson Tide were ranked number three in the nation in the preseason poll. That their defense would keep them in every game seemed assured, since the team returned twenty-three letter winners. Whether the offense could outscore its opponents was the real question, and the crucial uncertainty on offense was quarterback—the only position on the entire team not to return a letter winner. Although Bryant warned the press prior to the 1962 season that Namath "has no at-bats yet in college football," it was impossible for Tide fans not to be optimistic about the team's future. Never had Bryant seemed so enthusiastic about a recruit. He compared Namath to another Beaver County recruit he had landed while at Kentucky, Babe Parilli, a quarterback who finished fourth and third in the 1950 and 1951 Heisman Trophy voting, respectively, and who in 1962 played for the New England Patriots. A week before the game, a reporter asked if Namath had a weakness.

Bryant thought for a moment and replied, "Yes, he needs to improve the way he holds the ball for points after touchdown."[16]

Despite his accolades for Namath, Bryant remained his usual anguished self. "Frankly," he told the press, "unless we play some mighty good football, those Georgia Bulldogs may run us out of the stadium at Birmingham." He lamented the loss of Trammell to graduation, Mike Fracchia to a knee injury, and, much more tragically, Thomas Bible, who had drowned in a north Alabama lake. He thought the 1962 Tide was about 60 percent as good as the previous year's squad and predicted a 5–5 or 6–4 record. No one really bought it, of course. Georgia was improved, but its 3–7 record the previous year offered little hope for an upset of the defending national champions playing in front of a home crowd.[17]

Namath entered his first varsity season with a full, if simplified, playbook at his disposal. The offense was a standard T-formation—two running backs took their three-point stances about five yards behind the line of scrimmage, separated equally to create a triangle with Namath. Passes were either play-action, where Namath faked a handoff to one of the running backs before setting up for a pass, or a straight dropback with a primary receiver. In both cases, Namath would throw the ball to a primary receiver or scramble from the pocket. The running plays were similarly predetermined. But despite the simplicity of the plays, there was a large variety of them, and Alabama's offense was nothing like the "three clouds of dust" approach of the power teams in the Big Ten Conference. Bear believed that a smaller, quicker team would always beat a larger, slower one, even if the latter were physically stronger.

Alabama received the kickoff, but Namath looked nervous in front of the record crowd of 54,000. On first down he ran for three yards, but botched the signals on second down and took a one-yard loss. On third and six, Namath missed Richard Williamson on a short pass, and it looked as if the transition from Pat Trammell to Joe Namath might be rough. Cotton Clark punted, and Georgia began its first offensive series in their own territory. After two running plays, Georgia's junior quarterback, Larry Rakestraw, threw a pass that Eddie Versprille intercepted at the Georgia 47-yard line.

Namath gathered his team and calmly called an "out-and-up" for Williamson—a play that required Williamson to run a short pattern to Namath's right, stop, then proceed down the sideline at full speed. The success of the play depended on fooling the defensive back covering Williamson into "jumping the route," that is, charging at Williamson after his initial hesitation. Namath took the snap, then stood motionless in the pocket looking at Williamson for the entire play. Williamson made his quick stop and Namath faked a pass, further convincing the defender to make a run at the receiver. When Williamson broke toward the end zone he was five yards clear of the defender. Namath threw an arching pass that virtually fluttered toward Williamson. "All I had to do was catch it," the receiver said. And he did. At the 15-yard line the ball floated over his left shoulder and dropped into his open hands, which remained close to his body. He pulled the ball into his stomach and four steps later scored the first touchdown of Namath's college career.[18]

To the Alabama fans in attendance, Namath's 53-yard touchdown pass was a reason for celebration, and they erupted in cheers. For Alabama's players and coaches, the touchdown confirmed Bryant's unmatched optimism for his northern quarterback—the first in what was sure to be a line of validations for Namath's trip into the tower. For others, who knew only of Namath and his reputation, the pass was a revelation. No one in the Southeastern Conference had thrown a ball like that since Parilli a decade earlier at Kentucky. And even he had never looked that calm and polished in his entire career, let alone his first varsity game.

Alabama added a safety in the first quarter to make the score 9–0, and Namath threw his second touchdown pass late in the second quarter, a 10-yard connection to Cotton Clark, to end the half at 15–0. In the third quarter, he led Alabama on another touchdown drive, again passing to Clark to make the score 21–0 and end his evening at quarterback. He was 10 of 14 for 179 yards and three touchdowns. The *Birmingham News* called it "as auspicious a debut as a sophomore quarterback ever made for anybody." Jack Hurlbut replaced Namath, and the Crimson Tide defense never allowed Georgia near scoring position. The final score was 35–0.[19]

In the locker room after the game, Namath answered questions from the press. Elated with the victory and his debut, he gave appropriately modest responses to the simple questions lofted his way. Bryant abruptly broke up the festivities. He pointed to a group of Crimson Tide seniors gathered across the room and said, "Y'all get away from that popcorn quarterback. Get over to those boys who won the game." Namath felt blindsided. All of the troubles he had had acclimating to the South seemed to rush back over him. He had survived the heat, the humidity, and most of the racism. Now what seemed to be his last safe haven, the football field on game day, had lost its feeling of sanctuary. He had played the game to the best of his ability, lost himself in the competitive air of the evening, and stood respectfully before the reporters, then was reprimanded by Bryant for doing so.

Bryant's brusque style signified no rebuke however. Lee Roy Jordan, one of the seniors to whom Bryant had directed the press, heard the "popcorn quarterback" remark. He was one of the players Bryant depended upon to make sure the team remained cohesive. When players chose to sit with their girlfriends rather than their teammates, team leaders like Jordan made sure Bryant never witnessed it. Moving slowly over to Namath, Jordan said, "Joe, you just don't know the man. You just don't know him yet." He assured Namath that there was always a rationale behind even the harshest of Bryant's comments. The coach maintained a distinct caste system for his team, and the seniors were on top, no matter how well a sophomore played. The seniors recognized this system and maintained its structure. Sometimes, as on this occasion with the press, Bryant stepped in where the seniors could not. "It's not against you," Jordan suggested, "it's for us. For the seniors."[20]

Namath remained shaken. Although Bryant may have seen Namath as "all worldly-wise," he was merely a nineteen-year-old in an alien land with few friends. He was impressionable, lonely, and childish. He had little in common with the students at the university, and really only one thing in common with his teammates. He was the precocious youngest child of a divorced, indulgent mother. In short, he was not used to criticism. "Enough of this shit," he thought. "What else do I have to do here?"[21]

What Joe needed were friends outside of football. If he could just find a few people to make his life more like it had been in Beaver Falls, Tuscaloosa would be more livable. He had already tried to import a friend to Alabama during semester break of his freshman year when he invited Krzemienski to transfer and join him. "Coach Bryant really wants you down there," Namath told his old receiver. "He thinks we could have something special." Krzemienski turned Namath down, choosing to finish his career at Michigan State.[22]

So he had to find local companionship. Instantly, Namath fell into the company of a group that replaced not his former friends, but rather his mother. Wayne "Peanut" Morrison played football in the Tuscaloosa region but lacked the ability to play for the Crimson Tide. Even by Bryant's lenient standards, Peanut was too small. But he loved Alabama football and tried to help the cause in any way he could. As word spread that Namath was having trouble adjusting to the South, Peanut called upon three women he thought might be able to help. Mary Krout, Ruth Burchfield, and Bessie Asbury followed the Crimson

Tide like groupies, but were not the kind of women around whom a college athlete built his romantic fantasies. They were old enough to be the players' mothers, and that's just how they acted toward Namath. With genuine southern hospitality, they invited Joe Willie to their Tuscaloosa home for meals and advice. To be sure, they hoped to keep the future star on the Crimson Tide, but more important to them, they wanted to make Namath's southern experience memorable. The match between Joe and the three women not only succeeded, it also kept him connected to them for the rest of their lives. Namath always felt comfortable around older women and needed a homey sanctuary from school and football. Moreover, the "three ladies," as they became known, loved to cook, and Namath loved to eat.[23]

No one, though, became better friends with Namath than did the Crimson Tide's team manager, Jack "Hoot Owl" Hicks. Hicks had good times and bad troubles written all over his wide-open Ernest Borgnine face. His nickname resulted from his all-seeing, enthusiastic, wide-eyed look, which, combined with his down-home bowl haircut, made him look just like a hoot owl. Occasionally an upperclassman player demanded that Jack demonstrate his "hootowlness." With a blink but without hesitating he would dash outdoors, climb the closest tree, and commence "hoo-hoo-hooing." It never failed to get a laugh.

Hoot Owl grew up about twenty miles from the Alabama campus in the small town of West Blocton. The place looked like something out of *The Andy Griffith Show*, with a filling station serving as the headquarters of cultural affairs. Set in between Tuscaloosa and Birmingham, the sacred sites for the Crimson Tide, it became known as "Piss Break," since its central location made it the perfect place for drunken students to stop and relieve themselves. The people of West Blocton were united in their passion for Alabama football. The town had a fine football team in the late 1950s, and a number of its players ended up in Tide uniforms. Hicks played tackle for the West Blocton Tigers, but did not make the team at Alabama. Instead, before he started his freshman year in 1957, he accepted the job of team manager. The position not only provided him with a scholarship, no small thing in itself, but also offered the chance to travel with the team to places most other students never saw. Moreover, it placed him inside the most important group on campus. In 1961, after four years at Alabama, he was still a manager and had several years of classes remaining.

As varsity manager, Hicks spent little time around the freshmen and did not get to know Namath during the 1961 season. During spring camp in 1962, though, he and Namath developed a close friendship. On spring break that year, the two took their first of many road trips, traveling to Panama City, where Namath caught his first glimpse of the Florida beaches that he came to love. Had Hoot Owl known Namath's personality before they met, he would have realized that the immediate attention Namath showed the team manager was by no means fleeting. Throughout his youth, Namath kept so few close friends that most of his peers came to the conclusion that he was, for all of his confidence and bluster, actually shy. In high school, he remained close to a couple of teammates, but that was the extent of the star athlete's social circle. He felt much more comfortable in small groups and, for all of his seeming egalitarian revelry, actually had little patience for people he did not warm to immediately. Hicks he liked. Like Whitey Harris had done for him in high school, Hicks kept Namath entertained with his biting sense of humor and general disregard for accepted decorum.[24]

So Namath found his Tuscaloosa niche—three women took the temporary place of Rose and one Hoot Owl replaced everyone else. Bryant continued to be a stern and sometimes tactless taskmaster, but the benefits could not be denied. Heading into the second game of the 1962 season, Namath led the number-one-ranked team in the nation.

There was still a bit of confusion as to his ethnicity, though.

Following the Georgia game, the *Atlanta Journal* described Namath as "the slender swathy [*sic*], American-born Italian from Beaver Falls, Penn." That the paper meant to term Namath "swarthy," not "swathy," was a simple typo. That it turned him from Hungarian to Italian held a deeper meaning. He was one of the wretched refuse, of a mass of humanity that required little further delineation. His family had washed onto Ellis Island sometime at or near the turn of the century, and now he had washed into the Southeastern Conference.[25]

———

Alabama had a short week after the Georgia win, traveling to New Orleans for a Friday night game against Tulane on September 28. By any statistical estimation Tulane was a poor team—they had won two games in 1961, scoring only 60 points all season, and appeared to be even weaker in 1962. But there was still something for Bryant to grab on to in terms of motivation. The "New Orleans jinx" referred to the Tide's troubles in Tulane Stadium, including the narrow 1962 Sugar Bowl victory over Arkansas and also their 1960 tie with a Tulane squad that ended that season at 3–6–1. Even the national champions of the previous year had to fight off a stubborn Green Wave team, 9–0, in Mobile. "We expect as always a long game," Bryant said before the contest. "Against Tulane we always get one."[26]

On Alabama's opening drive, Eddie Versprille took a simple handoff through an enormous hole for 37 yards to the Tulane 28-yard line. A few running plays later, with Alabama at the seven-yard line, Namath displayed one of his less noticeable, but equally crucial, attributes. Hunched over center, he called the signals looking to his right, took the snap, and shoved the ball into Cotton Clark's gut. As three Tulane players converged on Clark, tackling him three yards short of the goal line, Namath pitched the ball he had pulled back from Clark to Butch Henry, five yards to his left, who trotted into the end zone without being touched. It was a simple play of football beauty, and one that Namath had already perfected. His huge hands helped, of course, but it was the deception and timing that put him in another category—he not only performed the play physically, but sold the entire fake with a practiced nonchalance. So effective was the fake that Bryant initially gave Clark credit for the touchdown on his highlight show.

In the second quarter, Namath demonstrated another attribute when he pitched to Clark, ran hard to the right, leading his offensive line and the Tulane defense in that direction, and opened up a cutback lane for Clark to score an 11-yard touchdown. On this play, as he was swarmed under, he showed that he was not afraid to take or give a hit. Namath ran for a touchdown and threw for another in the second quarter. At halftime, Alabama led 36–6, and the New Orleans jinx was over. Another Namath touchdown pass and two-point conversion in the fourth quarter ended the rout at 44–6.[27]

Namath had many physical attributes that helped him on the football field, but none were as unique as his hands. Here, as he poses for a photograph with some of his running backs, his right hand dwarfs the football. (Bryant Museum)

While a good football game was always heralded in the region, it was the political football going on in Mississippi that made real news, and Governor Ross Barnett was again at center stage. On Saturday, September 29, 1962, the evening before James Meredith was scheduled to register for classes, Barnett used a football game to present his call to arms. That night in Jackson, the seventh-ranked Rebels played the Kentucky Wildcats. With only a 7–0 lead, the Ole Miss players entered the locker room at halftime. While the players ran off the field, Barnett made his way to the 50-yard line. Before he spoke, the scoreboard displayed a new state fight song, entitled "Never, No, Never," that left little room for subtle interpretation. Although the line "We will not yield an inch of any field" seemed innocuous enough, it was quickly followed by the more blatant "it's to hell with Bobby K." As the song ended, to the frenzied cries of 43,000 spectators waving Confederate flags, Barnett gave his most famous exhortation. "I love Mississippi!" he shouted. "I love her people! Our customs! I love and respect our heritage!"[28]

If Barnett desired a violent opposition by his constituents, he got his wish. Rioting ensued in Oxford and two people were killed in clashes with the state National Guard. In Washington, the Kennedys also tried to take advantage of Mississippi's football mania to end the violence in Oxford. On the night of the rioting, Bobby Kennedy phoned Ole Miss's head coach, Johnny Vaught, and asked for his assistance in subduing the crowd. Vaught refused, choosing instead to confine his players to their dormitory, telling them, "I don't know what's going to happen, you don't know what's going to happen, and Ross Barnett damn sure doesn't know what's going to happen." At least one player, Buck Randall, escaped captivity and attempted to quell some of the violence.[29]

The following night President Kennedy, expecting a peaceful

matriculation of Meredith and unaware of the intense fighting on the campus, gave a speech, once again keeping football close to the surface. Kennedy's words seemed meant for a different time and place:

> In 1945 a Mississippi sergeant, Jake Lindsey, was honored by an unusual joint session of the Congress. I close therefore with this appeal to the students of the University, the people who are most concerned.
>
> You have a great tradition to uphold, a tradition of honor and courage won on the field of battle and on the gridiron as well as the University campus.[30]

James Baldwin and Martin Luther King Jr. regarded the speech as "lacking moral conviction" and thought it patronizing to compare "war heroes and football stars to rioting students and yahoos in Oxford that awful Sunday night." Indeed, whether "the gridiron" belonged alongside a Medal of Honor winner in a speech on a night of hatred and death was questionable. Nevertheless, the president could not picture the South and its universities without seeing a football field.[31]

Alabama returned to its football field the next week, but despite the easy victory over Tulane, they had dropped to number two in the country. Still, the Tide stood as a 38-point favorite when it hosted Vanderbilt at Legion Field in Birmingham. Alabama played sloppy football, though, as Clark fumbled away a punt in his own end zone, giving Vanderbilt an early lead, 7–0. Angry with himself after failing to convert a third down, Namath came off the field and threw his helmet toward the bench in disgust. As he sat on the bench, Bryant joined him, placing his arm around Joe's shoulder and speaking in a low voice. From a distance, it looked as if

Bryant was offering up fatherly advice to his disappointed quarterback. He was not. Speaking in a low hiss, Bryant said, "Son, if you ever throw that goddamned helmet or do anything like that again, I will personally drive you back to Pennsylvania." "But Coach," Namath countered, "I'm just mad at myself." "Then stop actin' like a chile!" Bryant said as he rose from the bench.

It was the other side of an old adage that Bryant used to prevent his players from celebrating too much in the end zone after a touchdown—"Act like you been there before." Namath had just found out that Bryant's stoic philosophy about on-field behavior also included demonstrations of anger. It was not the first time Bryant had yelled at Namath. On the practice field, he had screamed at his young quarterback from his tower, "God damn it, Namath, you do what I tell you when I tell you!" As Namath slunk back toward the huddle with his head down, he offered a mumbled, "Okay," setting off Bryant again. "And call me sir," he yelled. "And look me in the eyes when I'm talkin' to you!"[32]

Namath led Alabama on a four-play drive, tying the game on a tackle-eligible pass to Butch Henry. On the play, Namath slipped and almost fell on the slick turf, but managed to keep his balance and deliver on target one of his weaker passes. At halftime, the score was 7–7.

Namath regained his strength in the third quarter when he reverse-rolled to his right, then hit Williamson with a 34-yard pass over the outstretched arms of two Vanderbilt defenders for a touchdown. Williamson made a nice adjustment on the ball, running backward for a few steps to cradle the pass into his arms, and Bryant regarded it as "one of the most beautiful catches of the year."

Another great catch by Williamson in the fourth quarter set up a field goal to end the scoring at 17–7. Bryant praised Vanderbilt's tenacity, but the closeness of the game really came down to

Alabama mistakes, including four fumbles and Namath's first varsity interception. Benny Marshall of the *Birmingham News* predicted that Bryant's happiness in escaping with a win over Vanderbilt would not last throughout the week. "Pop might have a lesson or two to administer in the privacy of the Alabama practice field this week while preparing for Houston," he wrote. "Just in the family."[33]

Marshall was right—three days after lauding Vanderbilt on his television program, Bryant lit into his own team. "We have very few people with genuine desire," he told the press after Wednesday's practice. "We've got a lot of folks out there who ought to be doing something else. They're just wasting our time, and theirs."

On October 13, Houston made the trip to Tuscaloosa for the Tide's first home game of the season. After Ohio State lost to UCLA, Alabama once again sat atop the college poll. Houston led 3–0 in the second quarter, but a bad snap on a punt and a recovery by Jordan put Alabama ahead, 7–3. Namath did not have a good game. He lost a fumble at his own 18-yard line, but the defense prevented a score. His best play of the game came after one of his worst. Late in the first quarter, he threw a pass that was intercepted by Gene Ritch, who looked as if he was going to return it for a touchdown. In pursuit, Namath managed to avoid a blocker and force Ritch out-of-bounds at the Alabama 11-yard line, some 70 yards from the spot of the interception. Again, the defense held Houston out of the end zone. Namath split time with Hurlbut in the second half, and Alabama won 14–3. Namath had corrected some of his errors, but it was the first game in which he had been outplayed by Hurlbut. It was also another ugly win that would anger Bryant.[34]

The sloppy performance dropped Alabama to number two once again, this time behind the Texas Longhorns, as the Tide prepared for a trip to Knoxville. Bryant and the press singled out Hurlbut as one of the few players worthy of praise in the Houston game and anticipated a greater role from the junior quarterback. Bryant had never won a game as a coach in Knoxville, so there was talk of a Tennessee jinx. Namath played well, using a variety of methods to complete passes. On a play early in the game, he rolled to his right, jumped, and completed a pass to Bill Battle to set up a field goal. In the second quarter, he dropped back, listed ever so slightly to his left, and drew the defense with him. Then, abruptly, he turned to his right and hit an uncovered Benny Nelson for a 35-yard touchdown pass. It was another of his subtle moves that did not freeze the defense so much as it shifted them to the wrong side of the field. Bryant tried to protect the lead by playing for field position, punting on third down on one drive. But Tennessee scored to make it 12–7 at the end of the third quarter, and it appeared as if they might defeat the Tide once again. Namath responded with one more bit of deception as he pump-faked a pass, allowing Williamson to get behind the defenders for a completion to the three-yard line. Alabama scored from there, and once more under the guidance of Hurlbut put the game out of reach at 27–7.[35]

Jack Hurlbut had come to Alabama, like Namath, on the recommendation of a third party. One of Bryant's famed "Junction Boys" of Texas A&M was Jack Pardee, who in 1960 played professionally for the Los Angeles Rams but also owned a business in Houston. When Pardee heard that Rice's young star quarterback had left school, he immediately wrote to Bryant. Hurlbut was a country boy and did not assimilate into the challenging academics at Rice. Although he averaged an 85 at Aldine High School, he received all D's and two semesters of scholastic probation at Rice. Regardless, Bryant offered Hurlbut a scholarship in August 1961. "Jack is going to leave very early Monday morning the 29th, and should be there not too late the same nite," Hurlbut's father wrote to the coaching staff. "Altho we have told him if he gets too tired he should get him a cabin and rest before finishing the trip." Like Namath, Hurlbut arrived on the eve of the 1961 season. Unlike Namath, he was already a sophomore.[36]

———

Two days after the Tennessee game, Alabamians received news that pushed football from their thoughts. President Kennedy again appeared on national television, this time seated in a makeshift studio in the Oval Office. "Good evening, my fellow citizens," he began. "This government, as promised, has maintained the closest surveillance of the Soviet military buildup on the island of Cuba. Within the past week unmistakable evidence has established the fact that a series of offensive missile sites is now in preparation on that imprisoned island." Then he gave one of the more frightening pronouncements in modern history: "It shall be the policy of this nation to regard any nuclear missile launched from Cuba against any nation in the Western Hemisphere as an attack by the Soviet Union on the United States, requiring a full retaliatory response upon the Soviet Union." The address terrified Americans, raising the specter of a nuclear confrontation.[37]

Several days after Kennedy's speech, the *Tuscaloosa News* published an editorial warning that although "Tuscaloosa could hardly be considered a prime target for Red Missiles launched in Cuba," its location in the southeastern portion of the United States meant that it was within the range of the warheads and might receive significant damage from an attack on another town. More importantly, the town needed to gear up its civil defense system in case its citizens were required to provide "massive assistance in the event of a nuclear attack on Birmingham, Montgomery, or Columbus, Miss."[38]

On October 27, as the U.S. Navy tracked four Soviet submarines carrying nuclear warheads, Alabama played the University of Tulsa on a beautiful Indian summer day in Tuscaloosa. In an attempt to get his younger players some varsity experience, Bryant used a three-team platoon system, having the Red (two-way) team, the White defense team, and the Blue offense team share snaps throughout the game. The Tide started fast, forcing a Tulsa fumble on its opening drive and giving Namath's offense the ball on the Tulsa 22. Two minutes later Namath scored on a one-yard sneak. Hurlbut took over in the second quarter and led Alabama on a long touchdown drive, and Clark returned a punt 91 yards for a score just before halftime. Alabama continued its dominance in the second half. With Auburn assistant Vince Dooley and other scouts in attendance, Bryant offered up a variety of wrinkles for his future opponents to ponder. In the end, they learned little other than that Alabama was loaded with talent, easily beating Tulsa 35–6.[39]

By the time Alabama boarded its buses for Starkville, Mississippi, on Friday, November 2, the Cuban Missile Crisis was over and the state could once again concentrate solely on football. Alabama played against Mississippi State that Saturday for the Bulldogs' homecoming game, but the crowd was a sparse 25,000 and the competition was lopsided. Namath ran for 16 yards and completed two passes on the first drive of the game, before Clark scored on a four-yard run just five minutes into the contest. In the second quarter, Namath rolled slightly to his right, stopped, and just before taking a jarring hit from a defensive lineman threw a 15-yard pass across the middle of the field, hitting Battle in stride. The receiver rumbled into the end zone, making the score 14–0 at halftime. In the third quarter, Joe faked a handoff and hid the ball behind his right hip before ripping a pass into the end zone, again to Battle. The final score was 20–0, and even Bryant had little criticism of his team. Namath ended probably his best game thus far with 75 yards rushing and 150 passing.[40]

Alabama had its homecoming the next week against the University of Miami. Most of the attention was given to Miami's junior quarterback, George Mira. Mira had gained national attention during the 1961 season when he had made a spectacular play against Florida. To avoid defenders, the right-hander had shifted the ball to his left hand and thrown a strike to one of his receivers. Alabama reporters, however, focused on senior center/linebacker Lee Roy Jordan, who was receiving Heisman Trophy consideration from some of the writers. "He'll be trying to imagine what Mira will be wanting to do," Bryant said, "trying to guess with him." As for Alabama's own quarterback, Alf Van Hoose of the *Birmingham News* gave the first strong indication that Namath was truly accepted into the Bryant mold—the game, he wrote, would be a contest between "Miami's brash George Mira and Alabama's quiet but confident Joe Namath."[41]

Miami entered the game with only one loss, to a very good LSU team, but was unranked. The first half was a defensive struggle. Neither Mira nor Namath had much success, and the Hurricanes led 3–0 at the half. In the second half, Namath changed the game. He ran an option to the right before cutting back across the field for 40 yards. On the play, he showed quickness in making the upfield cut and in outrunning most of the defense. A few plays later, Clark scored, giving the Tide a 7–3 lead. Another Clark touchdown and a botched snap for the extra point that resulted in a two-point conversion increased Alabama's lead to 15–3. After that the game was never close. Namath threw for a touchdown and ran for another, and Hurlbut scored one as well, giving the Tide a 36–3 victory. With 205 yards passing and 65 yards rushing, Namath completely outplayed Mira.[42]

Heading to Atlanta to play Georgia Tech on November 17, Alabama was 8–0, ranked number one in the country, and on a 19-game winning streak—they had tied Texas in the 1960 Bluebonnet Bowl but had not lost a game since their defeat to Tennessee on October 15, 1960. In all, it amounted to 26 games, or two years, without a loss. Although Georgia Tech was 5–2–1 and unranked, memories of the 1961 game gave the contest the feeling of a grudge match. Just two days before the contest, Furman Bisher, in an article for the *Saturday Evening Post* titled "College Football Is Going Berserk," revisited the 1961 game, claiming that Alabama had played unnecessarily violently in a "tooth-jarring" brawl with Georgia Tech. Tech coach Bobby Dodd claimed that because of Bryant, his team now hit harder in practice than it had done in games a decade ago. Auburn coach Ralph "Shug" Jordan said, "Since Bear Bryant came back to Alabama, it's the only kind of game which can win." Bisher further argued that Bryant expected Marine Corps fitness from his players and "left a trail of discarded athletes who couldn't or wouldn't meet his 120 percent demands for conditioning." Mentioning other coaches but clearly singling out Bryant as the greatest villain, Bisher called "for a return to sanity" led by the coaches, or else "football will surely be called to face a general public indictment."[43]

Between the natural rivalry and Bisher's well-timed article, the crowd was more rabid than ever. Whiskey bottles flew around and out of the stands, several nearly hitting Bryant on the sidelines. None of the 52,971 fans at Grant Field, some of whom had bought scalped tickets for upwards of a hundred dollars, could have asked for a better game.

The combination of the sloppy field from pregame rainstorms plus his wariness of Georgia Tech's large, fast defensive linemen led Bryant to devise some bold formations for his offense. His most unique setup put both Namath and Hurlbut in the same backfield, with Hurlbut behind center and Namath about eight yards farther back. From this position, Hurlbut could take the snap and run a play or sprint into motion before the center snapped the ball to Namath in the deep shotgun. As a result, Hurlbut played as important a role in the game as Namath.

Georgia Tech head coach Bobby Dodd placed his quarterback, Billy Lothridge, in similarly unique positions, sometimes lining him up in veritable punt formation to run a pass play. For the first two quarters, neither scheme generated any points. The only score came late in the second quarter, after Namath threw an interception that Mike McNames returned to the Alabama 14-yard line. McNames scored a couple of plays later to give Georgia Tech a 7–0 lead at halftime.

The second half was as hard-hitting as the first. Only an Alabama fake punt from its own end zone prevented either team from getting the ball into the other's territory. With a little more than six minutes left in the game, Lothridge prepared to punt from deep in his own territory. He mishandled the snap and began to scramble for an opening to kick the ball. After narrowly avoiding several Alabama players, he let go a marvelous punt, seemingly avoiding disaster, but after a brief bit of confusion the referees declared that Lothridge's knee was down at his own nine-yard line, giving Alabama the break it needed. Cotton Clark scored from two yards out on fourth down, and it looked as if the game would be tied.

But Bryant played to win. He replaced Namath at quarterback, sending in Hurlbut to try for the two-point conversion. Hurlbut sprinted to his right on a quarterback option but never really looked to throw the ball. With the Georgia Tech defenders playing the run, Hurlbut went down before reaching the goal line. The score remained 7–6.

With five and a half minutes remaining, Alabama successfully ran an onside kick and took over at the Georgia Tech 33-yard line, needing a field goal to go ahead. On first down, Namath faked to his left, reverse-rolled to his right, and threw perhaps his weakest pass of the entire season. It lacked any of his normal spin, fluttering into triple coverage where it was intercepted by Lothridge. Lothridge took off for Alabama territory, but at the Tide's 45-yard line he seemed to drop the ball at the mere sight of Lee Roy Jordan. Alabama recovered and marched into Tech territory.

From the Georgia Tech 29-yard line, Namath kept the football on a roll-out option and ran for 15 yards. With a little over one minute left and the ball on the Tech 14-yard line, Bryant stuck with his game plan and replaced Namath with Hurlbut under center. Hurlbut threw a pass that got deflected between two Alabama receivers and intercepted by Don Toner to end the game.[44]

After the contest, Bryant claimed that he made a few errors in judgment, but overall this game was just one of those times when the defenses prevailed in "a reckless, tooth-jarring football game." "Champions don't settle for ties," Benny Marshall of the *Birmingham News* wrote of the two-point conversion attempt. The next year's Alabama yearbook might have been correct in its effusive praise of Coach Bryant's decision to go for two: "Alabama had the chance late in the game to kick for a one point PAT (point after touchdown) and thus gain a tie. Champions don't play for ties." Continuing the praise, the sports editor of the 1963 *Corolla* wrote, "Little over a minute to go and the Tide was rolling in. Bama may well have elected to go for the field goal, with a good position, the wind at their backs; yet champions score touchdowns—not field goals—and a touchdown was what the Big Red had marched this far to get."[45]

In the aftermath of the loss and amid the distraction of the *Saturday Evening Post* article, Bryant prepared his team for the Iron Bowl, the rivalry game between Alabama and Auburn. Held at Legion Field in Birmingham, across the street from a bar named The Tide and the Tiger, the game decided the top team in the state at a site both teams used throughout the season. Auburn had started the 1962 season with five straight victories, before losing to Florida. After that, they defeated Mississippi State by a touchdown, then lost to Georgia and tied Florida State. By the time of the Alabama game, Auburn's hopes of a successful season had faded. Bryant never would have taken Auburn lightly, but the loss to Georgia Tech had turned him into the angriest man in the state. That Alabama had two weeks to get ready for Auburn only made the preparation twice as intense. If Bisher thought Bryant required 120 percent from his players before the Georgia Tech game, he would have calculated that percentage much higher in the weeks after it.[46]

Prior to kickoff, Bryant seemed as friendly as ever, especially with Shug Jordan. "Do you think State's got much chance against Ole Miss?" he asked the Auburn coach. "Georgia looked good against us," Jordan said. "They might play Tech a real good one." Bryant replied, "I said it all summer and I still say it. They've got some fine-looking football players at Georgia." "Gonna be a good crowd," Jordan said as he scanned the stadium. "Well, I'd better be getting along, Shug," Bryant said as he started toward his bench. Then, turning with a big grin on his face, he added, "I wish you all the bad luck in the world." "Same to you," Jordan replied. "See you after the game, Paul."[47]

Bryant's friendly demeanor belied his and his team's intensity. On the opening kickoff, Butch Wilson—"a gangling galloper from Hueytown"—took the ball 92 yards for an Alabama touchdown. At the end of the first quarter, Namath led the Tide on its fifth offensive drive of the game. At the 17-yard line, he kept the ball and ran around the end for the team's second touchdown. Alabama then stopped Auburn and blocked its punt attempt and recovered for a third touchdown, making the score 21–0 at halftime. Namath ran a quarterback sneak for a touchdown in the third quarter, led the team to a field goal, then threw a 16-yard score to Williamson on the first play of the fourth quarter, ending his day at quarterback and the scoring at 38–0.

In his three quarters of work, he completed only four passes, but two of them were for touchdowns. As the game ended, it looked as if Alabama was playing its best football. Jay O'Neal summarized the affair when he said, "I never saw an Alabama man knocked off his feet all afternoon." That had to worry him since he was the backfield coach for the Oklahoma Sooners, Alabama's Orange Bowl opponent.[48]

Namath's first varsity season was superb. He broke Alabama records in throwing for 1,192 yards on 76 completions, and tied school records in throwing for three touchdowns in a single game (versus Georgia) and 13 for the season. Not record-setting but still impressive, he also ran for 229 yards on 70 carries, adding another four touchdowns on the ground. He finished third in Alabama history with 1,421 total yards.[49]

With the semester and regular season ended, Namath went to Beaver Falls for Christmas vacation with his brother Sonny and his family. Sonny had served as an instructor at the Redstone Arsenal in Huntsville in 1962, and as a result was able to watch almost all of Joe's sophomore season in person. Back in Pennsylvania, the brothers spent Christmas Eve putting together a pair of bicycles for Sonny's two daughters. After several frustrating hours, Joe turned to his brother. "You know, Sonny," he said, "you're an officer in the Army training guys how to use nuclear missiles and I'm

an industrial arts major, and both of us can't put together a goddamned bike!"[50]

———

As much as any bowl game in recent memory, the 1963 Orange
Bowl was a politicized event. Capitalizing on his success in the
Cuban Missile Crisis, President Kennedy arrived in Miami like a
conquering hero. He met with a large group of Cubans now living in Miami; Jackie Kennedy saluted the recently freed soldiers
of the Bay of Pigs invasion in Spanish; and he promised to return
their tattered battle flag to them "in a free Havana." The game
also spoke to the Kennedy administration's determination for civil
rights. Alabama represented the Deep South, Kennedy's most
recent target for desegregation, and the Oklahoma football team
served as an example of peaceful desegregation, as Sooners head
coach Bud Wilkinson had broken the color line in 1956 when he
recruited Prentice Gautt. Wilkinson was also a close friend of President Kennedy and had political aspirations of his own.[51]

On New Year's Eve, something truly bizarre occurred when
Julian Lackey, one of the Alabama boosters, presented Bryant with
a copy of the Oklahoma game plan. No one was sure if it was real
or a plant meant to throw Alabama off in its preparations. To be
safe, Bryant put in extra time in one of the hotel's large meeting
rooms, where he drilled his defense using chairs to represent Oklahoma players. Lee Roy Jordan participated in the drills but did
not find them all that helpful. Still, it was a strange incursion that
spoke to Bryant's dedication in preparing his team.[52]

Just before kickoff, Wilkinson gathered his team in the locker
room. "Gentlemen," he said. "I'd like to present the President of
the United States." Kennedy addressed the team. "Well, fellows, as
you know, Bud is head of our physical fitness program," he said.
"So I thought I'd drop by to see somebody who was physically fit."

He then wished the team well and went to his seat in the stands. Some fans of Oklahoma later claimed that Wilkinson had made an error in introducing the president to his team right before they took the field, arguing that it distracted them from the game. Whether Kennedy's appearance in the Oklahoma locker room hindered the Sooners' performance is debatable, but unquestionably Kennedy's failure to greet the Alabama team in a similar manner motivated the Tide. Bryant took special care in letting his team know that the president's decision not to visit them was an insult. "You boys realize," Bryant told his squad before the game, "that the president is over there in the Oklahoma locker room congratulating who he thinks is goin' be the winner of the game."[53]

Alabama won the coin toss, a silver dollar presented to Lee Roy Jordan by the president, and prepared to receive the opening kick-off. Oklahoma attempted an onside kick, but it was not well placed and Alabama recovered the ball in excellent field position. After three productive runs, Namath faced second down with five yards to go. Taking the snap, he rolled to his left, stopped, and threw an inaccurate pass into the hands of a Sooner defensive back.

Oklahoma could not move the ball, though, and Namath got another chance to run the offense four plays later at the Alabama 40-yard line. On first down, he completed his first pass of the game, a five-yard toss to Billy Battle. After moving the ball to the Oklahoma 30, he faced a third down and three. He took the snap and immediately put the ball into the gut of his tailback before pulling it back for a pass. So quick was Namath's motion that he had to fire the pass over the head of his back, who had not yet had time to make it to the line of scrimmage. The pass went to Richard Williamson for a five-yard gain to the Alabama 25.

On first and ten, Namath dropped back and faked a pass while still in retreat—an enormous mock pass that, had it been released, would have traveled 50 yards. But the ball remained in his hand and, stopping in the pocket, he eyed his receiver and shot the ball on a slight arc from his 32-yard line halfway into the end zone, where Williamson cradled the first score of the game.[54]

Bryant liked to refer to Williamson as "saucered and blown," but few outside the region understood the nature of the phrase. It referred to the old-time method of pouring coffee into a saucer and blowing on it to cool it down—specifically, it meant that it was "ready." Namath consistently found Williamson to be ready; he was his favorite receiver, and the two developed a great rapport. One thing Williamson and Namath developed was an understanding spoken only by the speed of a pass. Namath's ability to "throw a player open" usually entailed his deft touch in leading his receivers out of harm's way, but also included the occasional fastball. When that happened, Williamson understood that he needed to secure the catch and quickly get down.

In the second quarter, with the score still 7–0 and the ball on the Oklahoma 34-yard line, Namath threw Williamson a fastball, targeting him at the 15-yard line between two Oklahoma defenders who blistered Williamson immediately after the completion. After a run for no gain, Namath took the snap, faked a handoff to Eddie Versprille, and kept the ball on an option. Running to his left, he veered toward the Oklahoma defender and feigned a move to his right, causing the defender to wobble ever so slightly. When Namath pitched the ball to Cotton Clark to his left, the defender was off balance just enough for Clark to run around the end for a touchdown. It was the subtlest of plays, the kind that displayed the fullness of Namath's talents. At halftime, the score was 14–0.[55]

Amid the 73,380 spectators sat President Kennedy, looking so good in a dark tailored suit with a starched shirt as white as his teeth, Wayfarer sunglasses, and a Cuban cigar that he could just as well have been a guest at a Hollywood party or casino trip as at a football game. As the bands performed their halftime routines, Kennedy spotted Martha Campbell, a nineteen-year-old Alabama cheerleader from Scottsboro, and summoned her to his box. Campbell complied, and Kennedy introduced her to Peter Lawford and Florida governor Farris Bryant before saying, "Your team is doing mighty well, isn't it?" Despite being a speech major, she could not remember her name and immediately started crying. Kennedy laughed and wished her well. The next day the *Miami Herald* reported, "Even Presidents notice strawberry blondes."[56]

The strength of the Sooners' attack was its running backs, Joe Don Looney and Jim Grisham, but Alabama contained them during the first half. In the second half, Oklahoma continued their game plan. But it became apparent that as good as the two runners were, the Alabama defense was better. The game turned into a succession of short offensive series followed by punts, as Alabama traded yardage for time off the clock, twice punting on third down. Only a poor Oklahoma punt halfway through the third quarter put Alabama in position to score. Namath completed a couple of short passes, but helped his team most with a scramble to the Oklahoma 19-yard line. Several plays later, from the seven-yard line, he tossed his worst pass of the game, overthrowing his receiver in the left side of the end zone. Alabama kicked a short field goal to make the score 17–0. Throughout the game, Oklahoma could not move against Alabama's defense. Lee Roy Jordan ended the game with an astounding 31 tackles, prompting Bryant to remark that "if they stay in bounds, Ole Lee Roy got 'em."[57]

Immediately after the game, ABC's Jim McKay interviewed Namath on national television. "We have found ourselves down here on the field, Joe Namath the great sophomore quarterback from the University of Alabama. Congratulations, Joe, on a great football game," he began. "Thank you, thank you," Namath answered, as Hoot Owl perched his head just behind Namath's right shoulder and into the view of the camera. "Was there a turning point in this football game that you saw?" "Well," Namath said, looking down, toward but not directly at the microphone, "those two fumbles Oklahoma had hurt 'em a lot, that was the big thing, that helped us out." "You sure gave a great, cool performance for a fellow in his first year of varsity football," McKay said. "Were you at all jittery or nervous when you first started the ball game?" "Well," Namath replied, this time looking up and squinting into the bright sunshine, "you always are in a big game. You got a team out there working with you like the rest of the guys from Alabama, a real good team, you don't have to worry too much about it." "Who's going to win the Southeastern Conference next year, Joe?" "Well," Namath replied, this time flashing just a bit of a smile, "I hope we do." "Alabama, huh? Congratulations to you again."[58]

In the locker room, as Bryant hugged Namath, a photographer asked in a worried voice, "Who's that with the coach—how do you spell his name?" "That's Namath...N-A-M-A-T-H," Bryant boomed in response. "But don't worry about it. You'll learn how to spell his name in the next couple of years." It took only thirty-seven seconds in front of the camera and one hug in the locker room to complete Namath's trip from "popcorn quarterback" to Joe Willie, the face of Crimson Tide football.[59]

James Wallace "Wally" Butts Jr. was one of the greatest football coaches in the history of the University of Georgia Bulldogs. Between 1939 and 1960 his teams went 140-86-9 and appeared in the Orange, Rose, and Sugar Bowls. But by the early 1960s his fortunes had changed and what was left of his career and reputation were on the line. (Hargrett Rare Book and Manuscript Library / University of Georgia Libraries)

7

"With Every Force at My Command"

Here was a publication tied by tradition to high professional standards, and here was a writer prodded by every element in his background to strict journalistic integrity, entangled together in ineptitude like a couple of drunken sailors.

—Frank Graham Jr.

BY THE IDES of March in 1963 Bear sensed that something bad was about to happen. Down in Florida, where the sportswriters had gone to cover spring training, there was more talk about Bryant than Mickey Mantle and Willie Mays. Rumors were easier to come by than sunburns, and sportswriters close to Bear—Alf Van Hoose of the *Birmingham News*, Fred Russell of the *Nashville Banner*, and New York Yankees broadcaster Mel Allen—kept the coach apprised of the talk.

In fact, there seemed to be too many, too specific rumors. "From New York to Florida," wrote Benny Marshall of the *Birmingham News*, "almost as if on a carefully charted trail, the story has been spread.... Rumors have pyramided." Every sportswriter seemed to have heard or read something.[1]

"The story they were getting in bits and pieces," Bryant later wrote, "was that Wally Butts, the athletic director and former coach of the University of Georgia, and I had fixed a game—bet on it." There was talk that somebody, maybe Furman Bisher, had a photostat of a $50,000 check Bryant had written as a payoff, that Bear and Wally had fixed the 1962 Alabama-Georgia game, and that Bryant had also thrown the Alabama–Georgia Tech contest, his team's only loss of the season. It was all going to be documented in the *Saturday Evening Post*, rumormongers claimed.[2]

Finally Tom Siler, a reporter for the *Knoxville News-Sentinel* whom Bryant deeply respected, called and asked for a statement about the yet-to-be-published piece. "Hell, Tom, I can't say anything. I haven't seen it," Bear answered.

"Well, *I've* seen it. And it's a helluva story," Siler replied. He had spent time with Bisher in Florida, and the Atlanta sportswriter had shown him proofs of the *Post* article. Bear had no doubt that in some way that "pissant" Bisher was involved with the entire sordid episode.

Well before the story hit the newsstands, administrators at the University of Georgia were in full crisis mode. By the spring of 1963 rumors and scandals swirled around Wally Butts, becoming part and parcel of a life that had been unraveling for several years.

Most everybody liked Wally, which was part of his problem. He had become head coach at Georgia in 1939, the same month that Hitler invaded Poland, and over the years he had amassed a fine record, including an undefeated team in 1946, a passel of SEC titles, and victories in the Rose, Sugar, and Orange Bowls. But in the mid-1950s his teams had begun to lose more often than they won, settling into a state of mediocrity.

Perhaps not coincidentally, as the fortunes of his teams declined, Butts's personal life became a subject of more Georgia conversation than the price of peaches. People who trafficked in such talk said that Wally had become a member of Atlanta's "Night League," an active player in the capital's saloon and gambling scene. A friend and Georgia alumnus commented that the coach was seen "in public places over there, such as nightspots and so forth, with groups, girls, and so forth." Added to his public drinking, he had acquired a young mistress, whom he made no effort to hide. He traveled and drank in bars with her, and expected the University of Georgia to pick up most of the tabs.[3]

It was a sad sight. As one of his daughters later wrote, "If Dad has a fault, it is an obsession about growing old. . . . He actually thought people would *admire* him if he was seen with a young girl." And so he was seen, causing considerable consternation among the alumni, who blamed Wally's wayward behavior for the decline of Georgia's football program. What mama or papa would send their boy to play for that coach? alumni asked. Wally couldn't even recruit in the talent-rich Atlanta area.[4]

In late December 1960 a group of administrators and alumni forced Butts out. They offered him a deal: Resign as coach and he could stay on as athletic director. The only other option was to hold fast and lose both positions. On Christmas Eve the Atlanta papers announced that effective December 31, Butts was no longer coaching Georgia. "I've had every honor a coach can get. This'll probably add ten years to my life," he told reporters. Newspapers printed the fiction that it was Wally's decision. But no one in the Night League was fooled. He had become an embarrassment, but after compiling a 140–86–9 record deserved a soft place to land.[5]

The two years after his ouster had been no picnic. John Griffith, the new coach, wanted nothing to do with him, and in turn Wally missed few opportunities to undercut Griffith. Furthermore, with more free time he had greater opportunities to participate in Atlanta's splendid nightlife. Rumors circulated that he drank too much, gambled for too-high stakes, and couldn't pick a lucrative investment if his life depended on it. It was said that if he had bought stock in Coca-Cola, the company would have immediately lost market share and gone into bankruptcy.

And now he and Bear Bryant were linked to the most sensational scandal in football history.

———

Coincidentally—but in the end importantly, for the two stories became linked—the unraveling of Wally Butts occurred during the same period that the *Saturday Evening Post*, one of the country's most venerable and respected literary institutions, was also attempting to restore its youth by means of a radical face-lift.

The origins of the *Saturday Evening Post* stretched back to Benjamin Franklin's *Pennsylvania Gazette*, founded in 1728, and among its writers the publication boasted Edgar Allan Poe, James Fenimore Cooper, and Harriet Beecher Stowe in the nineteenth century; and Edith Wharton, Ring Lardner, William Faulkner, and F. Scott Fitzgerald in the first decades of the twentieth. Under the editorship of George Horace Lorimer, it had become the voice of conservative America, booming the general credo that what was good for big business was good for the nation as a whole. It was the magazine of Norman Rockwell's version of FDR's Four Freedoms, as well as the artist's covers that trumpeted the wholesomeness of white, Anglo-Saxon, Protestant, rural America.[6]

In the 1950s, however, the *Post* began to slide gracefully into old age. Its Rockwell covers could still entice a smile and a tear, but it was written for an older America that no longer existed. Otto

Friedrich, an editor at the magazine, later wrote, "The *Post* was widely considered to be old and stodgy, edited by the old and stodgy to be read by the old and stodgy." It was like one of its great heroes, General Dwight D. Eisenhower—a valiant leader during the war years of the 1940s, a steady hand during the Cold War crises of the 1950s, but ready to retire to his farm by 1960. It was not the youthful and vigorous magazine for John Kennedy's America.[7]

To turn the *Post* around, the board of directors named Clay Blair Jr. as the new editor. Friedrich described Blair as something of a dark lizard, a pudgy, black-haired, dark-eyed nervous man whose tongue flicked in and out of his mouth as he talked in sharp, staccato movements. He posed as a no-nonsense straight shooter, but had advanced his career at the *Post* by stabbing his patrons in the back. His biography in the magazine's promotional materials contained serious exaggerations and several outright falsehoods, and perhaps his most important single attribute was an uncanny talent for self-promotion.[8]

In November 1962, at his first meeting with the magazine's editors, Blair described his vision for the new *Saturday Evening Post*. He demanded a magazine that would "generate electricity" and arouse controversy, the sort of rag that a person would have to read if he or she wanted to know what everyone else was talking about. Its stories would launch crusades, make and break careers, commence a new golden age of bare-knuckle journalism. Blair asked for "sophisticated muckraking," a marriage of the zeal of the Progressive Era *McClure's* and the literary quality of the *New Yorker*. It would appeal to a younger audience, the next generation of power brokers, and would be must reading for everyone inside the Kennedy administration.

Norman Rockwell schmaltz was out. New covers would be

timely and edgy. The opinion page would henceforth contain the opinions of people who mattered, men like Admiral Hyman Rickover and Edward Teller. Pointing to the most recent magazine, which featured an article by Bernard Fall on the threat posed by North Vietnam and the beginning of a regional war, Blair expressed savage dissatisfaction. The story, he said, was about "gooks," and, he explained, "The American people don't want to read about gooks. If we have to do a story about gooks, we ought to tell it in terms of what the Americans are doing out there, not what the gooks are doing."[9]

It didn't take Blair and his closest associates long to show what "sophisticated muckraking" looked like. In a January 1963 memorandum he complimented his staff for turning the *Saturday Evening Post* ship in a new direction. "You are putting out one hell of a fine magazine. The articles are timely, full of significance and exclusivity." How exactly did he measure such things? "The final yardstick: We have about six lawsuits pending, meaning we are hitting them where it hurts, with solid, meaningful journalism."[10]

That January, national reporters once again had turned their attention and the eyes of America on Alabama. In some southern states race talk had somewhat abated, or at least gone underground and away from the easy hearing of northern reporters. Five southern governors took the oath of office that month. In their inaugural addresses, two didn't mention segregation, and two struck moderate positions on the matter of race.

Only one, George Wallace of Alabama, defied the law of the land and went on the offensive. Standing in the portico of the Alabama State Capitol in Montgomery, Wallace issued an open challenge to the forces of change in Washington, D.C. Where he stood, he noted, was significant. It was the same spot that Jefferson Davis had been sworn in as the president of the Confederate States of

America, the "Cradle of the Confederacy," the "very Heart of the Great Anglo-Saxon Southland."

Standing before his people like William Travis before the gates of the Alamo, he told the gathering, "Today we sound the drum for freedom as have our generations of forebears before us done, time and again down through history." It was the moment to send a message to "the tyranny that clanks its chains upon the South. In the name of the greatest people that have ever trod this earth, I draw the line in the dust and toss the gauntlet before the feet of tyranny...and I say...segregation now...segregation tomorrow... segregation forever."[11]

The speech made Wallace a target of the national press. "Reporters were drawn to him like biologists are drawn to the unexpected emergence of an old virus they believed had been exterminated," wrote Gene Roberts and Hank Klibanoff. And Wallace wore the bull's-eye like a badge of honor, smiling, defiant, always ready with a quip or an insult. His face—the set jaw, a slight sneer on his lips, a flattened boxer's nose, and cold, dark, defiant eyes—was the very image of pugnacity. He challenged reporters to take their best shot, invited their harsh characterizations.[12]

If Wallace was the face of southern resistance, Alabama was its ground zero. And in that winter of American discontent, reporters on the race beat as well as sportswriters looked to Dixie for their stories. The *Saturday Evening Post* had begun its assault even before Wallace's inaugural address. Furman Bisher's diatribe "College Football Is Going Berserk" had appeared in October 1962, and led to Bryant's libel suit in January 1963. But Clay Blair was almost as pugnacious and defiant as Wallace, considering lawsuits as a clear signal that he was landing punishing punches. In fact, at least partially because of Bryant's suit, Blair took another swing at Alabama and its most famous coach.

In March 1963, the *Saturday Evening Post* ran two stories attacking the state of politics and football in Alabama. Birmingham-born Joe David Brown had attended the city's public schools and graduated from the University of Alabama before moving away to earn a living as a foreign correspondent and a novelist, but in his *Post* article, "Birmingham Alabama: A City in Fear," he despaired that the city he loved had not so much changed as hardened. The city he knew as a youth and as a reporter for the *Birmingham Post* had followed Eugene "Bull" Connor, the gravel-voiced, outspoken, flamboyant city commissioner of public safety, and other race baiters over to the dark side of political demagoguery. While the price and demand for steel plummeted, creating severe economic hardships in the hardscrabble steel town, Ole Bull, "a jug-eared, paunchy, overgrown country boy who...made his name a household word in Birmingham by the uninhibited corn-pone way he announced baseball games over the radio," had ranted and raved and mesmerized the city's citizens by charging that their only problems were integration and outside agitation. "He has bellowed defiance at the Supreme Court, offered to fight the Attorney General, [and] vowed that 'blood would run in the streets' of Birmingham before it was desegregated," wrote Brown.[13]

Diane McWhorter, a privileged young white girl in Birmingham in 1963, recalled that Brown's exposé "went after Our Way of Life and its chief guardian, 'Ole Bull,' finding little to praise in his hometown except the new Bank for Savings skyscraper." In fact, it was much worse than that. Brown reserved his most stinging attacks for the onetime moderates of the city. Even the "handsome and vigorous" Art Hanes, the city commissioner who had once seemed like the emerging foil to Connor, had voted with staunch segregationists to close Birmingham's park system, including playgrounds, golf courses, and community houses, rather than see whites and blacks enjoying the same public spaces. Sounding remarkably like Bull himself, Hanes announced, "I'll never give up either to integration or Communism. They are one and the same as far as I'm concerned. . . . I don't think any of you want a nigger mayor . . . or a nigger police chief . . . but I tell you that's what'll happen if we play dead on the park integration."[14]

The results of Birmingham's intransigence on race, Brown concluded, were devastating. It had become a city without a future, mired in the past and lagging behind other northern and southern cities in growth, economic development, cultural events, and social advancement. Outsiders considered it a bad place to live and raise a family, the Metropolitan Opera and other theatrical companies bypassed it, and northern manufacturers were as likely to relocate there as they were to move lock, stock, and barrel to Bombay. Yet for all its many problems, Brown saw little hope for change. In the final analysis, the real political power in Birmingham was in the hands of the KKK—the Kluxers. They were the ones whom elected officials sought to please, the people whom moderate residents feared to offend. As Brown's aunt Margaret cautioned, "Be careful what you say or the Kluxers will burn a cross in front of my house." That fear, Brown concluded, "is the real shame of Birmingham."[15]

———

While Joe David Brown was still writing his piece on his hometown, an odd story was circulating among a group of University of Georgia supporters. Sometime that winter, George Burnett, an undistinguished Atlanta insurance salesman who was known to pass a bad check or two, told the remarkable tale to a lawyer in the Birmingham firm of Beddow, Embry & Beddow, which just happened to be representing Curtis Publishing Company, the parent of the *Saturday Evening Post*, in its suit against Bear Bryant. The

Post at the time was looking for dirt on Bryant, following the general libel defense theory that one could not inflict libelous damage on a person with an unsavory reputation. Since the story involved Bryant and promised to destroy his reputation, the Alabama firm assumed quite correctly that Curtis's Philadelphia firm of Pepper, Hamilton & Scheetz would be interested in the information. The nearly unbelievable tale made its way up the corporate food chain until Phil Strubing, a partner at Pepper, passed it on to interested parties at the *Post*. As far as Clay Blair was concerned, he now had Bryant by "the short hairs."[16]

Bear's lawyer got a copy of the *Saturday Evening Post* story before it reached the newsstands and drove it from Birmingham to Tuscaloosa. At four in the morning, outside his office, Bear read it under the headlights of his car. He didn't even wait to get to his desk. The piece was written by Frank Graham Jr., the son of a well-respected New York sportswriter, who was transitioning from covering sports to focusing on nature and conservation topics. He seemed to be, and was, an unlikely writer for a sensational piece of muckraking. A *Post* editor later described the thirty-eight-year-old Columbia graduate as "a bespectacled, scholarly sportswriter, whose leisure taste runs to baroque music and lyrical poetry, and whose idea of 'flash' is a battered Renault Dauphine." But in "The Story of a College Football Fix," the mild-mannered Clark Kent turned into a crusading Superman in accusing Bryant and Butts of a crime that promised to end their careers and land both of them in prison.[17]

It began with a sensational teasing precede, or introductory box:

Not since the Chicago White Sox threw the 1919 World Series has there been a sports story as shocking as this one. This is the story of one fixed game of college football.

Before the University of Georgia played the University of Alabama last September 22, Wally Butts, athletic director of Georgia, gave Paul (Bear) Bryant, head coach of Alabama…all the significant secrets Georgia's football team possessed.

The corrupt here were not professional ballplayers gone wrong, as in the 1919 Black Sox scandal. The corrupt were not disreputable gamblers, as in the scandals continually afflicting college basketball. The corrupt were two men—Butts and Bryant—employed to educate and to guide young men.[18]

The precede was signed "The Editors," but it was written by the *Post*'s sports editor, Roger Kahn, who had been one of the biggest advocates of the piece. Bisher believed that the recently hired Kahn "wanted to hit the scene with a splash" and ignored the crippling problems with the story. Even though they had both written for *Sport* magazine, Bisher had little use for Kahn, later observing that "Kahn is one of these writing people caught up in his own trance. He fancied himself as a thwarted infielder, but only in his own mind. He threw like a girl. Yet he wrote of playing catch and his on-field experiences without a blush." In "The Story of a College Football Fix," Bisher notes, Kahn's "hand was engaged in the rewriting and the graphics, but his face was out of sight." Still, Kahn's precede was more damning than the actual content of the story.[19]

Graham's exposé fell far short of Kahn's 1919 Chicago Black Sox comparisons. He began his story, "On Friday morning, September 14, 1962, an insurance salesman in Atlanta, Georgia, named George Burnett picked up his telephone and dialed the number of a local public-relations firm. The number was Jackson 5-3536. The line was busy, but Burnett kept trying. On the fourth or fifth attempt, he had just dialed the final number, when he heard what he later described as 'a series of harsh electronic sounds,' then the voice of a telephone operator said: 'Coach Bryant is out on the field, but he'll come to the phone. Do you want to hold, Coach Butts, or shall we call you back?' "[20]

It was an intriguing opening—an average morning, an everyday John Q. Citizen, an innocuous telephone call, then suddenly some wire is crossed somewhere in the complex core of the Atlanta phone system and Mr. John Q. is privy to a private phone call. So what that Graham made a mistake in the first sentence and the actual date of the call was Thursday, September 13? So what that the *Saturday Evening Post* story fact-checker was asleep on the job, if, in fact, the story was ever really fact-checked? The opening paragraph reads like an Alfred Hitchcock thriller starring Jimmy Stewart. George Burnett, like the reader, was about to hear something not meant for his ears.

Butts holds, waiting for Coach Bryant to arrive in his office. After a brief pause, Bear arrives, abruptly saying, "Hello, Wally. Do you have anything for me?" According to Burnett, who unashamedly stayed on the line and even began scribbling notes, Butts proceeded to outline some of the offensive and defensive schemes Georgia planned to use in their season-opening game against Alabama. At the end of the conversation Butts even agreed to call Bryant on Sunday with additional details.

The game, Joe Namath's debut, was no contest. Led by Namath's brilliant passing and running, Alabama soundly defeated Georgia 35–0. But according to Graham's reporting, augmented with interviews conducted by Furman Bisher, the Georgia coaches and players believed there was something suspicious about Alabama's game plan. "They seemed to know every play we were going to run," commented quarterback Larry Rakestraw. End Mickey Babb recalled Alabama players taunting them. "'You can't run *Eighty-eight Pop* [a key Georgia play] on us,' they'd yell. They knew just what we were going to run and just what we called it." Sam Richwine, Georgia's trainer, added simply, "They played just like they knew what we were going to do."

After the game, the Georgia team tried to forget the humiliation and move ahead with the season. In truth, the Alabama game showed that the Bulldogs were a badly flawed team, and they limped through a 3–4–3 season, including losing their final game of the year against their major rival, Georgia Tech, 37–6, almost a perfect bookend to the loss to Alabama at the start of the season. But while Georgia struggled, Graham wrote, Burnett was "living in his private misery." To tell or not to tell, that was his question. To expose what he knew and "create furore, perhaps even national scandal," or to "remain silent, ignoring wrong?" Finally, after the season, he roused himself from his Hamlet-like reverie and told his story to Georgia officials, and eventually to the *Saturday Evening Post* for a payment of $5,000.

After Georgia head coach John Griffith learned about the Butts-Bryant call he yelped with outrage. He was quoted toward the end of the article as saying bitterly, "I never had a chance, did I? I never had a *chance*." That was exactly the point, Graham concluded. "When a fixer works against you, that's the way he likes it."[21]

———

Bryant's anger rose as he read the article. "It was so crammed full of lies and half truths I couldn't believe it," he later wrote. Since he was by his car and his headlights were already on, he told his driver to slide over and got behind the wheel himself, speeding to Lake Martin, where both he and Mary Harmon and the Roses had summer cottages.[22]

He walked into the Rose cottage at six-thirty in the morning. Tommye Rose was making coffee when Bear showed her the article. She told him that he "ought to sue them or shoot them or something," before her language became uncharacteristically colorful and she went to wake up her husband.

By the time President Rose came into the room Bryant's anger had mixed with nausea. Rose was direct. "Paul, let's get your lawyers."

Rose, of course, already knew some of the basics of the story. In early March he had talked with the University of Georgia's president, Dr. O. C. Aderhold, in Birmingham. By then University of Georgia officials and the state's attorney general had already scrutinized and investigated almost every part of the story, but Rose decided against a similar approach. In a March 6 letter he told Aderhold that he had "spent a great deal of time investigating thoroughly" the substance of the Bryant-Butts conversations, including several meetings with Coach Bryant. Rose had concluded that the two coaches talked mainly about new rules interpretations. It is dubious if Rose had actually discussed anything with Bear before that morning, because his letter to Aderhold seems to confuse the Graham article with the earlier one written by Furman Bisher about violence in college football.[23]

For the rest of the day Bear circled the wagons. He knew now, positively, that Rose was on his side. His next stop was his lake cottage, where he received tears and support. Then he drove back to Tuscaloosa and met with his team in Friedman Hall. Although Frank Graham Jr. was the author of record, Bear assumed it was the work of Furman Bisher. Voicing his opinion of Bisher, Bear began, "This [man] has done this, and I want you to know what has been said before anybody else tells you." He then read the entire story out loud, pausing occasionally to add details.

As he read his anger increased, partially because the Georgia game had been such an unchallenging affair. Accurately pointing out that "Georgia could do nothing right, and Alabama could do nothing wrong," Graham had written, "Georgia made only 37 yards rushing, completed only 7 of 19 passes for 79 yards, and made its deepest penetration (to Alabama's 41-yard line) on the next to the last play of the game." Bryant stopped reading for a moment, lost in deep contemplation of the rushing statistic. "Why, hell," he said at last, "that's just too damn many yards." If he wasn't otherwise occupied, he might have sent the team out on the field for their lackadaisical performance.[24]

His players believed him. They knew that Bryant always expected the truth from them, and, like it or not, he insisted on speaking it to them. "All he ever told us was to tell the truth," Lee Roy Jordan said of his coach. As for the Alabama-Georgia game, Jordan told reporters, there was no collusion, just a heavy dose of Joe Namath. "Joe just ate them up with his passes," he said. Namath also knew that the charges were ridiculous. "I called every play of that game," he later said, "so I *know* the game was not fixed." Still, many of the players appeared shocked by the seriousness of the accusation.[25]

After talking with his team it was time for the lawyers. In Birmingham, Bryant and Rose met with Winston McCall to plan strategy. The article was not yet on the stands, and the three men agreed that the wisest approach was to get in front of the story by denying it before anyone read it. Bear's approach to any personal problem was directness—look a man in the eye and say what was on his mind. Strip away the varnish and just say it. In part, his bluntness accounted for his legendary personal charisma.

Television allowed him to address a statewide audience, so he decided to book fifteen minutes of airtime. His problem was money. A few investments that had gone bad had emptied his pockets, and he lacked the finances to buy airtime. But the men who sponsored his television show—Sloan Bashinsky of Golden Flake potato chips and Preacher Franklin of Coca-Cola Bottlers—told him not to worry. They didn't need commercial time and Bear didn't need to pay.

On Sunday afternoon, March 17, Bryant spoke to Alabama. But before he talked to the people he answered the questions of Fred Nichol, a public prosecutor and a lie detector expert, in Room 914 of the Bankhead Hotel. The questioning took almost two hours. Then, flanked by Rose, McCall, Board of Trustees member Winton Blount, Southeastern Conference commissioner Bernie Moore, and several other University of Alabama officials, Bryant emerged from an elevator, rushed through the lobby, got into an automobile, and headed for the television station.[26]

Bryant walked into the same studio he had used for the previous five years, Sunday afternoons, September through November, for his enormously popular *Bear Bryant Show*. In the corner was a table with a simple nameplate: COACH BRYANT. He was dressed conservatively—dark suit and a crimson-and-white-striped tie. His face was drawn and serious, and he was in no mood for small talk. His eyes seemed to have darkened to an intense blue. He was there to say his piece and then get out.

With more Alabamians watching the show than any previous broadcast, Bryant immediately went on the offensive, denying the *Saturday Evening Post*'s charges. "I welcome this opportunity," he began, "to tell the people of Alabama that these charges are false in every sense of the word. I want to take this time to deny them with every force at my command. Never in my life have I attempted to fix or rig a ball game either as a player or a coach." He emphasized each word, speaking with solemnity mixed with anger. To support his point, he remarked, "Ladies and gentlemen, I have nothing to hide and volunteered to take a lie detector test before a professionally recognized expert in order to insure my friends of the truth of what I say." Took and passed, he added.

He expressed no doubt about the origins of the article. He had filed a $500,000 suit against the *Post* for Bisher's "College Football Is Going Berserk," and now the magazine was doing a little unsportsmanlike piling on of their own. "With this [suit] in mind," Bear said, "it is more obvious to me than ever that this article is another malicious attempt to destroy my reputation for honesty and integrity in order to affect the presentation of my case in the pending suit." And the television audience didn't have to take his word. Read the article when it comes out, he suggested. "I think it'll make you mad like me, and I think you'll agree that it is a series of misleading inferences."

Several times Bear repeated his denial of the accusations. But he became most incensed when he spoke about the implications of the charges on his players. The game-fixing accusation suggested that his boys were not good enough, that they needed an edge to defeat a weak Georgia squad. The article, then, impugned not only his honor but also the talent of the Alabama players. Alabama had won because they had a better team and played harder, smarter, tougher football.

He admitted that he had information about the Georgia team. "Certainly we did. We have information on and about every team we play." His staff worked tirelessly scouting opponents and developing game plans. However, he noted that the editors and writers at the *Post* were not as diligent. Without talking with him or getting his response to their fanciful tale, the magazine inferred that he and Butts had rigged the game and profited by the results. "This I absolutely deny," he repeated.

His talk didn't last long, but its impact was incalculable. Bryant spoke the language of the South—of honor and integrity and esteem. For him, such words had powerful and personal meaning. His idea of honor combined both how he viewed himself and how he was regarded by others, and was the basis of his reputation. It wasn't enough for Bear to know that he had done nothing wrong; his reputation required that his community recognize that he was guiltless. His need for a public forum, his constant denials, and his plea that he had nothing to hide were not simply public relations ploys. He spoke with heightened sincerity because he was sincere, and his reputation meant everything to him. The southerners who watched and listened to him understood that he spoke from the deepest reaches of their shared culture.

In the hours and days after Bryant's public denial of any wrongdoing, Alabama residents rallied to his cause. "Prominent Montgomerians, Fellow Coaches Back Bear," headlined the *Montgomery Advertiser*. "Support Pours in for Tide's Bryant," echoed a headline in the *Birmingham News*. The general tenor of the responses was that Bear wouldn't do it, couldn't do it, and didn't do it. No one in the *Post*'s offices was saying anything, and wherever Bear went he repeated his denial. Speaking at a YMCA engagement in Wichita, Kansas, on Sunday night, he fixed his blue eyes on his audience and said, "I've had some vicious criticism, but my head is high, my back is straight, and I can look you in the eye."[27]

On Tuesday, March 19, "The Story of a College Football Fix" reached the newsstands, and although Alabamians helped to boost the *Post*'s circulation, readers were outraged. The story, they concluded, was much ado about nothing. George Burnett had heard a few minutes of coaches' talk and let his imagination roam wide and wild. "If it lived up to advance billing, the story wouldn't be on Page 80," opined columnist Benny Marshall. "You put that kind on Page 1....Old *Confidential* [a gossip tabloid], in its keyhole peep-ingest days, couldn't have done better with less."[28]

Alabamians defended Bear with every force at their command, but Georgians treated Butts like a leper. In early January the executive committee of the University of Georgia's athletic board had voted unanimously to force Butts to step down as athletic director, and told him so a few weeks later. Butts appealed to President Aderhold. At a meeting that lasted more than two hours, Aderhold listened as Butts enumerated his various financial woes, which included a string of poor investments and disastrous choices. If he lost the income from his job at the university, he would be ruined. Aderhold sympathized with his old friend's plight, but said there was nothing he could do. Butts's only choice was to resign or be fired. On January 30, Butts issued a statement that he had decided to resign as Georgia's athletic director to concentrate on his business activities.[29]

At about the same time, University of Georgia officials began to investigate George Burnett's claim that he had overheard a conversation that sounded ominously like a plan to fix a game. At the request of M. Cook Barwick, an attorney and former FBI agent who handled the investigation for the Georgia Athletic Board, Burnett took and passed a lie detector test. When Butts was hauled into a meeting and coldcocked with the charges, he denied fixing any games but conceded that the conversation may have taken place. But his fumbling claim that it was all just coaches' talk did not inspire confidence in any of his supporters at the tense meeting.

To make matters worse for Butts, he was no friend of Georgia's governor, Carl Sanders. He had opposed Sanders in the 1960 gubernatorial race and the governor had not forgotten or forgiven. When he learned of the case, Sanders decided to use his executive authority to launch an official investigation. In the last two weeks of March, Attorney General Eugene Cook gave his fullest attention to the investigation, reporting back to Sanders on April 1, shortly after the *Post* article had shocked readers across the country.

Cook's thorough investigation carefully laid out the facts. Telephone records confirmed a sixteen-minute call between Butts and Bryant on September 13, and all evidence established that Burnett heard the conversation, which, Cook claimed, "was not casual and general football conversation." Telephone records also confirmed that Butts and Bryant spoke again on September 16. When Butts was first confronted with Burnett's accusation he refused to speak under oath or be tape-recorded, and his own story was confused and inconsistent. Similarly, Rose's response to the evidence was contradictory. Cook's conclusions were tempered by the gambling laws of Georgia. He found no evidence to implicate any player on Alabama's or Georgia's team, and technically no evidence that Butts had violated Georgia's criminal laws. But he thought the conversations between Butts and Bryant were "unethical and improper, and unsportsmanlike, and that the furnishing of information might well have vitally affected the outcome of the game in points and margin of victory."[30]

Cook's conclusions offered Butts hope of avoiding prison, but bode poorly for Bryant's reputation and career. They confirmed most of Burnett's story, if not his entire interpretation of the facts. Furthermore, Cook demonstrated that Butts was in dire financial straits and had gambler contacts, adding potential motive for his actions. Cook was less concerned with Bryant, but Bear was also smeared by his association with Butts. For a man as proud of his reputation as Paul Bryant, a coach who told his players to tell the truth and play hard but always by the rules, even a whiff of scandal was intolerable.

———

Newspapers and magazines across the nation opined on the sensational article, and not all were as generous to Butts and Bryant as those in Tuscaloosa, Birmingham, and Montgomery. Many echoed the judgments of the Cook Report. Something odd had transpired during that short telephone conversation. Perhaps it was not illegal, but it certainly seemed wrong. Red Smith, one of the nation's leading sportswriters, thought that there was nothing in the charges that amounted to "widespread corruption," but if what the *Saturday Evening Post* had charged was true, Butts's and Bryant's conduct was "unseemly." *Sports Illustrated*'s Dan Jenkins concurred. He doubted that either man had committed a crime, but it seemed clear that Butts had committed "a profound indiscretion" that "raises questions of ethics—not only the ethics of Wally Butts and Bear Bryant but of virtually the entire football fraternity, which has become fond of pregame conversations." The bottom line, a coach told Jenkins, was, "Maybe we talk too much to each other. I know we all try to con one another a little bit. But if I had to be one of the two men in that conversation, I would rather be the listener than the speaker."[31]

The findings of the Cook Report and the plans to launch a national congressional investigation also emboldened the editors at the *Post*. The leaders of the magazine staked out a sanctimonious high ground in an April 27 editorial written by Roger Kahn. "We have a radical philosophy at The Post. We believe that anyone who rigs a football game should be exposed," it began. When presented with Burnett's tale the editors simply could not in good conscience dismiss the report. "It is not enough to say 'absurd,' which is only a mask for lethargy. It is not enough to say 'too hot to handle,' which is a mask for cowardice. It is not even enough to say, 'This could hurt a great game.' The name of our game is not football. It is truth." In short, with righteous indignation, the magazine had to investigate and expose. And the magazines that now questioned the report, including *Newsweek*, *Time*, and *Sports Illustrated*, demonstrated only their inability to compete with the *Post*'s crack staff.[32]

The editors at the *Post* criticized southern supporters of Butts and Bryant as well as other news and sports magazines. The suggestion given by the *Birmingham News* to readers to burn their copies of the *Saturday Evening Post* "brought back warm memories of the Third Reich," commented the magazine's editor. Southerners viewed such statements as new examples of the North telling the South how to behave, and placed into the civil rights conflicts of the times, it drew an immediate and not surprising response. "It's a strange thing that those who are the loudest in decrying McCarthyism are sometimes the worst in practicing it—reserving for themselves, while denying it to others, the right to indict, try, and convict without giving the man his day in court," wrote an editor for the *Greensboro Watchman*. The problem, the editor thought, was "the urban mind of the East, busy finding an 'angle' to every human action."[33]

In the magazine's assault on Bryant, the Greensboro editor saw a more general northern attack on the South. Bryant is a "winner," a southern winner, and therefore a target for northern writers, and the *Post*'s editors were simply engaging in "the national pastime of baiting the South." Lee Roy Jordan also thought that jealousy accounted for the attacks. "I sincerely believe that somebody is using this opportunity to attempt to degrade Coach Bryant. I guess that is the price you have to pay to be the best . . . and I know he's the best football coach in the country."[34]

Throughout Alabama that was the message—Bryant was the best and therefore a prime target for the biased reporting of the northern editors at the *Saturday Evening Post* and their southern henchman

Furman Bisher. To show their support, southerners rallied around the Alabama coach. Within a week of the publication of the story, President Rose spoke out in favor of Bryant, the University of Alabama's Board of Trustees unanimously passed a resolution affirming their belief in his "personal integrity," the radio station WTBC called on the Alabama legislature to outlaw the sale of the *Saturday Evening Post* in the state, Alabama alumni called for an FBI probe to clear the coach, and resolutions were introduced in the state legislature denouncing the magazine. Governor George Wallace even said his piece: "I don't know anything about it, but I'll tell you this—*The Saturday Evening Post* is the sorriest authority on the truth."[35]

On the night of March 19 more than 4,000 students at Alabama voiced their support of Bryant by taking to the streets in an impromptu demonstration. In "the biggest display of student spirit in the history of student spirit," the students marched to the Student Union, read resolutions defending their coach, cheered for him, stomped their feet, and beat on whatever was around to beat on just to make noise. Cheerleaders waving pompoms and Colonel Carleton K. Butler's Million Dollar Band gave the proceedings a pep rally atmosphere. When Bryant, wearing a suit and carrying a trench coat over his arm, finally appeared in front of them the decibels rose to even greater heights.[36]

Looking grim but obviously pleased by the turnout, Bear gave a weary smile and said, "You should save that applause for folks like Lee Roy Jordan. You know, I never thought I'd be getting more publicity than Lee Roy." Then he turned serious, telling the students that he honestly appreciated their loyalty, and that his team was "sacred" to him, "especially when they win." He added, "The Good Lord willing, we'll keep on winning." He assured them they had not heard the last from him. "I'm an old man," he said, "but I still have some fight, and I'm tough. . . . One thing you can bet your life on is that I would never sell out this team for a 10 gillion to one odds for 10 gillion dollars." With that, he said the students and his players should get back to their studies.

Within days, the students and other Alabamians had more to celebrate. On March 24, Bryant's attorneys filed suit against the *Saturday Evening Post*, demanding that the magazine publicly retract the article. No one expected the *Post* to budge on its position. The demand simply satisfied a preliminary requirement of Alabama law and paved the way for a libel suit. When the *Post* refused to print a retraction, Bryant sued for libel, now claiming $5 million in actual and punitive damages. The $5 million, of course, was over and above the $500,000 that he had demanded in his earlier suit against the magazine, and separate from the $10 million that Butts was demanding. Altogether, then, the two coaches hoped to win $15.5 million from the *Post*.[37]

For all their sanctimonious bluster, the men behind "The Story of a College Football Fix" were now entertaining nervous second thoughts. Clay Blair had hoped that the story would cause a sensation. It had. He had also thought that he would receive help with the story from the *Atlanta Journal*, where Furman Bisher was sports editor, the kind of support that heavily publicized the story and then ran with it. He didn't. When the story hit the stands Bisher was in Florida covering baseball, and he was suddenly so silent about the article that one would have thought he had never read it or heard of George Burnett, Wally Butts, or Paul Bryant. Furthermore, the sports editor of the *Atlanta Constitution* was similarly uninterested in the *Post*'s coup. Sports columnist Max Moseley of the *Montgomery Advertiser* considered it odd that when every southern newspaper was covering the affair, Atlanta's two papers, which had the finest sports coverage in the South, wouldn't touch it. "Maybe they have a good reason for bypassing the biggest news in the [Southeastern Conference] in years."[38]

Bisher's silence was the most inexplicable. After all, before the article was published he had talked incessantly to other sportswriters about the story. So when the article appeared, writers, coaches, and knowledgeable fans saw Bisher's fingerprints all over it. Tom McEwen, sports editor of the *Tampa Tribune*, commented that Bisher, who had already attacked Bryant for brutal coaching techniques and the University of Alabama for "building a football factory," had secretly supplied material to Graham.[39]

Alabama attorney general Richmond Flowers sought the reasons for Bisher's quietness. On March 27 he called on Bisher to do what Burnett, Butts, and Bryant had already done—submit to a lie detector test "for us to ascertain whether or not he wrote, or collaborated with, or had any connection whatsoever with the original article that appeared in *The Saturday Evening Post*." Bisher responded that he was already involved in a lawsuit with Bryant and would certainly not take any lie detector test in Alabama, but he might take one in Atlanta. He never did. And at the time he made no statement on his part in the story.[40]

Later, more than forty years later, Bisher did comment, claiming that the Graham article wasn't the problem. The real culprit was Roger Kahn's overblown precede that likened the Butts-Bryant affair to the 1919 Black Sox scandal. The *Atlanta Journal* had agreed to work with the *Post* on the release of the story, but, Bisher claimed, when he saw the galley proof of the layout he immediately telephoned the managing editor at the *Post*. The conversation was brief and to the point:

"I've just looked at these proofs. You're not going with this, are you? There's no resemblance between this case and the Black Sox scandal," Bisher said.

"Well, we decided that if we were going with it, we were going all the way," answered the editor.

"You've gone all the way, all right, and then some. I don't see how you can do this."[41]

The conversation ended the *Atlanta Journal*'s participation in the story, which increasingly took on a North versus South subtext.

In his apartment in Brooklyn, Frank Graham Jr. had also begun to reappraise the story and the editors he thought he could trust at the *Post*. The sad truth was that Graham had been swept into Blair's muckraking, crusading current, and not only could he not get out, he didn't want to get out. He had become the point man for the Big Story, an inside player for a scoop that promised to shake up the world of sports and restore sanity to college football. It was heady stuff—a tiny group of tough editors and writers, jackets off and sleeves rolled up in the *Post*'s New York offices, whispering together, planning their assault on the sports establishment. They acted in secret, confiding in as few people as possible, everything on a need-to-know basis, marching lockstep toward the brink.

"As in a classic disaster," Graham later observed, "the wheels, once set in motion, could not be stopped. A sense of excitement, of inebriated delight in pulling off the coup, held together those who were in the know." At one point, "in a moment of good fellowship," Blair told Graham not to worry. No matter what happened, the *Post* would stand behind him. And a *Post* lawyer assured him that there was little to worry about: "Even if Butts sues, the case will never go to court. The attorney general has the evidence, and Butts will get to trial before he can get a suit off the ground."[42]

"Looking back on the incident," Graham wrote, "I am amazed at my naïveté, but it pales by comparison with the men who were making the final decisions at the *Post*. They had extraordinary faith in what they perceived to be their allies in Georgia. The attorney general was, in effect, going to carry the legal burden for the magazine by prosecuting Butts; the *Atlanta Journal* was going to carry the public relations burden by breaking the story in its pages on the same day that it appeared in the *Post*." Surely everything in the *Post*'s complicated scheme would go as planned.

The reality of the magazine's position became apparent when the *Atlanta Journal* backed out of the arrangement, leaving the *Post* to manage its own public relations in the South. And although the Cook Report suggested that if Burnett's interpretation of what he had overheard was true, then Butts had acted unethically in his conversation with Bryant, the Georgia attorney general had discovered nothing that proved the two coaches had fixed the game. In less than a week Graham concluded that the *Post*'s and his own reputation were in trouble. Under Blair's leadership the *Saturday Evening Post* had assaulted "the citadels of iniquity" in the South, attacking the foundations of its social system and football culture, characterizing virtually all of Dixie as racist, violent, and depraved. Below the Mason-Dixon Line, Graham wrote, the *Post* had become "a magazine for nigger-lovers." Yet after Butts and Bryant filed suit, the magazine's lawyers would have to defend its charges in Georgia and Alabama courtrooms.

Making the looming prospects worse, Graham knew that he and his editors at the *Post* had engaged in shoddy journalistic practices. Graham had banged out his draft in one night based on an incomplete set of notes and spotty research. He had not studied the tapes taken during the Burnett affidavit nor seen the insurance salesman's notes from the telephone conversation. In addition, when he revised his draft to include a few quotes Bisher had obtained in Georgia, neither he nor anyone at the *Post* verified the hearsay statements. And because of Blair's emphasis on secrecy, incredibly, "there had been no semblance of the fact-checking process that is routine in the office of every major magazine." Graham, Kahn, and the other editors just ran with Burnett's story without checking dates, scores, or other easily verifiable facts. "It was as if," Graham wrote, "another whispered question, another telephone call to Atlanta, would shatter the secrecy and with it the *Post*'s investment in this exclusive story."

Perhaps Graham felt the ground shift under his feet when he was deposed in the Butts case. Butts's lawyer asked him a simple question: Had he talked to Coach Griffith and several of the Georgia players he quoted in his article? He said he had not. Instead he had "reconstructed" their quotes from interviews with Burnett and others. On a story of this importance, he or a fact-checker at the *Post* should have verified the quotes, Graham knew. So he didn't add that "in the haste and secrecy surrounding the article's publication, no one contacted Griffith or the others quoted."

———

While the *Post*'s poorly laid plans fell apart and Graham had time to reconsider everything he had done or should have done, Bear Bryant suffered through sleepless nights, knowing he had not conspired to fix any game but fearing that he could not prove it adequately enough to salvage his reputation. "Oh, my, the nightmares," he later wrote. Many nights he woke up at some bewitching hour, soaked with sweat, unable to get back to sleep. He just sat in a chair and worried, mostly about the toll it was taking on Mary Harmon and his family. The nightmares would last for several years. Most nights he slept alone in an effort to isolate his wife from his torment.[43]

That spring the Butts-Bryant story was the talk of Dixie, often on the front pages of Alabama newspapers. The U.S. Senate's McClellan Committee sent investigators south, as did the Internal Revenue Service. Richmond Flowers continued his investigation, and Southeastern Conference officials did some digging of their own. If Butts and Bryant were found guilty, college football would face its most serious crisis in more than fifty years.

It was a bad time for sports in America. On March 21, Sugar Ramos beat featherweight champion Davey Moore in a title fight in Los Angeles. A few days later, Moore died of the injuries he sustained, again raising questions concerning the brutality of boxing. Then, in mid-April, National Football League commissioner Pete Rozelle indefinitely suspended star players Paul Hornung of the Green Bay Packers and Alex Karras of the Detroit Lions for betting on league games and associating with gamblers and "known hoodlums." Rozelle fined other players. But nothing rose to the level of the charges against Bryant and Butts.

The trial was set for August, promising to make the summer in Dixie even hotter. But in the spring, no one knew just how much so.

Governor George Wallace became the face of segregation in Alabama in the 1960s. Here, he shows his fighting demeanor as a boxer while attending the University of Alabama. (W.S. Hoole Special Collections Library, The University of Alabama)

8

The Greatest Performance of His Life

Someday, as it must happen to each of us, Wally Butts will pass on where neither the *Post* nor anyone else can then bother him. Unless I miss my guess, they will put him in a red coffin with a black lid with a football in his hands, and his epitaph will read, "Glory, glory to Old Georgia."
                                                            —William Schroder

He stares down most of them, and he sues the others.
                                        —John Crittendon, on Bryant and his critics

CALLS FOR FREEDOM and change dominated the summer of 1963. In Berlin, before 150,000 people crowded outside the city hall, President John F. Kennedy intoned, *"Ich bin ein Berliner."* "All free men, wherever they may live, are citizens of Berlin," he said. The problem was that all people were not free enough. So they clamored, marched, protested, and took the most extreme measures to publicize their plight. In Saigon that summer a Buddhist monk dramatized the repressive regime of President Ngo Dinh Diem by setting himself on fire and burning to death on a city street. Other Buddhists followed his example. In Addis Ababa black leaders formed the Organization of African Unity, pledging to support anticolonial movements. In Washington, D.C., Martin Luther King Jr. stood in front of the Lincoln Memorial and addressed more than 200,000 demonstrators. "I have a dream," he said, drawing out the last word so long that it felt like a prophetic vision.

Far from being immune to King's dream and the drift of world events, Alabama was on the front lines of the battle for freedom. Once again, race was one of the two most important topics of all discussions from Mobile to Huntsville. The other, of course, was football. Many white Alabamians were on the defensive, branded as hardened racists and resentful of attacks on their way of life. And to make matters worse, one of their icons stood accused of fixing a football game. That summer, at a university in Tuscaloosa and a courtroom in Atlanta, the two most important men in the state engaged in separate, desperate struggles. Almost simultaneously Bear Bryant and George Wallace had risen to power, attracted national attention, and become powerful symbols inside and outside the state. Both white southerners educated at the University of Alabama, both commanding audiences when they spoke, they represented two different and distinct dreams for Alabama during what writer Howell Raines called "the midnight of its humiliation."[1]

Like many Alabamians born in the 1940s and early 1950s, Raines gloried in Bryant from the first season he coached Alabama. He vividly recalled the night of September 27, 1958, riding in the backseat of his father's 1957 Dodge to a family hunting camp near the Florida border. It was Bear's first game at Alabama, and the Tide, woeful for the previous three or four seasons, were matched against the powerhouse Louisiana State University Tigers. Listening to the game as it faded in and out on a "maddeningly intermittent signal," he thrilled at the Tide's 3–0 halftime lead, and even when the Tigers came back to win a close game, Howell and his father and brother recognized that "here was a coach to be reckoned with." The collapse of a section of stands in Mobile that night was eerily symbolic of the end of the old Ears Whitworth regime. There was a new man in charge, and a new era for Alabama football.[2]

By the early 1960s the promise of that night in Mobile had been fulfilled. After winning the national championship in 1961, Bryant and Pat Trammell attended the National Football Foundation and College Football Hall of Fame dinner at the Waldorf-Astoria, where they received the MacArthur Trophy as the year's outstanding team. There the coach and his captain, dressed in tuxedos, shook hands and chatted with President Kennedy. Later that evening, Kennedy also addressed by telephone a Sugar Bowl pep rally in Tuscaloosa. This sort of recognition, these shining moments, received considerable attention in Alabama. Coming less than six months after the Freedom Riders had reached the Anniston city line, the Waldorf-Astoria event reflected a different side of the state.[3]

As an Alabama fan who attended graduate school in Tuscaloosa, Raines shared the sheer joy of Bear's success. He went to as many games as he could, watched some on television, and listened to others on the radio. Years later he would write, "It can, after all, never be as good again. And believe me, to have been in the city of Tuscaloosa in October when you were young and full of Early Times and had a shining Alabama girl by your side—to have had all that and then to have seen those red shirts pour onto the field, and, then, coming behind them, with that inexorable big cat walk of his, the man himself, The Bear—that was very good indeed."[4]

But what Bryant gave Alabama was more than just victories,

though they should not be discounted. "Bryant represented our aspirations," said Raines. "Alabama was full of Moro Bottoms and parents who worked in cotton mills and steel mills for the sole purpose of seeing their kids go to college and move up a step on the social ladder." When Bryant recruited their sons he wore a coat and tie and said, "I came from Moro Bottom and look what football brought to me. If you give me your son I'm going to make sure he graduates." At a moment when Alabama was moving from a rural, agricultural society to an urban, industrial one, Bryant's look, message, and history of success were powerful magnets.[5]

Parents caught between the old and the new Alabama took note of how Bryant looked and behaved. Shug Jordan, Auburn's coach who beat the Tide like a rented mule during the mid-1950s before Bear showed up, had a different approach to rural boys. He said, "Come to Auburn. We ain't highfalutin. We got plenty of boys on the team like you. Heck, you can even wear your jeans to class." By the end of the 1950s it was not a line that many parents wanted to hear. Bryant, in contrast, talked incessantly about class—acting right, talking right, dressing right, and playing right. A photograph taken in December 1959 when Alabama was in Philadelphia for the Liberty Bowl illustrated the point. It showed Trammell and a few of his teammates out on the street wearing coats, ties, and snap-brim hats. The message received was clear: "Bear can take 'em to town and dress 'em up right."[6]

If Bryant spoke to Alabama's better angels, Wallace communicated with its worst. He represented a past that still had a claw grip on the state. After he lost the 1958 gubernatorial election by seeming weaker on segregation than John Patterson, Wallace had vowed to his campaign leaders, "Well, boys, no other son-of-a-bitch will ever out-nigger me again." From that point Wallace pandered to the dark side of Alabama's history. Unlike Bryant, he embarrassed most of the old Alabama elite, who arched their eyebrows and sniffed at any of their number who supported him. They might have to deal with the politician, but they did not have to invite him to dinner at the Birmingham Country Club or the Tuscaloosa Country Club. Wallace, however, did not play to the Mountain Brook gentry. He catered to Alabamians' fears—fear of change, fear of losing their jobs, fear of the emerging culture, and, worst of all, fear of integration.[7]

With his underdog sense of inferiority and pugnacious competitiveness, Wallace struck a vein that ran deep in the state's cultural soil. Raines wrote that to reach the governor's mansion, "the slick-haired little pol with the spittle-stained cigar jutting from his truculent pan of a face" signed "a pact with evil that required him to publicize the fiction that Alabama's police and courts were powerless to prevent violence up to and including murder." But the truth is that he led the citizens and whipped up their passions as adroitly as Bryant commanded his team. And almost every white person in the state who knew better kept quiet out of fear of the Klan or social opprobrium. There is an old southern adage that a man shouldn't wrestle with a pig because he'll just get muddy and the pig will enjoy the romp. In the early 1960s, few Alabamians wanted to get muddy.[8]

A man like Paul Bryant, who had tussled with a bear and had influential ties in affluent anti-Wallace circles in Birmingham and Tuscaloosa, might have wrestled with the pig. He might even have won the match—perhaps even have altered the civil rights struggle in Alabama. But that summer he had other thoughts on his mind.

———

During the 1962 season the racial unrest that was beginning to convulse Birmingham and would move Alabama toward the election of Wallace began to spill over into relations between the state's most important economic center and the University of Alabama. The 1961 expansion of Denny Stadium's seating capacity from 25,000 to 43,000 certainly threatened the hold of Birmingham's Legion Field on Alabama's major "home" games and gave the university leverage in its efforts to force the city to upgrade their main stadium. Beyond that not insignificant economic clash, Bull Connor and his supporters considered the university soft on race. Editorials in the *Crimson White*, the school's moderately liberal newspaper, frequently raised howls of complaint in other parts of the state.

A small but clear indication of the growing rift occurred after the 1962 Alabama-Georgia contest, the contest that saw Joe Namath in his first varsity game lead the Tide to an overwhelming 35–0 victory.

As pleasing as the result was for most Tide supporters, the evening in Birmingham did not end well for everyone. Clement Seelhorst and several friends had driven to the game from Tuscaloosa, parking six blocks away from the stadium in a black section of the city to avoid getting caught in the postgame traffic. But after the game they could not find their car. Perhaps they had a few drinks at the game, and not unlikely they were celebrating the Alabama victory with a couple of boisterous cheers. Whatever the case, they were in a fine mood and creating no problems, but the more they looked for their car, the more confused and loud they became.[9]

"We saw some colored boys standing on the street," Seelhorst later wrote Birmingham officials, "so we told them that we would give the one that found the car fifty cents." A policeman saw the exchange between white and black youths and decided that it did not bode well. In no time a paddy wagon pulled up beside Seelhorst and two of his friends. One of Connor's policemen ordered them into the vehicle. When the Alabama students tried to explain, the cop told them to "shut up and get in the wagon."

They were hauled to the station. When one of the students asked what they had done, the policeman in charge called him a "punk" and said he was drunk, though no sobriety tests were administered. Then they were searched and thrown into a holding cell. It was a "beauty," Seelhorst recalled, with "vomit and urine wastes all over the floor."

They stayed four or five hours in the cell. No phone calls, no explanation, no relief from the stench. Finally the police fined the students thirty dollars and released them.

President Rose asked Bull Connor to look into the matter, and the commissioner of public safety responded promptly. The arresting officers said the boys were loud and drunk. Their yells of "Roll Tide Roll" had upset Mary Kress, "a negro female," and the police had simply stopped the students from "disturbing negro residents" and prevented what might have been an ugly racial incident. Bull concluded that the "three young bucks" got exactly what they deserved. "They could have caused a great deal of trouble between the whites and Negroes by the way they were acting down in that Negro community around Midnight." And any other story the students told was just damnable lies, including their estimation of the cleanliness of Birmingham cells. "They must have thought we should have a rug on the floor and a radio or television set in each cell for them," Bull observed.[10]

President Rose realized that Birmingham was Bull's city, and he promptly dropped the matter, thanking him for "going to all of the trouble to get this information together for me." The boys, Rose insisted, would be given an appropriate lecture on behavior by the dean of students.[11]

The episode was over. But President Rose, the students at Alabama, and the citizens of the United States had not heard the last of Bull Connor and his police force. Nor would civil rights activity in Alabama vanish from the headlines. In November 1962 George Wallace outtalked and outcampaigned the enormously popular and controversial two-term governor "Kissin' Jim" Folsom and a gaggle of other Democratic politicians to win the gubernatorial election. He had run as an uncompromising, unrepentant segregationist, who throughout—and after—demonstrated no inclination to soften his stand, no matter how modestly. During one exchange with reporters in the lobby of Birmingham's exclusive Tutwiler Hotel, meeting place for the Big Mules and other moneyed southern interests, Wallace addressed the recent decision by the City Commission to close parks, empty swimming pools, and pour cement in the holes of the public golf course rather than yield to a court order to desegregate. "We have to make sacrifices and do without things if we want to stand up for what we believe in," he said. At home and abroad there could be no "appeasing niggers." Shifting the subject by a few degrees, a reporter asked Wallace's opinion of Attorney General Robert Kennedy. A person filing a report about the session noted simply that "his reply was too revoltingly obscene to be repeated."[12]

After the election, however, none of his public comments, and few of his private ones, were judged too obscene to repeat. In fact, they gave him the publicity and the notoriety he craved, making him, along with Bull Connor, a visual symbol of the unchangeable, racist South. Wallace's "segregation forever" speech and Connor's use of high-powered fire hoses and police dogs against protesters became the sound bite and the snapshot of the South in the national media. In the summer of 1963 the civil rights movement and the segregationist South would clash in two Alabama cities separated by less than sixty miles. While millions of Americans watched on television, three men—Wallace, Connor, and Martin Luther King—in two cities, Birmingham and Tuscaloosa, waded into the current of modern history.

———

Joe Namath decided to stay in Tuscaloosa after his sophomore year. He had spent the summer of 1962 there as well, retaking an English composition course that he had failed. It had been a fine summer. He had made more friends, "dated" more coeds, and enjoyed immensely the fact that he was not working in the Babcock & Wilcox Steel Corporation or one of the other steel mills in the Beaver Falls area. It was hot in Tuscaloosa, but not blast-furnace hot.[13]

The coaching staff asked Vito Capizzo, a transplant from the Northeast who had tried out for football but was too small and slow to make the traveling team, to look after Joe that summer. Vito shared an apartment with other students across from Foster Hall, and Namath was a frequent and welcomed visitor. "The best thing about Joe," Capizzo remembered, "was that he was O-negative blood type and the rest of us were B-positive. When we sold our blood once a month for spending money we only got fifteen dollars a shot, but Joe got thirty dollars. We knew when Joe had donated because he would always show up at the apartment with steaks." Vito said Namath also picked up extra money from his summer job painting the steps in Denny Stadium. It had been a good summer of cheap beer, low-stakes card games, and late-night adventures, a time when Joe had to bum money for gas from one friend to drive another friend's car. It was his last summer that he could go anywhere without hearing someone say, "Look, there's Joe Namath."

He had an even more cushy job in the summer of 1963. The coaching staff got Joe and Hoot Owl Hicks jobs at the Gulf States Paper Company. Their duties were a bit ill-defined and consisted mostly of showing up sometime in the morning and taking off sometime in the late afternoon. But when they were on the job, they were expected to be ready to answer questions and talk friendly-like about the past and upcoming football seasons. "It wasn't too taxing," Hoot Owl recalled, "but sometimes our throats got dry and we'd go to some establishment equipped to fix the problem."[14]

Tied, as it were, to the grueling and malodorous task of making paper, the two paid very little attention to what was in their local newspaper. If they had, they would have read that the trail of university desegregation was winding toward the University of Alabama. Mississippi, Alabama, and Georgia had stood for almost one hundred years like three blocks of segregationist granite, the bedrock of the South's consensus that any change on the race issue was a lamentable one. "Segregation now, segregation tomorrow, segregation forever" may have been Wallace's words, but it was the South's creed. But the civil rights movement, which had been chipping at the granite with tiny hammers for decades, was now working with blasting caps and dynamite. In January 1961 the University of Georgia quietly desegregated. In October 1962 the University of Mississippi desegregated after volleys of gunfire, violent clashes, and the late arrival of armed federal troops. After Mississippi it was a certainty that Alabama would be next.

Far from fearing the challenge to his university's segregationist policies, Governor Wallace seemed to welcome it. He had always loved a good scrap, and he had never shied away from the sight of blood. It seemed he had been in one ring or another all his life. Twice he won the Alabama Golden Gloves championship, and he was a ferocious battler on the university boxing team that he captained. In 1939, the *Crimson White* sportswriter commented, "George Wallace, undefeated bantamweight, showed real class in winning over Fisher of Tulane by a technical knockout." A photograph showing Wallace tearing into his bloodied and over-matched opponent captured perfectly his physical presence and personality—heavily muscled in his arms and chest, jaw jutting forward, and teeth bared, he swings from the floor, eschewing defense and going for the knockout.[15]

With a flat pug nose, Wallace looked like a boxer, and on the stump he moved like one. As he spoke he constantly rolled his shoulders and shifted his weight, looking like an experienced pugi-list sliding, feinting, and looking for an opening. Words shot from his mouth like punches, some sharp, clipped, and rat-tat-tat like snake-quick jabs, others slow, heavy, and lethal like a Sonny Liston haymaker. While he spoke his face seemed to twitch, moving rapidly from a sneer to a mocking smile to a belligerent defiance. Everything added up to a mesmerizingly effective performance, touching the deepest passions and emotions of his listeners.

His message of "no, no, never" found its most powerful image in the schoolhouse door. Promising to personally and physically resist any order to integrate Alabama schools, he said, "And when the court order comes, I am going to place myself, your governor, in the position so that the federal court order must be directed against your governor.... I shall refuse to abide by any such illegal federal court order even to the point of standing in the schoolhouse door, if necessary."[16]

The image touched every sacred political and social belief of the intransigent white South. No one has analyzed it better than scholar E. Culpepper Clark. "Racism was the muscle and sinew of white anger," he wrote, "but it was so interlarded with tradi-tional suspicions of power and privilege that race itself could not be separated from other themes of the powerless: localism versus federalism, the working many versus the monied few, southern-ers versus Yankees, farmers versus bankers, average citizen versus pointy-headed intellectual, individual ballot versus bloc voter, little/big, light/dark, white/black, and so on until the majority race in Alabama was transformed into a conscious minority, victims of an overwhelming international colored majority." Like some sort of social magician, again and again, in front of cheering crowds across the state, Wallace plunged his half-clenched fist into a black top hat and rescued a defenseless white rabbit.[17]

One southerner who was inordinately unnerved by Wallace's magic act was university president Frank Rose. Since taking office he had convinced activists on both sides of the desegregation divide that he was on their side. But the election of Wallace began to seriously cramp his style. One senses Rose began to squirm once Wallace received the Democratic nomination to serve as governor. In a letter of congratulation that ominously lacked specificity, Rose nevertheless attempted to curry favor. "We have watched with a great deal of interest your concern for the major problems facing the people of our state," he wrote. "We have indeed been heartened by your proposals to solve these problems." Rose did not say which problems or proposals, and he must have known that Wallace was primarily interested in the politics of race.[18]

Rose's courtship included a good dose of football. Even before it was announced that Alabama and Oklahoma would play in the 1963 Orange Bowl, Rose passed the information along to the next governor together with an invitation for him and his wife to attend the game as guests of the Roses. Of course, he added, "we will be delighted to pay the expenses of both of you from Alabama and return." The trip, Rose added to Wallace, would provide "the much needed rest that you so richly deserve."[19]

Wallace showed little interest in spending much time with Rose, but he did book himself into the exclusive Fontainebleau Hotel and accepted the president's offer to foot the bill. In addition, he requested and received twenty-four tickets for himself and his circle of supporters. Rose unctuously complied, providing two dozen choice 50-yard-line tickets as well as invitations for the various pre- and postgame activities. Wallace's message was clear: He was in charge and Rose would carry the water bucket.[20]

At the same time as he was trying, with mixed success, to cozy up to Wallace, Rose was sending out covert signals that he was the stouthearted Kennedy man in Alabama. He had known Robert Kennedy for years, and the two seemed to be friends. "[Dr. Rose] was on our side," JFK later observed. "At least as he talked to us, he was on our side." But as Rose's options narrowed, and his ability to please two masters began to vanish, he inched closer to Wallace. Historian E. Culpepper Clark claimed that the university president "seemed to operate from no fixed compass." More accurately, true north on his compass pointed toward his own self-interest. To be generous, he worked for the best interests of the University of Alabama. To be blunt, he was after what was best for him.[21]

But what was best for Rose and his university? It was clear that Wallace controlled the state's purse strings, and if Rose crossed him he would retaliate. Ever the fighter, Wallace always punched back. It was equally clear that history had locked arms with the civil rights movement. On Good Friday, March 12, Bull Connor's police arrested Martin Luther King during a protest march and imprisoned him. A week later his "Letter from Birmingham Jail" was printed in newspapers across the country. Charged by a group of white clergymen with being an "outsider" and interfering with matters that were none of his business, King wrote, "I am in Birmingham because injustice is here.... Moreover, I am cognizant of the interrelatedness of all communities and states. I cannot sit by in Atlanta and not be concerned about what happens in Birmingham. Injustice anywhere is a threat to justice everywhere.... Whatever affects one directly, affects all indirectly.... Anyone who lives inside the United States can never be considered an outsider anywhere within its bounds."[22]

King's eloquent plea for simple justice and his assertion that no man—or community—is an island focused the attention of America on Birmingham. Throughout April and May, in full view of reporters and television cameras, the demonstrations and marches continued unabated. Police used fire hoses and police dogs to break up demonstrations of schoolchildren, arrested hundreds of protesters, and through their inaction condoned vigilante attacks against blacks. Klansmen held rallies and burned crosses, a bomb exploded in the A. G. Gaston Motel, and scores of blacks were injured in riots. Photographs on the front pages of newspapers convinced President Kennedy to dispatch federal troops to the city to quell the violence. By then, Birmingham had become a war zone, led by a commissioner of public safety with a narrow interpretation of who constituted the "public" and no concern whatsoever about "safety."

During that spring of intolerance in Birmingham, Wallace and the Kennedy administration moved toward a final confrontation in Tuscaloosa. The federal courts had ordered the University of Alabama to desegregate, and they rejected such delaying tactics as finding reasons to reject all black applicants. In December 1962, for instance, Rose had brushed aside the issue by rejecting three black applicants because of the "pressure of enrollment." It was all aboveboard, he announced, and all applicants had been informed of the process. Yet Vivian Malone, the only black applicant known by name, said she had not been told of the decision to close enrollment. Soon after the episode, the courts blocked Rose's tactics. Under court order, the university processed and accepted the three applicants for summer admission. All Rose and the trustees could do then was plead for "law and order" if the black students enrolled.[23]

In the beginning of June the weather was mild by Alabama standards. The skies were partly cloudy, but there was no rain, and the temperatures hardly reached into the eighties. But with the showdown that was scheduled for summer enrollment only a few days away it seemed unbearably hot. U.S. district judge Seybourn H. Lynne ruled that the powers of state sovereignty do not embody the right to obstruct justice, and Wallace did not have the right to stand in the schoolhouse door. In response the governor pushed out his chin and promised defiance. On June 5 he addressed a statewide television audience. He was going to stand in the door, and that was that. What happened to him, he said, was unimportant. "What is of more consequence is what happens to liberty and freedom and constitutional government." As he framed the story, he would not stand against desegregation but for justice and the American way.[24]

As Wallace prepared literally and symbolically to make his stand, and Vivian Malone and James Hood got ready to enroll at the university on June 11, authorities in Tuscaloosa planned for the end of an era. State troopers raided several establishments near campus, seizing dynamite, pistols, and tear gas guns. In the days following a local Klan rally, the Tuscaloosa County deputy sheriff made twenty-one arrests, most on weapons charges. Most of the Klansmen had permits to carry pistols, but state officials had revoked all permits during "the racial crisis" in the city. In addition to handguns, the sheriff uncovered bayonets, cotton hooks, nightsticks, and a variety of other deadly weapons. Grand dragon of the Ku Klux Klan Robert Shelton complained about the arrests, but the authorities ignored his protests.[25]

Summer registration was scheduled to begin on Monday the tenth, but in an effort to avoid the first-day crush of students and buzz of excitement Rose decided that Malone and Hood would not enroll until Tuesday the eleventh. In preparation, on Friday night police barricaded the campus, cordoning off the streets surrounding Foster Auditorium and setting up roadblocks at key intersections along University Avenue. On its front page the *Crimson White*, the school newspaper, listed the police "Ground Rules" for students. Students were required to carry summer IDs at all times, observe a 10 p.m. curfew, not congregate in groups of more than three, and report any rumor that they heard immediately to the dean of men or to the police. Everything was in shutdown mode as officials hoped for the best and prepared for the worst.[26]

Enrollment took place in Foster Auditorium, and Wallace planned to stand in the door at the north entrance of the all-purpose hall. The best vantage point from which to watch the stand was Bear Bryant's office in Little Hall, less than a block away. It was on the southwest corner of the ground floor of the building, and its windows offered an unobstructed view of the north entrance of Foster. Since Bear was out of town, Rose and the trustees decided to gather in Bear's air-conditioned office to watch the governor's performance.[27]

After breakfast in the President's Mansion, an antebellum structure that looked like it belonged on the set of *Gone with the Wind*, Rose and his guests met the trustees in Bear's office. Some sat in chairs, others stood, looking toward the "schoolhouse door," which Clark noted "was neither little nor red." It was an impressive entrance to an otherwise unimpressive building—six columns, three doors, the picture of Greek symmetry. A small semicircle had been painted in front of the center door, looking eerily like a tiny proscenium stage for Wallace to act out his operatic drama.

The group watched as Wallace arrived at Foster. They saw the cordon of 150 patrolmen assigned to separate enrolling students and curious onlookers from the governor's position, and if they glanced up at the roofs of the surrounding buildings they might have seen even more troopers armed with rifles. It had been a nice early summer morning, but by 9:30 waves of heat had begun to roll across the campus, moving the thermometer into the nineties. The day was getting decidedly hotter.

Shortly before 11 a.m., Rose saw a motorcade of three cars stop in front of Foster. Nicholas Katzenbach, head of the on-ground federal operations in Tuscaloosa and a veteran of the desegregation of the University of Mississippi, got out of a car, flanked by several other authorities, and approached Wallace, who was standing nervously in front of the auditorium's doors. Katzenbach and Wallace exchanged a few words, which hardly anybody in the crowd heard. In essence, Katzenbach asked for the governor's assurance that neither he nor anyone under his control would prevent the enrollment of Malone and Hood. It was an order of the United States president, he said. Wallace refused to give the assurances requested. Katzenbach insisted again, making it clear that Wallace could not and would not prevent him from executing his orders.

It was the confrontation that Wallace expected. Before leaving his stage he moved close to the podium and read a statement. It sounded like something out of the antebellum South, an address that could have been written by states'-rights theorist John C. Calhoun, retracing the relationship between federal and state governments. It was dead logic from a distant past, a bow to the Lost Cause and the ghosts of the Confederacy. In five minutes it was over and Wallace stepped back into the doorway of Foster, bracketed by two beefy patrolmen. Katzenbach tried to reason with him, attempted to convince him of what they both knew was true, that with or without his support, Malone and Hood were going to enroll for classes. Wallace stood unmoved, arms crossed, chin jutting forward defiantly, not even dignifying Katzenbach's words with a response.

At that point, Katzenbach returned for Vivian Malone and escorted her through the cordon of patrolmen to her designated dorm, Mary Burke Hall, just across the south parking lot from Foster. Dressed neatly in a pink skirt-and-blouse outfit, her hair done up like one of the Supremes, she walked with incredible dignity and composure. Fully recognizing that all eyes were on her, she even managed a slight smile.

After checking Malone into the dorm, where she was welcomed by the dorm mother and ate lunch with a group of other coeds,

Katzenbach called Attorney General Robert Kennedy for further orders. Both Kennedys agreed it was time to federalize the Alabama National Guard and force Wallace to comply with the order. In the next few hours this was done, and General Henry Graham of the Alabama contingent of the 31st Dixie Division was helicoptered to Tuscaloosa to force Wallace's hand.

Joe Namath and Hoot Owl Hicks, standing in the shade of a tree, were just outside the entrance of Foster Auditorium at about three-thirty when General Graham approached the north entrance. Joe had registered for a class the day before but while fiddling around with his new ID card had accidentally poked a pencil through it. Now he was back to get a new one. But the relaxed atmosphere of the previous day was gone. Namath thought Foster looked like a war zone.[28]

As Namath watched, unsure of what it all meant, the final act in the drama began. Graham looked every inch a general—tall, erect, gray-haired, and all business. He moved toward Wallace, saluted the governor, and said, "It is my sad duty to ask you to step aside, on order of the president of the United States." Wallace asked only to say a few words, and Graham agreed. The governor delivered a short address, hitting a few of his favorite constitutional points. He also asked for everyone to remain "calm and restrained," asserting that Alabama was "awakening the people to the trend toward military dictatorship in this country."

That was it. Wallace got into a patrol car and departed for Montgomery. A handful of spectators applauded his short speech, while many more breathed a sigh of relief. The men in Bear's office shook hands and congratulated each other on how they had handled the crisis. And Vivian Malone and James Hood returned to Foster and enrolled at the University of Alabama. Joe kept his eyes on Malone. She was the star of the show. Rose, Katzenbach, Graham, even Wallace—they played only walk-on roles.

On June 11, 1963, after Governor George Wallace dramatically blocked the entrance to Foster Auditorium, Vivian Malone enrolled for classes at the University of Alabama becoming, along with James Hood, one of the first African American students at the school in the 1960s. (Library of Congress)

Prompted by the events in Tuscaloosa, that night President Kennedy went on television and addressed "the moral crisis" facing America. "Now the time has come for this nation to fulfill its promise," he said. "The events in Birmingham and elsewhere have so increased the cries for equality that no city or state or legislative body can prudently choose to ignore them." With surgical precision he cut to the heart of the matter, demonstrating the statistical and moral costs of discrimination in America. Linking the issue to foreign policy, he noted, "We preach freedom around the world, and we mean it, and we cherish our freedom here at home, but are we to say to the world, and much more importantly, to each other, that this is the land of the free except for the Negroes; that we have no second-class citizens except Negroes; that we have no class or caste system, no ghettoes, no master race except with respect to Negroes?" Kennedy emphasized that the time had come for the nation to fulfill its ideals and constitution and to make it possible "for every American to enjoy the privileges of being American without regard to his race or his color."[29]

Kennedy's address stirred millions of Americans from all parts of the country. Combining phrases that alluded to Abraham Lincoln and Martin Luther King, promising justice and opportunity for all Americans, it spoke to the country's highest ideals.

Not many hours later, in Jackson, Mississippi, civil rights worker Medgar Evers had just returned home after working late into the night. As he walked from his car to his house, a man hidden in a honeysuckle thicket across the road squeezed off a single shot. The bullet ripped into Evers's back and exited through his chest. He died a short time later—and with him Kennedy's hopes for a peaceful resolution to America's "moral problem." Evers was the first of the major political assassinations that would convulse the nation during the next ten years.

During the rest of the week, while federalized troops and local police guarded the campus of the University of Alabama and while Malone and Hood began their classes, the school's most famous person and the football team's leading player were nowhere near the swarm of activity. Bryant was about as far away from Tuscaloosa as physically possible while still being in the continental United States. He was a featured speaker at a coaches' clinic in Montana. Namath was on campus, but his only contribution to the cause was to go into business with Hoot Owl. The pair earned a tidy profit by buying sandwiches and Cokes off-campus and selling them to guardsmen at wildly inflated prices.[30]

But the civil rights battles in Alabama in the early 1960s spilled onto Bryant's program, even if he tried to keep the political world locked outside his compound. Reporters employed simple, direct analogies. Political writers reported the violent, unlawful tactics of Birmingham's Bull Connor, the Alabama Citizens Council, and the Ku Klux Klan. Sportswriters accused Bryant's team of unnecessarily violent, and even illegally brutal, behavior. As proof they offered the brouhaha over the Holt-Graning affair and Furman Bisher's *Saturday Evening Post* "College Football Is Going Berserk" piece. Political writers explored the depths of educational, social, and cultural segregation in the South. Sportswriters dwelled on Alabama's all-white team that played before all-white spectators. In short, for many the Crimson Tide football team reflected the sins of the state of Alabama.

In the summer of 1963, Bryant had to go into an Atlanta courtroom to attempt to salvage his career and reputation. It was a daunting task. Even before he reached the court, he faced two serious challenges. First, his fate was tied to Wally Butts's. The Atlanta trial was *Wally Butts v. the Curtis Publishing Company*, not *Paul Bryant v. the Curtis Publishing Company*. If Butts lost the verdict, Bryant's chances of clearing his name decreased significantly. Though Bear never said so, it must have felt like he had jumped into a deep lake with a millstone tied to his neck.

Before the story broke, Butts's personal life was a mess; after it broke, all other aspects of his life nosedived. "Things have been hell and the only thing that has sustained me is the support of my true friends," he said. Since losing his job as Georgia's athletic director, he had sold his stately redbrick home, moved into an apartment, and experienced enough free time to watch his finances plunge downward. Once in high demand on the rubber chicken circuit, where he charmed groups with his southernisms and understated sense of humor, he was now deprived of most of those easy paydays. He appeared a few times in Alabama, undoubtedly arranged by Bear, and occasionally the old Wally resurfaced. "I had some hot information for Auburn," he told one group, "but they wouldn't accept my call. Word's out that I'm calling collect now."[31]

Bear's second challenge was the venue of the trial. Many

southerners, and particularly Alabamians, regarded Atlanta as the farthest southern borough of New York City. The city "too busy to hate," they thought, was a city busily working to disassociate itself from the parochialism of the Old South and to become the center of the New South. Even before the word came into everyday speech, civic leaders in Atlanta were cultivating a "sunbelt" image for their city. And in no southern location was Bear more of an outsider. It was in Atlanta that journalist Furman Bisher had led the attack against his teams and coaching methods. And it was in Atlanta's Grant Field in 1962 at the Alabama–Georgia Tech game that some rowdy Yellow Jacket fans threw liquor bottles at Bryant. Given the recent history between Bryant and Dodd, the prominent role Bisher played in both *Post* articles, and the long-standing rivalry between Alabama and Georgia Tech, Bear might have preferred a trial in Auburn more than Atlanta.

But Atlanta it was, and in the months before it opened it generated more heat and controversy than any southern trial in decades. "Not since the steaming summer of 1925, when two old orators, Clarence Darrow and William Jennings Bryan, voluntarily argued the theory of man's ascent from the ape on the courthouse lawn at Dayton, Tenn., has the South been as emotionally aroused over a trial as it is by the one that is scheduled to begin in Atlanta," commented Dan Jenkins of *Sports Illustrated*. "It's the biggest topic of conversation in the South since secession and may have almost as far-reaching effects," added Jim Murray of the *Los Angeles Times*.

Throughout that spring, august committees from Alabama and Georgia to the capital in Washington, D.C., had investigated the case, dissecting the truthfulness of the main participants and its implication for sports and America. George Burnett, Wally Butts, and Bear Bryant had all taken lie detector tests—and all passed, creating headlines and prompting articles about the general trustworthiness of the different machines and techniques. Everyone, it seemed, had had their say. Burnett had told his story to university officials, Georgia state investigators, the *Saturday Evening Post* editors, and about everyone else between Atlanta and New Orleans. Butts and Bryant had told theirs in front of television cameras and auditoriums full of loyal supporters. The facts were well known. Only the truth was as elusive and as slippery as an eel.[32]

At ten o'clock on the morning of August 5, in Room 318 of Atlanta's Post Office and Court Building, Wally Butts's $10 million libel suit against the Curtis Publishing Company, parent company of the *Saturday Evening Post*, began. A classic Depression-era federal structure, featuring granite exteriors, marble interiors, and wide stairways, the building no longer served its twin function as a post office, but it remained an imposing, and intimidating, court of law. Everything about the building sounded a note of quiet solemnity, from the disabled veteran manning a candy stand on the first floor and the old-fashioned manually operated elevator to the portraits on the dark mahogany walls of Room 318 and the grandfather clock that had died years before at 9:40. Presiding over the trial was District Judge Lewis "Pete" Morgan, a Kennedy appointee noted for a stiff but courteous manner and judicial seriousness that belied his informal nickname.[33]

A round, sad-faced Wally Butts, dressed in a dark suit and a Georgia Bulldog red tie, dragged himself into the courtroom like a condemned man. One reporter commented that he looked "grim and tired." Although his wife, three married daughters, and an assortment of friends sat behind him in a show of support, Butts had painful reasons for concern. In the years before the *New York Times v. Sullivan* (1964) decision, the burden of proof in a libel case rested squarely on the defendant. Butts, the plaintiff, did not have to prove he was innocent; the *Saturday Evening Post* had to prove he was guilty, or at least of such low character that the article could not have caused further damage to his reputation. Butts knew as he entered the courtroom that the *Post*'s lawyers would portray him as a slimy trafficker of team secrets, a gambler, a fixer of a football game, and a man of cheap and tawdry habits. They undoubtedly planned to paint a picture of him as so low-down and depraved that the jury would dismiss the case with cries of "throw the bum in prison." For his part, Butts hoped to win a staggering verdict, and he had convincing reasons to support that hope. But he knew that win or lose, by the end of the trial he would be so splattered with mud that he would never again be clean.[34]

Pursuant to the "too despicable to libel" strategy, the *Post*'s lawyers had spent weeks digging for all the dirt they could unearth about Butts and Bryant. They even hired journalist Bard Lindeman and another investigator to go to Lexington to check out Bear's years as the coach of Kentucky. The men heard a few unsupported rumors but learned nothing of real substance. At one point, Lindeman tracked down a man familiar with the town's gambling scene and asked whether Bryant had ever bet on football or basketball games. The gambler looked hard at him and said, "I ought to punch you in the nose!"[35]

Few lives can withstand thorough scrutiny and a malicious interpretation of the findings, Wally Butts's less than most. From the opening day in court, lead *Post* lawyer Welborn Cody, an outstanding varsity baseball player at the University of Georgia, an offspring of a socially prominent family, and a partner of a leading Atlanta law firm, assaulted Butts's reputation. Balding, reserved, and mild-mannered, Cody was an excellent attorney, experienced in insurance defense work and libel suits.

William Schroder was widely considered one of the top trial

lawyers in the South. The former Notre Dame football player, University of Georgia freshman coach, and standout law student defended Butts. Henry Troutman, the senior partner of the respected Atlanta firm of Troutman, Sams, Schroder & Lockerman, was a close friend of Butts, perhaps giving Schroder an even more personal interest in the case. Regardless, Schroder's style was to wait for a mistake or injudicious opinion and attack with speed and energy that must have pleased the coach.[36]

The jury, twelve white men who obviously relished the chance to have a front-row seat at one of the biggest events of the year, was selected without much fanfare in less than an hour and a half. Then the opposing counsels laid out their positions. The *Saturday Evening Post* article accused Butts and Bryant of conspiring to fix the 1962 Alabama-Georgia game, which the Tide won 35–0, Cody said, adding that the charge was true and he planned to prove it. "We intend to show that the information was calculated to affect the results of the game." In his opening statement Cody said nothing unexpected.

Nor did Schroder unveil any surprises. He said the article was "utterly false" and he planned to prove it. He was not interested in winning the trial on some abstract technicality, or because of a lack of clear proof on the part of the defense lawyer. He sought to vindicate Butts and to restore the man's reputation. Schroder's passion contrasted sharply with Cody's cooler, more scholarly delivery, emphasizing his belief that he represented a wronged man, a good coach and faithful employee of the University of Georgia who had his faults, certainly, but deceitfulness and betrayal were not among them.[37]

The jury could see the sadness on Butts's face. Cody's defense was hindered by the lack of his own wronged man. A number of men had played a role in the publication of "The Story of a College

Football Fix"—most prominently Clay Blair Jr., Roger Kahn, Frank Graham Jr., and Furman Bisher. But none of those men were sitting beside Cody or anywhere else in the courtroom. It was as if Cody were defending a man without fingerprints, the specter of a defendant, detached from the decisions he made, the words he wrote, and the damage he inflicted. Tired and worn as he was, Wally Butts still aroused human emotions. Cody's missing defendants evoked little more than mild curiosity.

Cody began the defense case by reading the article to the jury. Well written, dramatic, and suspenseful, it made a compelling indictment of Butts and Bryant. A compelling indictment, that is, if it were true in all its parts and interpretations. To support the article, Cody also entered into the record the toll ticket of the phone calls between Butts and Bryant, establishing that the calls Frank Graham wrote about had occurred.[38]

To verify the facts of the story Cody called George Burnett to the stand. Burnett's appearance contrasted sharply with his dramatic story. Benny Marshall, who covered the trial for the *Birmingham News*, wrote that the key witness was "a beginning-to-be-fat fortyish...dark complexion, with a hair-line going thataway, a deep, low voice and a look that seems to say: 'I wish I were somewhere else.'" Dressed in a conservative, baggy dark suit, he looked like the last person one would expect to be at the center of a sports-related drama. But here he was, and looking at his notes as he answered questions, he confirmed that Graham's portrayal of the phone calls was accurate. He did not seem so much uncomfortable on the witness stand as detached, answering questions in a flat, businesslike voice as if he were recounting his activities on some uneventful day. As for the notes he had jotted down as he listened to the Butts-Bryant conversation, Burnett admitted that they made almost no sense to him. He didn't know the difference between an "overshift" and an "undershift," or if they were actual football terminology. Such terms, his testimony made clear, were inside football talk, and he was not an inside football man.

Schroder's probing cross-examination demonstrated that Frank Graham and the other men involved in the article were similarly not inside football people, and, more importantly, not very careful about the "facts" in "The Story of a College Football Fix." After eliciting that Burnett knew very little about football and had been paid the considerable sum of $5,000 for his story, Schroder turned his attention to the article itself. He established that the article had the wrong date for the crucial phone call—September 14, 1962, instead of the actual date of September 13. But the problems with the article did not end on that insignificant error. Under a withering cross, Burnett admitted that he had not made a number of critical charges—including that the game was "rigged" or "thrown" or was a "sellout"—that Graham attributed to him. Nor, Burnett said, had Graham ever seen the notes he had taken during the conversation. Furthermore, Graham had not shown him the article so that he could fact-check it. The impression that Schroder's questions and Burnett's answers conveyed was that Graham had played fast and loose with the facts of the case and had not taken the extra steps to ensure the accuracy of his devastating charges.

By the time Burnett left the witness stand on the second day it was clear that Schroder would not challenge that the crucial call occurred. Rather, his case revolved around two issues: first, that Burnett had no idea what Bryant and Butts were talking about and misinterpreted the conversation; and second, that Graham and the *Post* were guilty of incredibly sloppy, journalistically unprofessional work far below accepted standards. Even the witnesses that Cody called seemed to confirm Schroder's central lines of attack. J. D. Bolton, a University of Georgia official who was present when Butts was first presented with Burnett's story, admitted that Wally said, "No doubt the guy heard what he said he heard. I don't blame him for placing the interpretation that he did on the conversation.... But he was mistaken. It's just conversation, ordinary football talk among coaches, and you know I would never give old Bryant anything to help him hurt Georgia."[39]

Once again, the specter of coaches' talk swept across the courtroom. Was it some sort of mysterious code, some arcane language, incomprehensible to the ordinary person? To shed light on coaches' talk, Cody called Georgia coach John Griffith to the stand. The thin, quiet Griffith was not exactly a hostile witness for the defense, but he was hardly an enthusiastic one either. He was a losing football coach at a university with a proud football tradition, a coach whose job was on the line, and he clearly did not relish the opportunity to criticize two important men in his profession. Certainly, he suggested, there was a small germ of intelligence in the notes Burnett took on the Butts-Bryant phone call, but not much. Actually, Butts's report would have been more accurate in 1961 than 1962. And as for offensive and defensive formations, Georgia and Alabama ran pretty much the same ones. Clearly Griffith did not see much in Burnett's note that looked like inside dope.[40]

He was a better witness for the plaintiff. Schroder had only to nudge Griffith to get him to admit that he and his players had been badly misquoted in the article. Graham's story quoted Griffith as stating, "You know, during the first half of the Alabama game my players kept coming to the sidelines and saying, 'Coach, we've been sold out. Their linebackers are hollering our plays while we're still calling the signals.' " Asked about the quote, Griffith said, "I don't remember it." The article also quoted Griffith as lamenting, "We knew somebody'd given our plays to Alabama, and maybe to a couple of other teams we played too. But we had no idea it was Wally

Butts." Again, he said he had never made the statement. Finally, Schroder asked Griffith about his last quote in the article, his sad, bitter, disillusioned realization: "I never had a chance, did I? I never had a *chance*." Wasn't the quote "absolutely inaccurate?" Schroder asked. "Yes," the coach answered.

It was clear to virtually everyone in the courtroom—and every journalist covering the trial—that Cody's defense of the Curtis Publishing Company was absorbing crippling punishment. If it had been a boxing match, the referee would have stopped it. And the few Georgia assistant coaches who were called to try to repair Griffith's damaging testimony did little to buttress Cody's case.

At this point, however, Cody surprised everyone. He took a deep breath, looked at the jury and then the judge, and rested his case. That was it. Clay Blair Jr., Roger Kahn, and Frank Graham Jr. never had to venture to Atlanta to tell their stories. And Furman Bisher, who lived in Atlanta, did not have to brave the traffic to drive to the Post Office and Court Building. Legal scholar James Kirby, the SEC official observer at the trial, was as stunned as the spectators and Butts's lawyers. "They had fully expected the writer and the editors of the article to be put on the stand by the *Post* to defend their handiwork and, at least, to testify to their belief in its truth when they published it." But Cody chose to limit the damage. Under cross-examination Burnett had demonstrated conclusively that he knew almost nothing about the intricacies of football, and Griffith had admitted that he had no idea of the origins of the quotes attributed to him. Cody evidently decided that he did not want to call another witness who would help the plaintiff's case.[41]

In the early afternoon when Cody rested his case, Bryant was en route from Birmingham to Atlanta, assuming that he would not take the stand until the next day, Thursday, August 8. Bereft of his star witness, Schroder chose to lead off with Frank Graham Jr. Of course, Graham was hundreds of miles away from Atlanta, but Schroder had his deposition, which he read to the court. Schroder read the brief, matter-of-fact answers from the deposition in a flat, matter-of-fact voice, giving the reporter an air of casual, uncaring nonchalance. In the deposition Graham admitted that his fact-checking had been spotty, and that the words "rig" and "fix" had been added by his New York editors. The overall impression of the deposition—and especially Schroder's performance in it—was that Graham and his editors were more concerned with the sensational charges in the story than the actual facts, and that they did not try to question Butts or Bryant, confirm statements given to Furman Bisher, or give much thought to the harm the exposé might cause.[42]

That harm was given a face the next day. Bear Bryant arrived at the courtroom dressed fashionably in a seersucker jacket, white shirt, light tie, dark slacks, and alligator shoes. On a hot, humid southern day, he looked cool and composed, but he was in no mood for small talk. James Kirby thought he seemed "grim and preoccupied." A mutual friend introduced Kirby to Bryant on the steps outside of the courthouse, and when Bear learned that Kirby was the SEC representative he disdainfully brushed by the lawyer and moved up the steps. He had not come to Atlanta to meet new people or to exchange pleasantries, especially with a conference representative who Bear believed should have been investigating the *Post*'s editors, not standing in judgment of him.[43]

The night before, when Schroder and Butts's other attorneys had gone over the case with Bryant, he could sense their concern. He was edgy, angry over the charges, and bitter about the entire affair. He had come less to answer questions than to attack his accusers. "Wally's lawyers were afraid I'd be too hostile," he later wrote, and his appearance in the courtroom did nothing to alleviate their worries.[44]

An angry Bear Bryant was a cause for alarm. In his mellowest of moods, after a few glasses of scotch and in the company of good friends, he still dominated a room, not because he tried to but because he just did. He intimidated some people, frightened others, and just plain cowed the rest. Former player Bobby Marks's remark about Bryant—"I don't know what he had, but he had a lot of it"—applied to virtually all circumstances. It was impossible to say exactly why he was such a forceful personality, but he undeniably was. And in a courtroom, a man so singularly dynamic, so impossibly center-stage, was dangerous. Bear was a blunt man, and he would speak his mind.

In his report to SEC commissioner Bernie Moore, Kirby wrote that Bryant's testimony "was marked by an almost arrogant domination of the proceedings. He freely volunteered information beyond the scope of the questions, ridiculed questions, and by the power of his personal presence overwhelmed all in the court room. He was deadly serious." The description, of course, missed the point that Bear was just being Bear. Oblivious of the setting, he answered questions in his own way and at his own pace, unconcerned with measuring out judicious legal responses with teaspoons. If an attorney asked what he thought was a stupid question, he treated it like a foolish question by a sportswriter after Alabama lost a close game. He made no attempt to disguise his contempt.[45]

Bryant's friends better understood his emotions that day in court. Alabama sportswriter Benny Marshall told John Forney that "Bryant on the witness stand was the embodiment of barely-controlled fury, as if it were a real effort for him not to get off the witness stand and tear his accusers apart by hand. He said the malevolence in every aspect of him, his absolute conviction he had been wronged beyond repair, hypnotized the entire courtroom."[46]

Schroder began his direct examination of Bryant with a

question about the September 13 phone call from Butts. "Sir," Bear answered, "I don't know whether he made the call or not. I don't remember. According to the records of the telephone company which I have seen, of course, the call was made." The force of his delivery made it clear that he was not attempting to evade the question or in any way dance around it. The impact was more that of a busy man who made and received hundreds of calls, and the one between Butts and himself—one of many between the two—was simply not memorable. But when Schroder asked if Butts gave him any inside information about Georgia's game plan, he answered authoritatively, "Absolutely not, and had [he], I wouldn't have taken it, because he is for Georgia and I am for Alabama." It was that simple, he repeated. He liked Wally, and they were friends, but he asserted that anything Butts told him about Georgia would be worthless because of his support of the Bulldogs.[47]

After Bryant stated that the *Post*'s charges were totally false, Schroder turned to Burnett's infamous notes, passing a copy of them to the coach. Bryant looked at them, holding them out at arm's length, then confessed, "I don't have my specs. I left them on the plane." That set off a scramble to aid the coach. Several jury members offered their reading glasses, as did Schroder. Bear tried Schroder's, but the prescription was not to his liking, then borrowed a pair of Wally Butts's glasses, which suited his needs. As he grumbled in a low voice throughout the brief episode, the touch of frailty only increased his appeal. Misplacing his "specs" and fumbling through the embarrassment of borrowing a pair—a touch of George Washington quelling the Newburgh conspiracy— made the mythic coach seem more mortal, just another man who was adjusting to the effects of aging.

Bryant handled the document with the dismissive disdain he believed it deserved. Point by point, he discussed the material in the notes, going to a blackboard, diagramming plays and formations, and explaining carefully and in great depth that the words the insurance salesman jotted down—and that the men at the *Saturday Evening Post* believed constituted a conspiracy to fix a football game—were at best trivial but on the whole meaningless. Watching Bryant, Kirby noted that the "jurors and spectators alike—even the judge—were held spellbound" by his magnificent performance. Many people in the courtroom were undoubtedly mystified by the coach's technical discussion of the game, but he left an indelible impression in their minds that Burnett knew nothing about football strategy, techniques, or formations.[48]

Bryant denied that he and Butts had talked about the details in the notes, but even if they had, the contents were worthless. "Those notes, as far as I am concerned, would not help me one iota," he said. His staff had worked several months on their scouting report for the Georgia game, had finalized it before the phone conversation, and had changed nothing after Bear and Wally talked. Anything worth knowing in the notes Bryant already knew. If he didn't, he remarked, "I oughta be bored for a hollow head." There were, of course, things that he would have liked to have known—Georgia's game plan, its strategy according to where it was positioned on the field, its repertoire of first-down plays and big-down plays—but Burnett's notes contained no information on such important matters.

No doubt, Bear confessed, the insurance salesman had heard him and Wally talk about football. "You can't get two coaches together when they don't talk about that," he said. But they did not talk about anything relevant to the Alabama-Georgia game. And most assuredly Bryant did not sit in his university office and discuss rigging a game.

Finishing his examination of Bryant, Schroder returned to the

Post's allegations. After reading Kahn's precede comparing Butts and Bryant to the notorious Chicago Black Sox fixers, he asked, "Did you and the plaintiff in this case, Wallace Butts, throw, fix or rig the outcome of the Georgia-Alabama game as you have been charged with doing by the *Saturday Evening Post*?"

The room by this time was deathly quiet, and every eye was on Bryant, who seemed to visibly stiffen at the question. "Absolutely not, and if we did we ought to go to jail," he answered before turning his attention to the men behind the article and adding, "and anybody who had anything to do with this ought to go to jail, because we didn't. Taking their money is not good enough."

The words alone did not convey the feelings behind them. The statement was the emotional height of Bryant's testimony, the perfect time for Schroder to say that he had no more questions and turn the angry coach over to Welborn Cody. The contempt Bear harbored for the men at the *Post* swept over the mild, soft-spoken defense attorney. Some observers thought Bryant intimidated Cody, and perhaps he did, but more likely after a few questions the Georgia lawyer realized a vigorous cross would not help his case. Bryant had won over the jury, and after ten minutes Cody announced he had no further questions.[49]

Bear's job was done and he was free to leave the courtroom. But after rising from the witness chair and taking a few steps, he asked, "Can't I wait for my boys?" It was a perfect finish. The next three witnesses—Jimmy Sharpe, Charley Pell, and Lee Roy Jordan— were Alabama players, Bear's Boys, come to court to testify that there was no way the game could have been rigged without their knowledge. "All Coach Bryant said was to tell the truth," recalled Jordan, "and that was the truth—the whole truth and nothing but the truth." Bryant's concern for his players completed the circle that had begun with the "specs" comment. It testified, in effect, that here was a hard, bitter, angry man, but a man of deep human compassion as well.[50]

Seated inside the rail just behind Butts, James Kirby had a ringside seat for Bryant's testimony. A law professor at the University of Tennessee with an extensive legal track record, he labeled Bryant's appearance "a virtuoso performance," convincing everyone in earshot that he was not the sort of man who asked for or needed any illegally obtained information to win a game. "Bryant continues to be," Kirby wrote years later, "the single most awesome figure this writer has ever seen in a courtroom, including lawyers and judges."[51]

———

Some trials are decided before the jury ever retires to deliberate; some are even finished well before the final witness is called and the opposing attorneys make the closing arguments. *Wally Butts v. the Curtis Publishing Company* ended when Bear Bryant asked if he could wait for his boys. Other witnesses approached the stand, put their hands on the Bible, and had their say. Wally Butts was one of them. On August 9 he got his chance to deny the charges under oath. Looking tired, even broken, the once confident man repeated much of what the jury had already heard—that he talked to Bryant often, that he didn't recall the full substance of the conversation, that he emphatically was not party to a fixed game.

The most touching moment in Butts's testimony came in the redirect. As he had done with Bryant, Schroder read the precede of the article and then asked, "Does that editorial contain any truth insofar as you, Coach Wallace Butts, the plaintiff in this lawsuit, is concerned?" "No," Butts answered. "And I would like to explain that for a time I hid from people, but not anymore. I am looking them in the eye because it is not true." As he spoke his own eyes filled with tears and he quietly sobbed. He clenched his fists, trying to compose himself. Failing that, Kirby observed, "he stumbled from the stand and slumped into a chair at his lawyers' table." During a short recess spectators remained seated, some crying themselves, numbly quiet and respectful of the former Georgia coach, the "Little Round Man," once the toast of Atlanta.[52]

If Schroder needed any more drama, the *Post*'s editor in chief, Clay Blair Jr., provided it. Although Blair did not testify, Schroder read his deposition into the record. In one section the editor was asked if he had received a telephone call from Butts's daughter Jean. Blair recalled that he had, adding that she was trying to discover if "we were doing a story, I think, or if we were, when it would be out, something like that." She was so emotional that Blair could not determine precisely what she wanted. Asked to explain his answer, Blair said, "Well, my impression was that she was trying to find out (a) if we were doing an article on her father, and (b) if we were, when it was coming out. It seemed to me that was what she was trying to get at, but it would be presumptuous here or any other time for me to try to interpret what any woman is really getting at when she talks to you."[53]

"Did you tell her an article was going to be published concerning her father?" Schroder asked.

"I swear to you, I can't remember," Blair answered. "I am not trying to dodge your question. I am—I get a hundred phone calls a day, you know, more or less, and it is hard to remember, but I don't know whether I told her specifically whether we were coming out with this article or not."

Blair was in the courtroom beside the magazine's lawyers at 3:03 p.m. on August 19 when the closing arguments concluded and the jury departed the courtroom to deliberate. He was with the lawyers at 10:25 the next morning when the court marshal announced that the jury had reached a decision and was returning to the court. Though it was a sizzling August morning, spectators ran into the courthouse and up the steps to claim their seats for the reading of the verdict.[54]

The legal niceties were all followed—the judge asked if the jury had reached a decision; the jury foreman said yes and handed a slip of paper to the marshal, who showed it to the judge. Judge Morgan looked at it impassively and handed it to the court clerk sitting to the right of the bench. "The clerk will read the verdict," he said. She began to read, "We the jury find in favor of Wallace Butts." The clerk announced that the jury had awarded Butts $60,000 in general damages and $3 million in punitive damages. It made the total package the second-largest libel award "ever in the world."[55]

Blair appeared stunned by the verdict. Looking like he had missed the important detail, he turned to one of his lawyers and asked, "Did she say *three* million?" Perhaps the specter he saw was the ghost of the *Saturday Evening Post*'s future.

For the second time Wally Butts began to sob. Surrounded by his wife and daughters, all of whom were also in tears, he sat in his chair, unsmiling, looking every inch a defeated man. Aware of the pressure Butts had carried for months, Schroder leaned over to him, whispering, "Let it come, Wally. Let it come, boy." Only later would Butts manage a smile for the cameramen, but it looked forced, the smile of a boy who had stubbed his toe and any second might start crying again.[56]

Still later that day Bryant called Butts. "Hey, Wally," he said. "What happened to the rest of it?"

———

The trial was over. Sportswriter Benny Marshall said that Coach Bryant was twenty feet tall before the accusations and was still the same height after the verdict. Friends of the coach assumed he would be bitter and belligerent, nursing a grudge like a glass of thirty-five-year-old scotch. They were right. "Bryant is bitter. He is belligerent," wrote Marshall. The accusations and the intense two-week trial, Bear said, had been hard on his family, and by occupying so much of his time had forced him to commit an "injustice" toward the University of Alabama. Now it was time to get back to work. In a month the Tide would play its season opener against Georgia, and before then the coaching staff had to develop a game plan and prepare a team. "I'm going to be at bat a lot from now on, I'll tell you," Bear said. That was a Bryantism for long, long days on the job, paying back the university for the time he owed.[57]

During the season Bryant ignored his two multimillion-dollar suits against the *Saturday Evening Post*. After Alabama's 1964 Sugar Bowl game, he turned his attention back to the lawsuits. By then the Atlanta trial judge had ruled that Butts's $3,060,000 award was "grossly excessive" and had reduced it to $460,000. After income tax deductions and lawyers' fees Butts cleared less than $100,000. It was sobering information for Bryant. It hardly made the effort, publicity, toll on his family, and risk of another trial worthwhile.

As the date of Bryant's trial approached, the nagging worry and the sleepless nights returned. How could he control what the *Post* and other publications said about him? How many people were there nursing a grudge against him, or just out for their fifteen minutes of fame? "You begin to think anything can happen, and anything can be said," Bryant wrote. "One of the things that crossed my mind was they'd bring in some sensational witness who would testify to some lie, that I'd done this, that, or the other."[58]

In early February Bryant settled his suits out of court for a tax-free payment of $300,000. The entire amount was paid to him as compensatory damages—direct payment for emotional suffering, loss of salary, and loss of status in the football community—which carried no tax burden. Had part of the payment been in punitive damages it would have been taxed as regular income. This arrangement meant that Bear actually received more money than Wally Butts. Given the 75 percent tax rates for high incomes, the *New York Times* estimated that Bryant would have to have received more than 2.5 million in taxable dollars to equal the settlement.[59]

Bear wasn't satisfied with the settlement—he would have rather seen his accusers behind bars than receive their money. But he did enjoy the tax-free aspect. Whenever he talked about the settlement he would say, "I got $300,000," pause a moment, and add, "and it was tax free." Jim Murray, one of Bryant's harshest critics, even had to tip his hat at the payout. "The biggest money-making story about the South ever written was not 'Gone With the Wind,' it was 'The Story of a College Football Fix.'"[60]

The settlement was also paid the way Bear wanted it. After the settlement was reached, the *Post*'s lawyers said they would send a check the next day. "I don't want your check, I want money," Bryant said, a not-so-subtle suggestion that he did not trust the company's financial status. The next day he received cashier's checks for the full amount.[61]

———

The two great crises of the summer were over. The University of Alabama, with the aid of the federal government, had weathered the interference of George Wallace and desegregated. Although it would continue to be a slow, painful process, it had been done. And Bear Bryant had gone to Atlanta, testified, and returned to Tuscaloosa with his reputation and career intact. Although his worst calamity was over, his troubles were not.

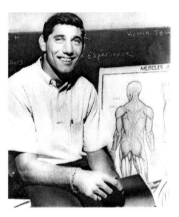

Despite his substandard SAT scores and the fact that his study habits were not stellar, Namath never incurred any academic problems while majoring in industrial arts at Alabama. Here he sits in a physical education classroom. (Bryant Museum)

9

"Living Like Yankees, Playing Like Barber College"

Unless you carry the gipsy eyes
That see but seldom weep,
Keep your head from the naked skies
Or the stars'll trouble your sleep.
—Rudyard Kipling, "Gipsy Vans"

O N SUNDAY MORNING, September 15, 1963, Frank Cicatiello drove toward the Birmingham airport with his friend Jimmy Walsh and Walsh's sister. She was heading home to New Jersey after a visit with her brother and his friends, including Joe. It had all been great fun to be part of the student body as the new semester began, when all of the students returned to Tuscaloosa with the kind of optimism that greets the beginning of a new school year, where every class and classmate looks interesting. The University of Alabama had more reason to be optimistic than most schools—it survived the summer of its desegregation without the kind of violence that convulsed the campus of Ole Miss and seemed on the verge of a very special rebirth as a southern institution not bound by all of the region's racial animosity. And the football team once again looked like a national power. But nonviolence in integrating the University of Alabama did not mean the state had escaped its past.

Cicatiello drove the borrowed Chevy on State Route 7, which became First Avenue in the Birmingham city limits. It was a drive he had taken numerous times to Birmingham in general and Legion Field specifically. At Tenth Street, things got a bit crowded. Cicatiello thought little of it, since it was a Sunday morning. At Fourteenth Street, it became apparent that this was no ordinary traffic jam, as cars tried desperately to get around others in a frenetic dash through the side streets. He knew that something serious had happened, and his thoughts were confirmed as he approached Sixteenth Street and saw a small army of state troopers and national guardsmen lined up with shotguns ready to fire at anyone attempting a left-hand turn. It was a scene that had become commonplace over the summer—the kind of war zone landscape that had turned Birmingham into "Bombingham." Sirens roared and dust filled the air just west of where they passed on their way to the airport. Fall had arrived in Tuscaloosa with the start of classes at the university, but it seemed summer was not yet over in Birmingham.[1]

What Cicatiello and the Walshes saw was the aftermath of the Sixteenth Street Baptist Church bombing, a segregationist response to the federal court order to admit five black students to public schools. The blast killed four young black girls working on their Sunday school lesson, "The Love That Forgives," and once again focused national and international attention on Birmingham. Martin Luther King Jr. delivered a eulogy for three of the girls, as the city braced itself for another round of violence. President Kennedy responded by dispatching two mediators to Birmingham—former army secretary Kenneth Royall and former West Point football coach Earl Blaik. Like at Ole Miss when he tried to enroll Johnny Vaught in halting the violence, Kennedy seemed unable to approach the troubled South without at least a nod to its passion for football.[2]

In Tuscaloosa, the students may not have looked at football as a remedy for the state's racial strife, but it certainly offered a respite from the stress. George Wallace and Bull Connor had the summer, but Bear Bryant got the fall. There was every reason to have high expectations—the team was ranked number three in the country, behind Southern Cal and Ole Miss, and there was little doubt that it had a quarterback ready to lead the team to a national championship. Joe Willie was no longer the unknown commodity taking the field for his first season. He was now a veteran leader, familiar with Bear and his methods, and the proverbial big man on campus. What could go wrong?

In a picture in the 1962 *Corolla*, Alabama's annual, two attractive coeds appear looking up at someone in slight surprise. "So that's the 'Bear,' huh?" the caption reads. "I always thought he had a halo." That Bryant was a football messiah was a common refrain among the fans. For the coaches and players, though, a more fitting analogy was military in nature—Bear was "General Bryant," the coaches were lieutenants, and the players were the infantry.[3]

Like a general, Bryant led by a combination of knowledge and intimidation, and no one wilted under his presence more than Larry "Dude" Hennessey. Hennessey played for Bryant at Kentucky in the early 1950s and joined the Alabama staff as ends coach in the fall of 1960. From the start, he fell under a kind of spell when Bryant was near. At coaches' meetings he stuttered and stammered, barely able to get across any information regardless of who asked so long as Bryant was in the room. Out of the offices he was even worse. Once, at Indian Hills golf course in Tuscaloosa, he was finishing off the best round of his life and beating a couple of other coaches by a few strokes. As he stepped up to his ball and prepared for a three-foot putt for birdie, Bear, who had been eating lunch at the clubhouse, came to watch. The rest of the threesome—and probably Bryant himself—knew that Hennessey was in trouble when Bryant asked, "Who's winning?" All eyes went to Hennessey, who by this time could barely hold his putter. With Bryant watching, Hennessey knocked the first putt fifteen feet past the hole, four-putted the green, and lost the match.

Hennessey's behavior was even more humorous when Bryant was out of sight but much in mind. The Bryant home sat behind the third green at Indian Hills, and although Bryant was rarely there during the spring and summer golf season, Hennessey became so fearful of a chance meeting while searching for a ball or addressing a shot that he made it his habit to skip number three altogether. He once walked directly from the number three tee to the number four tee even though everyone knew Bear was in West Germany on a goodwill tour of military bases. On another occasion Hennessey, returning home from a late night at a bar, hit the side of a slow-moving train that regularly ran through Tuscaloosa. Stopping the train, the conductor recognized Hennessey and, knowing how employees of the athletic department feared being caught in embarrassing situations, offered up a solution: "You fix yours and I'll fix mine, okay?" Hennessey shouted back, "Yeah! Don't tell Coach, will ya?"[4]

Howard Schnellenberger was no Dude Hennessey when it came to Bryant, but he still understood the military-style hierarchy of the coaching staff. Bryant recruited him to play at Kentucky, but when Bear took the head coaching job at Texas A&M in 1953, the All-American end played out his varsity career for Blanton Collier. It was a good fit for Schnellenberger, as Collier was an offensive innovator who came to Kentucky after serving as an assistant on Cleveland Browns head coach Paul Brown's staff. With Cleveland, Collier tutored Otto Graham and helped lead the team to eight consecutive championship games, first in the All-America Football Conference, then in the NFL. Working with Paul Brown was a revelation—the coach literally created the game's first playbook, was the first to use game film to prepare his team, and invented the facemask. He designed the pro-style offense from which all other professional offenses emerged. Collier soaked up Brown's methods and gained a reputation as a friendly but studious coach. Three years into his career as Kentucky's head coach, he brought back Schnellenberger as his ends coach.

An old adage, usually ascribed to Woody Hayes, held that when you threw the ball three things could happen and two of them were bad. Bear's analysis was a bit more brutal. If you throw the ball, he said, "someone in the stands might have a gun and shoot the receiver." When Namath came to Alabama, Bryant put aside his fear of assassins and began a decade-long acceptance of the forward pass.[5]

Schnellenberger brought Brown's system to Alabama. For Joe, it was not as complicated as it appeared to someone unfamiliar with the position of quarterback. He had a couple dozen base plays, about eight per down (four runs and four passes), with minor variations depending on the yardage needed for a first down. Under center, he decided whether to stay with the play called in the huddle or audible to a different play based upon the defensive alignment, usually

262 • RISING TIDE

dictated by the location of the strong safety.

dictated by the location of the strong safety. At the line he began his signals with a color—either a "hot" color, a predetermined word that the coaches changed every game to let the offense know that Joe was changing the play call, or a "decoy" color, a word that told the offense that the play called in the huddle remained intact and the rest of Joe's audible was a fake. He needed to remain consistent in his cadence and volume on these signals to keep from tipping the defense as to an audible and its color. After the snap, he continued to read the defense as he began his drop—for a passing play, three, five, or seven steps behind the line of scrimmage, depending on the length of the receiver's route. Again, consistency and the speed of his drop were the most important factors. Then he needed to see the field and decide which receiver *would be* open, then throw the ball to where that player *would be* positioned.

Joe learned to read defenses in Beaver Falls. His cadence needed no work and he had the quickest dropback of anyone in the game. In the pocket, he saw the field "generally" rather than "specifically," meaning that he never became too focused on any single defender and was able to find the open receiver quickly. He stood squared to the defense when preparing to throw, a position that enabled him to pass to either side of the field without any additional shifting of his body. He never "danced" or "floated" while scanning the field, but stayed where his linemen expected him to be as they blocked. Then he released the ball, quickly but not hurriedly and at the proper speed.[6]

Offensive linemen carried the plays in from the sidelines. Paul Brown called his plays with "messenger guards," interchangeable offensive linemen who shuttled in and out on each down. He had developed the system at Massillon High School on a cold day while sitting in his car, which he'd parked on the sidelines. There Brown cracked his window and relayed the plays he wanted run to his linemen, thus staying warm. Schnellenberger put his own twist on this system. He may have trusted Namath to run the offense, but he did not put much faith in the offensive linemen shuttling in the plays. He was not about to risk a game and his job on some "dumb-assed guard remembering to call a 3-6 firetrap on two." So he wrote the plays on small bits of paper and had the guards hand them to Joe. On strips a little larger than a fortune from a Chinese cookie, Namath read off the play. Then, to make sure that there was no evidence for the opposition to capture, he ate the paper. "It was that," Schnellenberger reasoned, "or send Hoot Owl onto the field to pick up the trash."[7]

On September 21, Alabama opened its season against Georgia at Sanford Stadium in Athens. It was a day short of the anniversary of the *Saturday Evening Post* "fix" game, but if that provided motivation for an Alabama victory, no one, especially Bear, was letting on. Georgia won the coin toss and elected to kick off. On third down on the first drive, Namath fumbled away the football at his own 26-yard line. A few plays later, Georgia scored a touchdown and set off the crowd of 44,000 surprised but happy fans.

Namath drove the Tide into scoring position the second time he had the ball, but again turned the ball over, this time on an interception. The Alabama defense held, and Joe got the ball back for the third time. After a series of runs by Mike Fracchia, in his first game back after his knee injury, Alabama set up at the Georgia 47-yard line. The defense cheated to the line as Namath called out the signals. Recognizing the coverage, Charlie Stephens ran a deep route behind the pressing safety and found himself alone at the 15. The pass was short, and he came back to the 20 to catch it, then, allowing the safety to overrun him, reversed field for Alabama's first touchdown of the season. Alabama added a field goal late in the second quarter and led 10–7 at the half.

In the third quarter, the Tide stopped Georgia and after a short punt took over deep in Bulldogs territory. A few good plays advanced the ball inside the five-yard line. But then Namath fumbled again. Fortunately for him, the Georgia offense fumbled the ball back immediately, and Fracchia ran in for a touchdown to give the Tide a 17–7 lead. After Georgia fumbled again, and Fracchia scored again, Namath's day was done. Alabama added a safety and Hurlbut threw a 41-yard touchdown pass, ending the scoring and the game at 32–7.[8]

After the game, Benny Marshall of the *Birmingham News* focused on ending the *Saturday Evening Post* controversy. "The score now for three years of Bryant vs. Griffith, Crimson Tide vs. Bulldogs, is 99 to 13," he wrote. "And what this establishes is that Coach Bryant of Alabama didn't need Butts last year or the year before, or any year, to be master of this situation." He also welcomed Fracchia "back on beam," but the game itself was a sloppy affair, not worthy of the preseason accolades lavished upon the Crimson Tide. "Joe Namath is still Joe Namath," Marshall added, "though his first half was not his sparkling best." Marshall was being kind—Namath had played poorly, fumbling twice at crucial spots on the field and throwing an interception that halted a scoring drive. Even his touchdown pass was underthrown and but for Stephens's exceptional effort would not have resulted in a score. For Alabama and its fans, it had been a nice victory by a healthy margin but far from a great game.[9]

Although Bear told the press that the *Saturday Evening Post* case added nothing to his desire to beat Georgia, his postgame comments had more malice than usual. "Georgia is not as good as I thought," he said. When asked to elaborate, he answered, "I mean as a football team. I honestly thought they had a chance to have a real fine football team." After that dismissal, he questioned his offense. "I felt like if we'd run at 'em straight a little more we might have been better off." If it was a message to Schnellenberger, it got through. As the team prepared for its next game with Tulane, there would be a bit more attention paid to wearing down an overmatched opponent, and considerably more emphasis placed on the running game.[10]

Heading into its second game, Alabama was ranked number two in the nation behind defending national champions Southern Cal. But before the Tide took the field for the evening game against Tulane in Mobile, they already knew that Oklahoma had defeated USC that afternoon. With a strong performance, they had a chance to take over the top spot in the poll.

In front of a crowd of a little over 32,000 fans seated under threatening skies in a sopping heat, Namath brought his offense onto the field and proceeded to hand the ball off for the first seven plays of the drive. On the eighth play, he threw his first pass, a completion from the 12-yard line to the four. Two plays later, he sneaked over for his first rushing touchdown of the season and a 7–0 lead.

In the second quarter, Alabama faced a fourth and inches at the Tulane 32. Namath, standing over center, peered at the defense bunched to stop another quarterback sneak, took the snap, and flipped the ball out to Benny Nelson, who weaved his way to a touchdown. After an interception return for a touchdown, Alabama led 21–0 at the half.

In the second half, Alabama worked to increase its lead. Midway through the third quarter, the Tide scored on another perfectly executed pitchout from Namath, and with twenty-three minutes left and the game under control, Bryant rested Joe, replacing him with sophomore Steve Sloan. For Namath, it was a workmanlike but unremarkable performance that Alf Van Hoose of the *Birmingham News* compared to "Grant's march on Richmond, the frontal assault with superior manpower."[11]

When the Associated Press tabulated the votes for its September 30 poll, Oklahoma was number one, having leaped over Alabama based on its 17–12 win at Southern Cal. It was a legitimate choice. Oklahoma beat a team that had not lost in a year, and Alabama beat a team that had not won in a year. Still, for Alabama fans the results were disappointing.[12]

Benny Marshall tried to build the tension before the next game against Vanderbilt by asking Bryant if he thought at all about Vandy in terms of the Howard (now Samford) team that tied Alabama in 1935. "Alabama elected me to our all-opponents team," Bryant said as he remembered his poor showing as a player that day. But his heart was not really in the joke. As Marshall wrote, "The third week of football season is not a laughing time."[13]

It was another muggy night, this time in Nashville, and both squads matched the damp weather, as neither team did anything on the first four series of the game. Finally, with the ball at midfield on a second and eight, Namath brought his team to the line and drew the defense in close to the center with a series of quick signals. When the defense dove toward him at the snap of the ball, he jumped and shot a lateral out to Nelson, who took the ball to the outside and outran the safety for a touchdown. After a Vanderbilt score, Namath returned and continued to set up run plays to the outside with his snap counts and quick pitches. Deep into Vanderbilt territory, he ran an option and, just before being hit by several defenders, stopped and passed to Nelson for 17 yards. After Fracchia dove into the end zone from one yard out, the score was 14–6 at halftime.

When Nelson took the second-half kickoff 97 yards for another touchdown and Namath once again drove the team to the one-yard line midway through the third quarter, it looked as if Alabama was in complete control. On second down at the one, Joe fumbled the snap and Vanderbilt took over. Then, on his next possession, he again fumbled away the ball on the Commodore 41. Alabama's defense held, and the final score was 21–6.[14]

Although he was praised for his handling of the ground game and throwing precise passes, Namath's fumbling was an issue. He was four of six in passing for 45 yards, but for the second time in three games he had fumbled the ball away twice. For the season, he was 14 of 28 for 184 yards, with one touchdown pass and one interception, hardly All-American statistics. Bear was quick to acknowledge how proud he was of the victory, but he was not happy. "We're not tough," he said. "We've just got a nice bunch of boys, and they play like nice boys." As he prepared his team for its first game in Tuscaloosa, his concern bubbled over into cynicism. "We're living like Yankees and playing like Barber College."[15]

The Monday after the Vanderbilt game, Bear called for a 5:30 a.m. team meeting and "peeled the paint off the walls." He voiced his disappointment more calmly to Benny Marshall, telling him that the worst thing was his "wanting them to be so good so bad." He also said that Namath's poor play was nothing to worry about, regarding it as the same as Sandy Koufax getting knocked out of a game. "I don't think having a bad night helps your morale much, but that doesn't mean anything if you've got class. Joe's got class." Bear was correct—Koufax had been knocked out of several games over the summer of '63, including a first-inning departure against the Giants when he gave up five runs while getting only one out. The problem was that Koufax started forty games and Namath got only ten chances each regular season. The other problem was that Koufax could lose a few games and still win the World Series, which was what happened in 1963. If 1962 proved anything, it was that Joe needed only to lose one game to lose the national championship. Bryant ended the interview with a burst of confidence. "No sir! I'm not worried about our quarterbacking," he said. "Jack Hurlbut was throwing the ball better Tuesday than he has in a long time, and Joe's running real well, too." Bear seemed to have a relief pitcher in mind already.[16]

Bryant also promised to toughen up the team, but since Mondays were "heavy class" days, he had to wait until the evening to start the process. Joe attended classes that day, and while no one ever said he was not intelligent, no one ever accused him of working too hard in the classroom either.

At most schools the classroom was a place where mostly bad things could happen to a football player. Namath's major was industrial arts, and all he sought to do was pass through the classrooms with as little notice from the professors as possible. But the fear that an error might jeopardize his time on the football field always hung over his days. On one occasion, Dr. Clark, his professor in a sheet metal and woodworking class, asked him, "Are you sure you're in this class?" Well into the semester and preparing to take an exam that week, Joe immediately got up and ran from the classroom, across campus to the coaches' offices, and grabbed Mike Daniels, the academic advisor to the football team. Daniels assured him and Clark that Joe belonged in the class, was on the roster, and should be given the exam. It had been an innocent error, caused primarily by Clark's daft personality (years later he was arrested in Memphis for impersonating a naval officer), but the idea that anything might hinder the progress of his football career scared Joe.[17]

The tough preparation did not eliminate Thursday "dress-up" day, an Alabama football tradition that allowed the players to pose for a photograph in slightly altered practice attire. The "costuming," as the newspapers generously referred to it, consisted mostly of players tying their shirts up in the middle, creating an effeminate look that the Dallas Cowboys cheerleaders would make famous. Joe stuck with a regular practice jersey without the knot, but added a wide strip of cloth around his forehead in the style of a kamikaze.[18]

The Florida Gators came to Tuscaloosa on October 12 with a record of 1–1–1. They lost their season opener to Georgia Tech 9–0 in Atlanta, tied Mississippi State 9–9 at home, then beat Richmond by a touchdown. Bear never took an opponent lightly, especially a conference foe, and looked upon Florida as if they were Y. A. Tittle's New York Giants coming to town, despite their middling record. "Florida has the greatest potential of any team in the Conference," Bryant wrote in the pregame itinerary. "We face our greatest challenge. When opportunity meets challenge the result is a clear cut victory to the team who is best prepared and who carries out that preparation, both physical and mental, in Denny Stadium this Saturday. That team will be Alabama!!!!"[19]

Florida was motivated too, as the team realized that its well-liked coach, Ray Graves, was under pressure to turn the season around. At the beginning of the second quarter, trailing 3–0, Namath lined up the team at midfield and threw a short pass to Charlie Stephens that bounded off his hands into a defender's arms. Alabama's defense stopped Florida twice deep in scoring position, first from the three, then from the six, without allowing any more points before halftime.

In the third quarter, Namath threw another interception. The crowd groaned at the turnover, then surged in support of its defense as they seemed to realize that this was not going to be an easy game to win.

Halfway through the fourth quarter, Florida scored a touchdown, and it looked as if the game might be over. No one left the stadium, though, as Namath led the team to the Florida 44. On fourth and 10, he threw a perfect pass to Jimmy Dill for 23 yards to keep the game in doubt. With three minutes left, Joe lined up the Tide at the one-yard line and, on his second try, took the ball over the goal line. In a move reminiscent of the Georgia Tech game a year earlier, Bear went for the two-point conversion to set up a potential game-winning field goal, but like the previous year the attempt failed, putting Alabama behind, 10–6. An onside kick was perfectly placed, but Alabama failed to fall on it and Florida recovered to give Bear his first loss at Denny Stadium.[20]

On the Thursday following the loss, the *Crimson White* ran an editorial entitled "Making Football Fun Again":

Last Saturday's loss brought to mind how much fun it used to be to go to football games back in the year one B.B. (Before Bryant), when the Crimson Tide lost sometimes. Back then a student could feel empathy with the team, since both student and team usually came out on the losing end of everything. Back then games were exciting: one never knew when the other team was going to score.

But gee whiz, it sure hasn't been fun in recent years, when you [knew] beforehand who was going to win. There has been no suspense left. The only thing we've had to worry about was whether or not it was going to rain, or how much peanuts were going to cost, or which belt to wear. And the only excitement has been when a fight started in the stands, or when somebody out of sheer boredom—drank too much and dived off the top of the stadium.

But things are looking up this year; maybe it'll be like old times. Thanks a lot, team—for making football fun again.[21]

It was meant to be humorous, but few around campus laughed, and no one seemed angrier than the school paper's sports editor, Lonnie Falk, who wrote a countereditorial the following week that assured readers on campus that the "Making Football Fun Again" column "was written by a member of the editorial board without any knowledge of the Sports staff"—the kind of person who not only disgusted Falk personally, but also hurt the university with his sentiment:

We do not hope to contend here that it cannot give any people joy to watch the home team lose. There are people of this sort in all walks of life. But to us it seems that they are closely akin to those who enjoy automobile races just to see the crashes, or go to a bullfight and cheer the bull.[22]

For Alabama fans, Falk stated the obvious—the university was football and football was the university, and to work against one was to harm the other. Crimson Tide football to a student was more than a game.

One thing the Florida game revealed was that the passing offense that Schnellenberger had expanded specifically for Namath was not working. Joe's leadership in the final drive looked heroic, but it was the heroism of defeat. He had played another poor game, completing 10 of 25 passes for 104 yards, with no touchdowns and two interceptions. Another thing the game showed was that the Tide was simply not strong enough to beat a decent team, even at Denny, without playing well itself. Bear's postgame analysis spoke to the systemic problem he had to solve. "I think," he told assistant coach Pat James, "that was the poorest conditioned team we've put on the field." The Tide fell from number two to nine in the nation.[23]

Before the next game against Tennessee, Bryant sat under the east stands of Legion Field in Birmingham with a cigarette and can of Coke. "It gets harder when you get the gray hairs," he said, the "harder" referring not to the game but to the wait before it. He was always pessimistic in front of the media, but this time Benny Marshall detected genuine concern in the Bear's voice—despite his pregame comments the week before, Bear had not anticipated losing to Florida, and he was trying to figure the direction of his team. After some private words in the locker room, he returned with the team, telling Marshall on his way to the field, "I'll see you after."[24]

Midway through the first quarter, Namath led the offense from its own 36-yard line, and it looked as if Bryant had once again overruled Schnellenberger's passing game for the afternoon. Alabama ran on seven of its first eight plays, with Nelson running in for a score from 36 yards. But after Tennessee fumbled the ensuing kickoff, giving Alabama the ball at the 26-yard line, Namath took the first-down snap and bounded back seven steps and looked for Dill. Dill's pattern took him past the defender to the end zone, then required him to come back to the goal line for the ball—variously known as a "comeback," "back shoulder," or "deliberate under-throw"—as the cover man overran him. Namath placed the ball perfectly, and Dill walked in for the score.

In the second quarter Joe continued to throw. He completed three passes to Tommy Tolleson to set up a three-yard jump pass that ended the first half 21–0. Then in the third quarter he threw for a touchdown on the Tide's opening drive and ran for one on its next possession, making the score 35–0 and ending his day. Sloan came in to finish off the game.[25]

In the locker room after the game, Bryant spoke over the sounds of a happy team. "We got more breaks today than I've ever seen a football team get," he told the press. It was true—Tennessee had fumbled the ball away six times—but the Bear's tenor seemed much more like his old "hangdog" ways than his pregame anxiety under the bleachers. As for his quarterback, Bryant said, "Namath was as sharp as I've ever seen him. He ran his game plan beautifully and his passing was excellent." This also was true—Joe's statistics finally read like *Sport* magazine had anticipated they would, completing 12 of 20 passes for 141 yards, with no interceptions, three touchdown passes, and one touchdown run. More importantly, he had led the team to a much-needed, dominant victory.[26]

After the Florida game, Bryant promised more physical practices. "We got to hit some this week and it helped," he told the press. "We'll hit some more next week, too. At least two days."[27]

After the Florida victory, the team returned to Tuscaloosa, a town Joe preferred to Birmingham. It was not that Tuscaloosa smelled any better than Birmingham—the paper mills filled the air with the stench of sulfur, reminiscent of raw eggs—but the campus was the rural paradise Namath had dreamed of when he left the grit of Beaver Falls. Trees and manicured lawns softened the odor from the mills, but for Joe it was the coeds that chased it from his senses. The most famous group of coeds were the "Bama Belles," attractive girls photographed and featured on the front page of the *Crimson White*. "Pretty Faye Fuller, sophomore from Miami, is this week's Bama Belle," read one of 1963's weekly installments. "The psychology major said she has only one complaint about 'Bama: 'Not enough dates.' She lives in 207 Mary Burke." The *Corolla* revisited the Bama Belles annually in a section titled "Beauties" that presented the coeds in a series of more professional studio photographs.[28]

Bebe Schreiber was a perennial Belle, a finalist for the *Corolla* Beauty Contest, and Joe's steady girlfriend. In the sea of southern belles, she stood out not only for her stunning beauty but also for her nonchalance. Even in the formal photographs, wearing a cocktail dress, high heels, and white gloves with her arm crooked at an unnatural angle, she looked completely real. While the other models wore their hair in extreme bouffants, Bebe's sat flat and almost unkempt. And while the other girls—all "M.R.S." majors— seemed to be on their way to the Rotary dinner at the country club with the husbands they met at a sorority mixer, she looked as if she were on her way to someplace different—an uncertain place, but one where she would know exactly what to do when she got there. She was also a lot like Joe—her parents had divorced, she had moved around, and although she came directly to Tuscaloosa from Atlanta, she did not consider herself "southern."

They went out on dates, often to Art's Char House, a steakhouse outside town, where Joe ate, drank, and sometimes lost his temper. She was his girl, and he was her steady, but it was not an exclusive relationship—at least not for Joe. And although she loved him, she saw that he was like a giant trying to fit into a phone booth. While she took a less well-trod path across campus, he was tearing a route that cut across hallowed ground. He looked, acted, and even smelled different than the crew-cut, Lava-scrubbed southern boys. To Bebe this made him exotic—a Magyar prince offering variety to a static campus—but to others he was simply dirty, a gypsy with habits that were not only different but also wrong. Joe cared little what others thought and became more comfortable moving away from the Alabama traditions he had acclimated himself to the year before. He was going to a place where even Bebe would not be able to follow.[29]

Be Be Schreiber

While Namath maintained an open social life at Alabama, he had a steady girlfriend in Bebe Schreiber. Schreiber was a perennial "Bama Belle," one of the featured coeds in the school newspaper and, here, in the annual *Corolla*. (Bryant Museum)

Back on the field at Denny Stadium against Houston, Joe played well for the second game in a row. On the Tide's second offensive series, he threw for 55 yards on three consecutive completions to put Alabama at the Houston nine-yard line, then finished the drive two plays later with a short touchdown pass. The crowd of 27,000 cheered what looked to be the beginning of a second straight blowout victory. But on the 85-degree day, Houston showed its conditioning and speed when Mike Spratt caught a 41-yard touch-down pass to tie the game just before halftime.

On Alabama's second drive of the third quarter, Joe bruised his knee after running to the Houston 35 and left the game to get it taped. In his absence, Hurlbut ran an option, pitching to Nelson, who rushed in for the Tide's second touchdown. Joe returned in the fourth quarter with the ball at his own 20 and quickly moved the team forward to the Houston 12. From there, he took a short drop and watched for his end, Ray Ogden, to cross the middle of the end zone. His first touchdown had been a looping pass that the receiver could have caught with eggs in his hands. This time he threw the ball at top speed to the six-foot-five-inch Ogden, who secured it against his chest. Leading 21–7 with five minutes left in the game, Bryant put in many of his reserves. Houston scored again to make the final an uncomfortably close 21–13, as Alabama's defense gave up 221 passing yards to the Cougars' two quarterbacks. "They made plenty of big third down plays," Bryant said. "That doesn't speak too well for our defense."[30]

Along with its population of coeds, Tuscaloosa had comfortable hangouts that Joe began to frequent. Most famous—infamous, really—was the Jungle Club. About two miles from campus, the bar got its name simply because it looked like a jungle—several booths were made of tree stumps, a tree grew through the middle of the main room, and woods surrounded the place. The propri-etor's personality matched the wild décor. When local authorities told him that he had to install a second door to comply with local fire codes, he did so at the back of the club. The only problem was that this door opened onto a thirty-foot drop. Motorcyclists periodi-cally rode into the bar, and the Ku Klux Klan once protested out-side and threatened to burn the club down when a black musician performed there. It served beer-to-go in cans, bottles, or Mason jars—it was, in other words, a place where Joe and Hoot Owl felt at home. They took advantage of the "to-go" policy sometimes to their own detriment. On their way back to campus one night, they were pulled over by the Tuscaloosa police. Since both had beers at the time, Joe threw both cans underneath their doorless Ford. But they were on a hill, and the cans kept rolling back to Namath until one of the policemen told him not to bother anymore. Recognizing the quarterback, he said, "Well, hello, Pain-suhl-vain-i-a kid," and began to search them, telling them that they were drunk and had been driving recklessly. Namath protested, saying, "I never had anything against police—except, you know, a couple of guys I didn't like—but now I know why you mothers are cops. You couldn't get a job anywhere else." The police were not amused and took the two to the local jail for a couple of hours of "sobering" time, then let them go without filing charges.[31]

There was good food in Tuscaloosa too, and no place was better than Dreamland, a barbecue joint that produced small batches of ribs and chicken for the town's black clientele. No place in Alabama would deny Bear entry, but Bryant respected the unwritten rules of segregation and never flaunted his status by going into "coloreds only" Dreamland. Instead, he sent Billy Varner, his black driver, into the restaurant while he waited in the car. "Chicken," he grumbled to Varner. "I'm not losing *my* teeth on those ribs." Varner tried to assure Bear that there was no danger of losing his teeth with an order of ribs. "Coach," he said, "you don't eat the bones." Bear remained steadfast in avoiding ribs, and there seemed to be some merit to his philosophy—Bryant kept all of his teeth his whole life, while Varner ended up with false ones.[32]

Billy Varner was one of the few people who saw the private Bear—not the stone idol or angry general he presented to others, but a man with foibles like everyone else. Varner had been a bartender and cafeteria worker when Bryant hired him after taking the job in Alabama. Bear often unwound with a bottle of whiskey in the backseat while Varner drove aimlessly around the state. Sometimes Bear's spontaneity got the better of Varner. Once he told him he wanted to go to Las Vegas, so Varner drove him to the Birmingham airport, only to be forced to join him on the trip. With just a single change of clothes, Varner went along, but got so angry that he decided to quit. Sensing his anger—which was not difficult to discern, since he never held back his feelings even with his boss—Bear gave Billy a note for his wife. Back home, as Billy told her the reasons he was fed up with the Bear—his all-night drives through the country, his "five minutes ago" mentality for getting things done and arriving places, and even his take-out orders from Dreamland—she listened quietly and nodded in agreement, while she slowly opened the note. Inside the folded paper, she found five hundred-dollar bills. "Oh, Billy," she said. "You can't quit. He *needs* you."[33]

November 2 was homecoming as the Tide hosted Mississippi State. The narrow victory over Houston had dropped them from number six to number seven in the national rankings, but at 5–1 they were still in the running for a national championship.

Alabama took a quick lead on a Tim Davis field goal after Mississippi State fumbled the opening kickoff, but found itself behind 6–3 following a long drive that ended with a one-yard touchdown plunge. Namath brought the offense back onto the field and immediately attempted a pass. From his own 39, he threw a bullet toward Stephens that defensive back Larry Swearengen cut off and ran back for a touchdown. MSU now led 12–3. Once again, Alabama was forced to play from behind.

With the ball back in his hands, Namath faced a fourth and four at the Mississippi State 40-yard line. Dill brought in a special play from Schnellenberger, and if Namath ate it he probably needed a couple of swallows to get it down. Taking the snap, he turned and handed off to Nelson, who ran a few steps before pitching the ball back to him on a flea-flicker. Finding Dill alone at the 15-yard line, Joe completed the pass for the Tide's first touchdown of the afternoon, cutting the Mississippi State lead to two points.

With a little over a minute left in the half Bryant called for an onside kick, and Namath was quickly back onto the field. After completing two quick passes and handing off once to put the team into field goal position, he threw one out-of-bounds to stop the clock. Davis kicked a short field goal to give Alabama a 13–12 lead and the homecoming crowd something to celebrate at halftime.

But the celebration ended once the game resumed. After a long kickoff return, Mississippi State took only five plays to retake the lead with its third touchdown of the day. MSU kept their lead until the fourth quarter. Then Namath led the team from near midfield to the one, hooking up with Stephens on an 18-yard completion to set up a first and goal to go. From there, he ran it in to tie the score, and Davis put the Tide ahead, 20–19. The defense held for the final seven minutes, and Alabama won its third straight game. Along with Davis, Namath again was the standout—throwing for 142 yards and one touchdown, and running for another. Even the interception returned for a touchdown seemed to be an acceptable price for having a dominant quarterback.[34]

The one-point victory over Mississippi State in Tuscaloosa provided little confidence for Alabama fans with Georgia Tech scheduled for the next contest. The good news was that Alabama remained at number seven in the AP poll and that Bryant had an extra week to prepare for the Yellow Jackets.

The week off also meant that Namath had a free Friday night, and on November 8 he and Hoot Owl went to the west side of town to watch a high school football game between the Druid Dragons and Ullman Wolfpack, two all-black high schools. The Dragons beat the Wolfpack 28–7, but Joe's presence was noticed by the home fans, who welcomed him as a discerning football aficionado and nonconformist. It was a small gesture against segregation, but still more than was necessary or expected, and well received by the black community.[35]

Watching Joe and Hoot Owl from a distance in the Druid stands was Dude Hennessey, a less visible but no less interested white fan. Dude was used to being inconspicuous where race and football mixed. Growing up in "Shallow South" Kentucky, he experienced less rigorous segregation and at sixteen played quarterback in an interracial exhibition game for the all-black squad, something that required him to wear long sleeves to hide his white arms. Hennessey realized that it was only a matter of time before black football players would play at Alabama, and he kept a close watch on black leagues throughout the state. Often, while watching a particularly fast receiver or overpowering lineman, he thought, "Jesus, what we could do with this guy!" For now, blacks did not even attend the Alabama games as fans. They were admitted for free to help fill the stands during the Ears Whitworth years. But in the Bryant era, selling out the stadium was not a problem, and the blacks returned to their place outside the stadium. "There wasn't any whites- and blacks-only stuff," Varner remembered. "Didn't need it, since weren't no blacks that could afford a ticket."[36]

On November 16, Georgia Tech came to Birmingham for the rematch of its upset victory the previous season. Furman Bisher did not miss the chance to revisit his feud with Bryant. "At any rate, it is more by legal command than by choice that I refrain from foisting myself upon that peculiar state of mind known as Alabama," he wrote the day before the game. "Oh, I still wave when I fly over, but only a few Auburn people wave back, and I'm not sure that some of them don't have their thumbs attached to their noses as they do." He also brought up the rumor that Namath and Mike Fracchia had gotten into a fistfight after the Florida game, before calling it "hogwash."[37]

For Georgia Tech, Alabama went back to the ground game. On the Tide's second offensive possession, Joe brought the team to the line at the Tech 44. Taking the snap, he turned and put the ball into his running back's gut, pulled it back, and made a quick pitch to Ogden on the right side. The Tech defense was fooled by the fake, and Ogden ran down the sideline, untouched, until he was hit in the end zone. After a Tech field goal, Joe began a drive from his own 23-yard line. He completed an 11-yard pass to Butch Henry, but the Tide devoted itself to running over the Tech line, as Benny Nelson scored from one yard out to make the game 14–3 at halftime.

Alabama stopped Tech at the one-yard line on the opening drive of the second half, but gave up a touchdown and two-point conversion on Tech's second possession. When the Yellow Jackets got the ball back, they moved to the Alabama 24-yard line and faced a fourth down and inches. As Bear had done the year before, Bobby Dodd chose to play for the lead rather than kick a field goal. Alabama held, then drove for another touchdown entirely on the ground. The Tide got a late interception and Namath snuck in for a touchdown to end the game at 27–11.

It had been a grinding affair—Alabama ran for 252 yards, including 53 by Namath. Joe threw the ball only three times, completing one for 11 yards total. Still, his play pleased his coach. "I feel

I must say this was Namath's greatest hour," Bryant said. "They kept calling me on the phone from the press box to tell me not to call plays since he was doing such a great job of it. I don't believe we called more than two plays all day."[38]

———

Alabama had another week off after the Georgia Tech game, but it turned out that most teams got an unscheduled one as well. On Friday, November 22, President Kennedy was assassinated. Like the nation, the world of college football was unsure how to respond to the tragedy. The majority of schools canceled games scheduled for the following day.

Joe was in class that afternoon when he heard the news. He was shocked and sickened. He paid attention to politics only when it infiltrated his world, but Kennedy *had* infiltrated that world just that past summer and had done so for the right reason. The campus was in shock, but there were also random comments of satisfaction that the person who desegregated the campus had been killed. It was a Friday afternoon, there was no game the next day, and his world seemed to have stopped. So he reverted to what he had learned as a child—he went to church with one of the few other Catholics he knew, Frank Cicatiello. They walked in silence to St. Francis Chapel on 5th Avenue, half a mile from the 50-yard line of Denny Stadium. It was a small church, never having to accommodate many students at one particular time, built in another bad year, 1929. For about twenty minutes, Joe and Frank sat and looked at the dark pews and white altar, and felt that nothing really made any sense.[39]

———

Eight days later, Namath was back in Birmingham for the Iron Bowl, Alabama's annual meeting with Auburn. Whatever problems he had with Birmingham in terms of its dirty sights and loud sounds, he had no problem with its sense of touch—specifically the touch of a booster palming money into his hand. It was illegal, but the NCAA tended to regard the exchange between alumni and other boosters with players as inevitable. Joe saw it as inevitable too—his inevitable graduation from the small gifts offered during recruitment to the largesse he warranted as a varsity player. It was even jokingly said that Lee Roy Jordan had taken a pay cut when he left Alabama for the NFL.[40]

But on Iron Bowl Saturday, Birmingham was an open city, and Auburn had its own version of Joe in Tucker Frederickson. Frederickson came from an area less traditionally southern than most places in the former Confederacy—from Hollywood, Florida, and South Broward High School, testimony to the saying about Florida that held that "the farther north you go, the more southern it gets." After arriving at Sewell Hall during his recruiting trip, Frederickson opened the bag he picked up at the Montgomery airport and three bottles of Jack Daniel's rolled out. "Now this," Auburn quarterback Bobby Hunt said, "is the kind of guy we've been needing to recruit all along." In actuality, Frederickson had picked up the wrong suitcase at the airport and was extremely embarrassed and worried that his Auburn career would end before it began. Head coach Shug Jordan laughed, understanding the mistake and not about to give up on this, the best-looking recruit he had ever seen. Like Namath, Frederickson turned out even better than anyone could have imagined both on and off the football field. Like Namath in Tuscaloosa, Frederickson was the most recognized and lionized student at Auburn.[41]

With Alabama ranked sixth and Auburn ninth in the nation, anticipation was high for the 1963 Iron Bowl. George Wallace tossed the coin into a 30-mile-per-hour wind, and Alabama chose to receive. Alabama knocked out Auburn's starting quarterback, Jimmy Sidle, on the Tigers' second play from scrimmage, but senior backup Mailon Kent led the team to a field goal. Namath brought his team to the Tigers' 39-yard line to begin a drive near the end of the first quarter. Three running plays took the ball to the Auburn five-yard line, and it looked as if Alabama was set to at least tie the game. Namath's attempted pitchout was broken up when Auburn's Howard Simpson crashed through the line and tipped, then recovered, the attempted toss to Ogden at the 15. Alabama got the ball back just before the half, but the Tide drive ended when an Auburn defender dove to intercept a Namath pass.

The second half began raggedly. After neither team was able to move the ball, Alabama's Benny Nelson fumbled inside Alabama's 10-yard line. Three plays later, Frederickson caught a touchdown pass to make the score 10–0.

When Alabama got the ball back, Namath once again could not seem to get his hands right, and fumbled. But the Tide held and got the ball back, and Nelson made amends for his fumble with an 80-yard touchdown run. On the two-point attempt, Joe faked a pass and dove behind his right tackle, barely getting the nose of the ball across the goal line to make the score 10–8.

After Alabama stopped Auburn, Joe had one final chance to pull out a victory. He completed two passes to Dill, moving the ball from the Alabama 20 to the Auburn 46 with less than two minutes remaining in the game. But a clipping penalty pushed the ball back to the Alabama 35. As 55,000 people stood, Namath threw two deep passes that fell to the ground incomplete, and the game and Alabama's second defeat was over.

Bryant gave all the credit to Shug Jordan, literally saluting him as his team carried him from the field. He also praised the work of his defense, but not the offense. "The penalties and fumbles did us in," he said. "We could never get any consistency on offense." It had been a bad day for Joe especially. He completed only four of

17 passes for 43 yards, with one interception, and again fumbled the ball away twice.[42]

───

The Auburn loss did not end the season, but it did end all realistic hopes of a national championship. Moreover, Namath seemed to have suffered a proverbial sophomore jinx. While his 1962 season had been a steady rise, both off and on the field, as he gained acceptance from his teammates and fans while showing a seemingly limitless capacity for improvement as a quarterback, 1963 lacked any sense of progress. Worse than simply regressing, Joe's journey through his junior season meandered almost haphazardly in its movement between completions and interceptions, touchdown runs and fumbles, and wins and losses.

Off the field too, Joe seemed to be wandering. It would not take long before he fumbled there as well.

No one became closer friends with Namath than team manager Horace Jack "Hoot Owl" Hicks, seen here on the sidelines with Joe and Coach Bryant. From nearby West Blocton, Alabama, Hicks became a cohort in almost all of Namath's escapades. (Hicks Collection)

10

The Rat Pack

Frequently the young man is slightly inebriated and the probability is that he and his cohorts are among the better known seducers of the campus, but no one sees any incongruity in this.

—Carl Carmer, *Stars Fell on Alabama*

A S A FRESHMAN NAMATH had struggled—away from his family, deep in what seemed like a foreign land, and surrounded by clean-cut faces and syrupy southern accents. "Y'all" and the whisper of elongated vowels had replaced "yinz" and the harsh sounds of the Pittsburgh area. But now he had come into his own. His role as starting quarterback definitely came with perks. For one thing, he was meeting new people and making more friends.

Occasionally, bored by a lecture, Joe passed class time by making mental lists. Instead of counting sheep, he tried to add up the number of girls he had slept with since arriving at the university. In 1963 only two million American women took the pill, and the fear of pregnancy was a constant side effect of promiscuity. But by his standards he was doing fine, even though he readily admitted that he was shy. "I'm not a very forward guy," he said a few years later. "There are so many times when I see a girl I'd love to get to know, but I won't approach her." He feared he'd say, "Hello, my name is Joe Namath, what's yours?" and all he would receive in return would be an empty "so what" stare that signaled the end of the conversation.

But even though he was shy, he had not exactly been lonely or celibate. So he counted, remembering some encounters, forgetting others. "I used to start making out lists to see how well I was doing," he admitted, "and I guess I was pretty close to 300 by the time I graduated."[1]

Individual sexual behavior, of course, is not a fit subject for statisticians. To be sure, Namath's number of 300 falls dramatically below Wilt Chamberlain's preposterous 1991 claim of 20,000 women—or 1.2 sexual conquests per day since turning fifteen. But the thought of Namath as a college student, still without significant funds, sleeping with seventy-five different women each year, approximately seven per month from September 1961 to May 1965—almost two per week—staggers the imagination. Namath said his estimate was "conservative," but even if it was an exaggeration, he was probably in the ballpark, and it suggests his celebrity standing in Tuscaloosa.

Tales of his sex life became legendary at the University of Alabama. A member of the track team recalled visiting Joe's summer apartment. He walked into the living room and saw a beautiful brunette, nude from the waist up, sitting on the sofa watching TV. He introduced himself, and before long was kissing the coed. At this point Namath, dressed for class in slacks and a crisp button-down shirt, came out of his room. He walked past the two, hardly throwing them a glance. But as he reached the door he looked back at his fellow athlete and said, "She just gave me a blow job." Then he was out the door, a smile on his face.[2]

Not all the friends he made were female. By the middle of his junior year he had formed some strong bonds with a few boys like himself, mostly northerners and football players, who had the same sense of humor and similar values. Namath didn't go in for Frank Sinatra or Dean Martin; he was Motown all the way. Nevertheless, he developed his own Rat Pack. They hung together, laughed together, drank together, and did "whatever" else together. It was that "whatever" that led to all the problems.

Although Hoot Owl was undeniably Namath's closest friend in Tuscaloosa, Joe remained a staunch northerner in habits as well as company. By the bye week of 1963, he had found and created a community of transplanted northerners that constituted his entourage. One of Namath's closest friends was Frank Cicatiello. Cicatiello had been a stud football player for Chaney High School, one of the more storied programs in Youngstown, Ohio. The high school's most famous alum was Frank Sinkwich, who played for Wally Butts at the University of Georgia and won the Heisman Trophy in 1942. In 1960, Cicatiello played alongside Ken Ambrusko, a highly touted quarterback. Like Namath and Krzemienski in Beaver Falls, Ambrusko and Cicatiello made the rounds together on recruiting visits.[3]

Unlike the other coaches from the Deep South, who only sent letters to introduce themselves to northern football players, Frank Howard of Clemson University took a slightly more aggressive tack. Rather than recruiting each of the Ohio Valley's potential players individually, he set up a "group recruit." The site for the meet-and-greet was a Youngstown restaurant named Cicero's, a mob hangout deep within one of the most mob-infested cities in America. Cicero's, in fact, became famous as one of the most dangerous locations in the nation for car bombings. Jokes swirled around Youngstown that it cost a dollar for a haircut and five dollars for someone to start your car, and that a "Youngstown tune-up" was the installation of a device that caused a car to explode upon ignition. The town's reputation reached a national crescendo when the *Saturday Evening Post* published a cover article in 1963 that detailed the town's mob violence.

On a night in early 1961, no car bombs exploded at Cicero's as a group of high school seniors heard about the glories of Clemson over their spaghetti dinners. Cicatiello and Ambrusko sat next to Namath and struck up an immediate friendship. The food was good but the critique was unanimous—none of the three were going to play football for a school in South Carolina, no matter how great the speakers made the coach and place sound. Ambrusko, for his part, had his mind set on Maryland, and Cicatiello planned to follow. Namath added that he too was leaning toward the Terrapins, but had not made his final decision.

Ambrusko and Cicatiello did in fact choose Maryland and were there together for their freshman season of 1961. Ambrusko played out his college career at Maryland, becoming a Terrapin legend when he returned a kickoff 100 yards to defeat the Roger Staubach–led Naval Academy in 1964. Cicatiello, on the other hand, ran into trouble when there appeared to be a discrepancy on his college board examination scores. As they had done for Namath, the Maryland coaches sent a message to Bear Bryant that there was another football player, unqualified for Maryland academically, immediately available for service farther south.

With Cicatiello, though, Alabama was more cautious, largely because of Namath, whose academic deficiencies were known across campus. Indeed, Frank Rose received a letter in March 1962, in response to the president's self-congratulatory report on Alabama's scholar-athletes, that left no doubt that Namath's appearance on campus was not completely aboveboard:

How can one be so hypocritical?

I happen to know that Joe Nameth [sic] (Alabama Frosh star) could not get to the Big 10 because of his scholastic record. (lower third)

Also, I am very familiar with the <u>ethical</u>?? method Mr. Bryant used in recruiting "Babe" Parilli for K.U. [sic, University of Kentucky]

Why don't you College Presidents "call a spade a spade" and quit hoodwinking the gullible football fan? No offense intended.

Sincerely, A Friend of Babe and Joe.[4]

Before he could enter and play for Alabama, it was decided that Cicatiello needed to prove his academic proficiency at another school. So he spent the fall semester of 1962 living at home and attending Youngstown State University.

Cicatiello finally matriculated into the University of Alabama for the spring semester of 1963 and moved into Friedman Hall. Since he had missed the 1962 season, he began his Crimson Tide football career during the spring practice. On the fourth day, he got his chance to show off his abilities when he was chosen to be the "bull in the ring." The "bull in the ring," or less dramatically the "circle drill," was exactly what it sounded like. One player was chosen to defend himself against a group of teammates attacking from all sides. For the Alabama coaches, it was a great drill to see a player's strength and mobility. It was also an excellent way to weed out those players not made for the Bryant system. For this, his first time in the circle, Cicatiello was nothing short of a maniac, as he not only defended himself against the outside invaders, but *threw* several of them back beyond their original position. He was, truly, a mad bull in the ring—a perfect player for Bryant's team.

The following day Cicatiello found Namath. Both Cicatiello and Namath majored in industrial arts and shared classes all across the academy. Most famous was an English class the two took, along with another dozen football players. By this time Namath was the king of the campus and the classroom was a place to hold court. He was still the class jester he had been at Beaver Falls High School, but not without a genuine sense of respect. He never attempted to humiliate any of his teachers. Perhaps this was out of fear for his football future, but Namath tended to want everyone in his presence to have a good time—even the professors. He also attempted to help the less popular, non–football players in class, encouraging them to speak to the various coeds, usually ending the prompting with, "Okay, if you ain't gonna talk to her, I will."

Amid all of the good humor and compassion, Namath still played the rogue from the North. If he sometimes seemed to have the whole world in his hands, it was partly because his hands were so damned big. Cicatiello watched in amazement as Namath cribbed notes during exams. "It's just not fair," Cicatiello told Namath after class. "Your hand is bigger than the fucking book we're supposed to read!"

Over the summer of 1963, the two made a trip north along with Hoot Owl to visit their families. Since it was considered rude to arrive empty-handed, Cicatiello and Namath borrowed Hicks's keys and took several bags full of Alabama gear. To Hoot Owl's great dismay, the pair presented footballs, jerseys, and even a helmet to their gracious hosts. It might have cost Hicks his job as team manager had they been caught, but this was Namath, and to his way of thinking there were few rules not worth breaking.

———

A good football player had allies on campus; a great football player, like Namath, had a coterie of bodyguards willing to take a symbolic bullet for him to continue playing football for Alabama. Other, less talented players were not forgiven for their youthful indiscretions. If he ever needed proof that there were clear lines of proper and improper misbehavior for a football player, Namath need look no further than another northern friend, Jim Somerville.[5]

Better known as "Java," a nickname he earned for his caveman-like demeanor on the practice field, Somerville also flouted much of the Alabama tradition. His drinking habit, for instance, circumvented the usual haunts for a more literal one, as he tended his evening binges on a cold piece of stone—the coldest stone there was, as a matter of fact. "Java, how come you always drinkin' in the graveyard?" Hoot Owl once asked. "Seems like the safest place to do it," he replied. Even though the graveyard was right across from Denny Stadium, Java was right; no one was going to look for him there. "These southern boys, even the coaches," he continued, "they're too afraid of the haunts!" Whereas most of the community welcomed Namath as a kind of roguish pet—a veritable Yankee mascot—they never warmed to Java. While Namath found willing coeds across the campus's surprisingly diverse population, Java got dates only with the girls from one of the school's Jewish sororities, almost all of them from New Jersey or eastern Pennsylvania. It took him over a year to get a date with a southerner, and she was no traditional belle, as she went on to receive a PhD and later became chair of Alabama's biology department.

All of his Yankee ways, though, would have been forgiven if Java had made a name for himself on the gridiron. He was similar to Namath—both were northern quarterbacks who had played football on integrated teams—but he was nowhere near as talented as Namath, and he never really impressed Bryant. Before long his precarious standing slipped beyond repair. In a freshman game against Tulane, Java played defensive back. Late in what he considered to be an excellent game, he was removed in favor of the son of an Alabama alumnus. Tulane immediately marched down the field and scored. When freshman coach Clem Gryska called for Java to return, Java replied, "Go get fucked!" With those three little words, he was permanently on the "shit list." Some indiscretions were profoundly more damning than others, and in football there was no greater sin than questioning a coach's decision. Java simply was not important enough to survive his outburst. That he never starred for the Crimson Tide meant that Java would never gain full entry into the community. That he broke a rule so sacred to the coaching staff meant that he became an outcast of the football family.

Java's failure served well as a counterpoint to Namath's success. Not everyone laughed about Namath's errors of youthful exuberance and impishness, to be sure, but whatever trouble Namath got into, it never occurred where it mattered most—on the football field.

Wilber T. "Wibby" Glover met Namath in Beaver Falls and followed him to Tuscaloosa in 1963. There, he became an important member of Namath's "carpetbagger" friends, kept an apartment off-campus, and sold Namath's gratis tickets for extra money. Here they celebrate Christmas with high school friend Larry Patterson's father while Larry played in the Sun Bowl for West Texas State. (Glover Collection)

Another northern import joining Namath's crew in 1963 was Wilber T. Glover, better known as Wibby. Unlike Cicatiello, Somerville, and Hicks, Glover was one of the few associates not affiliated with the football team.[6]

Wibby Glover was a testament to the old adage that it was not the size of the dog in the fight that mattered, but the size of the fight in the dog. Small in stature but fierce in nature, Wibby had a hair-trigger temper. As a youngster already smaller than most of his Beaver Falls classmates, he purchased a $60 boxing outfit from a local sporting goods store and set it up in his parents' garage. Working the heavy and speed bags late into the night— largely to the dismay of his neighbors, who railed against the 2 a.m. staccato bursts of the speed bag—Wibby got into excellent shape and developed extremely quick hands. They helped a bit in pickup basketball games, but served him even more in the street fights he regularly got into. Adding to his "little guy" short fuse was that he wore thick eyeglasses, and the phrase "four eyes" often preceded his fights. Glover's most famous fight ended with him and his opponent flying through the plate glass window of Nick's Bar. That fight might have been Nick's biggest claim to fame but for the fact that Nick's Bar was the front entrance to the Blue Room pool hall.

At the Blue Room in the summer of 1959, just after his graduation from high school, Glover met Namath. Although Namath had just finished his sophomore year of high school and was a full two years younger than Glover, the two became fast friends. A major reason for the quick friendship was that Namath was without wheels at the time and Glover, an auto body specialist, had a car. For Namath, Glover was nothing short of a perfect companion— a guy who hung out at the same places; was perfectly ready, able, and willing to fight; searched constantly for adventure, no matter how juvenile; drove an acceptable car; and, best of all, was of legal drinking age. In all senses, Wibby Glover met football coach Jake Gaither's famous qualifications for a great player—"agile, mobile, and hostile." And he could buy beer.

The benefit of their friendship, though, was not a one-way street on which Glover always drove. Namath may have been younger, but he possessed a confidence that Glover had seldom seen. Joe passed through the late nights of Beaver Falls not like a young punk, but like the most important guest at every party in town. He had yet to start a game at quarterback and would only start half the season during his junior year, but he seemed to believe that he was a sixteen-year-old local incarnation of Johnny Unitas. If he saw a pretty girl he had never met, he showed no signs of intimidation; if he watched the best pool player take someone's money, he challenged him to a game of nine-ball; and if someone seemed to be acting a bit too tough, he faced him down. Things did not always work out as he planned, of course. Sometimes the girl laughed, the hustler won, and the tough guy stared right back until it became clear that Namath might lose some teeth if he persisted. What Glover discovered, though, was that none of those failures even slowed the kid down. Nothing, in fact, seemed to matter much to Namath except for the confidence it took to have a good time.

Namath's confidence began to rub off on Glover. Rather than avoiding the rather touchy subject of Glover's eyeglasses, for instance, Namath incorporated their presence into the friendship, referring to Wibby as "Oliver Lenses." Namath did not even call Wibby "Wibby," but used the formal "Wilber T." Nicknames may have seemed insignificant to most, but for Glover it was important. Glover understood that Joe was attempting to draw him out of the shell that seemed to crack only when the smaller man used his fists.

So in 1963 when Namath suggested that Wibby move to Tuscaloosa, they each had something to gain from the other's presence.
Namath got a faithful friend from Beaver Falls living off-campus,
and Glover got a change of scenery without giving up the scene.

While Namath entered Tuscaloosa society as loftily as anyone
ever had—a star football recruit who had literally been raised into
the forbidden realm of Bear's tower—Glover crept in at its low-
est level. In Tuscaloosa Wibby found an apartment near campus
and a job with a construction company demolishing a theater. The
work was unbearable in the Alabama heat, and he served as the
crew's only white laborer. Still, even as he sat with shaking arms
from a day on the jackhammer or cold chisel, he did so in an apartment frequented by Namath and his fellow Crimson Tide athletes.
Although the athletic dorm was posh by any estimation, it was still
part of the university, and as such, full of rules, regulations, and
limitations. An apartment off-campus was like an open house—an
unchaperoned home with no chance of the parents returning—
and Glover's one-bedroom housing became one of the most famous
and well-used resorts in the Tuscaloosa zip code.

Glover's apartment was especially important for Namath, who
by 1963 was beginning to show signs of outgrowing his local celebrity. Few students in the history of the university had attracted as
much attention, and many male students watched their quarterback with a degree of awe. That Namath seldom endorsed himself was mostly because it was not necessary—there were plenty of
others doing it for him. Indeed, one of the more memorable and
accurate commentaries on Namath's lifestyle came from a classmate, who said that "there were two things Namath never had:
underwear and a wallet."[7]

Glover also served an important duty for financing the fun. He sold Namath's gratis tickets for home games, a traditional method for providing money for players while sidestepping NCAA regulations. Each player received four tickets for free and could buy up to six more at six dollars each. What they did with them was unmonitored, and Glover regularly took Namath's tickets to a well-heeled booster, ironically named Julian Lackey. Namath's tickets were especially sought after, as people liked to sit in the seats specially designated for the team's star players. In Namath's case, Lackey usually provided a few hundred dollars per home game.[8]

Lackey's support gave Namath a ready supply of cash, but that did not mean he wanted to spend it, as another of Namath's characteristics—never having a wallet—came from his practice of seldom paying for anything. Oftentimes, store owners regaled him with their wares. Clothing stores regularly contributed to Namath's wardrobe, hoping that he would be seen in their shirts or hats around town and on the road. Other times, Namath simply took what was not offered. Once, after he had spent time at a gas station fixing a flat tire on the doorless Chevy Joe and Hoot Owl drove, the station's owner discovered a store full of empty wrappers and bags, evidence of the fast-food feast Namath and Hicks had enjoyed while he worked. More commonly, though, Namath ate his way through the local A&P grocery store. Walking the aisles, he dined leisurely on a variety of items: a quart of milk in one aisle, a ham sandwich in the next, and a Moon Pie for dessert. In fact, these smorgasbords became so commonplace that Hicks or Namath often brought along a bottle opener so as to facilitate their consumption of RC Cola.[9]

If Namath believed that his feasts were going unnoticed, he was mistaken. The manager of the A&P knew exactly what was taken and who was taking from him. He turned a blind eye to Namath, but his acceptance ended there. Namath's celebrity, his value to the university's prestige and Tuscaloosa's pride, earned him favors not extended to other hungry shoppers.

One night in the fall of 1963, Namath, Glover, and Jimmy Walsh, another northern transplant from New Jersey, stopped at the A&P on their way to a party. Wibby decided to pick up some bologna, hiding it in his jacket and leaving the store. Outside, the store manager grabbed Glover by the arm as two Tuscaloosa police cars rolled into the parking lot with their blue lights flashing. "Beat it," the manager shouted to Namath and Walsh. "This doesn't involve you." Namath and Walsh remained, as the manager began to regale the policemen with a story of Wibby's outlandish offense. "This guy right here," he started, pointing at Glover but probably thinking of Namath, "he's just plain evil and bad. He comes in here and takes what he wants. Every time he's here he just walks out with everything he can carry." When the police made Glover empty his coat and pockets, they discovered not only the bologna, but about forty dollars in small bills. Glover had not stolen the money; he had come into the store with it, prompting the cashier to blurt, "Man, you crazy! You got forty dollars in your pocket and you stealing a dollar-fifty worth of baloney?!"

The police took Glover to jail, and he could hardly have been more frightened if the prison had been in Istanbul. As his stomach began to churn, he thought he might throw up. His biggest fear was that these policemen were going to put the Yankee on a chain gang and throw away the key—this was not Beaver Falls and he was not Joe Namath. After an hour, he was released. Walsh, a law school student, knew what to do and arranged for bail. Walsh also knew how to be a smart-ass. On their walk back to the parking lot, he serenaded the shaken Glover:

Saving nickels, saving dimes,
Working till the sun don't shine,
Looking forward to happier times,
On Blue Bayou.

For Glover, the crime meant a court date; for Namath, it meant a visit to Bryant's office. Sitting in Bear's famously low-slung couch, feeling like he was sinking into it, Joe listened to Bryant. "Joe," the coach began, "I understand that your friend got into some trouble." Shifting high behind his desk, he got to the crux of the matter. "Now Joe, we don't want anything or any*one* taking your mind off of where it should be, right?"

"Yessir," Namath answered, with sincere respect.

"Well, then," Bryant concluded, driving to the place he assumed Namath's respectful answer was pointing, "I think he's got to get out of here. He's got to go."

Then Namath did what so few had ever done—he surprised Bryant. "If he goes, sir, I go. He's a personal friend of mine."

The words shocked Bryant, but only for a moment. Recognizing in an instant Namath's sincerity and the fact that he might lose his quarterback to a minor violation not even perpetrated by one of his players, he regained himself and his position as the coach. "Okay," he began. "He made a mistake. Everyone makes mistakes. As long as he straightens himself out, he can stay."

In court, Glover waited in a large crowd of defendants. The language of the proceedings was not fit for a brothel. "This motherfucker done it!" began one argument. "Fuck that, motherfucker! I ain't done shit!" That the judge permitted the flow of indecencies almost to the point of physical combat did nothing to calm the still-horrified Glover.

As the last obscenity faded from the courtroom, Glover found himself alone. "Your Honor," he called, "what about me?"

"What's your name?"

"Wilber T. Glover."

"That case has been thrown out," the judge replied, beginning to walk out. "You can leave." Obviously someone had intervened, Glover realized, and he suspected Bryant himself.

Only after the court date did Namath tell Glover about his meeting with the coach. Wibby, hearing the story, burst out, "Are you crazy?!" It had been bad enough to spend an hour in jail for $1.50 worth of bologna, but Namath had risked his entire football career on the cheap meat.

That Sunday, Namath and Glover walked toward Morrison's Restaurant. It was a favorite of the two because it was a cheap and good cafeteria-style diner. The place loved them in return, as the wait staff fought over who got to bus Namath's tray and receive his phenomenal dollar tip.

On their way, they saw Coach Bryant and his family coming out of church. They moved toward each other, and Namath told Glover, "You have to apologize to him. Whatever you do, don't look down. Look him right in the eyes and tell him you're sorry that you made a mistake." Then, before waiting out of sight, Namath added something that only Bryant's players really knew: "He can tell if someone isn't sincere."

Seconds later Glover approached Bear. "Coach Bryant," he began, following Namath's advice to the letter and staring into the blue eyes, "I made a terrible mistake and I want to apologize and thank you for helping me out of this situation." Stomach churning, Glover concentrated on one thing: Do not blink.

In his signature gruff mumble, Bryant replied, "'S'okay, boy. Everon' makes mistakes." Then came the lesson. "You jus' need to use this as an example of how you learned somethin'." They shook hands and Glover returned to Namath.

Namath was as excited as Glover had ever seen. "That was incredible!" he whisper-shrieked. "I don't think you ever even blinked!"

The episode constituted more than another legal blip for Namath in Alabama. In fact, it came to define the selectively permeable boundaries for his mischievousness. That Namath's loyalty to his friends could not be called into question became abundantly clear to Bryant. Joe certainly understood that it was *he* who possessed carte blanche in Tuscaloosa, but he expected full coverage for anyone in his company. For Bryant, this was a newish situation that he hoped could be covered by his traditional method of turning every shortcoming into a life lesson. But he could not be sure. Moreover, the incident also showed the coach something of the northerner's cockiness. Not only had Namath stood up for his friend, but his friend had shown no sign of being intimidated by the great coach either. Glover was certainly grateful, but just as certainly not cowed—at least not outwardly. Could this be the beginning of a larger problem? That the local police, judge, and even the manager of the A&P could be counted on to overlook just about all of Namath's insubordinations was what Bryant depended on. But what would happen if Namath ran across someone outside the coach's influence? What if it had been Namath who had been thrown into a jail cell, even for just an hour? It did not take long for "if" to become "when."

———

Alabama had no game scheduled on November 23, 1963, as a result of the JFK assassination, so there was no change in their immediate schedule. After losing to Auburn 10–8 the following Saturday, though, the team had received another open date due to the ripple effect from the tragedy in Dallas. So as not to conflict with the postponed Army-Navy game on December 7, Alabama's game in Miami was pushed back one week. That meant there was yet another open week for the team, this time in the wake of a painful defeat. That trouble might find the idle hands of Namath and his friends was not guaranteed, but the layoff certainly increased the possibility.

Early on Saturday, December 7, 1963, Hoot Owl borrowed five dollars from Bebe Schreiber and bought a bottle of the aptly named Early Times whiskey. By afternoon, Hicks was drunk enough to take himself on a self-guided off-road tour of campus. Traveling west on University Boulevard, he turned left *across the sidewalk*, passing the Denny Chimes, through the three-hundred-yard field behind it, past the Amelia Gayle Gorgas Library, and over the Rotunda, finally making it back onto Capstone Drive. Amazingly, nothing happened to him.[10]

Most of that day, while Hoot Owl roamed the campus with little regard for the generally accepted rules of the road, Namath stayed inside and watched Navy beat Army, 21–15. Trying to keep up with Hoot Owl would have been foolish for Namath at this point in his drinking career. He rarely drank early in the day, and three drinks usually sufficed in making him drowsy enough to quit. Hoot Owl described it as "drinking like an Indian," meaning that Namath got as still and quiet as a cigar-store Indian after just a couple of drinks. So Namath waited and caught up with Hoot Owl later that evening, when they crashed a few campus parties. Like all of the football team, Hoot Owl and Namath belonged only to an unofficial fraternity known as the APEs, as in a bunch of gorillas, an abbreviation for their stature and demeanor around campus. Although their campus reputation had improved under Bryant, many students continued to view them as wild and unpredictable when they drank. Football players were still never denied entry into fraternity parties. Namath and Hicks were familiar with the Friday and Saturday night circuit of frat houses, and crashed as many parties as anyone affiliated with the team. This Saturday night was typical— Namath talked with one of the sorority girls at a party and sipped a beer, and Hoot Owl shouted insults at passersby.

The night had a different ending, though. After the party, Hoot Owl, still drunk, drove down Sorority Row with Namath riding shotgun. In front of one of the houses, Hoot Owl once again took to the off-road and drove through the front lawn. The girls looking out the window began shouting. About half of them yelled for Hoot Owl to get back on the road, that he was ruining their newly manicured garden and lawn. The other half recognized Namath and shouted hellos and good lucks to him. Quickly, Hoot Owl returned to the road, but it was a short trip. At the end of the street, which had no outlet to another road, the two ran out of gas. Seeing that the car behind them had Bibb County license plates, the county he came from and an obvious ally to their cause, Hicks asked for and received assistance from the driver. To get out of the street, though, they needed to stop traffic long enough to push their car around. Ever the quarterback, Namath got out of the car and gave signals for the other cars to pull over so as to clear a path. On the way back up the street, the house mother for the sorority with the tracks across its lawn recognized the doorless Chevy and took down its license number. It was not really necessary since everyone knew whose car it was and who the famous passenger was. Within the hour, a couple of the coaches had been notified, and they in turn told Bryant.[11]

On Monday, December 9, Bryant found Namath at the athletic dorm cafeteria. "Joe, somebody got in touch with me and said you were acting up Saturday afternoon. He said you'd been drinking and you were out directing traffic. I believe this gentleman for his word, but I'll take your word first 'cause I know you and I know you wouldn't lie to me. Is that story true?" Namath told him that he had not been drinking on Saturday afternoon, that he had been watching the Army-Navy game. "Were you drinking at all Saturday?" Bryant continued. "Well, yes, sir. I had a drink Saturday night," Namath responded, admitting that he had broken the rule about drinking during football season.[12]

After getting Namath's admission, Bryant called together his coaches to vote on the matter. As he went around the room, each coach thought that Namath should be spared suspension, that what had happened was not that big a deal, and that Namath was simply too important a player to be let go at such a crucial time in the year. Alabama was scheduled to play two nationally televised games, and Namath was the reason.

When the vote came to Gene Stallings, the mood of forgiveness quickly changed. Looking straight into Bryant's eyes, Stallings said, "If it had been me, you would have fired me, wouldn't you?" "Yeah," Bryant answered. "Well, let him go," Stallings concluded.

It was not that Stallings disliked Namath—on the contrary, he thought that Namath was one of the hardest-working players he had ever been around, a generally nice kid who treated Stallings's children with kindness and enthusiasm, and a person with an uncanny knack for making other people feel good. It was just that Stallings had more important things on his mind than football, and was beginning to look at life a little differently than in the past.

On June 11, 1962, his only son, John Mark, was born. Shortly thereafter, doctors diagnosed the infant with Down syndrome. For the first time in his life, Stallings felt unlucky. When his parents visited their newest grandson for the first time that year, Stallings talked nonstop about the newest Alabama star, Joe Namath, but noticed that the grandparents, like everyone else unfamiliar with John Mark's condition, handled him gingerly, awkwardly, and only briefly. It hurt him to think that his son caused immediate consternation even to his parents. Stallings's life seemed schizophrenic. By day, he coached some of the best athletes in the world; by night, he watched in pain as his son struggled to achieve even such simple tasks as taking a bottle. Stallings had always been a Yankees fan because they beat everyone they played, but after watching John Mark struggle every day of his life a new attitude came over him. He started rooting for the underdog, cheering for the players with less ability to succeed, and realizing that the worst thing for an athlete was to take his or her ability for granted. Most of these feelings hit him in full-blown intensity long after Namath's stint at directing traffic. Still, Stallings believed that if Joe was going to reach his full potential, coaches could not coddle him with a different set of rules.[13]

When Bryant left the room, the other coaches turned on Stallings. He had not only voted to suspend the best player on the team, he had all but guaranteed that the team would lose its bowl game. And the loss of a bowl game meant a loss of the coaches' bonus check, an indispensable windfall for an assistant coach in the early 1960s.[14]

Bryant returned to his office and cried before calling the coaches and Namath together. He told them that he had decided Namath should be suspended, and if anyone in the university tried to reverse the decision, he would resign. Namath told him not to do that, that he would take the suspension willingly, but asked him to call and tell his mother. Bryant agreed to call Rose, then told Joe to see Coach Bailey, who would arrange for a place for Namath to stay while he was suspended from the team. The length of the suspension was open-ended—as Bryant put it, "for the year, or forever, or until [you] prove something to me." Bryant offered to help Namath get into the Canadian Football League if he chose not to try to earn his way back onto the team the following year.

The next day Bryant and Coach Goostree flew to Tennessee on a recruiting trip. From there, Bryant contacted Rose Namath and told her that he had suspended her son. Naturally, she was upset with the decision. Later that day, though, she received a call from Art Catrino, the owner of Art's Char House, a restaurant across the street from the Alabama practice field. He told Rose that he would help take care of Namath while he worked his way back onto the team.[15]

On the practice field the next day, while the coaches called the players together to tell them that Namath had been in violation of team rules and was suspended for the remainder of the season, Hicks crouched in a distant corner. Tears streaming down his face, he pretended to gather some equipment. He had ruined Namath's football career. The next day, Coach Goostree told Bryant who else had been in the car with Namath, and Hoot Owl was also suspended from the team. Back again with Namath, Hoot Owl felt almost relieved.[16]

———

Along with Art Catrino, Namath had another ally in Tuscaloosa. Mary Harmon Bryant, the coach's wife, had always liked Joe. After hearing about his suspension, she invited him to dinner at the Bryants' house on Watermelon Road and pleaded his case to her husband. In actuality, she was preaching to the choir—Coach Bryant wanted nothing more than for Joe to return to the team for his senior year.[17]

It would take a bit of doing, but most people around the

university believed that Namath would make a successful return. Lonnie Falk, *Crimson White* sports editor, wrote about the suspension in an editorial in December that summed up the feelings of most of the students:

Most probably Joe Namath will ride again. At least this is the general opinion which runs through the more knowing strata of the campus.

The reasons are many.

They could be that Joe Namath has made a name for himself, and has associated himself with athletics at the Capstone. They could be that Joe Namath just wants to prove that he is the best college quarterback in the land. They could be lots of things, but most of all—the prime reason must be that Mr. Joe Namath, of Beaver Falls, Pa.[,] knows that he has made a mistake and wants to show that he is a big enough guy to realize it.

We here think he is.[18]

What Namath felt was a bit more complex. He certainly wanted to return, was loyal to Alabama, but still was stung that he was no longer on the team. He decided to return to Beaver Falls for the holidays. Glover and Hoot Owl agreed to make the trip to Pennsylvania with him. On their way out of town, Glover, who was driving, realized that he had forgotten his prized fedora. "Hold on," he told the other two. "I forgot my hat. We gotta go back." Namath told him to forget it, that the hat would be fine in the apartment, but Glover persisted. "Then let me out," Namath said. "Get your damned hat, but leave me here." Without a word Wibby made a U-turn, let Namath out of the car not far from the Jungle Club, and headed back into Tuscaloosa to retrieve his hat from off the bed in his apartment.

Waiting for his ride to return, Namath stood motionless in the empty parking lot. It was cold and he felt abandoned. His future, once again, was uncertain.[19]

TEAM PERSONNEL, Monday, December 9, 1963

	REDS	WHITES	BLUE	MIAMI OFF	MIAMI DEF
E.	Dill Stephens	Tolleson	Glimer	Shankles	Chambers
T.	Simmons	Durdy	Boler	Castleberry	Brand
G.	Lewis	Freeman	Mitchell	Casagrande	Vagotis
C.	McCollough	Crane	Carroll	Johnson	Calvert
G.	Allen	Wieseman	McClendor	Bird	Willoughby
T.	Kearley	Wright	Beard	Cicatello, Davis	King
E.	Stephens-Henry	Ray	Strickland	McLeod	Wheeler
Q.	~~Namath~~ *Hurlbut*	Hurlbut-Sloan	Sloan-Hurlbut	French	Sommerville
L.	Harris	Nelson	McGill	Bean	Miller
F.	Versprilli	Sherrill / Ogden	Bowman / Moseley	Duncan, G. Ray	Moon
R.	Andrews-Martin				

Fracchia On Off
Bates - Def

After Namath's suspension from the team in November 1963, Bryant chose Jack Hurlbut as his quarterback for the team's regular-season finale against the Miami Hurricanes. Here, Bryant literally scribbled Hurlbut's name over the crossed-out Namath on the team's itinerary. (Bryant Museum)

I I

Redemption Song

To Coach Bryant,
Thank you for the great help you've given me. You'll always
be the best <u>coach</u> and <u>man</u> that I'll ever be associated with.
                                                    Joe Willie Namath
                        —Signed photograph from Namath to Bryant

O N THE SIDEWALK surrounding the Denny Chimes on the
Alabama campus are the foot- and handprints of the Crimson Tide football captains. Visitors to campus often put their own
hands into the imprints, not unlike tourists in Hollywood touching
the physical records of movie stars at Grauman's Chinese Theatre. In
Tuscaloosa, beside a scrawled "Joe Willie," is a handprint so large that
most adult male visitors have trouble stretching their own hands up
to the second finger joint.

These were the hands someone had to fill for Alabama's final
regular-season game of 1963, as well as the 1964 Sugar Bowl. Since
both games were slated for national television, replacing Namath's

paws was going to be a public event. In the end, it took two hands to fill Namath's one.

Regarding the Namath suspension, Bryant dealt with the media in a typically detached manner. On Tuesday, December 10, sports pages from Birmingham to Beaver Falls ran Bryant's "infraction of training rules" quote. It turned out to be all the information journalists got, and as much as they seemed to require. Bryant was notoriously close-lipped, and after the row with the *Saturday Evening Post*, no sportswriter in America really wanted to press him.[1]

Alabama ended their regular season in Miami in their only nationally televised game that fall. Testimony to the game's national potential, it was twice rescheduled from its initial television spot, first from October until December 7, then again to December 14 so as not to conflict with the postponed Army-Navy game. CBS hyped the game as "the battle of the quarterbacks" in anticipation of a rare collegiate meeting between Namath and Miami's star, George Mira. Although Bryant claimed that he had not made a decision as to Namath's replacement, and might not until as late as Saturday afternoon, he penciled in Jack Hurlbut as the starter, literally crossing out Namath's name on the team personnel report of Monday, December 9, and scribbling a cursive "Hurlbut" above it.[2]

Along with the putative lineup for the Miami game, Bryant also addressed the Tide's opponent. In a handwritten itinerary that he distributed to the team, Bryant began, "#10 Mira—is a great Athlete without him they are just Another Team." He exhorted his team to reach "down and get that stuff that your Mother, Father & Good Lord gave you & using [*sic*] it for 60 min. come Sat."[3]

In Miami, the mood was generally one of disappointment. The Miami players commiserated with Namath, suspecting that the suspension had to do with alcohol and recognizing that it was a situation most of them had narrowly avoided for most of their careers.

Moreover, since the majority of the Miami roster came from east-ern Ohio or western Pennsylvania, they knew all about Namath and had looked forward to his visit.

Rich Niedbala felt especially bad for his old high school buddy on a personal level, but also lamented that there would be no great shootout between Namath and Mira. Mira, hailed by the press as "the Matador," threw the ball harder than anyone Niedbala had ever seen, even Namath. Namath, though, threw the ball with bet-ter touch. As much as he hoped his team would win the game, it was the game itself—the back-and-forth between his two good friends that would certainly have shot both teams up and down the field—that Niedbala had been looking forward to. So great were Namath and Mira that they could turn opponents and teammates from players back into simple fans of the game.[4]

George Mira was the star of Miami's team even before he played a down. As a Florida high school student he was an all-around ath-lete, an all-state football player who also pitched three no-hitters in baseball. The Baltimore Orioles tried to sign him, but he chose to play football at Miami, where he was one of only eleven Floridians on the 1963 team. Andy Gustafson, his ultraconservative coach, who had mastered the game as a Red Blaik assistant at Army, built Miami's offense around Mira during spring practice his freshman year. For a few years it paid off. Mira ranked first in pass completions in his junior and senior years. Notre Dame's coach, Ara Parseghian, called him "the quickest quarterback" he had ever seen.[5]

Parseghian was not alone in his assessment. Gustafson told a reporter, "George is the greatest passer I have ever coached.... A coach spends a lifetime looking for a boy who can throw like George. In a way, George reminds me of Ted Williams—kind of arrogant in a real confident way." Mira's delivery was like Williams's swing—picture perfect. If he had a fault as a thrower, it was that he threw the ball too hard, too often. His blockers claimed that the ball made a "wooshing" sound as it left his hands, and his receivers complained that it hurt their hands to catch his fastballs. But Gustafson lost no sleep worrying about his receivers. "It's a lot easier to find boys who can catch than ones who can throw."[6]

His statistics attracted attention. His good looks—conservative crew cut, bright smile, and Kingston Trio button-down shirts—made him a media darling. *Sports Illustrated* and *Sport* magazine featured him in articles, and it was Mira, more than Namath, who attracted television producers. Like Namath, he had a swagger and an easy smile, but Namath's star power was hurt by the racial traumas taking place in Alabama.

The 1963 season had not gone well, and Mira's stock had fallen. Despite his gaudy statistics (more than 300 completions in a day when few teams even threw the ball that often), Miami had lost six of their first nine games. They needed a win against Alabama to end the season looking like winners. Mira needed a win to improve his negotiating position with the San Francisco 49ers, who had already taken him in the first round of the draft. And Namath's suspension increased their odds. In addition to the loss of Namath and the proficiency and motivation of Mira, Alabama faced other disadvantages in Miami. The Orange Bowl, even on December 14, was one of the few places hotter and more humid than Tuscaloosa, and the heat took a toll on any team chasing after Mira. Then there was the emotional aspect of the game. It was not only to be Mira's final game as a Hurricane, but also the last contest for Andy Gustafson, who was retiring after sixteen seasons as head coach to become Miami's athletic director.

Some said it was God, others claimed it was Coach Bryant, but someone helped the Crimson Tide overcome all of these challenges, including Namath's suspension. Gary Martin returned the opening kickoff 100 yards for a touchdown, giving a much-needed score to an Alabama team whose offense was severely hindered by Namath's absence. A few minutes later, Miami fumbled on their own 13-yard line and Alabama recovered. Six plays later the score was 14–0. Halfway through the second quarter, Mira fumbled at his own 35 and Alabama was again in scoring position. A field goal made the score 17–0 at halftime and it looked as if Alabama would cruise to an easy victory.

But Mira and the rest of the Miami team were not yet ready to give up on Gustafson's last game, and got themselves together at halftime. Then Mira lived up to his billing, leading Miami in a frantic comeback effort. Miami went on four long drives in the second half. The first two ended deep in Alabama territory, but resulted in no points. The latter two ended with touchdowns and missed two-point conversions, putting the game at 17–12. Jackie Sherrill intercepted a Mira pass late in the game to secure an Alabama victory. The Matador had hit 24 of 48 passes for 301 yards to bring Miami within five points of the Tide, but ultimately left as a defeated hero.[7]

As in all proper fables, the slow and steady effort won the race, as Bryant's pregame itinerary—numbers 2c: *What one can contribute, not what one can receive*; and 2d: *When you win there is enough glory for everyone*—rang true loud and clear. Bryant stated how proud he was of his team, and Gustafson reiterated the sentiment. "Alabama was a beautifully drilled team—a typically Coach Bryant team," he said. "I will look forward to Monday afternoon not having to go to football practice." Playing the part of the tortoise to Mira's hare was Hurlbut, who threw for only 51 yards but made up for his pedestrian numbers in other ways. "Hurlbut was out there to block on the kickoff return Gary Martin turned into a touchdown, and he was there on defense to fight down Mira passes, intercept one, and almost another. No specialist, he," wrote Benny Marshall of the *Birmingham News*. "So Hurlbut got no headline," Marshall concluded. "He just tackled, and blocked, and knocked down passes, and handled the offense, too. Ole Miss scouted him, and Ole Miss will know Alabama has a good quarterback."[8]

The fact was that no one except Bryant knew who would start at quarterback in the Sugar Bowl, and he was not telling. For an article titled "I've Got a Secret," the *Birmingham News* featured a photograph of Alabama center Gaylon McCollough prepared to snap two footballs to Hurlbut and Sloan waiting behind him. Two days later, Bryant ended the mystery when he announced Sloan as the starter. "Hurlbut will probably have to play more defense than normally," Bryant said. If Bryant wanted a quarterback with a personal relationship with his mother, father, and the Good Lord, he could not have hoped for anyone better than the sophomore son of a Methodist car salesman.[9]

Unlike Namath and Hurlbut, Sloan came to Alabama after a lengthy recruitment process in which he received a full dose of the Crimson Tide treatment. From his senior high school football season through the summer of his arrival in Tuscaloosa, Sloan got a series of letters from Howard Schnellenberger that ran a course from the cloying adulation of a fan gushing at the potential of a formal commitment, up through a coach laying down the rules for an already captured player. Early on, Schnellenberger emphasized that Sloan was the Tide's number one recruit from Tennessee and possibly number one overall, profusely apologized for inadvertently calling one of Sloan's friends by the wrong name, and cheered on Sloan's basketball career. After Sloan signed his letter of intent, though, Schnellenberger pushed the recruit to withdraw from a high school all-star game ("the honor has already been extended to you...your playing would only jeopardize yourself"), lamented that he could not meet with Sloan more closely ("between your basketball now and your girl friend...I really haven't had the opportunity to speak with you as seriously as I have wanted to"), and voiced concern over Sloan's desire to continue to play on the golf team in college ("the thing is...to spent [*sic*] whatever time it takes to become a great football player").[10]

Schnellenberger's efforts paid off. Sloan went to Alabama before the 1962 season, bringing with him a legitimately high grade point average and the God-fearing work ethic that Bryant so dearly wanted in his players. Sloan's religious fervor ran toward the evangelical. Richard Williamson, Sloan's roommate, fell asleep every night to Sloan's Bible reading. "For the love of money is the root of all evil," Sloan orated, "which while some coveted after, they have erred from the faith, and pierced themselves through with many sorrows." Even in the Deep South, this kind of late-night preaching was a bit odd, but all things considered it was a minor peccadillo, and Sloan was a genuinely nice person.[11]

Sloan was also terrified. Since all but a few of Alabama's players practiced to go both ways, Sloan was not specifically a backup quarterback. Rather, he spent the 1963 season playing regularly in the secondary. That meant he racked up a lot of varsity action, but it also meant he had taken only a few snaps as quarterback all season, even in practice. It was not that he lacked confidence in himself, but he was not Joe Namath, not even Jack Hurlbut, and did not relish the opportunity to prove that fact in front of a national television audience in the Sugar Bowl. Even the Alabama press guide, written up before the season, seemed to mock Sloan. "Joe Namath... could be the greatest in the Nation," it read. "Steve Sloan...could be a good one."[12]

Without the northerner Namath, the Sugar Bowl of 1964 became truly the battle of the South—described variously as the clash of the recently desegregated, the battle for the soul of the former Confederacy, or, more cynically, the battle for the front of the bus. George Wallace and Ross Barnett were scheduled to be there as well.

In the locker rooms at Ole Miss, the lack of detail regarding Namath's suspension led to speculation. One of the Ole Miss players, from Alabama, went home over the semester break and added to his cache of Namath stories. He had already heard the tales of Namath's ostentatious arrival on campus, his apparent black high school girlfriend, and his northern arrogance toward southern tradition—all of which he retold as firsthand gospel to his Mississippi teammates. This time, his Christmas research trip provided him with his greatest scoop yet. "You know how they're saying that Namath was kicked off for drinking?" he told his captivated teammates as soon as they returned from Christmas break. "Well, I know the real reason. He got caught fucking a nigger!" The response was pure, unreconstructed pride, as the Rebel players cheered in euphoric glory.[13]

Racist motivation notwithstanding, Mississippi players knew that it was not the quarterback that gave Alabama its advantage, but rather Bryant's methods. Bryant's practices ensured that his team was in top physical condition, and his intensity created the most determined players in the nation. This produced a veritable "given" in preparing for a game against the Tide—no matter what else might occur on the field, an opponent could not wear out or outhit a Bryant-coached team.[14]

The buildup to the game included much more than a quarterback decision—it was a battle of the two greatest minds in southern college football, and Bryant and John Vaught volleyed comments as the game approached. "I wouldn't be surprised if it is not the best football game in the nation," Bryant confided, but Vaught thought in even higher terms. "I think we prepare the boy in football to compete under the most hazardous conditions," he said before the bowl. "You've got to win, even if you are selling insurance." He also indicated that he too could keep secrets. "We're just giving them the facts," he told the New Orleans press. "Later on, we will start the psychological buildup." Defending their own coach, the *Birmingham News* quickly brought up the fact that Bryant was not to be toyed with, psychologically or otherwise. "The fellow caught the bear easy, goes an old country story," Alf Van Hoose wrote. "Only to discover quickly he was in a tougher fix: How could he then turn him loose?"[5]

God seemed to be on Alabama's side as well, as the worst snowstorm in sixty-four years hit New Orleans, turning the Sugar Bowl into a cold and wintry mess. To the dismay of NBC executives, who were already upset with the advertising limitations of an all-Dixie matchup, and most of the 83,000 fans in attendance, the game was not defined by either of the two great coaches' acumen, but by 17 fumbles and four field goals.

On Alabama's second drive of the game, Sloan led the team 68 yards downfield, completing two passes on the way, before Tim Davis kicked a 31-yard field goal. Following a Mississippi fumble a few plays later, Davis kicked another field goal to put Alabama ahead 6–0. In what became the pattern of the game, Mississippi fumbled on their next possession and Davis added his third field goal of the half. At halftime, the score was 9–0, with Ole Miss having gained only 17 yards on the ground and no first downs.

In the third quarter, Mississippi quarterback Jim Weatherly threw an interception, setting up Davis's final field goal, a 48-yard effort that set the record for the longest in Sugar Bowl history. Mississippi scored a touchdown early in the fourth quarter to cut the lead to 12–7. With eight minutes left in the game, Ole Miss lined up at the Alabama two-yard line, but failed to score. Alabama's defense held the rest of the way in what turned out to be a record-setting event, as Mississippi fumbled 11 times and Alabama fumbled six. Although Sloan fumbled once, threw for only 29 yards, and failed to lead Alabama to a touchdown, he did what Bryant found most important—he won.[16]

Ross Barnett summed up the game as well as anyone when he asked, "Why is it the boys can't hold on to the football?" Watching the Sugar Bowl was one of the last official appearances for the outgoing governor. Since George Wallace could not attend the game because of the foul weather, a grand meeting of the South's two great segregationists did not occur in New Orleans. Vaught was not the most gracious loser, as he described Alabama as not as tough as some of the other teams he had faced. "Certainly," he said, "not as tough as the Tennessee team we beat this year." When asked why his team had fumbled so often, he reiterated his statement. "I'd be guessing," he said. "It wasn't that cold, the ball wasn't wet and they weren't hitting that hard." Bryant, on the other hand, was overjoyed with the performance, and showed it. After the game, he hopped onto a trunk and led the team in a few verses of "We don't give a damn for the whole state of Mississippi." When asked about Vaught's comment regarding the lack of hitting, Bryant shot back, "They were knocking out there, on both sides. Don't you ever think they were not."[17]

———

Namath and Hicks traveled to New Orleans to watch their team, pulling into the Tulane Stadium parking lot in a convertible with a whiskey bottle between them. After they came to a stop near the players' entrance, Hoot Owl jumped up through the open roof. Whiskey bottle in hand, he let out a traditional "Roooollll Tide!" Out the corner of his inebriated eye, though, he caught the familiar sight of Mary Harmon Bryant and quickly retreated into the car's interior. On or off the team, some things did not change.[18]

Indeed, Mary Harmon Bryant was to the drunken Hicks exactly what her husband was to the rest of the football-mad state: an immutable force that demanded the utmost respect. Namath was a great quarterback, as everyone in Alabama recognized, but his suspension proved that he was absolutely *not* irreplaceable. That the other players needed to step up their effort without Namath was true, but that was nothing above and beyond the call of duty on a Bryant-coached team. In fact, that was the essence of Alabama. No one wished Namath ill. On the contrary, all of the Crimson Tide nation hoped for his quick return to the starting lineup.

The *Crimson White* laid out the Namath-Sloan competition directly. "Reports came in that Joe Namath was one of the happiest of celebrants over that stunning Sugar win," Lonnie Falk began. "But we must wonder too, and publicly, if Old Joe wasn't, and indeed isn't, just a little fearful for his position come September." Falk then made a bold prediction: "With a full spring training and fall retouching under his belt don't bet that Sloan will be walking in the shadow cast by the Beaver Falls Bomber next season." Falk then went on to declare the Sugar Bowl the greatest single victory of the Bryant era and Sloan the winner of the "Bryant 101% effort award."[19]

Not yet twenty years old, Namath faced another Rubicon in his already fitful life. Whither Joe Willie?

———

In terms of housing, Namath could not have picked a worse time to get suspended. In 1964, Alabama opened its brand-new, state-of-the-art Athletic Residence Dormitory. The new dorm had two dining areas, special training tables for game-day meals, and rooms designed for two athletes with seven-foot beds and a bathroom in each. Other than the president's home, it was probably the poshest residence on campus.[20]

Along with his starting position and room at the athletic dorm, Namath also lost a couple of his best friends in town. In January, Wibby Glover's father died and he moved back to Pennsylvania. After redshirting in 1963, Frank Cicatiello lost his eligibility at Alabama and left for Southwest Louisiana, where he famously got into a fight and threw his helmet at Ray Blanco, a coach and the future husband of the first female governor of Louisiana.[21]

So Namath and Hoot Owl bedded down at a regular student dormitory and prepared for their comeback. Rooming across from one another, the two seemed unperturbed by their demotion in housing, as both continued to enjoy their celebrity status on campus. Namath, of course, was still Namath to the student body no matter his address, and he still enjoyed himself regardless of his downgraded status. Generally, he continued to entertain a large number of female guests and enjoy a drink every so often. Specifically, he got out of some minor trouble that accompanies life in a dorm. Music, for instance, was another of Namath's passions, especially the Motown sound of black musicians like the Supremes, the Four Tops, and Martha and the Vandellas. On one occasion, he blasted out one of his favorite songs, "Shake a Tail Feather" by the Five Du-Tones, on his dorm-room radio. On hearing the noise, the resident advisor rushed down the hall to reprimand the culprit. Upon discovering that it was Namath, he let the crime pass. A small bit of favoritism, to be sure, but it did Namath's ego good to realize that he had not lost all of his juice.[22]

Back on the field for spring practices, Namath quickly regained his spot as the team's number one quarterback. The *Crimson White* reported the good news. "With the second week of practice almost spent," read a caption under a staged photograph of a smiling Namath running the ball in uniform, sans helmet, "not too many

Tide fans were surprised to hear that Beaver Joe is back in his old number one quarterback spot."[23]

On May 8, 1964, the team played its annual A-Day football game, pitting Namath's Red team versus Sloan's White team. In front of the largest spring crowd in the history of Alabama football, Namath led the Reds to a 17–6 victory, throwing for two touchdowns and leading his squad to a field goal. The school paper might have already told the student body that Namath was back at the number one spot, but his performance removed any doubt as to the hold he had on the position. In his final column for the *Crimson White*, Lonnie Falk stressed Namath when he summed up his writing career. "It was written on these pages that Namath would make a return and reform—he has made that return and he has reformed," Falk wrote. "Both will be a credit to him. His return is a break that he richly deserves."[24]

The *Crimson White* ended the 1964 academic year with a few telling parting shots. In one editorial, the paper encouraged students to stand up for whatever they believed in, including a stance against George Wallace's segregationist platform, as the newspaper had done in the frightening days of the school's desegregation. Less seriously, the paper polled the coed population as to their opinion on the recent appearance of a "southern belle" from Georgia as a *Playboy* centerfold. "Would you do this?" it asked. Similarly, the paper asked the "Bama Babes" what they thought about the topless bathing suits just put on the market. The "topless" article even listed the measurements of two of those interviewed.[25]

For Namath it could not have happened at a better time—encouraging racial peace and reporting openly on *Playboy* magazine and topless swimsuits meant that things looked better than they ever had for the twenty-year-old All-American. Back at the number one spot for his senior season, Namath was poised to return to a better dorm and a greater notoriety.

———

Over the summer of 1964, Namath and Hicks took a memorable road trip to the World's Fair in New York. It turned into a prophetic travelogue.[26]

As always, they depended on the doorless brown Chevrolet to get them to the North in one piece. In this sense, it was a journey of faith. The radio blasted Ray Charles as they began to traverse Dixie. Through northern Alabama, into Tennessee, then following the border between Kentucky and Virginia, they passed through the Deep South and the Shallow South, bisecting the former Confederacy with little more consciousness of the act beyond the changing radio stations their trip offered. At West Virginia they entered the historical Union.

The first leg of the trip ended in Beaver Falls, where they stayed with Namath's mother, who invited the whole family over for a celebration. She made liver dumpling soup—the liver ingredient a carryover from the days of the Depression when chicken was scarce—and *golumpki*. With four sons and a daughter, Rose was familiar with insatiable appetites. Still, Hoot Owl, at 260 pounds, caused her a bit of pause as to whether she had made enough food. They visited Namath's old haunts, including the Blue Room pool hall, where Namath had won some money and fights, as well as some Ohio bars just across the state line where the drinking age was lower. They also went to see Namath's father. Hoot Owl knew that Joe's parents had had a rough divorce, but he also saw that the knot in their family was still tight, and that there was genuine love and respect between father and son.

Before continuing to New York, they took a side trip to Cleveland to see the Indians play the Yankees. They had no tickets to the game, but Hoot Owl promised some magic. "If we get over there," he told Joe, "I'll get us in." Namath was skeptical that Hoot Owl had any connections at all, let alone here in the North, but wanted to see the Yankees and figured that they could get in one way or another, regardless of Hicks.

When they got to Cleveland, Hicks called the hotel where the Yankees stayed. "I'd like to talk to Mr. Mel Allen," he began. To Hicks's surprise, Allen got on the phone personally and without an intermediary. "Mr. Allen," Hicks continued, "I know you don't know me, but I'm from West Blocton. I'm the football manager at Alabama and my friend, Joe Namath, and I want to see the Yankees game." Allen, also from West Blocton, replied that he knew Namath well, having voted for him on a preseason All-American ballot, and would leave tickets for them at the gate.

The tickets were as good as Hoot Owl's promise. Sitting directly behind the Yankees' dugout, Namath and Hicks saw their heroes so close they could have reached out and touched them. At one point, they yelled encouragement at Mickey Mantle as he came out to the on-deck circle. Late in the game he lined his eighteenth home run over the rightfield fence. The Yankees won 10–4, but one of the losing stars was Tito Francona, from New Brighton, Pennsylvania, just across the river from Beaver Falls. It all seemed a bit odd. Here they were, two kids from the University of Alabama sitting in box seats provided gratis as they watched a Beaver County ballplayer homer against the Yankees. Some things, all of a sudden, seemed a little closer at hand.

After a brief stop in Washington, D.C., to see Hatchet Hassan, they went to New Jersey to pick up Jimmy Walsh. Walsh, of course, had been in Tuscaloosa for "Wibby's bologna caper." Coming from New Brunswick, New Jersey, he too experienced a rough entry into Alabama. While Namath received his racist baptism in the bus station in Tuscaloosa, Walsh saw what he was in for as he drove into town on Highway 11. There, welcoming all visitors, was a large metal sign that read, WELCOME TO TUSCALOOSA, ALABAMA. HOME OF THE GRAND DRAGON OF THE KU KLUX KLAN. Other than that and the town's sharp paper-mill smell, it was lovely. After being introduced by Ray Abruzzese, Namath and Walsh struck up a quick and close friendship. It became closer when Walsh loaned Namath some money to help out a family member who had lost his job.[27]

They arrived in the city early in the morning, rolling into town through the Lincoln Tunnel. After adjusting their senses and sensibilities for several blocks in the valley of skyscrapers, Hoot Owl banked the car against one of 39th Street's curbs.

Catching the subway at 42nd Street, they were off to see the World's Fair. They knew they were there when they spied the Unisphere, a twelve-story hollow globe sponsored by the U.S. Steel Corporation. It was the centerpiece of the fair's "Peace Through Understanding" slogan, and looked huge even amid the enormity of the New York skyline. They "picture-phoned" each other at the Bell Telephone pavilion, a phone system that allowed callers to see each other. Similarly, they watched television at the RCA pavilion, where there was an operating television studio as well as a bank of "color" televisions. And they ate constantly throughout the entire village.

As Namath strolled through the fair, he came upon a realization that most visitors to New York in 1964 eventually understood. Holding the World's Fair in New York City was redundant. Even without the fair, New York already held the whole world within its environs. The other cities Namath knew—like Pittsburgh, Cleveland, and Birmingham—had the same basic structure through which one could gauge movement. Walk through Pittsburgh for a bit, and the buildings grew shorter, a clear indication that the central city was gone. That kind of philosophy did not work in New York City. Turning down street after street, heading north one time and west another and then south and east, Namath continually confronted yet another matrix of activity.

One particular structure that caught Namath's eye was Shea Stadium, which loomed near the fairgrounds. The Mets were terrible, having won only 23 games at this the midpoint of the season. But football was played in Shea as well. A new team, in fact, would be starting there in the autumn. The old Titans of the American Football League were moving from the Polo Grounds to Shea, changing their name in the process.

At night, things got even better, with an explosion of sights and sounds. Returning to Manhattan well after midnight, Namath, Hicks, and Walsh wandered around for a few more hours, not wanting it to end. It had been a big deal, a trip they would never forget. When they got back to their car on 39th Street, something strange had *not* happened. The car had not been ticketed. Perhaps the New York police simply could not believe the sight of a doorless car with Alabama plates in the heart of the city, and they gave it a one-time break. Regardless, Hicks climbed into the driver's seat and they headed back to New Jersey. As they pulled out, Namath remarked that the whole thing seemed like a dream.

———

Back on campus, Namath and the rest of the Tide prepared for the season. Most analysts thought that they would be a good, but not great, team by Alabama standards. They were ranked sixth nationally, but still second in the SEC behind the top-ranked team in the country, Ole Miss. Benny Marshall of the *Birmingham News* predicted a 5–0 start for the Tide, but added that the final five games would rough up their record. It was, as he put it, a "wait-and-see team."[28]

It was a strange and sometimes tragic return to football for the region. It had been a brutally hot summer, and throughout the Deep South football players sweated through sweltering practices. On September 1, Richard Ellzey, an eighteen-year-old sophomore fullback for Ole Miss, collapsed on the practice field after fielding a punt. Doctors attempted to revive him, but he died almost immediately. An autopsy revealed that Ellzey had died from a congenital condition causing a vessel of the heart to collapse. Doctors had treated him for asthma, but in fact he suffered a series of heart attacks prior to his death. The entire team flew to Meridian for his funeral, as the remainder of the conference hoped to avoid a similar tragedy.[29]

Perhaps the heat made Bryant even more testy than usual. Or it might have been his unwillingness to forget or forgive. One day Furman Bisher showed up for a preseason interview with Bryant. Bear refused to talk to him. After three hours of waiting, Bisher left the campus under the direction of a security guard. That Bisher thought he could meet with Bryant to talk over Alabama's prospects, as he said was his intention, did not go over well with the coach. Clearly, Bisher had hoped to get some sort of reaction from Bryant, and he succeeded. The university in short order supported Bryant and released an official statement declaring that the athletic department "believes [Bisher] has not been objective in his attitude toward the university."[30]

On the field, Bryant practiced a two-platoon system for the upcoming season, designating, but not completely relegating, players to one side of the ball. Beginning in the 1964 season, a coach could substitute as many players as he wanted on any down so long as the clock was stopped. If he wanted to substitute, a coach could call a time-out to do so. When the clock ran, he could substitute up to two players at a time. The system was named by Red Blaik, the head coach of Army, who, along with Fritz Crisler of Michigan, helped start the system in the aftermath of World War II and spoke of most things in military jargon. It was abandoned in 1953, but slowly worked its way back into the NCAA rulebook. Most coaches welcomed the change as a way to better use the specific abilities of their players, but some, like Shug Jordan of Auburn, did not. "College football is now out of the educational field and into the entertainment field," he said. "Football is now a game where coaches will strictly exploit the talent of a particular boy without having to particularly teach him anything."[31]

Bryant most likely agreed with Jordan's assessment of the two-platoon system, but he also understood that it was the new law of the land. He planned on maintaining his "best 11 in the game" approach, and made sure that offensive players learned defense and defenders learned offense. In keeping with his proven ability to adapt to the rules of the game, though, Bryant practiced and perfected the two-platoon system for his own purposes. Moreover, he seemed downright pleased with his team. "Let there be reassurance for those of Paul Bryant's friends who might have fretted because the Crimson Tide is in its second week of practice and scarcely one unhappy word or angry roar has been heard from the coach of this football team," Marshall wrote. "Paul Bryant has NOT lost his voice."[32]

One reason for Bryant's calm was that Namath was looking better than ever. Although it was well known that Bryant preferred to grind the ball on the ground, it was equally well known that Bryant used the tools he had. "Recall that Bryant had a fellow named Babe Parilli at Kentucky who was quite a passer," Max Moseley of the *Montgomery Advertiser* wrote. "Passing was Kentucky's main offense that year." That Parilli and Namath came from the same county in Pennsylvania probably did not matter, but the circuit between the two quarterbacks might have been neatly completed had Moseley mentioned it. At any rate, and no matter who was reporting it, Namath was clearly the key to the 1964 Alabama team.[33]

Just before the season opener, Bear got back into his usual form. After announcing that Namath and Mike Hooper would serve as captains for the season opener, he spoke of Georgia as if it were an NFL all-star team. "Those big old tackles, we might never get them stopped," he told the media. "They might run over everything we've got." No one bought it. By this time in his career, Bryant was a continual and recognized poor-mouther when it came to assessing his own talent and an exaggerator extraordinaire when it came to his opponents' ability. Even the mostly flattering *Montgomery Advertiser* referred to Bryant as the "Sad Bear" and ran a photo with the caption "Weeping Again!"[34]

In the autumn of 1864, General William T. Sherman prepared for his march across the South. Before setting off, he telegraphed General Grant. "I can make this march," he wired, "and make Georgia howl!" Although no one in Alabama, at least no one hoping to survive until sundown, would ever compare a local hero to General Sherman, Namath had an awful lot of "Uncle Billy" in him, especially when it came to Georgia. A century after Sherman's famous telegraph, another northerner made Georgia howl.[35]

Ironically, probably the only one involved in the Georgia-Alabama game who knew the Sherman quote was the new Bulldogs coach, Vince Dooley, who was making his debut in the September 19 opener at Tuscaloosa. While serving as an assistant coach at Auburn, Dooley had received his master's degree in history and was preparing to continue on for a PhD when he received a call from the athletic director at Georgia. Did he want a head coaching opportunity? Only thirty-one years old, Dooley accepted the offer, confident that he could go back to his study of southern history and a career as a professor if coaching did not work out. After facing the Namath-led Alabama team in his first season, it looked as if Dooley might have to return to the library sooner rather than later.[36]

The "big old" tackles of Georgia that so worried Bryant never bothered Namath, as he returned to varsity football the same way he started it, with a sound thrashing of the Bulldogs, 31–3. Namath accounted for 222 total yards of offense (57 more than Georgia's team total), including 167 passing, as well as three rushing touchdowns. Also impressive was Namath's ability to move the team on lengthy, time-consuming drives. Two of Alabama's scoring drives were over 70 yards, and two others were over 60. "Quarterback Joe Namath," the decidedly anti-Alabama *Atlanta Journal-Constitution* reported, "the man with the golden arm, turned the golden anniversary affair between Georgia and Alabama into a personal homecoming celebration." What was even more impressive was that Georgia was a fine team destined for a bowl game.[37]

On September 26, Alabama played Tulane in Mobile. Tulane was not much of a team, having won only one game in the past two years, and lost its first game of the season 31–0 to Texas. Scoreless after one quarter, Alabama put together two long drives in the second quarter for a field goal and a Namath touchdown run. In the second half, Alabama continued its domination, scoring 26 more points to Tulane's six. In all, Namath threw for 123 yards and one touchdown, and ran for another 52 yards and two more scores, leading Alabama to a 36–6 win. With Sloan nursing a dislocated finger and relegated to defense only, Namath played the entire game and led the Tide on all of its six scores. Still, Bryant found something to complain about. "We had no quickness whatsoever," he told the papers. "I thought Namath had another fine night," he conceded. "He made some awfully good calls out there tonight." Some humor came from Tulane's ineptitude, as the team appeared confused when preparing to kick off after scoring their first touchdown of the season. One

Tulane sportswriter quipped snidely that the team had never been schooled on what to do after actually scoring.[38]

The next week, October 3, Alabama hosted Vanderbilt in Birmingham. Vanderbilt's offense had yet to score on the year, and it looked as if the game would be another easy one for the Tide. But Alabama again came out flat and undisciplined, committing three special teams penalties, including two roughing-the-kicker flags. At halftime the game was scoreless. Four minutes and eight seconds into the second half, Namath threw a touchdown pass to Hudson Harris for the first points of the game. In the fourth quarter, a Vanderbilt defender taunted Namath, shouting, "Hey number twelve, what's your name?" On his way back to the huddle, Namath replied, "You'll see it in the headlines tomorrow." He then threw a touchdown pass to Tommy Tolleson, who made a great catch on a floater. It was Namath's 24th touchdown of his career, a new school record. The real highlight of the game, though, came on a Namath run. Nine plays into a drive that began at their own 10-yard line, Namath brought the Tide to the line of scrimmage at the Vanderbilt 15. Dropping back to pass, he straightened to freeze the secondary, then sprinted toward the defense, cut outside, and crossed the goal line. It was a small play in an already memorable season, but one that showcased not only Namath's ability to pass and run, but his remarkable acumen in presenting the two simultaneously with no sign of preferring either. He truly was playing like the best three-tool quarterback in the nation—arm, legs, and brain.[39]

After three games, it was looking like the official year of Joe Willie. For the first time in memory the emphasis on the Crimson Tide was centering on a single individual. The Tuscaloosa, Montgomery, and Birmingham newspapers wrote side-by-side articles about the games and Namath's personal accomplishments. "All-America Bidder," "Dapper Joe," "Mr. Everything," and the

"Reformed Quarterback" introduced the topic of Namath's brief but record-paced 1964 season. After three games, he had thrown for 538 yards and seven touchdowns, had run for another six touchdowns, and laid claim to the all-time Alabama record with 24 touchdown passes, breaking a mark shared by Harry Gilmer and Ed Salem. The *Crimson White* ran a special column listing seven current Namath records and another six within striking distance, and predicted that by the end of the season he "should go down as the greatest individual performer in Alabama history."[40]

Even Bryant seemed pleased with Namath. His quarterback was having another great season, but Bryant was most happy that Namath's public atonement was complete. He had not sulked or complained—at least not in public—and for Bryant that was the true mark of a champion. Now a senior leader, and one who had found his way back to the team with grace and penitence, Namath stood prepared to command the team in all possible ways.

On October 10, Namath and the Tide took the field at Denny Stadium in Tuscaloosa against North Carolina State. It was set to be a reunion of sorts, as one of N.C. State's standout players was Tony Golmont, Namath's old teammate from Beaver Falls. Golmont had accepted a scholarship to play wide receiver for the Wolfpack, but soon found himself on the other side of the ball playing cornerback. Golmont grew to enjoy defense, preferring to "dish it out rather than take it," and quickly became a hero there when he scored the team's first touchdown of the 1964 season on an interception return for a touchdown in N.C. State's upset victory over heavily favored North Carolina.[41]

The Beaver Falls reunion got a fair degree of attention. N.C. State's head coach, Earle Edwards, joked that he hoped "Namath will throw one to his old buddy," and "One or two for old times' sake would be fine with me." A large contingent of fans from

Beaver Falls, led by Joe Tronzo and a slew of Golmont's relatives, rented a plane to watch the game and, afterward, to spend the evening with Namath and Golmont.[42]

In the locker room, Namath got dressed for the game, but his mind seemed somewhere else. He put on his uniform and inadvertently put his thigh pads on backward. Then he put on his cleats, but did not tape up his feet and ankles. The thigh pads miscue was silly, but taping his feet was crucial. Alabama trainer Jimmy Goostree understood that taping ankles as stiffly as possible was the key not only to preventing twisted ankles but also in lessening the lateral give of the entire leg. Namath knew it as well and always taped his ankles and shoes prior to a game or practice. It was how he originally gained his "flashy appearance" of wearing "white" shoes. In actuality, they were standard black shoes covered with white tape. This game Namath jogged onto the field for the afternoon without the added support.[43]

Similar to the Tulane and Vanderbilt games, Alabama started slowly. After a quarter and a half, the game was scoreless. Namath played well enough, completing seven of eight passes for 52 yards, and looked as if he would soon lead another breakout for the Crimson Tide offense. No one in the crowd of 38,000, other than Bryant, who was always worried, seemed overly concerned that the game remained scoreless into the second period. Namath was moving the team, and soon, it seemed, the Tide would pull away from the Wolfpack as they had against Georgia, Tulane, and Vanderbilt.

A little over halfway through the second quarter, Namath drove the Tide across midfield. Standing over center, he spotted his old teammate Golmont to his left and called the signals and took the snap. He dropped straight back five quick steps and, with the coordination of a dancer, spun around, briefly turning his back to the line of scrimmage, and rolled back and to his left. After turning back toward the defense, he read the pursuit. It was a play no one in the country could perform better—not even Roger Staubach of the Naval Academy—where Namath had the option to pitch to a trailing running back, stop and throw from a standing position, continue to run and throw across his body in one motion, or run the ball himself.

Golmont had containment, so he shadowed Namath as his friend made his way across the field. Still behind the line of scrimmage, Namath dug his right foot into the soft turf and turned upfield. As Golmont broke toward the runner, Joe collapsed as if he had been shot. Golmont was still a few yards away from Namath, but closer than anyone else to the play. He ran up to his friend. "What happened, buddy?" he asked. Namath, still on the ground, replied, "I think I hurt my knee." As the medical staff ran onto the field, Golmont retreated to his huddle, fairly certain that Namath's injury was minor.[44]

Bear Bryant walks off the field as head trainer Jimmy Goostree works on Namath's right knee. The injury occurred against North Carolina State when Namath fell to the ground untouched after attempting to cut upfield. (Bryant Museum)

So intense had the rivalry with Georgia Tech become in the aftermath of the *Saturday Evening Post* suit that Bryant chose to wear a helmet for protection during the pregame warm-ups in 1964. Two years earlier a Tech fan had thrown a whiskey bottle that narrowly missed Bryant. (Bryant Museum)

12

"Joe Moves Like a Human Now"

Namath is the finest athlete I have ever seen—with the quickest hands. And he can run when trapped.

—Joe May, LSU scout, on the day Namath was injured

THE APPLAUSE SEEMED to build and ripple across Denny Stadium in the third quarter of the Alabama–North Carolina State game as the 38,000 spectators saw Joe Namath emerge from the locker room and jog toward the Tide bench. Namath had limped to the bench in the second quarter, and had to be helped into the locker room, but now, sportswriter Ray Holliman wrote, "he was trotting well enough to indicate that the injury may not keep him out long."[1]

Bryant knew better. He must have sensed that the slow jog was mostly for show, that his quarterback's knee was not just "slightly twisted," as the newspapers would report. Or perhaps he was just overly cautious. He had seen Mike Fracchia, a back who combined exceptional speed, quickness, and power as well as any he had coached, go down with a similar injury and struggle for years to regain his brilliant form. Bryant knew that Namath was too rare a talent to send back into the game. The knee "had swollen up and we got him off of it quick," he said after the game. "I had no intention of using him in the second half even if we had lost." And that, of course, did not happen. Junior Steve Sloan capably led Alabama to a 21–0 victory.[2]

The reports on Namath's injury were as varied as they were incorrect. In Beaver Falls, people read that Namath twisted his ankle when he was tackled by Golmont. Other stories correctly acknowledged that Namath had injured his right knee, usually listing it as having been twisted. The expectation was that Namath would miss the next game against Tennessee, but no more than that.[3]

In 1964, knee injuries relied more heavily on rehabilitation than surgery. Such injuries were classified in one of three categories—mild, moderate, or severe—with surgery recommended only for the last category. A standard method for diagnosis was the presence of blood and/or fluid in the joint. If there was no fluid, then the injury was considered mild; if there was just fluid, or a combination of blood and fluid, the injury was considered moderate; and if there was pure blood in the joint, the injury was severe. After draining Namath's knee and finding primarily fluid with perhaps a trace of blood, Alabama surgeon Ernest C. Brock Jr. decided not to operate. Rather, he prescribed a series of treatments including rest, local injections, compression bandages, cold packs followed by heat, splints, pressure dressings, and aspiration of the joint.[4]

On Monday Sloan practiced with the starting team. Namath spent the day, as well as the one before, flat on his back in the hospital getting his knee drained and undergoing medical tests. If his physician knew the precise extent of his injury—and it was doubtful he did—he did not tell the Alabama sportswriters who were sleuthing around the facility. Benny Marshall reported only that at some point on Monday Joe would rise to a vertical position, and blood would "course down through his knee." If it swelled again he would not play against Tennessee at the end of the week. But Marshall was confident that Namath's knee would not keep him out of many more games. Sportswriters used words like "strained" and "twisted" to describe the injury, not "torn."[5]

Information flowed out of Alabama's coaching quarters like the slow, vague, unsatisfying news coming out of the Politburo. An angry Bear Bryant took one call from his favorite columnist. "I thought he was going to be all right," he said. "But trainer Jim Goostree and the doctor had reexamined the knee. Now they're concerned." Goostree confirmed the report, mentioning something about an injured tendon leading into the knee and some possible cartilage damage, before adding ominously that Namath might not be ready to play against the Vols. "Right now, it doesn't look like he could be stable enough to do the job.... About all I can say now is that he is out indefinitely. Maybe that means two days, or a week. I don't know."[6]

By midweek Namath was out of the hospital and back on the practice field—or at least near the practice field. He walked briskly around the cinder track circling the field and played pitch-and-catch with another injured teammate. "He walks pretty good," an observer told Bryant, who just shook his head and answered, "You can't do much walking against Tennessee and the other teams we play from here in." "You just can't tell about knees," Bear continued. "Nobody knows about knees. X-rays won't show cartilage damage, if there is any. Past experience with Mike Fracchia... makes me mighty leery."[7]

Bryant's temper was never kindly in the week before a Tennessee game, and Namath's injury and the constant questions about its severity only added to his prickliness. Fifteen times his teams had taken the field against the Vols, and only four times had they left winners. Bryant's 4–8–3 record against Tennessee was the most glaring blemish on his career. In seven tries as Kentucky's coach he had never beaten the legendary General Bob Neyland, and he did not get a win against the Vols in his first three tries as Alabama's coach. Even though Tennessee's fortunes had declined in the early 1960s—the Tide had whipped them convincingly in 1961, 1962, and 1963—Bryant still fretted about the matchup. Now with Namath walking on a gimpy knee and Sloan untested before a really hostile crowd, Bryant arrived even earlier to begin his workday and departed his office even later.[8]

In 1964 Tennessee was rebuilding quickly under first-year coach Doug Dickey. He was a smart, persuasive man who generally knew what to say and how to get the job done. That year he impetuously traveled to Montgomery to recruit Alabama's biggest prospect, Richmond Flowers Jr. of Lanier High School. Son of the state's controversial attorney general, Flowers was one of the fastest runners in the nation and Bryant's top recruit. "I was just blessed with speed," Flowers said. "And it was an amazing amount of speed. I don't know where it came from but I had it. And I was white, which was at a premium back then." Several times Bear visited Flowers, and the recruit liked and deeply admired the coach, but he had one abiding and overwhelming fear. "The 'A-Club' at Alabama was notorious for its initiations. I had heard that those old boys in charge of it could get really mean and tough. And given the emotions around my father's position on desegregation, I don't think I could have survived the hazing." At the end of his official visit to Tennessee, Dickey took him aside and said, "Okay, Richmond, what is it going to take to get you to Tennessee?" Without hesitation, he answered, "Coach, I don't want any freshman hazed." That was a deal Dickey could shake hands on.[9]

During his freshman year Flowers learned the value of the deal. After a summer practice the players were eating lunch when a big lineman said, "Okay, Flowers. Up on a table! Let's hear you sing!" "Oh no," Flowers thought. "Here it comes. Everyone told me you can't believe anything a coach says during recruiting." For the fastest player on the team, he was the slowest table climber. He moved like he was going to the electric chair. Just as he was finally standing on the table Dickey walked by. "Flowers, get the hell off that table!" he yelled. "What do you think you're doing?" he excoriated the upperclassmen. "You players haven't earned the right to haze anybody. Until we develop a winning tradition around here there *WILL BE NO HAZING!*" "There's a man," Flowers thought, "who knows the right words to say."

And the words that he said in the week before the Alabama game were as mild as Ivory soap. "Alabama is a football team without weaknesses," Dickey purred. "They are great offensively, and great defensively." Although the Vols were 3–1, having lost only to Auburn 3–0, they were entering the heart of their conference schedule, and Alabama would test their capabilities. All Dickey would promise was to have his team at the stadium on time.[10]

After he arrived at the Knoxville Holiday Inn, Bryant did his best to avoid promises and social engagements. On Friday afternoon Tide publicist Charley Thornton reminded Bear that the Tennessee people had invited him to a reception for Alabama coaches and sportswriters. "I don't believe I can make it," Bryant said. But after checking on Namath and receiving a dismal report he had a change of heart. "Well," he told Thornton, "I reckon I better go. The last time we were here, I went to one of those receptions and we won a game."[11]

Almost 50,000 spectators filed into Neyland Stadium on a gorgeous autumn afternoon, most hoping that the famed Tennessee "trap" would once again snare Alabama, the third-ranked team in the nation. They waited patiently until the Tide got the ball to see whether number 12 (Namath) or number 14 (Sloan) jogged onto the field. It was Sloan. Namath remained on the bench, watching the Alabama offense sputter and make unaccustomed mistakes. During the game Tennessee defenders blocked three kicks—an extra point attempt, a field goal attempt, and a punt—recovered two fumbles, and snagged one interception. Although the weather was perfect and the field fast, Alabama managed less than 250 yards total offense.[12]

The Tide's defense, however, was in a stingy, larcenous mood. In addition to holding the Vols under 150 yards of total offense, they recovered three fumbles, intercepted two passes, and blocked several punts. One block gave Alabama a short field and Sloan led the team to the end zone. Defensive standout Gaylon McCollough fielded a second blocked punt "like Willie Mays" and returned it 22 yards for a score. David Ray added a 30-yard field goal to give Alabama an imposing 16–0 halftime lead.

Early in the second half Tennessee's Hal Wantland swept the right end for an eight-yard touchdown and followed it up with a two-point conversion run. Suddenly Alabama's secure lead was cut in half and Tennessee was back in the game. It seemed as if someone had turned up the amplified sound system in Neyland. Standing in the stadium, looking down at the Tennessee River and across the valley toward the golden-red mountains, it suddenly seemed a fine day to be clothed in orange.

At that moment, with momentum firmly behind the Vols, Namath ran onto the field. A day before the game his physicians had concluded that Joe had not torn cartilage. They told Bear that his quarterback had only a torn tendon, a condition that was painful but less serious. It was the reason that Joe could leave the hospital on Tuesday, walk around the track on Wednesday, and play with a heavily bandaged knee on Saturday.

To be sure, he did not play like he had earlier in the season. He did not throw blocks, run option plays, or even toss many passes. But he provided solid, mature leadership, protecting the ball, executing a conservative game plan, and leading the Tide down the field for another field goal. The final score: 19–8. But it kept Alabama in the running for a national title. Texas, the top-ranked team, dropped a one-point game to Arkansas, strengthening the Tide's national position.

———

Long before he was the Old Ball Coach, Steve Spurrier was a high school all-state football, basketball, and baseball player in Tennessee and a great quarterback at the University of Florida. He was only a sophomore in 1964, but a ferociously confident one who had led his team to four consecutive victories. Sportswriters commented that the 193-pound Spurrier helped to make Florida the best of Ray Graves's teams, including his 9–2 1960 squad. Always ready to publicly praise an opponent, Bear said, "Florida has one of the strongest teams that I've seen since I came back to Alabama a few years ago, except our 1961 National Champions. And . . . we'll have to play over our heads to win that big one."[13]

The game worried him. The combination of the previous season's loss and the hoopla that always surrounded a homecoming game soured his mood. All week he had made his team watch the Gators' previous year's 10–6 victory. It was like a horror movie without vampires and werewolves, Benny Marshall felt. And it got Bear thinking about scary things. He wanted his players to be like snakes for the upcoming game—"coiled and deadly." That was the way to play football: mean, ready to uncoil and hit when the center snapped the ball. But nagging him was Namath's condition.

He was penciled in to start the game, but Bryant said he was operating at only about 75 percent. "Joe moves like a human now," he reflected. "He moved like a cat before."[14]

Florida sportswriters agreed with Bryant—he had good reason to worry. Without Namath in the lineup to spread the defense, Alabama had no explosive runners, no halfbacks like Mike Fracchia, who was a threat to score from anywhere on the field. Joe Halberstein, *Gainesville Sun* sportswriter, made a list from the Alabama-Tennessee game to demonstrate that without Namath the Tide's offense lacked punch:

1. Alabama first down on the Vol 11—a field goal.
2. Alabama first down on the Vol 7—nothing.
3. Alabama first down on the Vol 30—fumble.
4. Alabama first down on the Vol 1—touchdown in FIVE plays, a fifth try possible because Tennessee was offsides on fourth down.
5. Alabama first down on the Vol 25—pass intercepted.
6. Alabama first down on the Vol 2—field goal blocked.
7. Alabama first down on the Vol 8—field goal good.

He believed the reason Bryant sent Namath into the Tennessee contest in the second half was to save the game. Sloan was a fine athlete, and a very good defensive back, but he could not keep 'Bama undefeated.[15]

Florida had not been 4–0 since before the Kennedy-Nixon election, and the week of the game the AP poll ranked the Gators ninth and Alabama third (Alabama had advanced to second on the UPI poll). "We can safely assume that football in the Sunshine State has arrived," wrote Harry Mehre, a leading columnist for the *Atlanta Journal*. The clash in Denny Stadium was the premier game of the week, and most likely would decide the SEC championship. Fittingly, scalpers were getting more than $100 for a ticket. Their only problem was that they had so few to sell. Bear had grown accustomed to such big games. "It's the biggest game of the week," he told reporters, "because it's the game we're playing this week.... Just as next week's game (Mississippi State) will be the next big one." But Coach Ray Graves was less blasé. A Miami newspaper headlined his feeling about the contest: GATORS WILL BEAT 'BAMA BECAUSE GOD IS ON OUR SIDE.[16]

The headline and story was pinned on the bulletin board in the Alabama dressing room. Affixed beside it was a picture of Gator players carrying an ecstatic Graves off the field after the previous year's game. No comment was added to either item.

The weather in Tuscaloosa on Saturday, October 24, was perfect—sunny and mild. Male students and alumni normally wore jackets and ties to the games, just as women dressed in smart outfits with corsages pinned to their bodices. But that was the code for a run-of-the-mill contest. Homecoming demanded that everyone step it up a notch, and they did. Splashes of fall color— yellow, orange, and especially crimson—moved into Denny as game time neared. The dress code was Sunday best, commented Howell Raines. "But not more decorous." And certainly not flashy or cheap. In Tuscaloosa, fashions had not yet turned the corner into the 1960s.[17]

Joe Namath led the Crimson Tide onto the field, but even in the pregame routine he moved like a tightrope walker over Niagara Falls. It seemed like he was thinking about every step, every physical movement. The way he bent over to take a snap, dropped back, planted his foot, released the ball—it looked more rehearsed than natural, more thoughtful than instinctual. Trainer Jim Goostree fully understood that Joe was damaged goods. "We'd better have

Steve (Sloan) ready," he had told Bryant on Wednesday. "One lick and Joe's knee could go again."[18]

To protect Namath—and to help Sloan, if Joe's knee didn't last—Bryant had installed a conservative game plan based on runs between the tackles, short passes, and draws. "I think we can beat them if our kicking game holds up and if somebody doesn't get hurt," Bryant told reporters. Although Spurrier was a talented sophomore, he was still only playing in his fifth varsity game, and Ray Graves also went with a limited game plan. The inevitable result was a game that featured punting and a fight for field position. For eleven minutes of the first quarter Namath did little more than take snaps and hand off the ball. He threw only two passes, completing them both for a total of 28 yards.[19]

The contest was still 0–0 when he attempted his first run. After a one-yard gain, he was hit and fumbled. Instinctually, he scrambled for the ball, but Florida recovered. As the players that had fought for the recovery got to their feet, Namath remained on the ground, clutching his knee, grimacing in pain. He had taken the one lick Goostree had talked about and his knee was gone again.

Namath watched most of the drive from the bench. With the ball on the 20-yard line, he struggled to his feet, waving off several teammates who moved to help him. Slowly, he began to walk, stiff-legged but not quite a limp, away from the action on the field and toward the entrance of the locker room. For a while no one in the stands noticed him. Then a few people in the bleachers behind the end zone saw him, and, forgetting the action on the field, they started to cheer for Joe Namath. Others joined the chorus of applause, standing and clapping and calling his name. He left the field, Benny Marshall wrote that day, "with the love of the multitude and its admiration, complete, ringing in his ears." There were moments, Marshall speculated, sealed off from the game, that he would be remembered longer than the tumult on the field. "This was one of them, the exit of Joe Namath of Beaver Falls, Pa., who for all I know might never play football for Alabama again."[20]

After the injury to his knee, Namath never played the game with the same athleticism he showed in his first two varsity seasons. In 1964 his future as a football player was in serious doubt. (Bryant Museum)

Not only had the play ended Namath's competition for the afternoon, but it gave Florida a field position break. Expertly mixing passes with runs, Spurrier moved Florida toward the end zone. Three minutes into the second quarter he tossed a nine-yard pass for a touchdown. With that score a game that had moved at the speed of a traffic jam suddenly quickened.

Namath was hurt, Spurrier had found his game, and Steve Sloan, the pious, rail-thin underclassman from Cleveland, Tennessee, found the expectations of a splendidly attired homecoming crowd on his back. He responded divinely. On the ensuing kickoff the Alabama returner was tackled on the 13. From there, Sloan was flawless. Like Spurrier, he adroitly mixed runs and passes, marching the Tide down the field in a 19-play drive that tied the score.

Later in the second half Namath returned to the sideline, an enormous ice pack taped to his knee. He sat and watched the game for a while, then rose and nervously stood behind his teammates and supported the team. He witnessed a terrific game. In the third quarter Spurrier engineered another drive. Twice he picked up crucial fourth-down conversions on the way to a touchdown. Florida led 14–7 going into the final quarter.

Alabama fought back. A long punt return gave Sloan a short field and he moved his team in for a score. The game was tied 14–14. Late in the quarter Alabama mounted another drive that ended in a 21-yard David Ray field goal. With time running out, Spurrier abandoned the running game, throwing on nearly every down. With no time-outs and the ball on the Alabama nine, the Florida field goal team sprinted onto the field and hurriedly got off the final play of the game. As Crimson Tide linemen dove to block the ball, Jimmy Hall attempted a 15-yard field goal. The ball twisted to the right and missed.

After the game, as Alabama players celebrated in the locker room, Namath avoided the sportswriters, not really wanting to answer questions about his injury. Instead he searched for Sloan. Seeing him, Joe walked over as quickly as he could. The two talked for a few seconds as Namath embraced his substitute. "That's what makes football teams, I think," Marshall wrote.

After the Florida victory Alabama was 6–0, ranked third nationally in both the AP and the UPI polls. Only Ohio State and Notre Dame were ranked ahead of them, though there was no chance of the Tide meeting either in a bowl game. Two teams on Alabama's schedule, Georgia Tech and LSU, ranked in the second half of the top ten. As in 1962, when Alabama had won their first eight games before losing a 7–6 contest to Georgia Tech, the Tide had a realistic shot at another national title. Ohio State still had to play nationally ranked Michigan, and Notre Dame was headed for a showdown with USC. Of the top three teams, none had an easy path to the title. The winner of the national title would have to win out.

Namath's knee was not so much day-to-day as hour-to-hour. Not only did Bear keep him out of any contact in practice, but he generally relegated Joe to the sidelines during any strenuous activities. Namath jogged slowly around the track, took his place behind the center for walk-through game-plan drills, and otherwise watched as Steve Sloan ran the team. It was not entirely Sloan's team quite yet—but it was not Joe's either.

The Tide played its seventh game on Halloween night in Jackson, Mississippi. With a record of 3–3, which included close losses against several good SEC teams and a handful of wins against weaker nonconference squads, Mississippi State did not appear to have the talent to compete with Alabama. But during an easy Friday practice Namath tweaked his knee again and looked doubtful for the game. Bryant would have to win or lose with Sloan.

Win or lose, that is, if Mississippi State took the field. For some time it did not look promising. Alabama poured onto the field to play the game, then waited, and waited some more. Perhaps Coach Paul Davis was delivering an especially stirring pregame speech to his players, or maybe the clock in the locker room was slow. For whatever plausible or implausible reason, the Bulldogs failed to come out for the kickoff until after the referee penalized them for delay of game. But once on the field, they looked like world-beaters, promptly taking the kickoff and marching toward Alabama's end zone. With a crowd of more than 45,000 in Memorial Stadium ringing cowbells and shouting encouragement, quarterback Ashby

Cook, fullback Hoyle Granger, and halfback Price Hodges ran play after play into the heart of the Tide's vaunted defense. The Bull-dogs, Atlanta sportswriter Jan Van Duser commented, "weren't supposed to be biting the powerful Red Elephants," but they were. On the final play of the first drive Hodges carried the ball through the center of Alabama's line, butted heads with the middle line-backer, and continued into the end zone. Mississippi State led 6–0, the crowd was cheering wildly, and Joe Namath was sitting on the bench.[21]

Namath's sole contribution to the evening's activities was to hold the ball on one field goal attempt. Beyond that he watched. His leg was so heavily bandaged that he looked like he had to struggle just to stand and move. Sloan, however, moved like a colt. He "bewitched, bothered, and bewildered" the Mississippi State defenders, commented one reporter. Not to be outdone by his out-of-state scribe, Alf Van Hoose of the *Birmingham News* wrote that the junior quarterback "passed like Joe Namath, ran like Steve Sloan, and masterminded Paul Bryant's attack plan like Pat Tram-mell." On the night of hobgoblins and witches he played like a monster, completing 14 of 23 passes for 176 yards and carrying the ball 14 times for another 48 yards. He did not toss an interception or lose a fumble in leading Alabama to a 23–6 victory.[22]

Mississippi State was less a test than an opportunity for Namath and the other injured players to rest before the Tide played three traditional SEC powers—LSU, Georgia Tech, and Auburn. With a thrilling 11–10 Halloween night victory over archrival Ole Miss, the Tigers from Baton Rouge had improved their record to 5–0–1 and their national ranking to eighth. Almost certainly the victor of the Alabama-LSU game would win the SEC and attract the best bowl invitation. The two squads had similar offensive and especially defensive traits, which was hardly surprising since LSU's

Charlie McClendon had played for and coached with Bryant. Bear genuinely liked Charlie, and McClendon held Bryant in awe, always addressing him as "Coach Bryant" and answering his questions with a polite "Yes, sir" or "No, sir."

The Tide and the Tigers were also plagued by quarterback injuries. Namath and LSU's Pat Screen were unlikely to play much, but their places had been filled superbly by Sloan and Billy Ezell, a thin junior from Greenville, Mississippi. Although Ezell's completion rate was under 33 percent, and his running was suspect, he had brought his team back in the Ole Miss game, and he possessed football smarts. "It's the main thing Ezell has going for him," McClendon said. "Football savvy. He can call a game. And pressure won't bother him."[23]

On game day, Bear awoke at 4:30 a.m. in his Holiday Inn room in Bessemer and pushed back the curtain to see what the weather promised. LSU was a big, powerful team, but not as quick as 'Bama, and Bryant did not want to play them in the rain. There were still stars in the sky, but rain was in the forecast and he didn't like the way it looked. By 6:30 he was up and off to work, agonizing over every detail, checking and rechecking his notes. At breakfast with his team he struck a familiar note. He liked to say that a football game was not a sixty-minute event, but more like thirteen or fourteen minutes of live action. There might be 150 or so plays in a game, almost all lasting for less than six seconds. That was not very long, he thought. He reminded his players, "Remember, do your job for six seconds, every play, and make something happen. Don't wait for it to happen. Make it happen. Do that, and you're going to win."[24]

After a steak breakfast he went for a walk with his quarterbacks—Joe Willie, Steve Sloan, and Wayne Trimble—and talked about strategy. Then he met with his coaches and discussed personnel.

The important thing was to have his best players on the field during those crucial six-second plays. Most importantly, he instructed, "in the clutch, when we know they've got to throw the football, I want Steve (Sloan) out there and I want Hudson (Harris), too. We're going to need them." Although both had been shifted to offense, Steve was an outstanding safety and Hudson a terrific cornerback. Bear liked to know that if the ball went up in the air he had the right boys on the field to go get it.[25]

When he finished talking, it was almost noon, time to load up the buses and go to Legion Field. He put on his hat, grabbed a raincoat, and looked once again at the sky. "It's a dog-goned shame," he told a reporter. "I mean the weather. The biggest crowd we ever had, and a day like this." Then he got on a bus and ordered a passenger to change seats. "You sit over there. I'm a little superstitious," he said as it began to rain.

Some 70,000 spectators crammed into Legion Field, the most that had ever assembled to watch a sporting event in Alabama. The list of state and regional dignitaries gave it a bowl game feeling. Even Hollywood was represented by Academy Award–nominated actor Chill Wills. One of the stars in John Wayne's *The Alamo*, whose line-in-the-sand theme was enormously popular in Alabama, Chill said he had come to Birmingham "to see the best football game in the land, since the rug has been pulled out from under my favorite coach, Darrell Royal of Texas." Meaning no snub to Bear, Wills was quick to send his best wishes to all his friends in Alabama.[26]

But even with all the activity in the stands, the gawking in Wills's direction, and the cheering for the Tide, the game began badly for Alabama. The field was slick, the LSU linemen strong, and the Tide players unexpectedly nervous. In less than four minutes, Alabama made its first miscue when John Mosley fumbled a punt and LSU recovered on the Alabama 21. In five plays Ezell piloted the Tigers toward the end zone, capping the drive with a 13-yard touchdown pass to Doug Moreau. LSU led 6–0, though the light rain had stopped and the sun was beginning to peek through the clouds.[27]

Late in the first quarter Alabama's punter, David Ray, followed his coach's advice to make something happen. He boomed a 67-yard kick that rolled dead on the LSU seven. Unable to move, the Tigers punted on third down, a short kick that Ray Perkins returned to the LSU 32. From there a series of running plays that featured Steve Bowman ended with the fullback bulling into the end zone from the one. But Alabama's 7–6 lead did not last long. Early in the second quarter Moreau kicked a field goal, giving the Tigers a 9–7 edge.

Namath watched the back-and-forth flow of the game from the sideline. He was suited to play but made no move toward the field until toward the end of the half. With time running out and Alabama needing a quick 10 or 15 yards for a field goal attempt, Bryant sent Namath in to throw a pass. Like an aged relief pitcher sent in to get one out, Joe half ran, half hobbled on to the field, called the play, took the snap, dropped back, and threw a perfect 12-yard strike. The pass set Ray up for a 37-yard field goal attempt, but the normally reliable kicker missed it.

The movement of the first half was noticeably absent in the second. Through a hard-fought third quarter Alabama's smaller players, outweighed on the line by 25 pounds a man, scrapped to hold the Tigers and get the ball back for the offense. But Sloan's offense went nowhere. It was mostly run three plays and kick, run three plays and kick. As the game entered the fourth quarter Bryant faced an important decision. If the contest was going to continue to be a defensive struggle—and it certainly appeared that that was the case—Bear wanted his best defensive players on the field. And that meant Steve Sloan at safety and Hudson Harris at defensive halfback. And if Alabama had to score more points, he needed to get Namath on the field.

"We were going to put Joe in there in the fourth quarter and put Steve in there at safety," Bear said after the game. Early in the quarter Bryant got some relief when Ray put the Tide in front 10–9 with a field goal. But all that really meant was that LSU would pass more. Midway through the last quarter, with LSU throwing on almost every down, Bryant sent in Sloan and Harris for an important third-down play. Harris, a square-jawed senior from Tarrant City, Alabama, read screen and moved forward from his position. His instincts were dead on. The quarterback overthrew his receiver by inches and Harris intercepted the pass, avoided a tackler, and ran 33 yards for the score. Alabama now led 17–9, and all Bryant wanted to do was get the game over. Keeping Namath on the sideline, he trusted his defense to keep the Tigers out of the end zone and Sloan to call running plays. Although LSU mounted two more drives, they did not score. Alabama remained undefeated and secured a hold on the SEC title.

————

Bryant and Namath had been there before—in Atlanta, favored to win, with everything to lose. In 1962, going into Alabama's mid-November game with Georgia Tech, they had been 8–0, ranked number one in the AP poll and number two in the UPI. They had traveled to historic Grant Field full of winning and made overconfident from reading their press clippings, faced a 5–2–1 Yellow Jacket team, and lost, failing by inches to convert a two-point conversion at the end of the game. "I think every one of us missed our blocks on that play," Lee Roy Jordan recalled more than a half century later. It was a painful loss, a bitter memory. Tide supporters said it was the kind of game that Pat Trammell would have found a way to win. He would have just threatened to kick the ass of anyone on the field who missed their assignment and then sauntered into the end zone. But Pat was gone, and so was a second national title.[28]

Yet there were no feelings of déjà vu. Everything about the 1964 game was palpably different. It might be that the two schools, both with rich football traditions, had never gotten over the 1961 Holt-Graning controversy. Neither the dapper, socially smooth Bobby Dodd nor Bear Bryant had handled the fallout very well, though supporters of each believed that their man had done nothing wrong. But the problems went deeper. Tide fans inside and outside the program thought Dodd and the Georgia Tech faithful were elitists who considered themselves better than the rubes in the rest of the SEC, and particularly the schools in the western half of the conference. By 1964 Dodd had dropped all but five of the other eleven SEC schools from Tech's home-and-home schedule, and Alabama was not in the privileged five. Georgia, Vanderbilt, and Tennessee were more to Dodd's liking than LSU, Mississippi State, Mississippi, and Alabama. The result was a distinct lack of good feeling by many members of the SEC for Tech. "It's common talk that some of the league's western members hold no fondness for Georgia Tech," noted the *Atlanta Constitution*.[29]

The bad blood spilled out at the conference's January 1964 meeting, when Dodd threatened that if the 140 Rule was not changed Tech would drop out of the SEC and become as independent as Notre Dame. The rule capped yearly football and basketball scholarships at forty-five, and limited the number of athletes on scholarship at any one time to 140. Its math was as simple as it was ruthless. If a school gave out forty-five scholarships a year and all the athletes stayed eligible, there would soon be 180 student-athletes on athletic grants. Only if scholarship athletes flunked out or dropped out could a university stay at or under the 140 number. Dodd maintained that his competitors intentionally and pitilessly "ran off" athletes who could not make the grade and help the program. Dodd refused to follow this policy, regarding a scholarship offered as something akin to a sacred contract. He would not intentionally force a boy off of the team to get his scholarship. The effect of his approach, he believed, put Georgia Tech at a competitive disadvantage. Instead of offering forty-five scholarships a year, Dodd offered only thirty-five, making sure that all his athletes had an opportunity to graduate. As he wrote in his autobiography, "We'd live with 10 boys a year, 20, 30, 40, 50, we don't give a damn how many boys you let us take. But don't tell us we gotta run 'em off."[30]

In the late January meeting the SEC presidents and athletic directors debated a revision of the 140 Rule, and it soon became clear that Dodd was not going to get the change he demanded. Before the final vote Tech's president, Edwin Harrison, asked to speak at the presidents' meeting. "Georgia Tech's interest is best served by withdrawal from the conference," he said, continuing that it would depart from the SEC effective June 30. Later he tried to say that the move was not simply about Rule 140, that Tech was a fundamentally different school than the others in the conference. "There is not another school in America like Georgia Tech trying to play football," he explained. But many at the meeting did not buy his argument. To Benny Marshall of the *Birmingham News* the substance of Harrison's discourse was, "We're out because, really, we're better."[31]

The brouhaha added a touch of desperation to the 1964 Alabama–Georgia Tech game. For the foreseeable future it was the last game in a great series that dated back to 1902, and Bear Bryant did not relish losing the final game to a school that had come to symbolize all of his recent troubles. "I won't deny my bitterness toward Tech," he later wrote. "And Atlanta, too, for that matter. I felt everything that had happened—the brutality issue, the first *Post* story, my suit, the 'fix' story, the Butts trial, all the heartaches—had sprung from the Chick Graning incident, from the way it was twisted to suit a rival viewpoint and then blown out of proportion by an unfair press." In his mind, Georgia Tech was not so much Bobby Dodd as the yahoos throwing whiskey bottles at him at Grant Field and, most of all, Furman Bisher—and he was not about to lose to Furman Bisher.[32]

In the week before the game Bryant wore two faces. He told reporters that the Tech game was important, yes, but no more so than any others. "I'd sure like to win, for the boys and for the University," he said, adding, "I'm selfish enough to want it personally, but it's no life or death proposition. And if they win, it won't be any upset." It was as if he had forgotten the 1962 loss that had cost him a national championship and all the bitterness associated with Atlanta. He was calm and deliberate, balanced, almost good-natured with reporters. If there was a pot to be stirred, he was not stirring.[33]

Away from the press, alone with his players, Bear was like a live wire, electric with energy and raw memories. "Strong feeling against Tech courses hotly through Alabama veins for any of a number of reasons," wrote John Underwood of *Sports Illustrated*. "Bryant's veins are no exception." Almost daily he talked to his players about winning and losing on the football field and in life. In his low, rumbling, mumbling style, he lectured that they were different from the big, talented, privileged boys who played at Tech. He had been coaching against Tech since before they were born, and had reached some definite conclusions: "Tech hits hard, but they don't hit hard all the time. They play tough, but they don't play tough all the time, because they don't live tough like we do." That was the soul of his message—that Alabama players had come from tough circumstances, worked hard, lived right, and met his unforgiving standards. The players were like him, Bryant suggested, winners because they had paid a higher price in life.[34]

Center Gaylon McCollough from Enterprise, Alabama, said as much to a national reporter covering the game. "In the spring, and then in the early fall, when it's two-a-day and dog-eat-dog, you think you'll never make it. You lie in your bed at night and you think, oh Lord, if I could only quit, if I could only get a day off. Every play is full out, and every workout is like a war. You go into every play like it was your last, you come back to the huddle keyed up for another. Then all of a sudden it's over, and the season's on, and it's easier. And now here we are with two games to go and a chance to go to another bowl game and win the national championship, and you know it's not every man gets this kind of chance."[35]

Even a player with a bum knee was determined not to miss out on such an opportunity. Though Namath moved laterally with great difficulty, he could still drop back and throw. The injury even improved his release. It removed the run option, previously available when he could not find an open receiver. Now it was drop back and throw. Find a receiver and release the ball. He was like a blind man whose loss of one sense magnified others. He was a sleight-of-hand ball handler and a passer. That was all he could do. So he honed those skills, becoming even better at each.[36]

And he was a leader. Bryant exuded the hard-edged confidence of a battle-hardened World War II general, someone along the lines of General George Patton. Namath oozed a different sort of confidence. It was less uptight, the smiling confidence of a new generation just coming of age. It was a more brash confidence, taking its cue from Cassius Clay/Muhammad Ali more than the aw-shucks athletes of the 1940s and 1950s. In 1964, bad leg and all, Joe Namath had it in spades.

At a pep rally in the gymnasium on the Thursday before the game Joe addressed the largest crowd of the year. "Two years ago," he said, "we went to Atlanta. We had won eight straight and were No. 1 in the country. We lost. This year we're 8 and 0, and we're No. 2. Saturday we're going to win in Atlanta, and we're going to come back to the No. 1 university in the country."[37]

His words were greeted by cheering students banging garbage-can covers. A teammate said that Joe's short speech sent shivers up his spine. How could Alabama lose? Coach Bryant had said that they would win because they were the products of a harder life. And Joe Namath had promised a victory. He had guaranteed it.

———

Several hours before the afternoon kickoff, Bryant led his team onto Grant Field for their ritual walkabout. It was usually a quiet time when players spoke in hushed voices and inspected the turf. Grant Field was a special place, hallowed in southern football tradition. It was the oldest campus stadium in the South, and football had been played there since 1905. In 1916 it had hosted the most lopsided game in the history of college football—Georgia Tech's 222–0 defeat of tiny Cumberland College. And of course, the 1962 Georgia Tech–Alabama game had been contested on the field. As far as football sites go, it was as solemn as the Rose Bowl or Yankee Stadium.

But there was no solemnity when the Tide players walked onto the field. It was a beautiful warm autumn day, and Bryant estimated that the stands were already about a quarter filled with boisterous Tech students yelling, "Go to hell, Alabama, go to hell!" and epithets significantly worse. Scoreboards on both ends of the stadium displayed the score: Georgia Tech 90, Alabama 0. Instead of giving the students the satisfaction of an acknowledgment, Bryant good-naturedly put on a red Alabama helmet and leisurely walked around the field. "I must have stood in front of the Tech bench five minutes, making believe like I was checking things out, making sure they could see me real good. They called me every name in the book, but I was ignoring them."[38]

By the time the players returned to the locker room Bear knew that they were ready to play, but in a quiet voice he framed the essence of a big game. It would last for only sixty minutes of clock time, and when it was over, it was over. Every player would remember the game the rest of their lives, reliving the high and low points in their minds. But once it had ended, they would never be able to change any part of it. The essence of football, he taught, boiled down to seizing opportunities, mastering the decisive moments. "In any big game there are five or six key plays that will decide the outcome," he said. "If you put out for five seconds on every play, you'll get your share of those key plays. You never know when they'll come, so you have to go all out every time."[39]

The scoreboard still had the 90–0 score when Alabama ran onto the field for the 46th game in the series. The announced attendance of 53,505 was the largest in the history of the Yellow Jacket stadium. The governors of both states, George Wallace and Carl Sanders, sat together, cheering as the bands and the teams entered the stadium. While the 'Bama band played "One Mint Julep," "Cotton Candy," "Days of Wine and Roses," and "Moon River," Bryant and Dodd, dressed in shirtsleeves, met and shook hands before their last coaching duel.[40]

Bryant had talked about the five or six key plays, and in the first twenty-eight minutes no Alabama or Georgia Tech player made one. Steve Sloan led the Tide on two drives into Tech territory. Both times Yellow Jacket defenders stopped Alabama and forced field goal attempts, which the usually reliable David Ray missed. Then, with less than two minutes remaining in the half, Tech moved for the first time into Alabama territory. Sensing an opportunity, Tech quarterback Bruce Fischer, tiny even by Alabama standards, dropped back to pass. Finding no open receivers and seeing an empty patch of parched grass in front of him, he tucked away the ball and ran. But he didn't tuck it tightly enough, and at about midfield the ball popped loose before he was hit. Alabama recovered the ball at the Tech 49-yard line.[41]

Fischer's fumble set off no alarms on the Tech sideline. Only a minute and forty-one seconds remained in a half in which neither team had done anything quickly or dramatically—in fact, neither had done much of anything at all. Perhaps, however, Bryant sensed some subtle shift in momentum; or maybe he was just playing a hunch. Whatever the case, instead of sending Sloan back into the game to safely run out the clock, he told Namath to take over the offense. Up until then Joe had taken the field for only a couple of uneventful plays.

Namath ran onto the field, an Atlanta journalist wrote, wearing "his throwing suit." Georgia Tech defenders batted down his first pass at the line of scrimmage, and tipped away a second before it reached a receiver. On third and 10, split end David Ray broke from the line of scrimmage, hesitated at about first-down distance, and then accelerated past the defensive back. As Ray neared the 17-yard line Namath fired a perfect "quail high blast" into his outstretched hands. Witnesses insisted that the ball seemed to "explode" out of Namath's hand in a tight, hard spiral that reached Ray on a trajectory that looked as flat as a tautly stretched rope. Ray was at the one-yard line before a Tech defender dragged him down from behind. On the next play, Steve Bowman dove through a sliver of a hole for the touchdown. With a minute and eighteen seconds remaining in the half Alabama finally had a 7–0 lead.[42]

Bryant followed Namath's perfect pass with a perfect call—an onside kick. Ray spun the kick off the side of his foot and it appeared as if a dozen players were trying to stick the slippery pig-skin to the ground. The play ended with a pile of Tide and Tech players fighting for the ball. When the bodies were scraped away like pieces of a wreck, Creed Gilmer, maybe the smallest defensive lineman in the SEC, was clinging to the ball on the Tech 48.

Namath trotted casually, confidently back to the huddle. His knee had held up for a series, his arm was loose, and if anyone at Grant Field had any doubt about what he was going to do they had left their seats to drink a Coca-Cola and eat a hot dog. Joe was not on the field to run out the half. He was there to pass, and he did just that. On the first play of the series he saw Raymond Ogden open at the 20 and hit him with another beautiful pass. Ogden caught the ball and ran to the three before he was tackled.

On the next play a Tech defender jumped in front of a receiver and almost intercepted a pass. He should have caught it, and he might have returned it more than 100 yards for a score. But he dropped it, giving Namath another chance. He needed only one. On second and goal he rolled out and flipped a soft butterfly of a pass to Ray for a touchdown. Namath added to his Alabama career touchdown total. But the record was not important to him. The win was.

And it was a win. With three key plays in less than two min-utes Alabama had ended the competitive phase of the contest. Even Bobby Dodd's friend Furman Bisher realized it. "In one brief moment of astounding perfection, coming at a time when it seemed Georgia Tech had successfully negotiated a battle of first half sur-vival, Joe Namath of Alabama came out of temporary retirement and plucked the hearts out of the Yellow Jackets' bosoms before the bugged eyes of 53,505 startled spectators."[43]

Namath stayed on the bench the entire second half watch-ing Sloan play his usual mistake-free but aesthetically uninspired game. And really, there was nothing that he could have done to top

Namath's artistry. Alabama accumulated another 10 points in the second half, and Tech managed to score a touchdown twenty-one seconds before the final whistle blew and Tide players hoisted Bryant onto their shoulders.

After the game a reporter asked Bryant why he kept Namath on the bench the second half. "We didn't want to pass much in the second half," he answered, and besides, "Joe's got a great pro career ahead of him and we didn't want to spoil it for him." But Bryant wouldn't have been himself if he had not added, "Of course, I'd played him 60 minutes if it meant winning the game." In the end, Joe did not need sixty minutes. He did not even need two.[44]

"I believe Joe can do just about anything," Bryant mused after the Georgia Tech game. He had no doubt that his quarterback would sign one of the largest professional contracts ever. But he wanted to send Joe off with a special memory of Tuscaloosa—a national title. After defeating Tech, Alabama received an invitation to play Texas in the Orange Bowl on January 1. And when Penn State defeated Ohio State, the Tide was solidly number two in both polls behind undefeated Notre Dame. Both teams, however, had their rival games to play—the Irish had USC and the Tide had Auburn. The title race was not over.[45]

But something odd was happening in Tuscaloosa. Since Bryant's return in the winter of 1957–58, the Tide had been unquestionably his. He was at the center of all newspaper and magazine stories about the squad, his players relegated to secondary, almost interchangeable roles. As great as Lee Roy Jordan and Pat Trammell had been at Alabama, they lived and played in Bear's long shadow. But now Namath had emerged from that shadow and attracted regional and national attention precisely because he was so different from Bryant and his teammates. Joe did not look, speak, or behave like Bryant's other boys, and it was not just because he was a northerner. It had nothing to do with North or South—Joe Namath was just different.

Sports Illustrated's John Underwood noticed it when he spent the week before the Georgia Tech game in Tuscaloosa. He wrote that Namath gave the team "a certain whimsy," but that was not exactly the correct word. Furman Bisher came closer when he labeled the quarterback a "non-conformist" who stood out in the Alabama locker room like a streetwalker at a Baptist church service. Casually smoking a cigarette as he answered questions about his brief, spectacular performance, Namath struck Bisher as wildly unlike his teammates, and perhaps even a new breed of athlete. "Nearly all Alabama players wear that death-row haircut," the columnist observed. "Namath wears his black hair in a natural cut, and gives you the impression of being a real swinging fellow. He conforms to nothing but the pattern of a remarkable quarterback." Namath, he continued, may have failed Maryland's entrance examination, but "he never failed anybody's examination as quarterback."[46]

Bisher was right. The player photographs in the 1964 Alabama programs display picture after picture of intense student-athletes dressed in jackets, white shirts, and ties, a few with slight half smiles, but most with grim, game-face expressions. Namath's photo stands out from the rest. Wearing a jacket and what appears to be a soft white shirt, buttoned fully but without a tie, he looks more like he's in a Hollywood publicity shot. He's tan, smiling, bright-eyed, and engaging, and far more glamorous than even a celebrated college quarterback has a right to look. In a cast of role players, he stands out like a matinee idol. While the others are stuck in the drab 1950s, Joe has already entered the Age of Aquarius.[47]

Nobody knew southern football talent like D. C. "Peahead" Walker. He started coaching in the late 1920s, and achieved success in the

1930s and 1940s at Wake Forest. He was a master of bestowing nicknames—he called all long-jawed players "Hogjaw" and any in the Wake Forest divinity school "Preacher," but was more inventive in other cases—and a legendary recruiter and evaluator of regional talent. By the early 1960s he had become the southern scout for the National Football League's New York Giants, which had the number one choice in the upcoming 1964 draft. And Peahead strongly believed that the top pick would be playing in the Thanksgiving Alabama-Auburn game—either Joe Namath or Tiger running back Tucker Frederickson would be a wealthy ballplayer very soon.[48]

"We like the way Namath throws," remarked Walker. "We like his quick release, his quick wrist, his good arm, his throwing accuracy. He can see the field. He has peripheral vision, and if his primary receiver is covered, he can locate another one. He's a good leader, a wonderful competitor, a fine athlete. He's got it all." The knee, of course, was a problem, but nothing that a surgeon could not fix. "Getting out that little piece of torn cartilage isn't nearly the problem for him that it might be for a running back."

Peahead was equally high on Frederickson, a big, handsome blond-headed fullback who could run, block, catch passes, and even play defense. If Namath was a renegade, Frederickson oozed a boy-next-door wholesomeness, very much in the tradition of Glenn Davis, Kyle Rote, and Frank Gifford. But with either player the Giants had nothing to lose—except money. Walker expected that Namath would receive the largest contract for any player out of the SEC. How much? Maybe, Peahead speculated, as much as $150,000, "counting salary over a normal three-year contractual span." Of course other sportswriters considered that figure outrageously high, putting the upper amount at about $100,000.[49]

But before the draft and the money, Alabama and Auburn had to play each other in Birmingham before a full stadium of rabidly partial Alabamians and a national television audience on NBC. The rest was all talk and speculation and newspaper filler, and Bryant made sure that his team knew it. The game was between Alabama and Auburn—the Crimson Tide and the Tigers—not Namath and Frederickson. It was a contest for state bragging rights, and as such the most important on the schedule. In the mid-1950s Shug Jordan's Tigers had pounded the Tide—28–0 in 1954; 26–0 in 1955; 34–7 in 1956; and 40–0 in 1957. In 1958, Bear's first year as coach of Alabama, the game had been closer, but the Tide still lost, 14–8. Since then Alabama had won four and only lost one, the debacle in Joe's junior year.

During those years Bryant had developed a healthy respect for Jordan and an unhealthy dislike of Auburn. He enjoyed telling the story about a 7 a.m. call he made one morning to Jordan or someone else in the football office. A female receptionist said that no one was in yet. Bear replied, "What's the matter, honey, don't you people take football seriously?"[50]

That was the difference between the two programs, he thought. Coaches and players at Alabama worked harder, played more intensely, and won because they wanted it more. And perhaps they carried just a fraction more dislike. How deep was Bryant's animosity toward Auburn? After Pat Trammell died of cancer toward the end of 1968, Bryant kept close to his wife and children, checking in from time to time, sending birthday and Christmas presents, making sure they received tickets to games, and just generally being there if they needed anything. When Pat Jr. was a senior in high school, Bear told him that he would pay for his college. He could go to any school he wanted, Bryant said—that is, "anywhere but Auburn." There was no need to ask if he was joking; Pat was bound for Alabama.[51]

The Thanksgiving Day game carried the promise of a perfect matchup. Auburn led the nation in defense, yielding just over 150 yards a game, and barely over 80 yards a game on the ground. The

Tigers employed a basic eight-man front (six linemen and two line-backers), with two defensive backs and a safety. And the safety was Tucker Frederickson, bigger and harder-hitting than most line-backers. The combination made it difficult for any team to estab-lish a ground game. And their offense had been steadily improving since their All-American quarterback Jimmy Sidle had badly injured his shoulder early in the season. Better than their 6–3 record indicated, Auburn approached the Alabama game as their bowl, and their opportunity to ruin their rival's season.[52]

Alabama played a more all-around game. Although they were not as stingy defensively as the 1961 team, only Florida had scored more than nine points against them. Moreover, when Namath was in the lineup their offense was significantly more explosive than in 1961. A few hard-hearted critics claimed that the Tide's backs lacked the speed to sweep the ends, but consistently throughout the season they had played effectively and with few errors. If Alabama had any weakness it was that without Namath they seemed plodding, almost like a group of racehorses waiting for the gates to open.

Legion Field was packed to the rim of its steel-and-concrete bowl on the magnificently sunny November 26 afternoon when the teams began the 29th installment of their rivalry. Of the 28 previous games, Auburn had won 14 and tied one, making it the only school in the SEC with a winning record against the Tide. In addition to the almost 70,000 spectators watching the game, the largest television audience of the regular season had dialed their channels to the contest. Among the observers at the game was Howell Raines, the future editor of the *New York Times*, earning his first byline for the *Birmingham Post-Herald*. He had secured the sideline pass he wore around his neck the hard way—by willingly, even eagerly volunteering to work the game on his day off for free, knowing that almost any other Alabamian would have paid dearly to luxuriate on the grass on which he was standing.[53]

While Raines and everyone else watched, the teams began the battle of position, kicking deep, excelling on coverage, and battling for yards like World War I soldiers fighting in no-man's-land. Then in the midst of the war of punts the Auburn replacement center made a mistake, lining a missile of a snap over the head of punter Jon Kilgore and 39 yards into the Auburn end zone. In a wild scramble Kilgore jumped on the ball, but it shot away from him in some sort of Newtonian reaction, and Steve Bowman corralled it to his chest as gently as a newborn child. The PAT failed, but with less than six minutes remaining in the first quarter Alabama led 6–0.[54]

Auburn was unfazed by the score. They stayed with their game plan to keep the ball on the ground, play for field position, and trust their defense to keep Alabama out of the end zone. All they needed was a break of their own. They got it in the second quarter when the Alabama punter, trapped deep in his end of the field, sliced a kick off the side of his foot. It nosedived out-of-bounds on the 29-yard line. In four plays, highlighted by Frederickson's 17-yard run and a three-yard touchdown burst, Auburn went ahead 7–6. The Tigers took the slim lead into halftime.

Auburn's Ben McDavid got every ounce of his foot into the second-half kickoff, driving it deep into Alabama's end zone. Raymond Ogden caught it about three yards from the end line. The smart play was to down the ball and take it on the 20-yard line. But Ogden was not known for his analytical thinking. "I knew from a female classmate who had dated Mr. Ogden that he was not a man you would look up for a discussion of *Lyrical Ballads*," Raines wrote. "On the other hand, once you put a football in his hands and got him pointed in the right direction, the result was pure Forrest Gumpian transcendence."[55]

This was one of those Gumpian moments. The ball dropped into Ogden's hands. Juggling it for a moment, he heard a teammate yell, "Bring it out." Then he began to run due south, almost like he had an important commitment in the Florida Panhandle. Watching from ground level, Raines lost the runner for a moment "in the fierce clot of blockers and attackers.... Then an alley opened up as if the white-clad Auburn players had been parted by Moses, and out of that immemorial fray, that moiling melee, that hurricane of hormonal Southern mayhem came Raymond Ogden, lengthening his stride like a thoroughbred.... He came loping past, his head back, his feet striking the ground but four times in ten yards. I suspect life has held nothing grander for him than that moment."

"One man had a pretty good shot at me," Ogden said with less lyrical rhapsody than Raines, "but someone took him out. The blocking was perfect.... I was just hoping nobody was going to catch me." No one did. Howell Raines is credited for coining the phrase "defining moment." Raymond Ogden's spectacular 107-yard kickoff return was the defining moment of the game. Steve Sloan followed the dash with a more mundane two-point conversion, giving the Tide a 14–7 lead.

Auburn, and especially Frederickson, continued their hard, rugged play, several times driving deep into Alabama territory. But the Tide held, and midway through the fourth quarter Namath threw a touchdown pass to Ray Perkins, increasing the lead to 21–7. The score gave the Tide all the insurance they needed. Auburn scored once more, but Alabama won 21–14.

In defeat, Frederickson performed like a champion, endearing himself to sportswriters and professional scouts. He ran the ball 22 times, gained 117 yards, scored a touchdown, excelled on defense, and played fifty-eight of the game's sixty minutes. It was when he was off the field that Namath led Alabama to its third score. In a game that sportswriters compared to war, Frederickson became a symbol of the southern warrior spirit. "Somehow," wrote John Logue of the *Atlanta Journal*, "the great causes are the lost causes.

In the absence of victory, Ivan Charles (Tucker) Frederickson here Thursday settled for Auburn immortality."[56]

Leaning on an empty oil barrel and sipping a Coke, Shug Jordan agreed with the assessment. "Gentlemen," he told a group of sportswriters, "I am sure that Tucker Frederickson today was the greatest football player within 3,000 miles of Birmingham. I played college football four years at Auburn, and watched it before that. And I have coached it at Georgia and Auburn for 32 years, and Tucker Frederickson can walk with any football player I ever saw." As for Alabama, Shug grudgingly admitted Bear had a good team, "but I don't think we'd take our hat off to them. If you know what I mean."

Celebration mixed with concern in the Alabama locker room. To the obvious question, Bear told reporters, "Sure, I think we're No. 1. We had to come from behind to beat four of the toughest teams in the nation, and we won all 10 we played. Who had done better than that?" He was more effusive in his praise for Namath, and he wanted it published. "I told you last year he wasn't a bad boy. I'll go further now and say that he has meant a great deal to this football team by his conduct both on and off the field and his great leadership."

Namath was more subdued. "All's well that ends well," he said. Then he asked about Steve Sloan, who had injured his knee in the second half. Joe knew what he was going through—the pain, anxiety, fear. He was still experiencing the emotions himself.

After he had showered he went to console his teammate. He found him with his knee so full of fluid and tightly bandaged that Steve could not bend it sufficiently to put on his sock. "Here, gimme that," Namath said. Kneeling on the floor of the locker room, he tenderly put the sock on his friend. "Then Joe Namath, who cannot miss being one of the great quarterbacks professional football has ever seen, ducked out of the back door of the dressing room."[57]

Two days later, USC defeated Notre Dame 20–17. On December 1 the voters in the AP poll took their hats off to Alabama and chose the Tide as the 1964 national champions. Students at Alabama celebrated with chants of "We're No. 1! We're No. 1! We're No. 1!" They streamed into Foster Auditorium cheering, "Roll Tide!," only to be drowned out by the Million Dollar Band. The jubilant rally was carried statewide on a radio hookup. Bear was in Montgomery, but he said a few words over the telephone, giving the players, staff, fans, and students all the credit for the achievement. Speaking at the rally, Namath gave Coach Bryant and his staff the most recognition. It was a wild, loud affair, prompting a journalist to write, "If this frenzy hits the streets, Tuscaloosa may have the National Guard here again asking the fans to hold it down."[58]

While cheerleaders at the University of Alabama jumped and clapped and students screamed until they were hoarse, Americans in other parts of the country observed the accomplishment more somberly. Once again an all-white team had won a national title without playing in a single integrated game. It was the last time it would happen, though no one knew it then. To many it was a clear sign of the desperately slow pace of change in America.

Once again, Jim Murray led the attack. "So Alabama is the 'National Champion,' is it? Hah! 'National' champion of what? The Confederacy? This team hasn't poked its head above the Mason-Dixon line since Appomattox.... This team wins the Front-of-the-Bus championship every year—largely with Pennsylvania quarterbacks. How can you win a 'national' championship playing in a closet? How can you get to be 'Number One' if you don't play anybody but your kinfolks?" As he had in 1961, Murray used the success of Alabama as an opportunity to condemn Bryant and the South, reminding millions of his readers that sports are never about just sports.[59]

Hobbled by a knee injury, Namath could still throw better than any quarterback in the nation. The question going into the 1965 Orange Bowl was whether or not he would get the chance. (Bryant Museum)

Epilogue

In a Class of His Own

THIRTY-FIVE DAYS SEPARATED Alabama's victory against Auburn at Birmingham's Legion Field and its New Year's Day game against the University of Texas in Miami's Orange Bowl. During that brief period the economic, social, and cultural foundations of college and professional football shifted. It was as if someone turned on the lights to reveal a new game.

It began with two decisions in the Empire City. New York had always been Janus-faced. There is the Wall Street New York, buttoned-down, gray-flannel-suit conservative with an eye on the bottom line and a nose for the next big deal. At the other extreme is the Times Square New York, Barnumesque, glitzy, full of unabashed hustlers and borderline con men on the make. The city's two football teams represented the two poles, which the 1964 NFL draft illustrated perfectly.

Two days after Joe Namath and Tucker Frederickson showcased their talents on national television, the National Football League and the upstart American Football League held their drafts. For weeks sportswriters had debated whom the New York Giants would select with their number one choice: the handsome, dependable Frederickson or the fragile, brilliant Namath.

Predictably, the Giants chose Frederickson, a player in the mold of Frank Gifford. It was a safe pick. He may not have been a great player, but he was more than dependable and his all-purpose versatility seemed to fit the team's profile. Just as predictably, the fullback immediately signed a low-six-figure contract, virtually ignoring the Denver Broncos, who had selected him in the AFL draft.[1]

Eleven names were called before the St. Louis Cardinals chose Namath twelfth in the first round. Some of the players picked before him would enjoy exceptional NFL or AFL careers—Dick Butkus, Gale Sayers, and Craig Morton among them. Others would have brief, uneventful stays in the pros. The AFL rated Namath higher. With the second pick in the AFL draft, the New York Jets chose the quarterback.

Unlike Tucker, Joe's season was not over, and until it was he could not ink a contract. But he could talk with representatives from both teams. And during the next month the constant talk—by Joe, by the Jets and Cardinals, and by sportswriters—drove his price ever upward.

Unlike his stylish but casual eleventh-hour admittance to the University of Alabama, Namath intended to enter into the world of professional football with at least a modicum of forethought. Like everybody else in America who read the sports pages of any newspaper, and especially in Alabama, he knew that professional football had undergone seismic changes.

In 1960, while Joe was leading Beaver Falls to an undefeated season, the American Football League began operations. The brainchild of Lamar Hunt, son of Texas oil millionaire H. L. Hunt, the AFL wanted a piece of the professional football business, which was taking off after the National Football League's 1958 thrilling sudden-death overtime championship game between the Baltimore Colts and the New York Giants. Although the AFL began in a splash of publicity, its first three seasons were marked by frustration, economic difficulties, and instability. While franchises in New York and Oakland struggled to stay afloat, and ones in Los Angeles and Dallas relocated, spectators criticized the AFL's flash-dash-and-pass brand of play. It was not up to the brutal standards of the NFL.

By the end of the 1963 season several teams in the league were clearly struggling. That year Harry Wismer's New York Titans franchise failed to meet several payrolls and filed for bankruptcy. But 1964 brought new hope, although it came too late to save Wismer, whose team was purchased by Sonny Werblin and renamed the New York Jets. In late January the AFL received a large cash infusion from the National Broadcasting Company. After failing to obtain television rights for the NFL, NBC paid $36 million for the rights to broadcast AFL games. It was a five-year deal—but for a league that was worried about its very survival, five years seemed like forever. The eight teams in the AFL now had the hard cash to embark on a bidding war for the finest college talent. And the ripples that had begun in New York boardrooms soon reached Tuscaloosa.[2]

With professional football increasingly embracing the passing game, Namath knew there would be a high demand for his services, even though he had not been the first player selected in either draft. He read the columnists who wrote that he could sign a three-year deal, plus a bonus, for as much as $100,000, even $150,000. Not long after the draft, Bryant asked Joe, "Do you have any idea what you're going to ask for?" Namath replied that he didn't, but that he liked the sound of $100,000. In that case, Bear advised, "You go ahead and ask them for two hundred thousand." Namath was shocked by the amount. "Well, hell," Bear reasoned, "you may not get it, but it's a good place to start. You may only get a hundred and fifty."[3]

Namath daydreamed about $150,000. To him it was a figure as impossibly high as $1 million. It was like Kennedy's promise to land a man on the moon, the kind of thing one dreams about but never imagines will actually happen. So when the representatives of the St. Louis Cardinals came to his dorm room in Tuscaloosa to talk money, Joe mentioned $200,000—and a new car, which he thought should be part of any contract. The representatives seemed shocked, and they left shortly after the discussion. But, Namath said, a few days later they got back to him, suggesting that the two hundred thousand and the car were his if he would sign immediately, before he talked with the Jets.[4]

"They went for it, huh?" Bryant said when Joe reported the Cardinals' offer. "Well, you got something pretty good going. You've got to talk to the Jets now."

Two hundred thousand was Namath's moon. He never thought that there was something out there higher than the moon. And he instinctively knew that the negotiations had gone beyond his limited financial talents. He had just advanced to the stage of carrying a wallet. But using the newest technology available once again— Joe had, after all, been the first player on his junior high team to use a facemask—he armed himself with an agent to aid in the negotiations. His new faceguard was named Mike Bite.

Years later, after finishing his masterwork and earning the beginnings of his small fortune, Mike Bite traveled to Lebanon. He was of Lebanese descent, but he seemed to have little in common with his ancestors. He looked and sounded as authentically Middle Eastern as the students attending the American University in Beirut. That he was young, had longish hair, wore decidedly Western garb, stayed at a hotel practically on the American campus, was Catholic, and could say only "son of a bitch," "fuck you," and a few other curse words in Lebanese—with an Alabama accent—did nothing to help him blend into his ancestral culture. That is, until he went to an open-air bazaar with George, a guide and translator, and decided he

By the beginning of 1965, Namath emerged as the top prospect in all of college football, and teams from both professional football leagues competed for his services. (Bryant Museum)

needed several water pipes known locally as *alghilli*. The negotiations started. "Fifteen dollars apiece," George translated. "That's what he says." "Fifteen dollars?! Fifteen dollars?!" (George relayed.) "Son of a bitch! Fuck you!" (No need for George.) "Finest quality, I assure you. I can go down only to thirteen dollars." "No way. Twenty-five cents apiece. That's all!" "Sir, you are stealing from my mother and family! Eleven dollars each!" "And *you* are stealing from *my* mother and family! Son of a bitch! Fuck you!" A crowd of locals formed to watch the proceedings. "Sorry, sir, you offer far too little." The merchant wrapped the pipes up in mock resignation. "Fifty cents each, but you throw in an extra one on the house." "All right, but you must buy thirty. I give you the thirty-first free. For eight dollars each." "Man, what have you got in your ears?!" And on it went, with George translating the nonvulgar portions of the conversation. In the end, Mike Bite bought five water pipes for $1.50 each. "You have stolen from my family, sir. From my mother and my children.

Are you happy?" the merchant concluded as he packaged the pipes for the American. "Yes, as a matter of fact, I am," Bite replied as he departed. The spoils of victory rained upon him from the observers and other vendors. Offers of free persimmons, dried fruit, and rides pelted the victor of the negotiation. The next day Bite sent George back to the market with ten dollars and the order that the money was for the vendor's mother and children. Not for the vendor himself, though, because he had lost the battle.[5]

Bite had attended the University of Alabama, and like Hoot Owl worked as a football manager. After graduation, he went to law school, graduating in 1956. Short, with small, dark eyes, a dark complexion, and a hook nose, Michael W. Bite *looked* like a B-film Hollywood lawyer who represented clients out to make a quick buck off some scam. The truth, however, was less dramatic. He was primarily a property lawyer who dealt with the humdrum world of real estate and mortgages.

One day, while golfing at Joe's Ranch House, a private club in Birmingham, Bite received a call from the young Namath, whom he had met through his ongoing association with the Alabama football team. "Hey, there's this guy named Werblin wants to know who my lawyer is. What'll I do?" With that, Bite began to work on the first and only personal service contract of his life.

Bite's greatest gift to Namath was his sheer naïveté regarding negotiations. He knew nothing of the established parameters surrounding an athlete's value and therefore had no mind to follow the traditional standards. He prided himself, rather, on interpersonal instincts: "I got good street sense. I know how to evaluate a situation. And money don't scare me. In this business, everyone's cold hard core is money. My job is to estimate how far down I have to go into that soft friendly exterior to get to that core. All of the fatherly advice and good buddy small talk—that's all a bunch of horseshit!

Everybody operates by the bottom line—by how it's going to affect him and his personal wealth. Sometimes the core is a lot deeper than expected; and sometimes certain people can lull you into feeling that they are genuinely concerned with your interest more than their own. But the core of selfish concern is always there, baby. *Always*."

So Bite approached the negotiation process with his and Joe's interests firmly in mind. To his way of thinking, someone was going to win and someone was going to lose during the process. His first target was the St. Louis Cardinals. To the people across the table from him, he appeared rigid, and sometimes downright silly in his demands. The Cardinals' representatives certainly felt so. They had entered the market for Joe Namath with a business-as-usual attitude and were surprised when Bite proved ignorant of the old-boy rules of the NFL. The Cardinals, in short, asked Bite to dance, and he quite simply had no idea what the music was and no intention of pretending to understand a single note.

The first meeting with Bill Bidwill, owner of the Cardinals, was at Tuscaloosa's Moon Winx Lodge, an establishment that undoubtedly had seen its share of negotiations, but not high-level football deals. "We are prepared to offer Mr. Namath…" Bidwill began. Every time Bite and Namath, who was also present, made counter-offers, Bidwill's response was invariably along the lines of, "Ohhh my God, woaaaahh, geeeeeeeeez!" And that's how it went. Bite felt the Cardinals' offer was too low in absolute terms—money, that is—but he also saw the Cardinals' approach to obtaining Namath's services as less than enthusiastic. "Sure, Namath has never played a down in professional football and, yes, he has had some knee problems in college," Bite conceded. "But you've got to see the larger picture. You've got to recognize what this boy *is* and what he's capable of *being* for your"—Bite made sure he did not use the word "team" at this point—"*franchise*."

"We recognize his potential, Mr. Bite, but there are many incoming rookies with great potential—"

"You're talking about football and I'm talking about a star!"

"I don't think I understand…"

But Bite understood all too well. St. Louis could think in terms only of football and not of stardom. It was a town of local television and local radio stations where local athletes advertised for used-car dealerships and dry cleaners. This idea of "stardom" as Mike Bite presented it simply did not exist in eastern Missouri. Football was what St. Louis had and football was what St. Louis offered.

"The Cardinals' football club is expecting to be competitive in the near future. We hope that Mr. Namath becomes an integral part of our program" is what they said, but "Small-time, small-time, small-time" is what Bite heard—loudly. He believed that they had no idea what they had sitting in front of them at the Moon Winx motel.

What Bite really wanted for Joe was all of the above. He wanted New York for Joe's career. He wanted money now. And he wanted the supreme competition of the NFL. The only team that could offer it all was the New York Giants, and although there were rumors that if St. Louis signed Joe they might trade him to the Giants, nothing was said to Namath and Bite about it. But if Bite and Namath could not get the New York Giants, they could at least get the New York part.

David Abraham "Sonny" Werblin understood exactly what Bite wanted. Unlike the NFL old guard—franchise owners such as Bill and Charles Bidwill of St. Louis, Wellington Mara of New York, Carroll Rosenbloom of Baltimore, Art Rooney of Pittsburgh, George Halas of Chicago, and George Preston Marshall of Washington—Werblin was not part of the football aristocracy. His world was entertainment, especially television. At the Music Corporation of America (MCA) he had earned a reputation for identifying, managing, and packaging talent. He knew how to spot, make, showcase, and sell stars. Over the years he had managed many of the biggest stars in the entertainment industry, including Dean Martin, Frank Sinatra, Elizabeth Taylor, Jack Benny, Gene Kelly, Abbott and Costello, and Ronald Reagan.

NFL owners had well-deserved reputations for parsimony. They threw around nickels like they were manhole covers. Although Werblin was a late arrival as an AFL owner, he knew what the league needed to succeed. There were plenty of good football players in America, but too few stars. And Americans loved stars. Werblin understood that money was a crucial factor in measuring stars. How much an actor made for a movie, the price an actress got for a television appearance—that helped define them in the constellation of stars.

Frank Lambert, an All-American punter for Ole Miss who was drafted by both the Jets and the Giants, learned this during his first negotiations with Werblin. Although he was the finest punter in the nation, he was still *only* a punter, and not drafted by the Jets until the tenth round. But Werblin dealt with him personally. "How much do you want to be paid?" he asked the player. Life in Hattiesburg and Oxford, Mississippi, had not exactly prepared Lambert for high-level New York negotiations, but he took a deep breath and answered, "Well, sir, I sorta thought that I should make something around what the top punters make." "No, no, no," Werblin began even before Lambert finished his sentence. "You don't want to make *as much* as the top punter. You want to make *more*!"[6]

More! Really, it was a simple concept. The best made the most. The one who made the most was the very best. He was the star. "It's something I learned from my theatrical experiences," Werblin said. "You can't do things cheaply. A million-dollar set is worthless if you put a $2,000 actor in the main role. To me the building of a football team is like building a show. You have to go all the way. And professional football has become one of the great entertainment mediums in the United States." Movies, television, football—it was all part of the same industry.⁷

Werblin met Bite and Namath in Los Angeles for the initial negotiations. Werblin's lawyer was Robert Schumann, a tax lawyer who also represented such Hollywood clients as Howard Hughes. (Schumann's offices were in Washington, D.C., but he flew out to the West Coast midway through the negotiations.) The experience was operatic. On December 6, 1964, the Jets' owner took Joe and Bite to see the Jets play the San Diego Chargers at Balboa Stadium. They went in a limousine driven by the actor who played the Lone Ranger on television. A better actor than driver, he immediately got lost and the three men ended up at the San Diego Zoo. The situation got worse when they finally made it to the game. Balboa Stadium was a rickety, sorry excuse for a professional arena, and there were only 16,225 people in attendance. On the field things did not look much better. The Chargers' quarterback, Malcolm "Dick" Wood, came from Auburn and had a rifle for an arm. The problem was that if he hit his receiver, which was a rare occurrence, he would knock him down. To make matters worse, this mediocre player led the Chargers to a 38–3 rout of the Jets. "We played baseball in *high school* in better stadiums than this," Bite thought to himself. "We played junior high football games in front of this many people. What the hell am I doing here?! Good God this is rinky-dink! Joe is a diamond compared to these guys. Where the hell are the Giants?"

For the time being, though, Bite was in negotiations with the New York *Jets*. Fittingly, Werblin was neither apologetic nor concerned with what occurred at Balboa Stadium. He had other ways of winning over a prospective client and intended on using them. What he lacked in football skills he more than made up for in personality and influence. It seemed to Bite that Werblin knew everyone in California. What kind of guy can get the Lone Ranger to drive them to a football game? The kind of guy who could also stop by and pick up Jane Wyman for dinner at Chase's. The actress, who appeared in such classic films as *The Lost Weekend*, *Magnificent Obsession*, and *The Yearling*, joined Werblin, Bite, and Namath for fondue. Throughout the dinner, other motion picture stars and executives came to the table to pay homage to Sonny. Suddenly for Bite it did not seem so rinky-dink anymore; he began to realize that this guy was important. Werblin made Namath feel just as special as all of the top actors in the restaurant. Made him feel that there was no real difference between a football player and a movie star in his world—it was all a matter of celebrity, publicity, and salesmanship. There was a definite excitement to it, but Namath remained cool. He sat unobtrusively while the visitors to the table came and went. Like a gambler, he took it all in. But Bite knew that the exterior cool hid a Beaver Falls–Alabama kid ready to move into Sonny's orbit.

First they had to negotiate. Bite equated negotiations to blowing up a balloon: You wanted as much as you could possibly get, so you blew hard; but you were always just a little bit away from busting the thing, so you needed to know when to stop blowing and tie it off. "Mr. Werblin"—and it was always "Mr." with Werblin, no "David" or "Sonny," and it remained that way for Namath and Bite (although they were "Joe" and "Mike" to Mr. Werblin) throughout their association with Mr. Werblin—"what we're looking for is something in the neighborhood of half a million dollars, with a few added incentives." Bite had pitched the big number and Werblin did not flinch—no "ohhhs" and "geeeeezes," just a stony cold complacency that might have been outrage or relief at the amount given, but nothing apparent. Maybe Mr. Werblin did not do business like the Bidwills, Bite thought. Maybe he just did not put on the whole production of feigning disbelief at large amounts of money but still felt the same trepidation beneath his mask.

Maybe, but Bite was about to bet it all that this time he was in the ballpark right from the start of the negotiations. It was just a feeling, but a good feeling was better than a bad one. "Joe, come here," Bite said as the meeting proceeded. They went into an adjoining room, out of hearing of Mr. Werblin. "Joe, get on your knees and say your prayers," Bite began, his poker face giving way to childish giddiness. "I'm gonna give a great big puff and we gonna bust this balloon or we gonna get out!" Bite genuflected dramatically and grabbed Namath and brought them both to their knees. "Oh Lord! I'm gonna blow real hard!" They returned. Mr. Werblin still looked calm. "This goddamned son of a bitch never gets tired!" Bite thought. "All right, Mr. Werblin, here's where we stand..." And that was it.

The price Bite wanted was $427,000 for three seasons. He had stretched the balloon as tight as it would get. Werblin was also pleased with the price. It was the highest amount ever paid to an athlete in a team sport in America. Joe Namath had a salary that would set sportswriters and Americans talking for months. A million dollars of free publicity, Werblin knew. With his signature on the contract, Namath would transcend the football field. He would become a marketable commodity. He would become a star.

And that was precisely what Werblin desired. "I believe the Jets have found a star, and that star is Joe Namath," he told Arthur Daley of the *New York Times*. "In all my theatrical experience I've met few Hollywood stars with the indefinable quality of being able to walk into a room and electrify everyone there by the magnetism of their presence—Clark Gable, Gregory Peck, Joan Crawford, and Marilyn Monroe. It's the same quality that Jack Dempsey and Babe Ruth had. My feeling is that Namath has much of the demeanor and attitude of Joe DiMaggio."[8]

Bite felt the same way, but he wanted guarantees as well as praise for his client. First of all, he demanded that Namath play in New

York. In an unprecedented move, Bite forced the Jets to install a "no trade" clause in the contract. "I damn sure didn't want them shipping his ass to St. Louis, Missouri, or Green Bay, Wisconsin." Or Balboa Stadium. Although Namath just wanted the most money he could get, Bite worried about the ability of the American Football League to make the best of his client. He battled feelings that he was leading his friend not to the promised land but to some fleeting, penny-ante, pissant, rinky-dink, rickety league. Where, he wondered, were the Giants? Could Sonny Werblin turn this new league around and field a competitive football team in the same home as the Giants, perhaps the most popular team of all team sports save the crosstown Yankees? New York was not St. Louis, but likewise the AFL was not the NFL.

Nor did Bite want to compromise the University of Alabama. Namath still had the Orange Bowl to play, and if he signed early the team might be sanctioned by the NCAA. Bite had read reports about Florida State and Oklahoma players who signed professional contracts immediately after the regular season and had been declared ineligible for the Gator Bowl. He did not want this to happen, partially because he wanted to do things aboveboard, partially because he supported the Crimson Tide, but mostly because he could not imagine what Coach Bryant might do to him if he screwed up. So he was very careful. When he and Namath went to Los Angeles, his law firm paid for both hotel rooms as well as their airline tickets. Namath claimed that he was so frightened of breaking any rules that when Werblin offered to buy him a Coke he insisted upon paying for it himself, perhaps a first in his college career. "It's a good thing he didn't offer to buy me a Scotch; I don't think I could have covered that," Namath added. Bite's firm would be reimbursed by the Jets only after the college season was over. So before the Orange Bowl game, he had the Jets' signature on the contract but not his and Namath's. This was a Machiavellian strategy that not only kept the Crimson Tide out of trouble with the NCAA, but also secured Namath's future. "If he went down in that game," Bite reasoned, "I'll go to the goddamned hospital bed and tell Joe, 'Put your John Hancock on this baby. We still got a deal!' "[9]

And then there was the car, the Lincoln Continental convertible that Namath had insisted on no matter whose contract he signed. Mr. Werblin, fortunately, had connections everywhere. The Lincoln Corporation sponsored one of his television shows and, calling in a favor, he expedited the delivery and had the car shipped to Miami in time for the Orange Bowl. Namath saw his car in the lot of the hotel where the team was staying. It was Jets green. He could not yet touch it, not until after the game, but he could look. It seemed a long way from the primed car he had driven around Beaver Falls with Whitey Harris and the doorless wonder he and Hoot Owl took on and off the roads in Alabama.

———

During the weeks after the Alabama-Auburn game, while Bite and Werblin went back and forth negotiating the contract, Namath and his teammates prepared to play the Texas Longhorns. The game, like Namath's contract, signaled a new age for football. Arguably they were the two best teams in the country. Earlier in the season the Longhorns had spent a month as the top-ranked team, but then Texas lost to Arkansas 14–13 when Coach Darrell K. Royal went for the win rather than the tie after a late-game touchdown. Texas won the rest of their regular-season games and carried a 9–1 record to Miami. Alabama, of course, was 10–0, and the Associated Press had already named them the 1964 national champions.

But the 1965 Orange Bowl game was greater than the records of Texas and Alabama. It was the first bowl game to be televised in prime time and, in the phrase of the day, "in living color." For thirty years, since the first Orange Bowl in 1934, the contest had been played in the afternoon, mostly in sunshine, though occasionally in driving rain and wind. Now, to meet NBC's football-filled schedule—the network had the rights to televise the Sugar, Rose, and Orange Bowls on January 1—the Orange Bowl would be played under the lights.

It was a dramatic and meaningful move. On January 1, 1964, the Sugar, Cotton, and Orange Bowls had all begun at the same hour, followed by the West Coast broadcast of the Rose Bowl. But NBC's 1965 EST lineup was: Sugar Bowl (2 p.m.); Rose Bowl (5 p.m.); and Orange Bowl (8 p.m.). "Armchair quarterbacks may require spring training to condition themselves for a rigorous football schedule," noted a *New York Times* reporter.[10]

The arrangement virtually guaranteed that the Orange Bowl would garner a prime-time ratings bonanza. In 1964 only 5.5 million homes watched the Orange Bowl, compared to 16.3 million for the Rose Bowl, which overlapped with the East Coast prime time. In 1965 the premier slot went to the Orange Bowl, and experts confidently predicted that it would be the most watched college football game in history. They were right. More than 25 million American homes had their TVs dialed to the game.[11]

The combination of format, time slot, and audience made it more than a game—it was a stage, a showcase for any player who could impose his will on the contest. One of the finest defensive players was Texas's junior linebacker Tommy Nobis, a good-natured, red-headed, freckled kid from Thomas Jefferson High School in San Antonio. He was one of the early proponents of weight training, and his combination of strength, mobility, and intensity was redefining the position of middle linebacker. Alabama's star, of course, was Namath. Recovering from his knee injury, it was his chance to show Sonny Werblin and millions of Americans that he was the best college quarterback in America. After four years of playing the game in the South, in the shadow of Bear Bryant and the legacy of Alabama's civil rights abuses, Namath finally had the national stage he wanted. Other quarterbacks might lead the nation in passing and win consensus All-American honors, but none—not Terry Baker in 1962, Roger Staubach in 1963, or John Huarte in 1964—had this stage for their final college game.

Bryant's constant concern was the state of his quarterback's right knee. Namath had been day-to-day since it had "given way"—a perfect orthopedic description—on October 10 in the North Carolina State game. At that time it had been drained and little if any blood had been detected in the fluid. Joe had reinjured the knee on October 24 in the Florida contest. This time when his doctor aspirated the knee there was blood.

Since the initial injury, Namath had practiced when he could and played when he had to, measuring the daily pain with such short descriptions as "not too bad," "pretty bad," and "it really hurts." Although the extent of his injuries would not be known until a New York surgeon repaired the damage in early February 1965, Namath had shredded his medial meniscus and stretched a ligament. The lateral and medial menisci are the knee's shock absorbers; when one was gone, the knee was constantly unstable.[12]

A sign in the Alabama locker room gave Bryant's general attitude toward injuries: "It's all in the mind." Namath could walk, he could jog, and if he had to, he could even run. But most of all, he could pass. Even more importantly, his team needed him. After going down in the Auburn game, Steve Sloan's knee seemed worse than Joe's. "Our record of recovery with these knees is not what you'd call a good one," Bryant told reporters. A few weeks before the Orange Bowl, Sloan still had trouble jogging, and he looked doubtful for the contest. But Joe was moving better than he had in weeks, and he assured Bryant that he would play.[13]

A week before the game the betting line favored Alabama by six points. Tulane was the only school to play both Alabama and

Texas, and Greenie players thought that Namath would make the difference. "He's got the quickest hands I've ever seen," said lineman Jim Besselman. "Namath has come up with the big play for Alabama every game." Defensive back Jim Davis agreed. With Namath, Alabama would win; without him, they'd lose. It was an opinion that was shared by virtually every reporter covering the game. Even Lou Maysel of the *Austin American-Statesman* announced in a headline, "Namath Praise Unanimous."[14]

Aware of the importance of Namath, Bryant handled him like a Fabergé egg. In practice he was an untouchable. Teammates could not even slap him on the back after a nice pass. Mostly he just walked through his assignments or ran a few plays for timing. But his knee was so wobbly that it was beyond total protection.

On Monday, just four days before the Friday game, Namath was quarterbacking a shadow drill. He took a snap, turned to hand off to a halfback, and dropped to the ground, clutching his knee in pain. "Oh, no, not this," Bryant groaned when he saw Joe go down. Later in the locker room, as Joe had ice packed to his knee, Bear talked to reporters. Running his hands through his hair, he explained the cold facts about knees. "It won't even start swelling badly until tomorrow. That's when it will hurt him ... then it will take a couple of days for the swelling to go down." Thinking over his options, he continued, "Sloan will start if he is able." But of course, Sloan was still hobbling around on a bum knee as well. "This is disheartening. It means we'll have to change our entire pattern of plays. We had planned our offense for this game around Namath. Sloan's at his best on option plays, but we threw the option out for this game because we didn't want to risk further injury to him."[15]

Stretched out on a training table, wincing in pain as Goostree probed his knee, Namath said, "I'll play against Texas." When Bryant looked at him, he repeated, "I'm okay, Coach. I'll be ready to play." It was a guarantee. Bear just shook his head, telling reporters, "He's just being...well, himself. I would have been surprised if he hadn't said he will play. He's just that kind of player."

But Bear was unconvinced. "As of now, Sloan is my starting quarterback," he said as he left the room.

———

The wind-whipped, driving rain had stopped and the Orange Bowl was filled for the nighttime finale of the bowl season. In the locker room under the stands, dressed in a short-sleeved shirt and black tie, Darrell K. Royal stood in front of a green blackboard. Sitting on benches facing their coach, Longhorn players waited for him to say something. Instead of talking, he turned to the blackboard and in a steady, elegant hand copied a recent headline from a Miami paper: "Nobody lives as tough as we do—P. Bryant."[16]

Pausing, giving his players time to think about the quote, Royal walked over to a watercooler and got a drink. Every eye in the locker room followed him. The players waited, tense, ready for action. Assistant coach Pat Culpepper recalled that Tommy Nobis was sweating, the cords of muscle on the back of his neck bulging. Then, still without a word, Royal returned to the blackboard, picked up a piece of chalk, and wrote, "B.S.—DKR." Finally he turned to his team and said, "Let's go!"

Both teams emerged from their locker rooms at about the same time. They were greeted by a blast of fireworks, the clang of cowbells, and an explosion of Rebel yells. Before them was the Orange Bowl, done up like a football version of Disneyland. There were elaborate floats, fake orange trees with real oranges Scotch-taped to their branches, and, just past the end zones, brightly colored coral reefs with an array of beautiful girls in bathing suits lounging on them. In the stands were 72,647 spectators, some drenched and still dripping water from the shower that had hit Miami less than an hour before kickoff. Although *The Jack Benny Show* and *The Jack Parr Show* had been bumped from their Friday time slots by the game, there were enough celebrities in the audience to make up for it. Jackie Gleason, the popular television personality and "adopted pet" of Miami, strolled onto the field with a blonde on each arm to watch the coin toss. From the stands former vice president Richard M. Nixon (accompanied by Bebe Rebozo), Governor George Wallace, and Princess Takako Suganomiya of Japan watched "the Great One" go through his act. So did millions of television viewers. The *Miami Herald* reported that it was the largest audience to ever witness a sporting event.[17]

The rain had stopped by game time, but the wind was still swirling with gusts of 15 to 20 miles per hour. Alabama won the coin toss and elected to take the wind and play a field position game. Without Namath in the game, Bryant assumed that his defense would contain the Longhorns and the game would be a tight defensive struggle. For most of the first quarter Bryant's assumption was dead on. Texas was able to make a handful of first downs but not mount a significant drive, and the Sloan-led Tide was hardly able to move the ball at all.

Then in an electric moment the game changed. On second and nine from Texas's 21-yard line, Alabama called a stunt, sending their defensive end inside the tackle. Texas called the perfect play. Ernie Koy took a pitchout, broke through the space vacated by the end, and raced 79 yards for a touchdown. It was the longest touchdown run by a Texas back in four years. Texas led 7–0.

Alabama had been behind several times during the season and always came back. On the next series, Sloan led his team on an impressive drive, mixing runs with short and long passes, including a 42-yard strike to Ray Ogden. But inside the 20, Sloan missed his receiver on third down, and the reliable David Ray attempted a short field goal. This time he missed.

The Longhorns took the ball on the 20, but gained only six yards in three plays. Koy's punt was high and long, driving Alabama back almost 50 yards, inside their own territory. But a penalty flag lay on the ground near the line of scrimmage. Offsides, Alabama. Texas kept the ball. On the next play substitute quarterback Jim Hudson threw a bomb to a streaking George Sauer, who caught the ball in stride and carried it into the end zone for a 68-yard touchdown play. Texas led 14–0, and if Alabama players were not panicking, they were beginning to ask themselves some hard questions.[18]

During the regular season only Florida and Auburn had scored 14 points against Alabama, and no team had scored more. Alabama prided itself on smart play and defense. But a boneheaded mistake—the tackle had lined up over the scrimmage line on the punt—had allowed Texas to keep the ball, and the vaunted Tide defense had been shredded on two long plays. In *Building a Championship Football Team*, Bryant's popular book on coaching, Bear listed five "*must nots*" in his ten "Defensive Axioms." Number one was, "The defense *must not* allow the opponent to complete a long pass for an 'easy' touchdown." Number two was, "The defense *must not* allow the opponent to make a long run for an 'easy' touchdown." With plenty of time remaining in the second quarter and an entire second half, it looked like Alabama was bent on surrendering all the "*must nots.*"[19]

After the score, Americans across the country watched a commercial and waited for the Texas kickoff. But on the Tide sideline, with a warm, humid breeze increasing his discomfort, Bryant had shed his rain slicker and sport jacket and replaced his checkered fedora with a beat-up Alabama baseball cap. "Sartorial splendor had been sacrificed to the urgency of the hour, and comfort," wrote Benny Marshall. Bryant was thinking, plotting a way to get back in the game. He needed something dramatic—and he needed it now.

Moving alongside Jim Goostree, he asked, "Can Joe play?"

"Yessir," Goostree answered. "Joe can play."

During the kickoff, Bear called for his team captain, the player he said was the finest athlete he had ever coached. With Joe at his side, Bear placed one of his big hands on his shoulder and said something into his quarterback's ear. Then he signaled a time-out.

On the Texas sideline Pat Culpepper had his back to the field while he gave instructions to the Horns' defensive team. But hearing a huge roar from the Alabama side of the field, he turned to see what all the commotion was about. He would never forget the sight. "There was Bear, hat on his head and arm around Namath, walking his quarterback onto the field. He walked him all the way to the hash mark, then turned around and walked back to the sideline." He had literally physically delivered Namath into the game.[20]

Namath's right knee was heavily bandaged, and he wore white soccer shoes with short cleats to prevent them from grabbing too much turf. After Bryant left his side Joe sprinted toward the Alabama huddle. With the Alabama stands exploding in excitement, the Tide band playing their fight song, and Namath flashing across the field in his new passing shoes, it was the dramatic moment the team needed. "I wish I could paint you a picture," Culpepper said. "I had no idea of what was going to happen, but there was a feeling that something was going to happen." Certainly the Alabama offense Texas had prepared for—the Steve Sloan option and short pass game—was off the table.

A mishandled kickoff had resulted in poor field position. The ball was on Alabama's 13-yard line when Namath took the field. He handed off to Wayne Trimble for a two-yard gain on first down. On second down he dropped back and threw a perfect pass to sure-handed sophomore Ray Perkins for a 25-yard gain. He hit Perkins for eight yards on the next play, then missed him on second down. After a one-yard run to midfield, Alabama faced fourth and one. All thoughts of playing for field position had vanished when Namath went into the game. He called a running play that picked up the yard. With the ball on Texas's 49-yard line, Namath completed an

11-yard pass to Trimble, and two plays later a 15-yard pass to Tommy Tolleson. The ball was now on the 23. Another completion to Wayne Cook advanced the ball to the nine, and a short run moved it to the seven. Joe finished the drive with a pass to Trimble in the end zone. The score was 14–7, and Alabama was back in the game.

The drive had seemed inexorable. "Namath dropped back seven yards to pass faster than anyone alive," Culpepper said. "We just couldn't get to him. We played an eight-man front, blitzed linebackers—nothing. We couldn't get a hand on him. He'd just drop back, look, raise up on his toes, and fire the ball. And I mean fire it. We had great linebackers, but Namath would throw the ball right between them. Tremendous velocity. And he'd put it right between the numbers." Almost fifty years after the game, Culpepper wrote, "To this day I have never seen a quarterback as accurate or with as quick a release as Namath on that New Year's Night." To make matters worse, water from the pregame storm had gotten in the telewriter, making it impossible for the defensive coordinator to send diagrams from the press box to the sidelines. They came out smeared and indecipherable, as blurred as the flight of a Namath pass.[21]

Pregame predictions of a defensive struggle now seemed foolish. With Namath in the game Royal knew his offense would have to score more than 14 points. Following Alabama's score, Texas mounted their own drive. The Longhorns opened up their throwing game, converted a fourth and one, and reached the Alabama 29-yard line. On fourth and five they went for a field goal, which was blocked by Creed Gilmer. David Ray scooped up the ball and cut for the open field but was hit from his blind side and fumbled the ball. Texas recovered on the Alabama 38.

Alabama rushers sacked Hudson on the next play, only to have it nullified by a holding penalty. Three plays later Koy bulled two yards into the end zone, giving Texas a 21–7 lead. Bryant's

"Defensive Axiom number 3" emphasized, "The defense *must not* allow the opponent to score by running from within your 5-yard line." Alabama had now failed to uphold their coach's three primary goals. And there was almost no time remaining in the first half.[22]

The second half belonged to Namath and Alabama. Although Texas altered their defensive strategy, effectively rushing only two men and keeping the rest back to stop the passing game, it had no effect on Namath. In Alabama's first possession, he marched the Tide down the field with surgical passes, including one to convert a fourth and eight. The final pass of the series was a 20-yard strike to Perkins. Both Nobis and linebacker Timmy Doerr dove toward the ball, but Namath had thrown it hard and low. As the linebackers fell to the ground Perkins caught the pass and lunged into the end zone. Alabama had narrowed the lead to 21–14.

In the press box New York Jets head coach Weeb Ewbank watched Namath pass Alabama back into the game. He bubbled like champagne. "Fabulous, fabulous, fabulous," he kept repeating, thinking about the contract he had in his pocket that was complete save for Namath's signature. It was an enormous amount of money, but…"Reminds me of Unitas," he said. "He doesn't have to be tutored. He could take a pro team right now."[23]

On the Texas sideline Royal realized that the best way to stop the Tide's fabulous quarterback was to keep him on the other sideline. That meant the offense had to grind out first downs. Led by Koy, they ate up some time, and their defense was able to get a stop, but by the end of the third quarter Namath was engineering another drive. On the second play of the fourth quarter Ray kicked a 27-yard field goal to cut Texas's lead to 21–17. Almost a quarter of play remained—and the last quarter virtually always belonged to Bear's team.

Throughout the game it seemed as if Texas had gotten every

break. Batted balls, fumbles, and officials' calls all seemed to go their way. But midway through the final period Alabama got a break when starting quarterback Marv Kristynik's pass was batted into the air and landed in the hands of Alabama guard Jim Fuller. With the ball on the Longhorn 34, Namath hobbled back onto the field. After a run lost two yards, he completed two passes that moved the ball to the six-yard line. On first down, power back Steve Bowman advanced the ball to the two. On second down he was stopped for no gain, and on third moved the ball to the one.

Darrell Royal apparently had read *Building a Championship Football Team* and noted Defensive Axiom 3, the same one Alabama had not upheld—don't allow your opponent to score by running from within your five-yard line. From the press box Texas's defensive coach had called "74 Goalline," which called for the seven down linemen to submarine under the Alabama blockers and allow Nobis and the other linebackers to make the tackle.

Namath saw what Texas was up to. "I thought I saw an opening. The time before...I could see the linebacker moving. I thought I could make it." Limping, hurting, and a signature away from making more than the president of the United States, he called his own number. It called for Gaylon McCollough to work with right guard Wayne Freeman to push back the Texas left tackle, opening a sliver of space for Joe to wedge through. But just before the snap, Nobis moved into the gap between the tackles, nose to nose with McCollough. Making an instant decision, McCollough snapped the ball and drove straight into Nobis.[24]

McCollough centered the ball, and, he wrote, "the two lines crashed into each other like 14 bulls, straining and twisting for all we were worth." He hit Nobis and fell into the end zone. "I looked for Namath. It was easy to find him. He was lying on top of me *in the end zone.* We jumped up and began to celebrate." One official indicated, "TOUCHDOWN!!"

Culpepper saw it differently. "On the snap of the ball, the Texas linemen beat the Alabama linemen to the punch and Nobis buried Namath as the Alabama quarterback tried to sneak to his left side." Later, after watching the film of the stand, defensive coach Mike Campbell told Culpepper, "Pat, not only didn't Namath score, not one damn Alabama jersey crossed the goal line."[25]

But the referees had no film to review. The line judge ran toward the play and asked, "Did he score?" "Yes," one official said. But the head official took the ball, placed it one foot away from the goal line, and signaled Texas ball.

Alabama did not get that close to the end zone again. The game ended 21–17.

Bear Bryant never complained. When McCollough said Namath had scored, Bryant replied simply, "If [Joe] had walked in there would be no question about it." Nor did Namath grouse. After the game a fan told him, "Good game, Joe. Good game, boy." Namath shook his head and said, "It wasn't good enough. It didn't get us over."

———

About 5,000 miles away from Miami, Sonny Namath sat at his kitchen table in the married quarters of Sullivan Barracks in Mannheim, Germany. Sipping a cup of coffee, he looked over the headlines in the *Army Times*. When he saw his own last name he read more closely. Something about the Alabama quarterback signing a big professional contract. That would be his little brother Joey, he thought. As he read, he made a face. "Oh, Christ, they made a mistake there."

"What's the matter, Sonny?" his wife, also a lifer in the Army, asked when she saw the look on his face.

He answered that "the stupid paper" never got anything right. She knew all about the *Army Times'* problems. It seldom got even the most mundane facts completely correct. Even items such as the ranks of Army officers inevitably got screwed up by the paper. "What'd they do this time? Make [General] Mark Clark a private?" she asked.

"No, they got a story about Joey signing a contract with the Jets. Got one too many zeros, though. Says here he got four *hundred* thousand!"

"Think they'd have caught something like that."

"Four hundred thousand. Ain't nobody in this world worth four hundred thousand dollars! Christ almighty, this stupid paper. You ever heard anything so silly?"

Reflecting on the amount, Sonny added, "They must have meant *forty* thousand. Jesus, he's really doing great. Joey got forty thousand dollars to play football! Did you ever hear anything so crazy? Forty thousand dollars to play football?!"

"Your little brother made the right decision, I guess."

"Good for Joe." Sonny drank his coffee and let the number sink in—the forty, not four hundred, thousand. "That's an awful lot of money just to play a game. Unbelievable. He's really doing great. Good for Joe. Good for Joey."[26]

With his former head coaches Bear Bryant and Larry Bruno flanking him, Joe Namath prepared for his new life in professional football with David "Sonny" Werblin, owner of the New York Jets. (Krzemienski Collection)

Acknowledgments

There is a misconception that because their names are on the cover of books, authors work alone in the writing process. Nothing could be farther from the truth. Authors may choose the words in and the emphasis of their books, but they are helped along the way by countless people. In the case of *Rising Tide*, hundreds of people helped. They answered questions, searched for documents, and made the story of Paul "Bear" Bryant, Joe Namath, and Alabama in the early 1960s come alive. Many agreed to multiple interviews, giving up time in which they could have been reading, writing, or fishing. To name them all would be next to impossible. The footnotes in the book point out many. But I have to single out a few.

In many respects this is an Alabama story, and people from or experts of the history of that state proved of immense aid. Paul Bryant Jr. took time from a busy day to share memories of his father and life at the University of Alabama. Delbert Reed shared generously in memories of a lifetime in and around Tuscaloosa. At the Paul W. Bryant Museum Library, director Ken Gaddy and his assistants Taylor Watson and Brad Green answered our questions, allowed us to look through boxes of materials, and located game films and photographs. No wonder the museum is such a popular site. E. Culpepper Clark, the foremost authority of the integration of the University of Alabama, could not have been more open or helpful. Howell Raines, who I'm certain has a better grasp of Alabama history than any person alive, spent hours introducing me to a world that was not my own. He made people and events from history books achingly real. George and Kay Rable listened to stories and provided lodging during a trip to Tuscaloosa. George, I had nothing to do with the Pittsburgh Steelers Terrible Towel that found its way onto your bust of Lincoln, a claim that Ed cannot make. And, of course, scores of players such as Lee Roy Jordan and Richard Williamson, and coaches such as Howard Schnellenberger, Gene Stallings, Larry "Dude" Hennessey, and Clem Gryska shared memories of their days with Coach Bryant and Joe Namath.

Several people aided with the research. Johnny Smith, my long-suffering friend, looked through some newspapers at the Library of Congress. C. J. Schexnayder helped with some loose ends in Birmingham and Tuscaloosa while he was conducting his own research on the Crimson Tide. Kurt Kemper also shared insights and documents from his research. Thanks to all for being part of a sharing profession.

We were also supported immeasurably by the good people at Fletcher & Company. Whether in New York or Hollywood, Christy Fletcher took time to answer questions, offer advice, render support, and move the project along. Thanks again Christy for everything. And Don Lamm was, as always, terrific, making me feel like he was my biggest fan. His enthusiasm is infectious.

Finally, the folks at Twelve believed in the book. Before he departed the press, Cary Goldstein shared his vision, edited the manuscript, and lent moral support. His assistant, Libby Burton, has been fantastic. She had an answer for every question, a solution for every problem, and just generally radiated hope and enthusiasm. Brian McLendon has been supportive since the day the proposal reached his desk. He recognized the book's audience and had ideas of how to reach it.

At home, my wife, Marjorie Traylor Roberts, lived with stories from *Rising Tide* and me. In a remarkable show of love and character, she never seemed to tire of either. But then, I was talking about Bear Bryant, Joe Namath, and Alabama football.

Randy Roberts

In Beaver Falls, the name Krzemienski preceded me and I received an openness and consideration that I probably did not truly deserve. Larry Bruno and Joe Tronzo revealed information with a candor that I assume had more to do with my last name than my incisive interviewing ability. The Namath family, as well, especially Frank and Rita Namath, never hesitated in their support of my research and told me stories of their "little brother" that had never been shared previously. Others, equally supportive and candid but too numerous to name here, appear in the notes for this book, but Wibby Glover needs to be singled out for his contribution.

No one provided as much information for this book as Horace Jack "Hoot Owl" Hicks. Hoot opened his memories and heart to me on what became our regular Sunday night phone conversations, as well as several visits to Alabama when we traveled his and Joe's stomping grounds. He became such a good friend that even my wife, a die-hard University of Miami fan, found it impossible not to cheer for the Crimson Tide on his behalf. In one very real way, Hoot Owl's love of this book's subject can be seen in the very existence of his son, whom he named Joseph Bryant.

My family helped immensely and, in many ways, groomed me for this story my entire life. My father, Edward Thomas Krzemienski, remains in death his brother's greatest fan. My mother, Helen McCullough Krzemienski, taught me the historian's greatest trait directly through her close relationship with the Namaths—how to remain solidly and accurately in the realm between iconoclast and fan and recognize the difference between identifying excellence and falling prey to hero-worship. More than anyone from my family, though, Tom Krzemienski opened up all of his memories to me and, somewhere along the line, ceased to be my uncle and became one of my very best friends. My wife, Beth, served as an incisive editor but, alas, due to her profound knowledge of college football, could never represent the "uninformed" reader we hope to reach. My daughter, Rosa Ethel, interrupted my progress by making me shift from my Word program to YouTube for installments of *Schoolhouse Rock!*; and my son, Edward Joseph, who won a national book award from PBS during the writing of this book, became a great colleague in the writing process. Most sons surpass their fathers—mine, I fear, did so as an author in the first grade.

Ed Krzemienski

Notes

PROLOGUE: THE TOWER

1 Jack "Hoot Owl" Hicks interview.
2 Howard Schnellenberger interview.
3 Larry Bruno interview; Clem Gryska interview; Larry "Dude" Hennessey interview.
4 Howard Schnellenberger interview; Eli Gold with M. B. Roberts, *Bear's Boys: 36 Men Whose Lives Were Changed by Coach Paul Bryant* (Nashville: Thomas Nelson, 2007), 201.
5 Frank Namath interview; Howard Schnellenberger interview.
6 Howard Schnellenberger interview.
7 Ibid.
8 Ibid.
9 Larry "Dude" Hennessey interview.
10 Gaylon McCollough interview; E. Gaylon McCollough, *Shoulders of Giants: A Facial Surgeon's Prescriptions for Life's Dilemmas* (Huntsville, AL: Albright, 1986), 50.
11 Joe Namath interview.
12 Howard Schnellenberger interview.
13 Joe Namath interview.

1. "Mama Called"

1 Bear Bryant held two memorable "first" meetings, one in December and the other in January. There is some confusion about what he said in which meeting, but the substance of his remarks was absolutely consistent.

2 Keith Dunnavant, *Coach: The Life of Paul "Bear" Bryant* (New York: Thomas Dunne, 2005), 138.

3 Tom Stoddard, *Turnaround: Bear Bryant's First Year at Alabama* (Montgomery, AL: Black Belt Press, 2000), 38–40. Unless noted the quotes from the meeting are from Stoddard.

4 Kurt Edward Kemper, *College Football and American Culture in the Cold War Era* (Urbana: University of Illinois Press, 2009), 118–19.

5 E. Culpepper Clark, *The Schoolhouse Door: Segregation's Last Stand at the University of Alabama* (Tuscaloosa: University of Alabama Press, 1995), 135–37.

6 Stoddard, *Turnaround*, 17–25.

7 E. Culpepper Clark interview; Clark, *Schoolhouse Door*, 137–41.

8 Clark, *Schoolhouse Door*, 139.

9 Ibid.

10 Paul W. Bryant and John Underwood, *Bear: The Hard Life and Good Times of Alabama's Coach Bryant* (Boston: Little, Brown, 2007), 107.

11 Stoddard, *Turnaround*, 35–36.

12 Ibid., 36.

13 Allen Barra, *The Last Coach: A Life of Paul "Bear" Bryant* (New York: W. W. Norton, 2005), 197; Mickey Herskowitz, *The Legend of Bear Bryant* (New York: McGraw-Hill, 1987), 110–12.

14 *Anniston Star*, November 20, 1957.

15 John Forney, *Above the Noise of the Crowd: Thirty Years Behind the Alabama Microphone* (Huntsville, AL: Albright, 1986), 12.

16 *Anniston Star*, November 22, 1957; Herskowitz, *Legend of Bear Bryant*, 114.

17 Herskowitz, *Legend of Bear Bryant*, 116.

18 This quote was covered in the major Alabama papers. See, for instance, *Anniston Star*, November 29, 1957.

19 *Anniston Star*, December 2, 1957.

20 *New York Times*, December 4, 1957.

21 Bryant, *Bear*, 61.

22 Paul Bryant Jr. interview.

23 Forney, *Above the Noise of the Crowd*, 19–20.

24 Dunnavant, *Coach*, 137.

25 Bryant, *Bear*, 49.

26 Stoddard, *Turnaround*, 60.

27 Michael Oriard, *Bowled Over: Big-Time College Football from the Sixties to the BCS Era* (Chapel Hill: University of North Carolina Press, 2009), 37.

28 Ibid., 55.

29 Jack Pardee interview, http://espn.go.com/eoe/junctionboys/pardee_qa.html.

30 Al Browning, *I Remember Paul "Bear" Bryant: Personal Memories of College Football's Most Legendary Coach, as Told by the People Who Knew Him Best* (Nashville: Cumberland House, 2001), 114.

31 Ibid., 79–85.

32 Ibid., 221.

33 Stoddard, *Turnaround*, 212.

34 Ibid., 133.

35 Ibid., 103.

36 Ibid., 137.

37 Gaylon McCollough interview.

38 Stoddard, *Turnaround*, 128.

2. "DIXIE'S PRIDE, CRIMSON TIDE"

1 Theodore Roosevelt, "The American Boy," *St. Nicholas*, May 1900.

2 For an outstanding treatment of southern football see, Leo Andrew Doyle, "Causes Won, Not Lost: Football and Southern Culture, 1892–1983" (PhD dissertation, Emory University, 1998).

3 Ibid., 187–88.

4 Ibid., 11–165; see also Michael Oriard, *Reading Football: How the Popular Press Created an American Spectacle* (Chapel Hill: University of North Carolina Press, 1993), 57–133.

5 Winston Groom, *The Crimson Tide: The Official Illustrated History of Alabama Football, National Championship Edition* (Tuscaloosa: University of Alabama Press, 2010), 33.

6 John M. Carroll, *Red Grange and the Rise of Modern Football* (Urbana: University of Illinois Press, 1999), 101.

7 John R. Thelin, *Games Colleges Play: Scandal and Reform in Intercollegiate Athletics* (Baltimore: Johns Hopkins University Press, 1994), 23; *New York Times*, June 11, 1925.

8 Doyle, "Causes Won, Not Lost," 189.

9 Ibid., 190.

10 Jack Temple Kirby, *Media-Made Dixie: The South in the American Imagination* (Baton Rouge: Louisiana State University Press, 1978), 65; H. L. Mencken, "The Sahara of the Bozart," in *Prejudices: Second Series* (1920), 136–54.

11 Doyle, "Causes Won, Not Lost," 191.

12 Ibid., 193.

13 For the game, see ibid., 193–96; Andrew Doyle, "1925," in Kenneth Gaddy, ed., *Twelve and Counting: The National Championships of Alabama Football* (Tuscaloosa: University of Alabama Press, 2009), 15–17; Groom, *Crimson Tide*, 41–47.

14 Doyle, "Causes Won, Not Lost," 196.

15 Ibid., 196–97.

16 *Roses of Crimson* (VHS, 1997); William Warren Rogers, Robert David Ward, Leah Rawls Atkins, and Wayne Flynt, *Alabama: The History of a Deep South State* (Tuscaloosa: University of Alabama Press, 1994), 459.

17 Rogers et al., *Alabama*, 459; Doyle, "Causes Won, Not Lost," 202.

18 Delbert Reed, *Paul "Bear" Bryant: What Made Him a Winner* (Northport, AL: Vision Press, 1995), 74–76.

19 Ibid., 71.

20 John Temple Graves, *The Fighting South* (New York: G. P. Putnam's Sons, 1943), 90–91.

21 John Matthew Smith, "'Breaking the Plane': Integration and Black Protest in Michigan State University Football During the 1960s," *Michigan Historical Review* (Fall 2007): 101–29.

22 Travis Sawchik, "Clemson's First Black Football Player Has Spent Lifetime Laying Foundations," *Post and Courier*, November 10, 2010, http://www.postandcourier.com/article/20101110/PC1602/311109944; Smith, "Breaking the Plane," 117.

23 Smith, "Breaking the Plane," 112.

24 C. J. Schexnayder, "Liberty Mutual: How the 1959 Liberty Bowl Led the Tide Down the Path Toward Integration," *Maple Street Press Crimson Tide Kickoff 2011*, 118.

25 Tom Stoddard, *Turnaround: Bear Bryant's First Year at Alabama* (Montgomery, AL: Black Belt Press, 2000), 215; *New York Times*, December 1, 1959; Frank Fitzpatrick, "Giving 'Em Fitz: Echoes of Trayvon Martin Incident in Death of Ex-Football Star Janerette," philly.com, April 3, 2012; Schexnayder, "Liberty Mutual," 119. Unless noted, the Liberty Bowl discussion is based on Schexnayder's article.

26 *Birmingham News*, December 2, 1959; *Montgomery Advertiser*, December 2, 1959.

27 Schexnayder, "Liberty Mutual," 119; Kurt Edward Kemper, *College Football and American Culture in the Cold War Era* (Urbana: University of Illinois Press, 2009), 130–33.

28 Schexnayder, "Liberty Mutual," 120; Bryant, *Bear*, 269.

29 Schexnayder, "Liberty Mutual," 120.

30 Ibid., 122; Dallas County Citizens Council to John Patterson et al., December 7, 1959, Frank Rose Papers University Archives, University of Alabama; *Montgomery Advertiser-Journal*, December 13, 1959.

31 *Montgomery Advertiser*, December 3, 1959.

32 *Birmingham News*, December 2, 1959.

33 *New York Times*, December 20, 1959.

34 Paul W. Bryant and John Underwood, *Bear: The Hard Life and Good Times of Alabama's Coach Bryant* (Boston: Little, Brown, 2007), 269.

35 Robert Weisbrot, *Freedom Bound: A History of America's Civil Rights Movement* (New York: W. W. Norton, 1990), 28–29.

36 For sit-ins, see Taylor Branch, *Parting the Waters: America in the King Years, 1954–63* (New York: Simon & Schuster, 1988), 272–311.

37 For Harrison in Birmingham, see Diane McWhorter, *Carry Me Home: Birmingham, Alabama; The Climactic Battle of the Civil Rights Revolution* (New York: Simon & Schuster, 2001), 157–74; Gene Roberts and Hank Klibanoff, *The Race Beat: The Press, the Civil Rights Struggle, and the Awakening of a Nation* (New York: Vintage, 2006), 229–55.

38 *New York Times*, April 12, 1960.

39 Ibid., 280.

40 For the Freedom Riders journal, see Raymond Arsenault, *Freedom Riders: 1961 and the Struggle for Racial Justice* (New York: Oxford University Press, 2006).

41 Ibid., 133.

3. THE RIVER

1 *Beaver Falls News-Tribune*, October 1, 1960.

2 Tom Krzemienski interview.

3 "1945 Beaver County Industry Report," "ORD Form No. 172, Pittsburgh District—Ohio River," Steel Industry File; and "Beaver Falls Industrial Map, 1943," Maps File; in Beaver Falls Historical Society, Carnegie Free Library, Beaver Falls, PA (hereafter cited as BFHS).

4 Beaver Falls versus Ambridge game film; Tom Krzemienski interview; Joe Namath interview.

5 Joe Namath interview.

6 "Beaver Falls City Map, 1945," Maps File, BFHS.

7 Joe Namath interview.

8 Cheryl Weller Beck, ed., *The Twentieth Century History of Beaver County, Pennsylvania, 1900–1988* (Marceline, MO: Walsworth, 1989), 371.

9 J. Thomas Jable outlines the Brailler and Fiscus claims and endorses the Heffelfinger claim in his article "The Birth of Professional Football: Pittsburgh Athletic Clubs Ring in Professionals in 1892," *Western Pennsylvania History Magazine* 62 (1979): 131–47.

10 Ed Bouchette, *The Pittsburgh Steelers* (New York: St. Martin's, 1994), 12.

11 Frank Namath interview.

12 Joe Namath interview.

13 Joe Willie Namath with Dick Schaap, *I Can't Wait Until Tomorrow...'Cause I Get Better-Looking Every Day* (New York: Random House, 1969), 127.

14 John "Sonny" Namath interview.

15 Frank Namath interview.

16 Larry Bruno interview.

17 *Beaver Falls News-Tribune*, October 8, 1960; October 22, 1960; October 29, 1960; Gary Harris interview.

18 *Beaver Falls News-Tribune*, December 30, 1960.

19 *New Castle News*, September 24, 1960; *Beaver Falls News-Tribune*, October 22, 1960; Tom Krzemienski interview; *Beaver Falls News-Tribune*, November 1, 1960; *Beaver Falls News-Tribune*, September 10, 1960.

20 Tom Krzemienski interview; Joe Namath interview.

21 Frank Namath interview; John "Sonny" Namath interview; Rita (Namath) Sims interview.

22 Joe Tronzo interview; Gary Harris interview.

23 Gary Harris interview.
24 Joe Ursida interview.
25 Gary Harris interview.
26 Joe Tronzo interview.
27 *Beaver County Times*, October 17, 1995.
28 Joe Tronzo interview.
29 *Beaver Falls News-Tribune*, November 15, 1960; Joe Tronzo interview.
30 Joe Tronzo, "Beaver Falls Wallops Aliquippa, 34–7," *Beaver Falls News-Tribune*, October 29, 1960; *Beaver Falls News-Tribune*, n.d.; Joe Tronzo interview.

4. THE PRIVILEGED SON

1 Tom Krzemienski interview.
2 Tony Golmont interview.
3 Rich Niedbala interview.
4 Larry Bruno interview.
5 Al Hassan interview.
6 Don Greco interview.
7 Hy Turkin and S. C. Thompson, revisions by Pete Palmer, *The Official Encyclopedia of Baseball*, 10th rev. ed. (South Brunswick, NJ, and New York: A. S. Barnes, 1979), 308.
8 Joe Tronzo interview.
9 Al Hassan interview.

5. PLAYING DEFENSE

1 John Forney, *Above the Noise of the Crowd: Thirty Years Behind the Alabama Microphone* (Huntsville, AL: Albright, 1986), 68–69.
2 Jack "Hoot Owl" Hicks interview; Paul W. Bryant and John Underwood, *Bear: The Hard Life and Good Times of Alabama's Coach Bryant* (Boston: Little, Brown, 2007), 159, 183.
3 Pat Trammell Jr. interview.
4 Mickey Herskowitz, *The Legend of Bear Bryant* (New York: McGraw-Hill, 1987), 125.
5 Delbert Reed interview; Bryant, *Bear*, 160; Pat Trammell Jr. interview.

6 Bryant, *Bear*, 161.

7 Allen Barra, *The Last Coach: A Life of Paul "Bear" Bryant* (New York: W. W. Norton, 2005), 224.

8 *Athens News Courier*, December 12, 1968.

9 Pat Trammell Jr. interview.

10 Bryant, *Bear*, 160.

11 *1961 Football Round-Up*, 33.

12 *Crimson White*, September 21, 1961.

13 Lee Roy Jordan interview. Unless noted, Jordan's quotes are from the interviews.

14 Lee Roy Jordan interview; Andrew Doyle, "An Atheist in Alabama Is Someone Who Doesn't Believe in Bear Bryant: A Symbol for an Embattled South," in *The Sporting World of the Modern South*, ed. Patrick B. Miller (Urbana: University of Illinois Press, 2002), 252.

15 Lee Roy Jordan interview; Doyle, "An Atheist in Alabama," 252.

16 Keith Dunnavant, *Coach: The Life of Paul "Bear" Bryant* (New York: Thomas Dunne, 2005), 155.

17 Bryant, *Bear*, 170.

18 Ibid., 160.

19 Lee Roy Jordan interview.

20 "The Paul Bear Bryant Story" (1990).

21 Allen Barra, *The Last Coach: A Life of Paul "Bear" Bryant* (New York: W. W. Norton, 2005), 250–53; Dunnavant, *Coach*, 162.

22 "The Paul Bear Bryant Story."

23 Forney, *Above the Noise of the Crowd*, 74.

24 *Atlanta Journal*, November 20, 1961.

25 Ibid., November 21, 1961; November 24, 1961; November 28, 1961; see also opinions on November 26, 1961.

26 Ibid., November 21, 1961.

27 Forney, *Above the Noise of the Crowd*, 74.

28 *Birmingham News*, November 26, 1961.

29 *Atlanta Journal*, November 21, 1961.

30 Bobby Dodd to Paul Bryant, November 22, 1961, Frank Rose Papers.

31 *Atlanta Journal*, November 23, 1961.

32 Bryant, *Bear*, 168.

33 Ibid., 170–71.

34 *Atlanta Daily World*, November 25, 1961.

35 *Los Angeles Times*, November 20, 1961.

36 *Atlanta Journal*, November 20, 1961; *Los Angeles Times*, November 20, 1963; Roy Terrell, "The Bear and Alabama Come Out on Top," *Sports Illustrated*, December 11, 1961.

37 Frank A. Rose to Daniel J. Haughton, November 29, 1961, Frank Rose Papers.

38 *Los Angeles Times*, November 29, 1961.

39 Kurt Edward Kemper, *College Football and American Culture in the Cold War Era* (Urbana: University of Illinois Press, 2009), 63–73; Kurt Edward Kemper, "The Smell of Roses and the Color of the Players: Football and the Expansion of the Civil Rights Movement in the West," *Journal of Sport History* (Fall 2004): 317–39.

40 *Atlanta Journal*, November 9, 1961; November 11, 1961; *Montgomery Advertiser*, November 19, 1961; November 20, 1961; *Birmingham News*, November 20, 1961; Kemper, *College Football and American Culture*, 138; John Forney and Steve Townsend, *Talk of the Tide: An Oral History of Alabama Football Since 1920* (Birmingham, AL: Crane Hill, 1993), 92.

41 Ibid., 140.

42 *California Eagle*, November 16, 1961; November 23, 1961; *UCLA Daily Bruin*, November 22, 1961.

43 *Los Angeles Examiner*, November 15, 1961; November 21, 1961.

44 *Los Angeles Times*, November 29, 1961.

45 Ibid., November 19, 1961.

46 W. R. Rivers to Norman Chandler, December 5, 1961, Frank Rose Papers; Kemper, *College Football and American Culture*, 144–45.

47 Frank A. Rose to Robert S. Johnston, November 22, 1961; Frank A. Rose to W. R. Rivers, December 19, 1961; Frank A. Rose to John Canaday, November 29, 1961, all in Frank Rose Papers.

48 Howell Raines interview was insightful on the southern character.

49 Bryant, *Bear*, 174.

50 Terrell, "Bear and Alabama Come Out on Top."

51 Herskowitz, *Legend of Bear Bryant*, 126.

52 *New York Times*, January 2, 1962.

53 Forney and Townsend, *Talk of the Tide*, 93.

54 Ibid., 94.

55 Ibid.

56 Frank W. Boykin to Bear Bryant, January 2, 1962, Frank Rose Papers.

6. BECOMING JOE WILLIE

1 Requisition form and accompanying literature, June 7, 1962, Bryant Papers, Paul Bryant Museum, Tuscaloosa, AL.

2 Joe Namath interview.

3 Frank Lambert interview.

4 Quoted in Frank Lambert, *The Battle of Ole Miss: Civil Rights v. States' Rights* (New York: Oxford University Press, 2010), 97–98.

5 Charles H. Martin, *Benching Jim Crow: The Rise and Fall of the Color Line in Southern College Sports, 1890–1980* (Urbana: University of Illinois Press, 2010), 282; Lambert, *Battle of Ole Miss*, 112.

6 Clem Gryska interview.

7 Ibid.

8 Gaylon McCollough, *Shoulders of Giants: A Facial Surgeon's Prescriptions for Life's Dilemmas* (Huntsville, AL: Albrigh, 1986), 51–52; Gaylon McCollough interview.

9 Joe Willie Namath with Dick Schaap, *I Can't Wait Until Tomorrow...'Cause I Get Better-Looking Every Day* (New York: Random House, 1969), 148–49.

10 Karlin "Butch" Ryan interview; Joe Namath interview.

11 Namath and Schaap, *I Can't Wait*, 149; Paul W. Bryant and John Underwood, *Bear: The Hard Life and Good Times of Alabama's Coach Bryant* (Boston: Little, Brown, 1975), 175–77.

12 Larry "Dude" Hennessey interview; Jim Goostree interview.

13 Frank Namath interview.

14 Game itineraries, Bryant Papers, Paul Bryant Museum, Tuscaloosa, AL.

15 Jack "Hoot Owl" Hicks interview.

16 *Knoxville News-Sentinel*, September 16, 1962.

17 *Montgomery Advertiser*, September 6, 1962; September 9, 1962; September 22, 1962.

18 *Crimson Classics* [DVD Recording], Georgia Game; Richard Williamson interview; *Birmingham News*, September 23, 1962.

19 *Birmingham News*, September 23, 1962.

20 Jack "Hoot Owl" Hicks interview.

21 Ibid.

22 Tom Krzemienski interview.

23 Jack "Hoot Owl" Hicks interview.

24 Ibid.

25 *Atlanta Journal-Constitution*, September 23, 1962.

26 *Birmingham News*, September 28, 1962.

27 *Montgomery Advertiser*, September 29, 1962.

28 Quoted in Lambert, *Battle of Ole Miss*, 113–14.

29 Taylor Branch, *Parting the Waters: America in the King Years, 1954–63* (New York: Simon & Schuster, 1988), 666–67; Frank Lambert interview.

30 "President John F. Kennedy, Radio and Television Address on the Situation in Mississippi, September 30, 1962," quoted in William M. Goldsmith, *The Growth of Presidential Power: A Documented History*, vol. 3: *Triumph and Reappraisal* (New York: Chelsea House, 1974), 1667.

31 Goldsmith, *Growth of Presidential Power*, 1665; E. Culpepper Clark, *The Schoolhouse Door: Segregation's Last Stand at the University of Alabama* (Tuscaloosa: University of Alabama Press, 1995), 146, 165–66.

32 Jack "Hoot Owl" Hicks interview.

33 *Birmingham News*, October 7 and 8, 1962; *Crimson Classics*, Vanderbilt Game.

34 *Birmingham News*, October 14, 1962.

35 Ibid., October 21, 1962; *Crimson Classics*, Tennessee Game.

36 Jack Hurlbut File, Bryant Papers, Paul Bryant Museum, Tuscaloosa, AL.

37 Michael Dobbs, *One Minute to Midnight: Kennedy, Khrushchev, and Castro on the Brink of Nuclear War* (New York: Knopf, 2008), 49–50.

38 *Tuscaloosa News*, October 25, 1962.

39 *Birmingham News*, October 28, 1962.

40 *Montgomery Advertiser-Journal*, November 4, 1962.

41 *Birmingham News*, November 8, 1962; November 9, 1962.

42 *Montgomery Advertiser-Journal*, November 11, 1962; *Crimson Classics*, Miami Game.

43 Furman Bisher, "College Football Is Going Berserk," *Saturday Evening Post*, October 20, 1962, 10, 15.

44 *Atlanta Journal*, November 18, 1962; *Birmingham News*, November 18, 1962, *Crimson Classics*, Georgia Tech Game.

45 *Tuscaloosa News*, November 18, 1962; *Birmingham News*, November 18, 1962; 1963 *Corolla*, 331.

46 Richard Williamson interview.

47 *Birmingham News*, December 2, 1962.

48 Ibid.

49 Don McDaniel, ed., *University of Alabama, 1963 Football Information and Record Book* (Tuscaloosa: Drake, 1963), 48.

50 John "Sonny" Namath interview.

51 Branch, *Parting the Waters*, 687.

52 *Crimson Classics*, "If they stay in bounds...," 1963 Orange Bowl, Alabama vs. Oklahoma.

53 Quoted in George Lynn Cross, *Presidents Can't Punt: The OU Football Tradition* (Norman: University of Oklahoma Press, 1977), 336; Lee Roy Jordan interview.

54 *Crimson Classics*, "If they stay in bounds..."

55 Ibid.

56 *Miami Herald*, January 2, 1963.

57 *Crimson Classics*, "If they stay in bounds..."

58 Ibid.

59 *Miami Herald*, January 2, 1963.

7. "With Every Force at My Command"

1 *Birmingham News*, March 16, 1963.

2 Paul W. Bryant and John Underwood, *Bear: The Hard Life and Good Times of Alabama's Coach Bryant* (Boston: Little, Brown, 2007), 199. Unless otherwise stated, Bryant's reaction to the story is from his autobiography.

3 James Kirby, *Fumble: Bear Bryant, Wally Butts, and the Great College Football Scandal* (New York: Harcourt, 1986), 19–33.

4 Ibid., 33.

5 Ibid., 20.

6 Otto Friedrich, *Decline and Fall: The Death Struggle of the "Saturday Evening Post"* (New York: Harper & Row, 1970), 7–18. Our discussion of the politics at the *Saturday Evening Post* is indebted to Friedrich's brilliant study. See also Kirby, *Fumble*, 55–66.

7 Friedrich, *Decline and Fall*, 13.

8 Ibid., 19–35.

9 Ibid., 34.

10 Ibid., 40.

11 The 1963 Inaugural Address of Governor George C. Wallace (January 14, 1963).

12 Gene Roberts and Hank Klibanoff, *The Race Beat: The Press, the Civil Rights Struggle, and the Awakening of a Nation* (New York: Vintage, 2006), 303.

13 Joe David Brown, "Birmingham Alabama: A City in Fear," *Saturday Evening Post*, March 2, 1963, 16–17.

14 Diane McWhorter, *Carry Me Home: Birmingham, Alabama; The Climactic Battle of the Civil Rights Revolution* (New York: Simon & Schuster, 2001), 319; Brown, "Birmingham Alabama," 17.

15 Brown, "Birmingham Alabama," 18.

16 For the chain of events that led to the *Post*'s article, see Friedrich, *Decline and Fall*, 41–42; Frank Graham Jr., *A Farewell to Heroes* (New York: Viking, 1981), 283.

17 *Saturday Evening Post*, April 27, 1963, 82.

18 Frank Graham Jr., "The Story of a College Football Fix," *Saturday Evening Post*, March 23, 1963, 80.

19 Furman Bisher, *The Furman Bisher Collection* (Dallas: Taylor, 1989), 18; Furman Bisher, *Furman Bisher: Face to Face* (Champaign, Illinois: Sports Publishing, 2005), 36–41.

20 Ibid., 81–83. The following quotes come from Graham's article.

21 Ibid., 83.

22 Bryant, *Bear*, 201–3, gives Bryant's reaction to the story.

23 Frank A. Rose to O. C. Aderhold, March 6, 1963, Aderhold Papers, University Archives, University of Georgia, Wally Butts Investigation. The Georgia investigation by Attorney General Eugene Cook was very thorough, amounting to several thousand pages of reports and testimonies. By contrast, there is virtually nothing in the Frank Rose Papers on the case.

24 Joe Willie Namath with Dick Schaap, *I Can't Wait Until Tomorrow...'Cause I Get Better-Looking Every Day* (New York: Random House, 1969), 181.

25 Lee Roy Jordan interview; *Birmingham News*, March 18, 1963; Joe Namath interview.

26 For Bryant's television appearance, see *Birmingham News*, March 18, 1963; *Montgomery Advertiser*, March 19, 1963; *New Orleans Times-Picayune*, March 19, 1963.

27 *Montgomery Advertiser*, March 19, 1963; *Birmingham News*, March 19, 1963.

28 *Montgomery Advertiser*, March 20, 1963; *Birmingham News*, March 19, 1963.

29 For Butts's resignation and reactions to Georgia's investigation, see Kirby, *Fumble*, 40, 48–54.

30 Memorandum from Eugene Cook, Attorney General of Georgia, to Carl Sanders, Governor of Georgia, April 1, 1963, Aderhold Papers, Wally Butts Investigation.

31 Kirby, *Fumble*, 67–69; Dan Jenkins, "Scandalous Notes," *Sports Illustrated*, April 8, 1963.

32 *Saturday Evening Post*, April 27, 1963, 82; Graham, *Farewell to Heroes*, 292.

33 *Montgomery Advertiser*, March 23, 1963.

34 *Montgomery Advertiser*, March 24, 1963.

35 *Birmingham News*, March 18, 1963; March 22, 1963; *Montgomery Advertiser*, March 19, 1963; Kirby, *Fumble*, 72.

36 *Tuscaloosa News*, March 30, 1963; *Montgomery Advertiser*, March 20, 1963; *Birmingham News*, March 20, 1963.

37 *Birmingham News*, March 24, 1963; *Atlanta Journal*, April 10, 1963; April 11, 1963.

38 *Montgomery Advertiser*, March 26, 1963.

39 *Birmingham News*, March 18, 1963.

40 Ibid., March 28, 1963.

41 Bisher, *Furman Bisher: Face to Face*, 39–40.

42 For Graham's experiences, see Graham, *Farewell to Heroes*, 279–98.

43 Bryant, *Bear*, 209.

8. The Greatest Performance of His Life

1 Howell Raines, "Goodbye to the Bear," *New Republic*, January 24, 1983, 10.

2 Howell Raines interview.

3 *New York Times*, December 4, 1961; Winston Groom, *The Crimson Tide: The Official Illustrated History of Alabama Football, National Championship Edition* (Tuscaloosa: University of Alabama Press, 2010), 108–9; E. Culpepper Clark, *The Schoolhouse Door: Segregation's Last Stand at the University of Alabama* (Tuscaloosa: University of Alabama Press, 2007), 146.

4 Raines, "Goodbye to the Bear," 11.

5 Howell Raines interview.

6 Ibid.

7 Dan T. Carter, *The Politics of Rage: George Wallace, the Origins of the New Conservatism, and the Transformation of American Politics* (New York: Simon & Schuster, 1995), 96.

8 Raines, "Goodbye to the Bear," 11.

9 Clement Seelhorst to the Birmingham Chamber of Commerce, September 23, 1962, Frank Rose Papers.

10 W. J. Haley, Acting Chief of Police, to Eugene "Bull" Connor, October 10, 1962; Eugene "Bull" Connor to Frank Rose, October 11, 1962, both in Frank Rose Papers.

11 Frank Rose to Eugene "Bull" Connor, October 18, 1962, Frank Rose Papers.

12 Clark, *Schoolhouse Door*, 153.

13 Vito Capizzo interview. Capizzo is the source for Namath's summer 1962 activities.

14 Jack "Hoot Owl" Hicks interview.

15 Suzanne Rau Wolfe, *The University of Alabama: A Pictorial History* (Tuscaloosa: University of Alabama Press, 1983), 169.

16 Clark, *Schoolhouse Door*, 154.

17 Ibid.

18 Frank A. Rose to George C. Wallace, May 31, 1962, Frank Rose Papers.

19 Frank A. Rose to George C. Wallace, November 27, 1962, Frank Rose Papers.

20 George C. Wallace to Frank A. Rose, December 6, 1962; Frank A. Rose to George C. Wallace, December 10, 1962; Frank A. Rose to George C. Wallace, December 12, 1962; Frank A. Rose to George C. Wallace, December 18, 1962, all in Frank Rose Papers.

21 E. Culpepper Clark interview; Clark, *Schoolhouse Door*, 170.

22 Martin Luther King Jr., "Letter from Birmingham Jail" (1963).

23 *Montgomery Advertiser*, October 20, 1962; October 21, 1962; December 4, 1962; *Birmingham News*, November 10, 1962; November 11, 1962.

24 *Birmingham News*, June 6, 1963.

25 Ibid., June 9, 1962; June 10, 1962.

26 *Crimson White*, June 9, 1963.

27 Clark, *Schoolhouse Door*, 222–37. *Birmingham News*, June 11, 1963; June 12, 1963. Unless otherwise noted, the details of Wallace's schoolhouse door stand are from Clark and the *Birmingham News*.

28 Joe Namath interview; Jack "Hoot Owl" Hicks interview.

29 John F. Kennedy, "Civil Rights Speech," June 11, 1963.

30 Jack "Hoot Owl" Hicks interview.

31 Dan Jenkins, "A Trial That Has the South Seething," *Sports Illustrated*, August 5, 1963.

32 Ibid.; *Los Angeles Times*, April 3, 1963.

33 Jenkins, "Trial That Has the South Seething"; *Birmingham News*, August 6, 1963; James Kirby, *Fumble: Bear Bryant, Wally Butts, and the Great College Football Scandal* (New York: Harcourt, 1986), 91–95.

34 *Birmingham News*, August 5, 1963.

35 Allen Barra, *The Last Coach: A Life of Paul "Bear" Bryant* (New York: W. W. Norton, 2005), 293.

36 Kirby, *Fumble*, 91–148. Kirby was the official observer of the Southeastern Conference at the trial, and his insights as well as observations of the personalities and atmosphere of the trial are astute. They are used here for additional details.

37 *Birmingham News*, August 5, 1963.

38 Ibid., August 5, 1963; August 6, 1953.

39 Ibid., August 6, 1963; *Atlanta Journal*, August 6, 1963; Kirby, *Fumble*, 104.

40 *Birmingham News*, August 7, 1963; *Atlanta Journal*, August 7, 1963.

41 Kirby, *Fumble*, 111.

42 *Birmingham News*, August 8, 1963.

43 Kirby, *Fumble*, 113; Paul W. Bryant and John Underwood, *Bear: The Hard Life and Good Times of Alabama's Coach Bryant* (Boston: Little, Brown, 1975), 224.

44 Bryant, *Bear*, 217.

45 J. C. Kirby Jr. to Executive Committee of Southeastern Conference, "Analysis of Evidence on Butts-Bryant Phone Call of September 13, 1962," November 12, 1963, Aderhold Papers.

46 John Forney, *Above the Noise of the Crowd: Thirty Years Behind the Alabama Microphone* (Huntsville, AL: Albright, 1986), 82.

47 *Atlanta Journal*, August 3, 1963. Quotes from Bryant's testimony come from the transcript of his testimony in the *Atlanta Journal*.

48 Kirby, *Fumble*, 115.

49 *Birmingham News*, August 8, 1963; August 9, 1965; *Atlanta Journal*, August 8, 1963; August 9, 1965.

50 Lee Roy Jordan interview.

51 Kirby, *Fumble*, 120–21.

52 *Atlanta Journal*, August 13, 1963; Kirby, *Fumble*, 126.

53 Kirby, *Fumble*, 134–35; *Atlanta Journal*, August 14, 1963.

54 *Birmingham News*, August 20, 1963; *Atlanta Journal*, August 20, 1963; Kirby, *Fumble*, 148.

55 The settlement was later reduced to $460,000.
56 Robert H. Boyle, "It's Not the Money, It's the Vindication," *Sports Illustrated*, September 2, 1963.
57 *Birmingham News*, August 22, 1963.
58 Bryant, *Bear*, 223.
59 *New York Times*, January 17, 1964; February 5, 1964; "Magazines: Balm for a Gloomy Bear," *Time*, February 14, 1964.
60 Howell Raines interview; *Los Angeles Times*, August 3, 1965.
61 Bryant, *Bear*, 223.

9. "Living Like Yankees, Playing Like Barber College"

1 Frank Cicatiello interview.
2 Taylor Branch, *Parting the Waters: America in the King Years, 1954–63* (New York: Simon & Schuster, 1988), 888–93.
3 1962 *Corolla*, n.p.
4 Jack "Hoot Owl" Hicks interview; Larry "Dude" Hennessey interview.
5 Mickey Herskowitz, *The Legend of Bear Bryant* (New York: McGraw-Hill, 1987), 125.
6 Howard Schnellenberger interview; John Madden with Dave Anderson, *One Knee Equals Two Feet (And Everything Else You Need to Know About Football)* (New York: Random House, 1986), 67–72.
7 Bill Nunn interview; Howard Schnellenberger interview.
8 *Birmingham News*, September 22, 1963.
9 Ibid.
10 *Atlanta Journal and Constitution*, September 22, 1963.
11 *Birmingham News*, September 29, 1963.
12 Ibid., October 1, 1963.
13 Ibid., October 2, 1963.
14 Ibid., October 6, 1963.
15 Ibid., October 6, 1963; October 7, 1963.
16 Ibid., October 7, 1963; October 10, 1963.
17 Jack "Hoot Owl" Hicks interview.
18 *Birmingham News*, October 11, 1963.
19 Florida Game Itinerary, Bryant Papers, Paul Bryant Museum, Tuscaloosa, AL.
20 *Birmingham News*, October 13, 1963.

21 *Crimson White*, October 17, 1963.

22 Ibid., October 24, 1963, 10.

23 *Birmingham News*, October 13, 1963.

24 Ibid., October 20, 1963.

25 Ibid.

26 Ibid.

27 Ibid.

28 *Crimson White*, August 8, 1963.

29 1964 *Corolla*, 259, 262–63; Jack "Hoot Owl" Hicks interview; Jim Somerville interview.

30 *Birmingham News*, October 27, 1963.

31 Jack "Hoot Owl" Hicks interview; Joe Willie Namath with Dick Schaap, *I Can't Wait Until Tomorrow…'Cause I Get Better-Looking Every Day* (New York: Random House, 1969), 151–52.

32 Billy Varner interview.

33 Ibid.

34 *Birmingham News*, November 3, 1963; *Jackson Clarion-Ledger*, November 3, 1963.

35 Jack "Hoot Owl" Hicks interview.

36 Larry "Dude" Hennessey interview; Billy Varner interview.

37 *Atlanta Journal-Constitution*, November 15, 1963.

38 Ibid., November 17, 1963.

39 Frank Cicatiello interview; http://www.stfrancisuofa.com/index.php?page=about-us.

40 Jack "Hoot Owl" Hicks interview; Frank Cicatiello interview.

41 Phillip Marshall, "Remembering Tucker Frederickson," http://auburn.scout.com/2/651692.html; Howell Raines interview.

42 *Birmingham News*, December 1, 1963; *Atlanta Journal-Constitution*, December 1, 1963; *Montgomery Advertiser-Journal*, December 1, 1963.

10. THE RAT PACK

1 Joe Namath interview, December 1969, in Stephen Randall, ed., *The Playboy Interviews: They Played the Game* (Milwaukee, OR: M Press, 2006), 312.

2 Jack "Hoot Owl" Hicks interview.

3 Frank Cicatiello interview.

4 F. M. Williams to Frank Rose, March 7, 1962, Frank Rose Papers.

5 Jim Somerville interview.

6 Wilber Glover interview. All Glover stories are from his interview.

7 Jack "Hoot Owl" Hicks interview.

8 Wilber Glover interview; Frank Cicatiello interview.

9 Ken Gaddy interview; Jack "Hoot Owl" Hicks interview.

10 Jack "Hoot Owl" Hicks interview.

11 Ibid.; Paul W. Bryant and John Underwood, *Bear: The Hard Life and Good Times of Alabama's Coach Bryant* (Boston: Little, Brown, 1975), 202.

12 Joe Willie Namath with Dick Schaap, *I Can't Wait Until Tomorrow...'Cause I Get Better-Looking Every Day* (New York: Random House, 1969), 185; Bryant, *Bear*, 202–3.

13 Gene Stallings and Sally Cook, *Another Season: A Coach's Story of Raising an Exceptional Son* (Boston: Little, Brown, 1997), 29, 31, 64–65; Bryant, *Bear*, 203; Gene Stallings interview; Howard Schnellenberger interview; Larry "Dude" Hennessey interview.

14 Larry "Dude" Hennessey interview.

15 Bryant, *Bear*, 203–4; Jack "Hoot Owl" Hicks interview; Rose Namath Szolnoki with Bill Kushner, *Namath: My Son Joe* (Birmingham, AL: Oxmoor House, 1975), 57–58.

16 Jack "Hoot Owl" Hicks interview.

17 Bryant, *Bear*, 204.

18 *Crimson White*, December 12, 1963.

19 Jack "Hoot Owl" Hicks interview.

11. REDEMPTION SONG

1 *Beaver Falls News-Tribune*, December 10, 1963; *Atlanta Constitution*, December 10, 1963; *Birmingham News*, December 10, 1963; *Tuscaloosa News*, December 10, 1963; *New York Times*, December 10, 1963.

2 Team Personnel, Monday, December 9, 1963, Bryant Papers, Paul Bryant Museum, Tuscaloosa, AL.

3 Team Itinerary, Miami Game 1963, Bryant Papers, Paul Bryant Museum, Tuscaloosa, AL.

4 Rich Niedbala interview.

5 "At Miami with George Mira," *Sport*, December 1963.

6 John Devaney, "At Miami They Leave It to George," *Sport*, November 1962, 81.

7 *Birmingham News*, December 15, 1963.

8 Team Itinerary, Miami Game 1963, Bryant Papers, Paul Bryant Museum, Tuscaloosa, AL; *Birmingham News*, December 15, 1963; *Montgomery Advertiser-Journal*, December 15, 1963.

9 *Birmingham News*, December 27, 1963; December 29, 1963.

10 Steve Sloan File, Bryant Papers, Paul Bryant Museum, Tuscaloosa, AL.

11 Richard Williamson interview.

12 Steve Sloan interview.

13 Frank Lambert interview.

14 Ibid.

15 *New Orleans Times-Picayune*, December 29, 1963; *Birmingham News*, December 29, 1963.

16 *Montgomery Advertiser*, January 2, 1964.

17 *Atlanta Journal*, January 2, 1964.

18 Jack "Hoot Owl" Hicks interview.

19 *Crimson White*, January 9, 1964.

20 1964 *University of Alabama Football Brochure* (Tuscaloosa, AL: Drake, 1964), 54–55.

21 Wilber Glover interview; Frank Cicatiello interview.

22 Jack "Hoot Owl" Hicks interview.

23 *Crimson White*, April 16, 1964.

24 Ibid., May 14, 1964.

25 Ibid., April 23, 1964; June 25, 1964.

26 Jack "Hoot Owl" Hicks interview.

27 Jimmy Walsh interview, from *Namath*, HBO documentary.

28 *Birmingham News*, September 13, 1964.

29 Ibid., September 2, 1964; Frank Lambert interview.

30 *Atlanta Journal*, September 10, 1964; *Birmingham News*, September 10, 1964.

31 *Detroit News*, January 13, 1964.

32 *Birmingham News*, September 8, 1964; September 9, 1964.

33 *Montgomery Advertiser-Journal*, September 13, 1964.

34 Ibid., September 16, 1964.

35 William T. Sherman, *Memoirs of General William T. Sherman, by Himself*, vol. 2. (Bloomington: Indiana University Press, 1957 [originally published 1875]), 152.

36 Vince Dooley interview.

37 *Atlanta Journal-Constitution*, September 2, 1964.

38 *Birmingham News*, September 27, 1964; *Montgomery Advertiser-Journal*, September 27, 1964.

39 *Birmingham News*, October 4, 1964; *Montgomery Advertiser-Journal*, October 4, 1964.

40 *Atlanta Journal-Constitution*, September 27, 1964; *Crimson White*, October 3, 1964.

41 Tony Golmont interview.

42 Joe Tronzo interview; *Beaver Falls News-Tribune*, October 19, 1964.

43 Jim Goostree interview; Joe Namath interview.

44 Tony Golmont interview.

12. "Joe Moves Like a Human Now"

1 *Montgomery Advertiser-Journal,* October 11, 1964.

2 Ibid.; *Birmingham News*, October 11, 1964.

3 *Beaver Falls News-Tribune*, October 12, 1964; *Birmingham News*, October 12, 1962.

4 Don H. O'Donoghue, "Surgical Treatment of Injuries to Ligaments of the Knee," *Journal of the American Medical Association* 169 (March 28, 1959): 1427; Howard Schnellenberger interview; Jim Goostree interview.

5 *Birmingham News*, October 12, 1964.

6 Ibid., October 13, 1964.

7 Ibid., October 14, 1964.

8 Ibid., October 15, 1964.

9 Richmond Flowers Jr. interview.

10 *Birmingham News*, October 16, 1964.

11 *Montgomery Advertiser-Journal*, October 18, 1964.

12 Ibid., October 18, 1964; *Birmingham News*, October 18, 1964.

13 *Montgomery Advertiser*, October 10, 1964.

14 *Birmingham News*, October 23, 1964.

15 *Gainesville Sun*, October 20, 1964.

16 Ibid., October 20, 1964; October 25, 1964; *Atlanta Journal*, October 23, 1964.

17 Howell Raines interview.

18 *Birmingham News*, October 25, 1964; Jim Goostree interview.

19 For the game, see, *Birmingham News*, October 25, 1964; *Montgomery Advertiser-Journal*, October 25, 1964; *Atlanta Journal*, October 25, 1964; *Gainesville Sun*, October 25, 1964.

20 *Birmingham News*, October 25, 1964.

21 *Atlanta Journal*, November 1, 1964.

22 Ibid.; *Birmingham News*, November 1, 1964; *Montgomery Advertiser-Journal*, November 1, 1964.

23 *Birmingham News*, November 6, 1964.

24 Ibid., November 8, 1964; Paul W. Bryant and John Underwood, *Bear: The Hard Life and Good Times of Alabama's Coach Bryant* (Boston: Little, Brown, 1975), 175.

25 *Birmingham News*, November 8, 1964.

26 *Montgomery Advertiser-Journal*, November 8, 1964.

27 Game coverage from *Birmingham News*, November 8, 1964; *Montgomery Advertiser-Journal*, November 8, 1964; *Atlanta Journal*, November 8, 1964.

28 Lee Roy Jordan interview; Jack "Hoot Owl" Hicks interview.

29 L. Mitchell Ginn, "The Day Tech Sports Changed Forever," *Georgia Tech Alumni Magazine*, March/April 2011, 72. The discussion of Tech leaving the SEC is largely based on this insightful article.

30 Ibid., 70.

31 Ibid., 73.

32 Bryant, *Bear*, 227.

33 *Birmingham News*, November 15, 1964; *Atlanta Journal*, November 9, 1964.

34 John Underwood, "'Bama's Big, Bold Bid in the Week That Was," *Sports Illustrated*, November 23, 1964.

35 Ibid.

36 Joe Namath interview.

37 Underwood, "'Bama's Big, Bold Bid."

38 *Birmingham News*, November 15, 1964; Bryant, *Bear*, 233.

39 Bryant, *Bear*, 232–33; Howell Raines, *The One That Got Away: A Memoir* (New York: Lisa Drew/Scribner, 2006), 297.

40 *Birmingham News*, November 15, 1964.

41 For the game, see *Birmingham News*, November 15, 1964; *Atlanta Journal*, November 15, 1964; *Montgomery Advertiser-Journal*, November 15, 1964.

42 *Atlanta Journal*, November 15, 1964.

43 Ibid.

44 *Birmingham News*, November 15, 1964.
45 Underwood, "'Bama's Big, Bold Bid."
46 Ibid.; *Atlanta Journal*, November 16, 1964.
47 *Alabama–North Carolina State Program* (1964).
48 *Birmingham News*, November 24, 1964.
49 *Atlanta Journal*, November 20, 1964.
50 Bryant, *Bear*, 5.
51 Pat Trammell Jr. interview
52 *Birmingham News*, November 23, 1964.
53 *Atlanta Journal*, November 25, 1964; Raines, *The One That Got Away*, 180–81.
54 Ibid., November 27, 1964; *Birmingham News*, November 27, 1964; *Montgomery Advertiser*, November 27, 1964.
55 Raines, *One That Got Away*, 179–80.
56 *Atlanta Journal*, November 27, 1946.
57 *Birmingham News*, November 27, 1964.
58 Ibid., December 1, 1964.
59 *Los Angeles Times*, December 4, 1964.

Epilogue: In a Class of His Own

1 *Atlanta Journal*, November 28, 1964; November 29, 1964; *New York Times*, November 29, 1964.
2 *New York Times*, January 30, 1964.
3 Joe Willie Namath with Dick Schaap, *I Can't Wait Until Tomorrow…'Cause I Get Better-Looking Every Day* (New York: Random House, 1969), 202.
4 Ibid., 202–3.
5 Mike Bite interview. Unless otherwise noted, the negotiation stories are from Bite's interview.
6 Frank Lambert interview.
7 *New York Times*, January 10, 1965.
8 Ibid.
9 Namath, *I Can't Wait Until Tomorrow,* 203.
10 *New York Times*, January 21, 1964.
11 Ibid.
12 Gilbert Cant, "A Joint for Next Season," *Sports Illustrated*, February 8, 1965.
13 *Birmingham News*, December 11, 1964.

14 *Miami Herald*, December 26, 1964; *Austin American-Statesman*, December 27, 1964.

15 *Miami Herald*, December 29, 1964; *Atlanta Journal*, December 29, 1964; *Austin American*, December 29, 1964; *Montgomery Advertiser*, December 29, 1964; John Underwood, "Fabulous in Defeat," *Sports Illustrated*, January 11, 1965.

16 Pat Culpepper interview; Pat Culpepper, "The Main Event: 1965 Orange Bowl vs. Alabama," http://insidetexas.com/news/story.php?article=1875.

17 *Miami Herald*, January 2, 1965; *Birmingham News*, January 2, 1965; *Montgomery Advertiser*, January 2, 1965; *Atlanta Journal*, January 2, 1965; *Austin American*, January 2, 1965. Unless noted, game coverage is from these papers.

18 Ray Perkins interview.

19 Paul "Bear" Bryant, *Building a Championship Football Team* (Englewood Cliffs, NJ: Prentice Hall, 1960), 27.

20 Pat Culpepper interview.

21 Ibid.; Culpepper, "Main Event."

22 Bryant, *Building a Championship Football Team*, 27.

23 Underwood, "Fabulous in Defeat."

24 John Forney and Steve Townsend, *Talk of the Tide: An Oral History of Alabama Football Since 1920* (Birmingham, AL: Crane Hill, 1993), 100–101: E. Gaylon McCollough, *Shoulders of Giants: A Facial Surgeon's Prescriptions for Life's Dilemmas* (Huntsville, AL: Albright, 1986), 79–80.

25 Culpepper, "Main Event."

26 John "Sonny" Namath interview; Sharon Namath interview.

Index

428 • INDEX

ABOUT TWELVE

TWELVE was established in August 2005 with the objective of publishing no more than twelve books each year. We strive to publish the singular book, by authors who have a unique perspective and compelling authority. Works that explain our culture; that illuminate, inspire, provoke, and entertain. We seek to establish communities of conversation surrounding our books. Talented authors deserve attention not only from publishers, but from readers as well. To sell the book is only the beginning of our mission. To build avid audiences of readers who are enriched by these works—that is our ultimate purpose.

For more information about forthcoming TWELVE books, please go to www.twelvebooks.com.

CPSIA information can be obtained
at www.ICGtesting.com
Printed in the USA
LVOW07s2020161217
560050LV00002B/134/P